SOCIAL EXCHANGE
Advances in Theory and Research

SOCIAL EXCHANGE
Advances in Theory and Research

EDITED BY

KENNETH J. GERGEN
Swarthmore College
Swarthmore, Pennsylvania

AND

MARTIN S. GREENBERG AND
RICHARD H. WILLIS
University of Pittsburgh
Pittsburgh, Pennsylvania

PLENUM PRESS • NEW YORK AND LONDON

Library of Congress Catalog Card Number 80-18170
ISBN 0-306-40395-1

© 1980 Plenum Press, New York
A Division of Plenum Publishing Corporation
227 West 17th Street, New York, N.Y. 10011

Printed in the United States of America

Contributors

HARUMI BEFU, Department of Anthropology, Stanford University, Stanford, California

EDNA B. FOA, Department of Psychiatry, Temple University Health Sciences Center, Eastern Pennsylvania Psychiatric Institute, Philadelphia, Pennsylvania

URIEL G. FOA, Department of Psychology, Temple University, Philadelphia, Pennsylvania

IRENE HANSON FRIEZE, Department of Psychology, University of Pittsburgh, Pittsburgh, Pennsylvania

HOWARD L. FROMKIN, Department of Psychology, York University, Downsview, Ontario, Canada

KENNETH J. GERGEN, Department of Psychology, Swarthmore College, Swarthmore, Pennsylvania

NELSON H. H. GRABURN, Department of Anthropology, University of California, Berkeley, California

MARTIN S. GREENBERG, Department of Psychology, University of Pittsburgh, Pittsburgh, Pennsylvania

EDWIN P. HOLLANDER, Department of Psychology, State University of New York, Buffalo, New York

L. ROWELL HUESMANN, Department of Psychology, University of Illinois at Chicago Circle, Chicago, Illinois

GERALD S. LEVENTHAL, Department of Psychology, Wayne State University, Detroit, Michigan

GEORGE LEVINGER, Department of Psychology, University of Massachusetts, Amherst, Massachusetts

WALTER R. NORD, Department of Business, Washington University, St. Louis, Missouri

FREDERIC L. PRYOR, Department of Economics, Swarthmore College, Swarthmore, Pennsylvania

BARRY SCHWARTZ, Department of Psychology, Swarthmore College, Swarthmore, Pennsylvania

C. R. SNYDER, Clinical Psychology Program, University of Kansas, Lawrence, Kansas

RICHARD H. WILLIS, Department of Psychology, University of Pittsburgh, Pittsburgh, Pennsylvania

Preface

Introduction

In developing scientific theory there is perhaps nothing more propitious than a compelling metaphor. If the metaphor is rich in imagery, complexly differentiated, emotionally evocative, and vitally wedded to the cultural lore, the theory to which it gives rise may enjoy a long and vigorous life. If the metaphor is sufficiently powerful, the theory may even be sustained in independence of systematic empirical support. Role theory is likely to remain prosperous so long as there is a thriving theater; decision theory experienced a dramatic rejuvenation with the development of the electronic computer; and, in spite of its archaic construction, Jungian theory will prevail so long as ancient myths and symbols continue to haunt us (cf. Smith, 1978). From this standpoint, the development of social exchange theory is hardly surprising. Experience with the marketplace is extensive in society, its images are both complex and richly evocative, its challenges are often exciting and its lessons sometimes painful. It is thus both intellectually and emotionally invigorating to consider the social arena in all its diversity as an extended market in which each individual seeks to maximize profits.

The economic metaphor is hardly new to the social sciences. The recent intellectual roots of contemporary exchange theory can be traced to the works of Claude Lévi-Strauss, Marcel Mauss, Karl Marx, and B. F. Skinner. The exchange orientation also embodies a sophisticated form of *Homo economicus*, and thus owes much to classic economic theory. However, the first clear articulations of the exchange orientation were provided by George Homans (1961), John Thibaut and Harold Kelley (1959), and Peter Blau (1964). Although the works were independently conceived, their similar vision of social relations is a compelling tribute to the pervasive strength of the economic metaphor. Each of the volumes essentially views the individual as hedonistically motivated (cf. Abrahamsson, 1970). All action represents a search for pleasure and/or a reduction of pain. Actions which succeed in gaining such ends will be maintained, and those which fail will be abandoned. In order to obtain rewards and reduce punishment in the social sphere, the individual must perform various behaviors. If others find these behaviors rewarding, they will furnish behavioral outcomes in return which may be of value to the individual. Thus, social life is constituted by a series of transactions in which rewards and costs (in the form of behavior) are being provided to others in exchange for behaviors that may be "consumed" by self.

A variety of compelling extensions immediately emerges from this view.

For one, the framework suggests that individuals may develop preferred types of exchanges, essentially those which provide them maximal payoffs. These preferred arrangements may then become reflected in the norms of the relationship, or indeed, of the society as a whole. Norm sanctions may often be established to reduce deviations from preferred exchange patterns, and such sanctions may often be elaborated in the legal codes of the society, and even buttressed by armed force. In this light, the one major task of socialization is to instill an appreciation of commonly preferred exchange patterns. Large-scale institutions, such as business and government, may also be viewed in terms of normative exchange arrangements governing more specific arenas of action. Leadership and power are further implicated. Where group leaders are needed, the individual who provides maximal profit to the group may obtain senior status. Differences in social power may be cast in terms of the ability of the individual to obtain costly behaviors from others at little expense to self. Social attraction may also be understood in terms of exchange: attraction is directly related to the profit which another provides.

Since its inception, the exchange framework has captured the interest of investigators throughout the social sciences. Within social psychology, the framework has been applied to such diverse phenomena as cooperation, competition, and conflict (cf. Deutsch, 1975), social conformity (Nord, 1969a), the development of leadership and status in informal groups (Harsanyi, 1966; Hollander, 1964), helping behavior (Greenberg, Block, & Silverman, 1971), norm formation (Thibaut & Faucheux, 1965), the search for uniqueness (Fromkin, 1972a), reactions to assistance (Gergen & Gergen, 1971), social attraction (Huessmann & Levinger, 1976), coalition formation (Thibaut & Gruder, 1969), the perception of pay (Weick, 1966), the distribution of pay in groups (Leventhal & Whiteside, 1973), the achievement of equity in intimate relations (Walster, Walster, & Berscheid, 1978), and self-presentation (Reis & Gruzen, 1975), to name but a few. Sociologists have found the framework fruitful in examining organizational behavior (Evan, 1966), interorganizational relations (Levine & White, 1960), the attractiveness of work roles (Yuchtman, 1972), the fairness of earnings (Alves & Rossie, 1978), administrative decision making (Gamson, 1966), anomie and deviance (Hamblin & Crosbie, 1977), collective decision making (Coleman, 1964a), social obligation (Muir & Weinstein, 1962), group cooperation (Schmitt & Marwell, 1977), and the distribution of power in society (Coleman, 1973; Emerson, 1972). Anthropologists have further utilized the exchange formulation in understanding such diverse behavior as gift giving (Befu, 1966; Lebra, 1973), reciprocity (Hollensteiner, 1964), ceremonial activities (Hogbin 1971), social structure in primitive cultures (Schwimmer, 1970), and primitive trade (Sahlins, 1972). Social psychologists with a cross-cultural perspective have also been much stimulated by the exchange perspective (cf. Gergen, Morse, & Gergen, 1979). Within political science, Waldman (1970), and Curry and Wade (1968) have relied upon the exchange framework to integrate understanding of wide-ranging political activities. Rapoport and Chammah (1965) have used a form of exchange theory to account for conflict, negotiation, and decision making in both the interpersonal and the international arenas. Within the field of law, Nimmer (1977) has adopted the exchange approach to account for decision making in the criminal justice system, and Lempert (1972) has applied the theory to relate contract law to norm formation.

The Present Volume

The purposes of the present compendium are several in number. Recent years have seen a number of invaluable syntheses of early contributions to the exchange orientation. Homans has undertaken a revision of his classic, 1961 work, and in his recent volume (1974) has done much to clarify, defend, and extend his initial formulation. Likewise, Thibaut and Kelley have further elaborated the suppositions contained in their initial work, integrating many relevant contributions ensuing since the publication of their 1959 volume. Although both abstract and formalized, the new work (Kelley & Thibaut, 1978) is important in its novel consideration of psychological processes of perception, motivation, and self-regulation. Other scholars have rendered detailed analyses of the exchange orientation, its potential and its shortcomings. Richard Emerson's essays (1972a,b) have done much to clarify inconsistencies in the initial writings and to flesh out the social-structural implications of the early works. Maris (1970) has usefully examined Homans's theoretical suppositions on the basis of their logical adequacy. In a highly thoughtful and carefully detailed volume, Chadwick-Jones (1976) has examined the structure of the initial formulations, and much of the research which they have spawned. Ekeh's (1974) examination of exchange theory is equally significant in its critical concern with the sociological and anthropological implications of exchange theory. Hamblin and Kunkel's (1977) edited essays in honor of Homans add further insight and substance to the developing orientation.

Yet, simultaneous with this impressive effort at critical syntheses and elaboration, other scholars have been absorbed with new departures. Novel lines of research have developed, interdisciplinary inquiry has fermented, innovative forms of application have emerged, and fresh lines of critical thinking have coalesced. Either because of its recency and/or its positioning outside mainstream social psychology and sociology, much of this work has not been integrated into the various syntheses of the past decade. However, it is important to give voice to this work, for not only does it demonstrate the continued vitality of the general paradigm, but it represents the initial impetus of the theory's third decade. The contributions represent the new voices in the arena, and as such demand critical attention.

A second major aim is more catalytic. As we have seen, the exchange orientation has flourished throughout the social sciences. However, within these disciplines investigators have often labored in ignorance or disregard of relevant departures in other disciplines. When such work has been discovered, the results have often been intellectually exciting and empirically productive. The use of economic exchange in anthropological field work (cf. Chapter 10), the reliance on cognitive developmental thinking to understand social-structural patterns (cf. Chapter 4), and the employment of basic operant conditioning derivatives to understand organizational relations (cf. Chapter 6) are exemplary of the fruits of such cross-fertilization. By bringing together major lines of thinking both within the various disciplines and within the interstices, it is our hope to facilitate further boundary-breaking endeavors.

Finally, our hope is that the volume will represent a useful step toward a unified conceptual view. Although there may be no fundamental unity among social events, it is both intellectually challenging and humanly satisfying to discover formal similarities among highly diverse phenomena. From this standpoint, it has been our attempt to assemble a group of investigations that employ a similar set of conceptual constructs, but grapple with the most diverse aspects of behavior. Through such varied exposure, a unification may be discerned, not only across behavioral contexts, but across levels of social analysis— from the psychological to the sociocultural. It is not that we believe this to be the only significant lens through which coherency is discerned, nor necessarily the most promising for all purposes. However, if the theoretical lens is to be useful at all, one must be trained in its employment. By focusing on highly disparate phenomena, the intensity of the training is much enhanced.

The contributions to the present volume are placed into three major sections. In the initial section we have included a series of innovative extensions of the original exchange formulation. These papers deal with highly general issues relevant to exchange in all walks of life. Issues of indebtedness, equity, uniqueness, and the structure of resources all receive attention. In the second section the focus sharpens considerably. The papers in this section all take a more detailed look at more specific domains. The papers deal with such diverse topics as group leadership, behavior organizations, and sex roles. The final part of the volume is concerned with the critical analysis of the exchange perspective. Significant new questions are raised concerning the reciprocity norm, the motivational basis for exchange, the empirical basis of the exchange approach, and the transhistorical durability of the orientation. In the same way that it is hoped the contributions in the preceding sections will open up new lines of thinking and research, it is hoped that the latter chapters will contribute to continued and much needed debate.

KENNETH J. GERGEN
MARTIN S. GREENBERG
RICHARD H. WILLIS

Contents

PART I   THEORETICAL EXTENSION

Chapter 1   A Theory of Indebtedness
MARTIN S. GREENBERG

Introduction 3
Definition of Indebtedness 3
Determinants of the Magnitude of Indebtedness 4
   The Donor's Motives for Aiding the Recipient 5
   The Magnitude of the Recipient's and the Donor's
      Rewards and Costs 6
   The Locus of Causality of the Donor's Action 8
   Cues Emitted by Comparison Others 10
Assessment of the Magnitude of Indebtedness 11
   Self-Reports 12
   Behavioral and Cognitive Attempts to Reduce Indebtedness ... 14
Comparison between Indebtedness and Inequity 21
Cultural Variations 23

Chapter 2   What Should Be Done with Equity Theory? New
Approaches to the Study of Fairness in Social Relationships
GERALD S. LEVENTHAL

Introduction 27
   The Problem of Allocation 27
   Issues in Equity Theory 28
A Multidimensional Approach to Distributive Fairness 28
   The Unidimensional Approach of Equity Theory 28
   The Multidimensional Approach of Justice Judgment Theory .. 30
   Judgments of Distributive Fairness 30
The Perception of Procedural Fairness 34
   Procedural Fairness Defined 34
   Structural Components in Cognitive Maps of the
      Allocative Process 37
   Justice Rules for Evaluating Procedural Fairness 39

The Relative Weight of Procedural Rules 46
The Impact of Perceived Fairness on Behavior 47
    The Importance of Fairness 47
    Activation of the Justice Judgment Sequence 48
    Concern for Fairness and Other Causes of "Fair" Behavior 51
    A Distinction between Fair and Quasi-Fair Behavior 52
Summary 53

Chapter 3   The Search for Uniqueness and Valuation of
Scarcity: Neglected Dimensions of Value in Exchange
Theory
HOWARD L. FROMKIN AND C. R. SNYDER

Introduction 57
Conformity as Social Exchange 58
Uniqueness Studies 59
    Uniqueness as a Neglected Cost 61
Uniqueness Attributes 63
    Scarcity 64
    Names 66
    Clothing 68
    Dates and Mates 69
    Beliefs 70
    Performance 72
Deindividuation and Uniqueness 73
Summary 75

Chapter 4   Resource Theory: Interpersonal Behavior as Exchange
EDNA B. FOA AND URIEL G. FOA

Introduction 77
Six Resource Classes 78
Relationship between Resource Exchange and
        Interpersonal Behavior 81
Differentiation of Resources in Childhood 82
Exchange Outcomes and Environmental Influences 84
    Relationship between Self and Other 84
    Relationship between Giving and Taking 85
    Relationship between Interpersonal Situation and Exchange 85
    Time for Processing Input 85
    Delay of Reward 85
    Optimum Group Size 85
Empirical Support for Resource Theory 86
    Homogeneity of Classes 86

Similarity and Substitution 87
Structure 87
Exchange...88
Effect of Restrictions 89
Helping Behavior 89
Recent Development 90
Differentiation of Resources in Hetero- and Homosexual Males ..90
Asymmetry in Generalization 91
Further Results 92
Rules of the Game 93
Application to Problems of Society 94

PART II   EXCHANGE THEORY IN SPECIALIZED SETTINGS

Chapter 5   Leadership and Social Exchange Processes
EDWIN P. HOLLANDER

Introduction 103
Leadership in Retrospect 104
Leadership as a Transactional Influence Process 105
Leader Legitimacy and Social Exchange 109
Idiosyncrasy Credit and Innovation 110
Leader Legitimacy and System Progress 113
Leadership Effectiveness and a Fair Exchange 115

Chapter 6   The Study of Organizations through a Resource–Exchange Paradigm
WALTER R. NORD

Introduction 119
Resource Exchanges in Organizational Analysis.................122
Historical Development......................................122
R–E Processes in Organization–Environment Relationships 124
Some R–E "Extra-Economic" Aspects of
    Interorganizational Relations 125
Organizational Coping 126
Interorganizational Networks................................127
Power and Dependence.......................................129
Implications of the R–E Paradigm for Intraorganizational
    Processes 131

Internal Processes: Some Macrolevel Studies .133
Internal Processes: Some Micro-Considerations 136
Conclusions 138

Chapter 7   Sex Roles, Social Exchange, and Couples
Richard H. Willis and Irene Hanson Frieze

Introduction 141
Role Expectations 142
    Ascribed and Achieved Status 142
    Evaluation of Male and Female Role Occupants 145
Partner Markets and Initial Formation 147
Intrinsic Compatibility 148
    Components of Compatibility 149
    Overall Compatibility 154
    Relations among Formation, Compatibility, and Stability 156
    Market Characteristics and Mean Compatibility 158
    Effects of Loners on Stability 159
Preliminary Research Support 161
Summary 162

*Chapter 8   An "Incremental Exchange" Perspective on the Pair
Relationship: Interpersonal Reward and Level of Involvement*
George Levinger and L. Rowell Huesmann

Introduction 165
Exchange Theory in a Sequential Perspective 165
    Incremental Exchange Theory 166
The Relate Model 168
    Simulation of a Romantic Involvement 170
The Meaning of "Reward" in Dyadic Interaction 173
    Dimensions of Reward 174
    Behavioral versus Relational Rewards 174
    Other Dimensions of Reward 175
    Adaptation Levels, Comparison Levels, and Gradients 176
The Meaning of Involvement 178
    Toward a Revised Model 178
Reconsidering the Simulation of Interpersonal Involvement 180
    Differing Levels of Involvement 181
    Toward a Revised Simulation of a Heterosexual Relationship . . .183
Conclusions 187
    Implications for Exchange Theory 187

PART III   CRITICAL ANALYSIS

Chapter 9   Structural and Motivational Approaches to Social Exchange
   HARUMI BEFU

Introduction 197
The Norm of Reciprocity and Normative Values 199
Mauss and Gouldner Compared 201
Rules of Exchange..202
Strategies of Exchange 203
Cultural Frame of Reference 204
Structural versus Motivational Approaches 206
   Introduction 206
   The Structural Approach 207
   The Motivational Approach 210
Summary...213

Chapter 10   The Myth of Reciprocity
   FREDERIC L. PRYOR AND NELSON H. H. GRABURN

Introduction 215
Anthropological Approaches toward Reciprocity and
      Some Hypotheses 216
The Ethnographic Setting of the Study 218
   The Society 218
   Data Gathering 220
   The Methods of Handling the Data 221
Testing Various Reciprocity Theories 224
   The Regression Analysis and Its Implications 224
   Reciprocity and Kinship Distance 229
   Native Interpretations versus Our Interpretations of
      Exchange Transactions 233
Summary and Conclusions...................................235

*Chapter 11   New Developments in Operant Conditioning
and Their Implications*
   BARRY SCHWARTZ

Introduction 239
The Experimental Analysis of Behavior: Methods
      and Assumptions 241
   Is Learning in Nature Biologically Neutral? The
      Ethological View 245
   Instinctive Drift 246

Taste-Aversion Learning 248
Is the Skinner Box Biologically Neutral? 250
Implications of Specialized Learning for Extensions
    of Operant Conditioning Principles to Human Affairs 254
Summary...258

Chapter 12   *Exchange Theory: The Transient and the Enduring*
  KENNETH J. GERGEN

Introduction 261
Enlightenment Effects: Exchange Theory as Prescription 263
Level of Abstraction and the Incorporation of Change 265
Theoretical Utility and the Exchange Orientation 268
    The Explanatory Function..................................269
    The Sensitizing Function 270
    The Organization of Experience 273
    The Integration Function..................................275
    The Generative Function...................................276
    The Value-Sustaining Function 278
Conclusion 279

References 281

Index 303

I

Theoretical Extension

ADVANCES IN THEORY

The initial works of the exchange theorists were clearly integrative in character. Homans, Thibaut, Kelley, and Blau all succeeded in demonstrating the power of a single framework to synthesize a broad array of empirical observations. Such work has essentially fashioned a vital and compelling perspective on human affairs. In doing so it also potentiated wide-ranging inquiry in the social sciences. Within positivist circles it is traditionally maintained that such inquiry should bear on the truth value of the initial formulation; investigation should properly be concerned with demonstrating the predictive capability of the inductively derived theoretical structure. However, such a view is highly constricting. The heuristic value of a theory may also be assessed on other and perhaps more important grounds. Does the theory stimulate others to reconceptualize or gain new insights into a given set of phenomena? Are new phenomena brought to light? Do convincing demonstrations of further applicability emerge? Are investigators prompted to make further distinctions among phenomena? All are significant criteria against which to judge the heuristic merit of a given theory.

In the present section, we have assembled a series of contributions giving striking testimony to the broad heuristic value of the exchange formulation. In the initial selection, Martin Greenberg utilizes the framework to launch a discerning inquiry into the nature of indebtedness. When rewards are received, the recipient acquires a cost, that is, the cost of obligation. Indebtedness is thus viewed as an aversive state having motivational properties—the greater the magnitude of indebtedness, the greater the aversiveness and the stronger the subsequent attempts to reduce it. Building upon the earlier work of Gouldner (1960), Greenberg details the determinants of the magnitude of indebtedness, and the various modes for its reduction.

In the second chapter Gerald Leventhal presents a clear alternative to traditional equity theory. As he argues, traditional theory is problematic, insofar as (a) it is "unidimensional" in its sole concern with merit or contributions of various kinds as inputs, (b) it considers only the final distribution of outcomes, ignoring the justness of the procedures used to arrive at the distribution, and (c) it tends to exaggerate the importance of equity, insofar as other motives are not given due consideration. To deal with such problems, Leventhal opts for a broader definition of equity, one emphasizing *fairness* or *justice*, and including on the input side not only merit or contributions, but also needs, equality, and other components. The research which he reports nicely demonstrates the value of this reconceptualization, and renders equity theory in this more comprehensive version far more applicable to social problems besetting the society.

Fromkin and Snyder's contribution (Chapter 3) shifts the focus from the structural costs of receiving to the specific commodity received. In particular, they maintain that within Western culture a strong value is placed on being treated as unique, and that to be treated as similar to others often has negative payoff value. Again, widespread empirical evidence is used to demonstrate the strength of the arguments. Not only does this inquiry elucidate a subtle and fascinating human need, but it demonstrates as well the importance of moving from a level of generalized reward to a more discrete level of analysis. In the original exchange formulation, the attempt was not so much to deal with specific costs and benefits as it was to demonstrate the utility of a wholly general model. Whether the model might be applicable to specific needs, and the range of activities that might be affected, were left largely unexamined. Fromkin and Snyder do much to compensate for these lacks, and in doing so open new vistas of research.

Both in the initial and the revised formulation of exchange theory, neither Homans nor Thibaut and Kelley attend to the problem of substitutability of payoffs. In general, it is assumed that various forms of "social capital" are interchangeable. The final paper in this section, by Edna and Uriel Foa (Chapter 4), focuses exclusively on this aspect of social exchange. Their effort is by far the most ambitious attempt to date to map the resource classes employed in social exchange. Assuming that *"what* is exchanged matters and therefore should be specified," they delineate six resource classes: love, status, services, information, goods, and money. And, as they argue, resources in certain classes are more substitutable than resources belonging to other classes. After laying out the theory and the supporting evidence, they move to a macrolevel of analysis, applying the theory to problems of society. Although speculative, their ideas on this subject are both stimulating and challenging. By spelling out the rules which govern the interplay between economic and social resources, they also provide a theoretical framework that can facilitate collaborative efforts among diverse disciplines to solve complex problems.

1

A Theory of Indebtedness

MARTIN S. GREENBERG

INTRODUCTION

The obligation to repay a benefit has long been noted by observers of human interaction. Democritus, for one, offered the following advice in the fourth century B.C.: "Accept favors in the foreknowledge that you will have to give a greater return for them." Four centuries later the Roman Seneca observed that "He who receives a benefit with gratitude, repays the first installment on his debt." Although the idea of an obligation to repay benefits has been recognized for centuries, it is only in recent years that its antecedents and consequences have been investigated empirically. The purpose of this chapter is to clarify the theoretical and empirical status of the indebtedness concept, and to illuminate its utility for understanding social interaction. The first section is concerned with defining indebtedness; the second presents hypotheses and relevant data regarding the determinants of the magnitude of indebtedness; the third contains a discussion of the various modes for assessing the magnitude of indebtedness, along with a review of the relevant empirical literature; in the fourth section, indebtedness is distinguished from the related concept of inequity; and in the last section, indebtedness is examined from a cross-cultural perspective.

DEFINITION OF INDEBTEDNESS

It is the thesis of this chapter that under a set of specifiable conditions the receipt of a benefit (i.e., an outcome having reward value) from another places the recipient in a psychological state of

MARTIN S. GREENBERG • Department of Psychology, University of Pittsburgh, Pittsburgh, Pennsylvania 15260.

indebtedness. *Indebtedness* is defined here as a state of obligation to repay another. This thesis is predicated on the assumption that there exists a norm of reciprocity, which, according to Gouldner (1960), states that "(1) people should help those who have helped them, and (2) people should not injure those who have helped them" (p. 171). The state of indebtedness is assumed to have motivational properties, such that the greater its magnitude, the greater the resultant arousal and discomfort, and, hence, the stronger the ensuing attempts to deal with or reduce it.[1] It is further assumed that the arousal and discomfort associated with this state lead to heightened alertness and sensitivity to opportunities for its reduction. Demosthenes probably had in mind the distress of being indebted when he warned that "To remind a man of the good turns you have done him is very much like a reproach." It is reasonable to speculate that the discomfort associated with indebtedness derives from early socialization experiences with the norm of reciprocity, during which individuals associate being indebted with (a) restrictions on their freedom of action (Brehm, 1966), (b) loss of power and status relative to the donor (Blau, 1964; Homans, 1961), and (c) anticipated costs of repayment.

Although indebtedness has features in common with the related concept of inequity (Adams, 1965; Walster, Berscheid, & Walster, 1973), the two should not be confused, as they differ in fundamental ways. In order to explicate these differences, further elaboration of the theory of indebtedness is first required; these differences will be discussed subsequently.

DETERMINANTS OF THE MAGNITUDE OF INDEBTEDNESS

There appear to be multiple determinants of the magnitude of indebtedness which are linked to each other in complex ways. The degree of indebtedness experienced by an individual at a given moment may reflect the influence of one or more of the following

---

[1] This is not to say that indebtedness itself is always aversive. Occasionally, indebtedness may be somewhat pleasant and, indeed, sought after, as when it facilitates the achievement of other and perhaps more important needs of the individual. For example, the obligation to reciprocate a benefit can give legitimacy to a rewarding interaction that previously lacked such legitimacy, and can, therefore, protect the individual from internally and/or externally imposed sanctions. Thus, a teenage girl who is dating a boy against the wishes of her family may willingly accept a gift from him, thereby incurring indebtedness in order to justify further interaction with him. However, it is postulated here that the sources of positive affect associated with the state of indebtedness are far less frequent and potent than the sources of negative affect.

determinants: they refer to the recipient's perception of (1) the donor's motives, (2) the magnitude of the rewards and costs incurred by the recipient and donor as a result of the exchange, (3) the locus of causality of the donor's action, and (4) cues emitted by comparison others.

The Donor's Motives for Aiding the Recipient

The recipient is likely to feel indebted to the extent that he perceives that in helping him the donor was more concerned with the recipient's welfare than his own. In emphasizing the importance of the recipient's perception of the donor's motives for helping, the present formulation represents an extension and elaboration of ideas first put forth by Gouldner (1960) and later refined by Schopler (1970).

We may reason that the recipient's greater concern with the donor's motives than with the donor's overt actions is probably a reflection of individuals' being socialized to identify and respond to the stable or dispositional elements in their world. Presumably, by identifying the stable elements in the environment, a recipient achieves a sense of predictability and perhaps control over that environment (Heider 1958). It can be speculated that requiring recipients to feel particularly obligated to reciprocate when the donor has acted for altruistic motives has adaptive consequences for both the recipient and the group. Given that individuals have limited time and energy resources with which to deal with their environment, it would be adaptive for individuals to invest their resources in reinforcing those stable dispositions in others which are maximally beneficial to themselves. That is, from the recipient's perspective, reinforcement of a donor's altruistic disposition constitutes a more stable and thus predictable outcome situation for the recipient than a less discriminating reinforcement of donor helping actions. From the perspective of the group, socializing recipients to feel obligated to reciprocate when the donor is perceived to have acted from altruistic motives serves to reinforce and maintain altruistic dispositions in group members, thereby enhancing group cohesiveness and cooperation.

Although much of the above discussion is admittedly speculative, there does exist empirical support for the proposed relationship between the donor's perceived altruism and the magnitude of the recipient's indebtedness. Greenberg and Frisch (1972) found that the perceived magnitude of the donor's motivation to help was significantly correlated with the magnitude of reciprocity. Moreover, Schopler and Thompson (1968) reported evidence showing that a favor performed in an informal (i.e., appropriate) context elicited greater reciprocity and attribution of generosity than a favor performed in a formal (i.e., inappropriate) context. Presumably, the inappropriate favor caused recipients to suspect that the donor was motivated by self-gain rather than by the needs of the recipient. Similarly, Lerner and Lichtman (1968) found that recipients of a favor were less likely to reciprocate when they discovered that egotistical motivations underlay the donor's seemingly gracious act than when such motivation was not implied.

The Magnitude of the Recipient's and the Donor's Rewards and Costs

The magnitude of indebtedness is in part an additive function of the quantity of the recipient's net benefits derived from the exchange (i.e., rewards minus costs) and the quantity of the donor's net costs derived from the exchange (i.e., costs minus rewards). This relationship is expressed by the following equation: $I = B + C$, where I refers to the magnitude of indebtedness, B refers to the recipient's perception of the quantity of net benefits received, and C refers to the recipient's perception of the quantity of the donor's net costs. The quantity of either person's rewards and costs is evaluated in terms of perceived need of the person to whom it relates. The greater the perceived need for a resource, the greater its reward value when received and the greater its cost when given up. In making this calculation, it is assumed that the recipient evaluates his own rewards and costs in relation to his own needs, and that he evaluates the donor's rewards and costs in terms of his perception of the donor's needs.

The basis for this determinant of the magnitude of indebtedness lies in its adaptive significance for the group and, ultimately, for the individual. Simply stated, it is adaptive for the group to reinforce help giving among its members, particularly help of a large magnitude. Consequently, it is assumed that the group socializes individuals into feeling pressure to reciprocate as a function of the magnitude of net benefits received. Furthermore, by requiring recipients to feel obligated as a function of the donor's net costs, the group increases the probability that potential help givers will be compensated for risks assumed as well as effort involved, thereby increasing the likelihood of their attempting to render aid. This help-facilitating function is similar to that noted by Gouldner (1960) when he referred to the norm of reciprocity as a "starting mechanism." It might be noted that viewing indebtedness as an additive function of the recipient's net benefits and the donor's net costs raises the possibility that the recipient can feel indebted to one who does not provide him with a benefit, but instead incurs costs while unsuccessfully attempting to render help.

The magnitude of the recipient's net benefits and the donor's net costs may influence indebtedness in yet another way: via the attribution of positive motives to the donor. The recipient may use the benefits received and costs incurred by the donor to infer the magnitude of the donor's motivation to help him. The greater the magnitude of benefits received and/or costs incurred by the donor, the greater the likelihood of the donor being perceived as generous and altruistic. This statement is qualified by Jones and Davis's (1965) suggestion that excessively large benefits provided by the donor might cause the recipient to question his motives, thereby decreasing the magnitude of felt indebtedness.

Examination of the empirical literature lends strong support to the proposition that the magnitude of indebtedness is positively related to the magnitude of the recipient's net benefits (Greenberg, Block, & Silverman, 1971; Greenberg & Frisch, 1972; Kahn, 1972; Leventhal, Allen, & Kemelgor, 1969; Pruitt, 1968; Stapleton, Nacci, & Tedeschi, 1973; Wilke & Lanzetta, 1970). The repeated positive findings regarding the relationship between the recipient's net benefits and the magnitude of indebtedness have been achieved with a number of different experimental designs involving help and no help conditions (Kahn, 1972), "high" help and "low" help conditions (Greenberg & Frisch, 1972; Pruitt, 1968), and three or more levels of help (Greenberg et al., 1971; Leventhal et al., 1969; Stapleton et al., 1973; Wilke & Lanzetta, 1970). It is noteworthy that in only one of the four studies employing three or more levels of prior help (Leventhal et al., 1969) was there a failure to obtain a positive monotonic relationship between the amount of help and the index of indebtedness. All the studies listed above utilized designs in which net benefits were varied by manipulating the amount of the recipient's rewards, while the recipient's costs were assumed either to be randomly distributed across conditions or nonexistent.

There has been far less research on the donor's net costs than on the recipient's net benefits. In two separate investigations using similar manipulations of donor's costs, Pruitt (1968) and Gergen, Ellsworth, Maslach, and Seipel (1975) found that of two donors providing an equal quantity of benefits, the one who gave from smaller initial resources received more help in return. Presumably, subjects perceived that it was more costly for the less affluent donor to give. Perhaps Aristotle had instances such as this in mind when he wrote, "We speak of generosity relative to a person's property. . . . it is quite possible that a man who gives less is more generous, if his gift comes from smaller resources" (Aristotle, 1962, p. 85).

Additional supportive evidence pertaining to the influence of the donor's net costs was provided in studies by Latané (1973) and Gross and Somersan (1974). Latané found that subjects were less likely to accept a coke when they believed it cost the other fifteen cents than when they believed it cost the other nothing. Presumably, subjects who were offered the costly favor felt that by accepting it they would be more indebted than did subjects who were offered the free coke. Consequently, they avoided acceptance of the favor. Similar reasoning can be applied to the Gross and Somersan study, which found that subjects requested less help when the potential helper's perceived effort was high than when it was low.

Conceptualizing the magnitude of indebtedness as a function of the recipient's net benefits and the donor's net costs raises an important question about the relative weights of these two variables. Consider, for example, two situations in which an individual needs help and someone offers it to him. In one instance, the individual receives the needed help while the donor incurs minimal costs. In another situation, the donor incurs high costs while unsuccessfully attempting to render aid. In which instance is the "recipient" more obligated to help the other? Are the recipient's rewards more heavily weighted than the donor's costs? Recent evidence seems to suggest so (Greenberg *et al.*, 1971; Greenberg & Saxe, 1975). Greenberg and Saxe, for example, presented subjects with one of two versions of a story concerning a hypothetical student who needed assistance in writing a paper. In one version, the student received help which was not costly to the donor. In the second version, a would-be donor unsuccessfully attempted to render help while incurring considerable costs. Subjects were asked to place themselves in the role of the student and to answer questions regarding feelings of obligation and willingness to assist the donor. Results indicated that subjects in the successful help condition reported feeling more obligated and more willing to help the donor than subjects who received unsuccessful and costly help. Taken together, these two studies strongly suggest that indebtedness is more a function of the recipient's net benefits than the donor's net costs. These data suggest further that the indebtedness equation be modified to reflect differential weighting of net benefits and net costs: $I = x_1B + x_2C$, where x_1 and x_2 are empirically determined weights and $x_1 > x_2$.

The Locus of Causality of the Donor's Action

The third determinant of the magnitude of indebtedness is the recipient's perception of the locus of causality of the donor's action. The obligation to reciprocate is expected to vary as a function of the recipient's perception that he is responsible for the donor's help attempt. Thus, it is proposed that the magnitude of indebtedness is greatest when the recipient perceives that the locus of causality resides in himself, such as when he *requests* or *pleads* for help. The magnitude of indebtedness is expected to be somewhat less when the locus of causality is perceived to reside in the donor, such as when the latter either *offers* or *imposes* help on the recipient. Finally, least indebtedness is expected when locus of causality resides in the environment, such as when the donor's helping act is perceived to result from either *luck* or *role obligations*. Thus, helping acts that are unintentional or chance-produced, or that derive from requirements imposed by others, are least likely to produce feelings of indebtedness, since the recipient is least likely to perceive himself as sharing responsibility for the helping action. Phrased somewhat differently, one might say that the magnitude of indebtedness is in part a function of the degree to which the donor is perceived to exceed intentionally the requirements of his role. Consistent with this view is Heider's (1958) observation that "We do not feel grateful [i.e., indebted] to a person who helps us fortuitously, or because he was forced to do so or because he was obliged to do so. Gratitude is determined by the will, the intention, of the benefactor" (p. 265).

The importance of locus of causality as a determinant of the magnitude of indebtedness is rooted in the belief that it is in the interest of the group to hold individuals accountable for the consequences of actions for which they are responsible. Socializing group members into feeling strongly obligated to repay help which they are responsible for obtaining is beneficial to the group in at least two ways: first, it ought to increase donor willingness to comply with requests for aid, because the donor would be more confident that his efforts will be reciprocated; second, the potential recipient's knowledge that he will be under strong obligation to reciprocate when he asks for help may cause him to think twice before requesting such help, thereby fostering a degree of self-sufficiency among group members.

The locus of causality variable may, of course, interact with one or both of the previously discussed determinants of the magnitude of indebtedness. For example, feeling less obligated to repay someone who helped him by chance or because of role obligations may reflect the recipient's difficulty in attributing positive motives to the donor. Similarly, when the donor is perceived to have acted in response to role requirements, the recipient may perceive that the donor's net costs are not very great, since the donor is likely to receive benefits from others for fulfilling role obligations. The empirical data with regard to locus of causality is highly supportive of the proposition linking perceived responsibility for the helping act and the magnitude of indebtedness. Recipients have been found to reciprocate more when the benefit received was intentionally given by the donor than when it was chance-produced (Garrett & Libby, 1973; Greenberg & Frisch, 1972; Leventhal, Weiss, & Long, 1969). Similarly, Goranson and Berkowitz (1966), Gross and Latané (1974), and Nemeth (1970) found that recipients were more likely to return a benefit when the donor's assistance was voluntary than when it was compulsory.

Data collected by Muir and Weinstein (1962) and Greenberg and Saxe (1975) lend further support to the prediction that the magnitude of indebtedness is greater when the recipient perceives that the locus of causality resides within himself rather than in the donor. Muir and Weinstein asked their subjects, "Do you feel more obligated if you ask someone for a favor or when they offer it to you without your asking?" High socioeconomic-status females reported feeling more obligated to repay a requested favor than one that was offered. Results for the low socioeconomic females were in the same direction but were not significant. Greenberg and Saxe manipulated locus of help initiation by presenting subjects with one of three versions of a story concerning a hypothetical student who needed assistance. In one version, the student *requested* help from another; in the second, help was *offered* to the student; and in the third, help was *imposed* upon the student by the other. A significant linear trend was obtained on the measure of obligation, indicating that feelings of obligation tended to increase as the locus of causality shifted from the donor to the recipient. In addition, there was a significant correlation ($r = .51$) between the measure of obligation and the subject's (i.e., recipient's) feeling of responsibility for the help attempt. Contrary to the present theorizing, no differences were observed on the measure of willingness to help the donor. In sum, then, existing empirical data tend to support the hypothesis linking perceived locus of causality with the magnitude of indebtedness.

Cues Emitted by Comparison Others

It is further proposed that the magnitude of indebtedness is a function of verbal and nonverbal cues emitted by comparison others. These "others" may consist of *witnesses* to the receipt of the benefit, *co-recipients* of the benefit, and/or the *donor* himself. It is hypothesized that this source of indebtedness becomes prepotent when the recipient perceives that the "objective reality" surrounding the helping event is ambiguous and confusing. When confronted with such a situation, the recipient will rely on social reality to confirm or label his state. This reasoning is very similar to that underlying the work of Schachter

(1964). Just as individuals have been shown to label their emotional state in terms of socially available cues, so might individuals use others to label their state of indebtedness. Although there presently exist no data pertaining to the influence of witnesses and co-recipients on the magnitude of felt indebtedness, one study has yielded data concerning the importance of the donor's beliefs on the magnitude of indebtedness. In a questionnaire study that examined subjects' "naive beliefs" about indebtedness (Greenberg, Mowrey, Steinberg, & Bar-Tal, 1974), the following question was asked: "If you were indebted to someone, how indebted would you still feel if you repaid the help-giver but he/she was unaware that you were the one who had helped them?" Subjects responded on a 7-point scale which ranged from "Still feel indebted" to "No longer feel indebted." It is noteworthy that 53% (42/79) of the responses fell between the neutral response position and the position labeled "Still feel indebted." This would indicate that, despite having repaid the benefit, the fact that the donor believed the debt still remained was sufficient to cause a substantial number of subjects to feel that they continued to be indebted to the donor.

In concluding this section on the determinants of the magnitude of indebtedness, it must be pointed out that the theory in its present form does not provide any formula or precise basis for weighting the importance of the four determinants. Neither can it be claimed that the variables are independent of each other. On the contrary, it has been contended that three of the determinants—the donor's motives, the recipient's and donor's rewards and costs, and the locus of causality—interact in a series of complex causal relationships. For example, it might be speculated that the locus of causality variable will have minimal impact on the magnitude of indebtedness when the recipient's net benefits are exceedingly large, as when the donor saves the recipient's life. In such a situation, the fact that the donor was fulfilling a role requirement (e.g., lifeguard rescuing a drowning victim) may be far less salient to the recipient than the magnitude of the benefit, and, consequently, may play a relatively small role in determining the magnitude of indebtedness. A more detailed statement concerning the precise nature of the interrelationship among the determinants of indebtedness must await further empirical research.

ASSESSMENT OF THE MAGNITUDE OF INDEBTEDNESS

The magnitude of indebtedness can be measured in terms of two broad response classes: (1) self-reports and (2) behavioral and cognitive attempts to reduce indebtedness. This section contains a review of the empirical evidence relevant to each measure and a discussion of problems inherent in their use.

Self-Reports

Indebtedness is assumed to be a conscious state involving both cognitive and affective components. It can, in most circumstances, be measured via self-reports. The cognitive-affective components are represented by (1) a feeling of obligation to repay the donor, (2) a feeling of discomfort and uneasiness, and (3) a heightened alertness to cues relevant to indebtedness reduction. Accordingly, self-reports ought to yield data which suggest that recipients feel obligated and uncomfortable and that they are searching for an opportunity to repay the donor. There are, however, several problems inherent in the use of such self-report measures. The first derives from Heider's (1958) distinction between "local" and "total relevance." Immediately after receiving a benefit, the recipient's attention is likely to be dominated by thoughts about the value of the benefit and its immediate positive implications rather than by concern about the costs of repayment. Therefore, immediately upon receiving the benefit, the recipient may cheerfully report his desire and perhaps obligation to repay the donor, and not be able to recognize and report any awareness of discomfort or distress. On the other hand, in situations where the recipient recognizes the costs of receiving the benefit and feels ensuing discomfort, he may not report his distress, because it could be construed as a sign of ingratitude toward the donor. Yet, if sufficient time passes so that the self-report is obtained after the recipient has repaid the donor, additional sources of error may be introduced. The recipient may prefer to view his act of repayment in the most favorable light, that is, as a generous, altruistic act, and not as an act motivated by a feeling of obligation. Moreover, the feeling of obligation itself may be difficult to report in situations involving long-standing relationships in which reciprocation of help has become routinized. In such situations, obligations are likely to become salient only when the routine is disrupted. An incident reported by Whyte (1955) in his description of "street corner society" well illustrates this point:

> While Alex and Frank were friends, I never heard either one of them discuss the services he was performing for the other, but when they had a falling-out over the group activities with the Aphrodite Club, each man complained to Doc that the other was not acting as he should in view of the services that had been done him. In other words, actions which were performed explicity for the sake of friendship were revealed as being part of a system of mutual obligations. (p. 257)

Despite these inhibiting factors, a number of studies have yielded self-report data showing that recipients experience feelings of obligation and discomfort upon receipt of a benefit. Bar-Tal and Greenberg (1974), Brehm and Cole (1966), and Greenberg and Shapiro (1971) found that recipients of help reported feeling more obligated to help a work partner. Greenberg and Frisch (1972) found that reported feelings of obligation were stronger among those who received deliberate as opposed to accidental help. Interestingly, when subjects in this study were asked to report how indebted (rather than obligated) they felt, they indicated feeling more indebted after receiving high as opposed to low help, as well as feeling more indebted after receiving deliberate as opposed to accidental help. These data suggest that subjects give slightly different interpretations to the terms *indebted* and *obligated*. Findings reported by Tesser, Gatewood, and Driver (1968) showed that subjects view indebtedness as synonymous with *gratitude*. Goranson and Berkowitz (1966) employed an interesting measure of felt obligation. They asked subjects to indicate the extent to which they believed most people would have expected them to work hard to help their supervisor (i.e., the donor). Results showed that those who received voluntary assistance from the supervisor believed more strongly that others expected them to help than did those who received compulsory assistance.

Somewhat less attention has been given to assessing the discomfort presumed to accompany indebtedness. Self-report measures of discomfort have been employed in four studies. In two of these, survey questionnaires were used. The other two were laboratory experiments in which self-reports were elicited after subjects actually received help from another. In the first of the questionnaire studies, Muir and Weinstein (1962) reported that all their respondents stated that they "like to do favors for others," whereas only 8.9% replied that they "like being obligated to others." Virtually identical results were obtained by Greenberg et al. (1974), who asked their subjects, "Do you generally enjoy being indebted to someone?" Indebtedness was defined for subjects as a "feeling of obligation to repay another." Only 9.1% responded yes to this question, compared to 90.9% who responded no. The first laboratory study of subject discomfort (Leventhal et al., 1969) tested the equity model in a dyadic situation involving a donor and a recipient. Results revealed that to the extent a subject received a share of the reward greater than he was entitled to, the subject manifested increased "concern" about the division of the reward and about changing it. The second laboratory study (Gross & Latané, 1974) showed that recipients of help who believed that they would be unable to reciprocate rated themselves as feeling less "comfortable," more "constrained," and more "confined" than those who expected to reciprocate shortly. Taken together, the findings reported here lend general support to the hypothesis that the state of indebtedness produces feelings of obligation and discomfort which can be assessed by self-reports.

Behavioral and Cognitive Attempts to Reduce Indebtedness

The magnitude of indebtedness can also be assessed by measuring the strength of attempts to reduce it. This hypothesis is predicated on the assumption that as the magnitude of indebtedness increases, there is a corresponding increase in the degree of effort and vigor directed toward its reduction. Two principal modes of indebtedness reduction are proposed. The recipient can behaviorally reduce his feeling of indebtedness by *reciprocating* the benefit, and/or he can *cognitively restructure* the situation. These modes of reducing feelings of indebtedness are assumed to complement each other, in that to the extent the recipient reduces his indebtedness via one mode, he will be less likely to employ the other. Each mode of reduction will now be described in greater detail, the purpose being to identify the conditions under which each mode is likely to be employed. It is assumed that in choosing a particular mode for reducing indebtedness, the recipient is motivated by reward–cost considerations, the mode that is less costly and more rewarding being preferred.

Reciprocation

The attempt to measure magnitude of indebtedness in terms of reciprocity behavior is complicated by the fact that reciprocity behavior can serve other motives in addition to indebtedness reduction. It is hypothesized that there are at least three motivational bases for reciprocating a benefit. Although each by itself is sufficient to motivate reciprocity, it is suggested here that a given act of reciprocity is likely to be multidetermined.

First, reciprocity may be motivated by the recipient's desire to receive future rewards from the donor. By reciprocating the benefit, the recipient is in effect reinforcing the donor's helping action, thereby increasing the probability of receiving such help in the future. This form of reciprocity motivation is often used to characterize the economic nature of man—the principal theme of exchange theorists such as Homans (1961) and Blau (1964). The major determinant for this type of reciprocity, which can be labeled *utilitarian reciprocity*, is the recipient's belief that the donor has the ability to provide him with future benefits.

Second, reciprocity may derive from the recipient's increased attraction to the donor following receipt of a benefit. It is assumed here that attribution processes (Jones & Davis, 1965; Kelley, 1967, 1971) mediate the recipient's increased liking for the donor. Attraction to the donor can result from a number of attributions made about the donor's motives, such as his liking for the recipient and his concern about the recipient's welfare. In this context, reciprocity fulfills several related functions for the recipient. First, reciprocity can serve to express to the donor the recipient's positive regard for him, such as when the recipient labels his help as "a token of my esteem." In addition, the increase in attraction for the donor may make reciprocation more rewarding for the recipient, since it would involve interaction with an attractive other. Finally, the increase in attractiveness following receipt of a benefit is likely to increase the recipient's concern for the donor's well-being. He will, therefore, be more sensitive and alert to the donor's needs, and thus be more likely to help when such need arises. The common thread underlying these instances of reciprocity is that each requires the mediating presence of increased attraction to the donor following receipt of a benefit.

In comparison with reciprocity based on utilitarian and attraction considerations, reciprocity motivated by the need to reduce indebtedness can be labeled *normative*, since it derives from internal pressure to conform to the norm of reciprocity (Gouldner, 1960). This form of reciprocity is not contingent upon external rewards as in the case of utilitarian reciprocity, nor is it exclusively dependent upon the recipient's attraction to the donor, as in the case of an attraction-mediated reciprocity. Rather, normative reciprocity is motivated by the feeling of obligation, the removal of which constitutes a reinforcement. Examination of the experimental literature on reciprocity reveals considerable support for the indebtedness-reducing function of reciprocity (Garrett & Libby, 1973; Goranson & Berkowitz, 1966; Greenberg *et al.*, 1971; Greenberg & Frisch, 1972; Kahn, 1972; Kahn & Tice, 1973; Leventhal *et al.*, 1969; Pruitt, 1968; Regan, 1971; Stapleton *et al.*, 1973; Wilke & Lanzetta, 1970). The conditions under which reciprocity is the preferred mode of reducing indebtedness are discussed below.

Conditions Affecting Use of the Reciprocity Mode

Reciprocity is likely to become the preferred mode of reducing indebtedness to the extent that the following conditions obtain: (a) the reciprocity response is made prepotent or salient, and (b) the recipient perceives that he has an opportunity to reciprocate.

Salience of the Reciprocity Alternative. It is hypothesized that the reciprocity response will become salient to the extent that the recipient has been reinforced in the past for reciprocating help and the present situation is perceived as similar to past situations in which reciprocity was reinforced. In addition, the behavior of others in the present situation or in the very recent past can increase the salience of the reciprocity alternative. Thus, it is hypothesized that observation of a reciprocating model in the recent past will heighten the salience of the reciprocity mode. Furthermore, actions by the donor or observers which indicate their expectation that the recipient should repay the donor will increase the salience of this mode of reducing indebtedness.

Perception of an Opportunity to Reciprocate. In order for the recipient to attempt to repay the donor, he must perceive that there exists an opportunity to do so. This, in turn, is contingent on the perception that (1) the recipient has the ability to help, (2) the donor is willing to accept help, and (3) reciprocation involves minimal costs for the recipient. The last contingency is based upon the assumption that in choosing to reciprocate the recipient selects what he perceives to be the most profitable option available to him. For example, while the recipient may perceive that he has the ability to provide the donor with needed help, he may not consider this a profitable opportunity when reciprocation entails high costs in terms of time and effort relative to other options. One factor that is likely to affect the profitability of reciprocation is the donor's need state. By providing the donor with much-needed resources, each unit of help is invested with greater value, thereby permitting the recipient to reduce his indebtedness more efficiently.

Indebtedness theory would predict, therefore, that the recipient, in his search for an opportunity to reciprocate, will be motivated to view the donor as both needing and willing to receive help. Accordingly, we might expect the recipient to be particularly vigilant regarding the donor's need for help. In addition, it is expected that the recipient will attempt to maximize his ability to provide the donor with needed help. Examination of the experimental literature on reciprocity behavior indicates that the recipient has usually been provided with the constituents of an opportunity to reciprocate, with the major focus being on the recipient's willingness to use this opportunity. Thus, we see that, typically, the recipient has been led to believe that on a second task he has the ability to provide the donor with needed assistance, usually at minimal costs, and that the donor is likely to accept such assistance. Examples of help that recipients have been asked to provide include: stacking papers (Brehm & Cole, 1966), purchasing raffle tickets (Regan, 1971), providing financial help either directly (Garrett & Libby, 1973) or indirectly (Greenberg *et al.*, 1971; Greenberg & Frisch, 1972; Pruitt, 1968), choosing to receive electric shocks (Lerner & Lichtman, 1968), and agreeing to wash a blouse (Schopler & Thompson, 1968).

Two experiments by Greenberg and Bar-Tal (1976) indicate that when one of the necessary components of an opportunity to reciprocate is absent, recipients appear motivated to establish its presence. In both experiments subjects were asked to solve two jigsaw puzzles. On the first task, subjects received varying amounts of help from a confederate. After informing subjects that on the second task they could interact and exchange information with each other, and prior to working on the second puzzle, subjects were permitted to examine a booklet containing solutions to their own and the confederate's puzzle. Results from the first experiment showed that recipients of help spent more time studying the solution to the confederate's puzzle than subjects who did not receive help. In the second experiment, study time was held constant, with the dependent variable being amount of information correctly learned concerning the solution to the confederate's puzzle. Consistent with the results of the first experiment, subjects who received prior help acquired more information concerning the confederate's puzzle than those who did not receive prior help. These results support the conclusion that motivation to reduce indebtedness stimulates exposure to and learning of information which is instrumental for reciprocation.

The relationship between indebtedness and the opportunity to reciprocate has been explored in a series of investigations in which the opportunity to reciprocate comprised the independent variable. Indebtedness theory would predict that it is more aversive to be in a situation where no reciprocation opportunity exists than in a situation where such an opportunity does exist. Hobbes (1651/1960) described graphically the condition of one who is unable to reciprocate a benefit:

> To have received from one, to whom we think ourselves equal, greater benefits than there is hope to requite, disposeth to counterfeit love; but really secret hatred; and puts a man into the estate of desperate debtor. . . . For benefits oblige; and obligation is thraldom [i.e., bondage, servitude]; and unrequitable obligation, perceptual thraldom; which is to ones equal, hateful. . . . Also to receive benefits, though from an equal, or inferior, as long as there is hope of requital, disposeth to love. (p. 65)

Consistent with expectations from indebtedness theory, experimental findings show that compared to people who are able to reciprocate help, individuals who are unable to reciprocate (a) demonstrate greater reluctance to request help (Greenberg, 1968; Greenberg & Shapiro, 1971; Morris & Rosen, 1973), and when help is received they (b) accept less help (Greenberg & Shapiro, 1971), (c) show less liking for the donor (Castro, 1974; Gergen *et al.*, 1975; Gross & Latané, 1974), and (d) feel less comfortable and more constrained and confined (Gross & Latané, 1974).

Since one of the components of the opportunity to reciprocate is the donor's need state, it is not unreasonable to speculate that in order to increase the value of the resources that he can provide, the recipient may engage in activities designed to increase the donor's need state and/or enhance the donor's dependency on the recipient for help. Conceivably, the recipient may actively prevent others from helping the donor since their assistance would deprive him of an opportunity to reciprocate. It must be kept in mind that an individual who is indebted is motivated to reduce his indebtedness, and is not necessarily desirous of seeing the donor benefited by just anyone, as would be true of a person who is highly attracted to the donor. What the indebted individual desires is that the donor be benefited at his hands. Writing in the eighteenth century, Adam Smith (1892) described eloquently the difference in motivation between one who is attracted to a donor and one who is indebted to him:

> All that his passion [attraction] desires, is to see him happy, without regarding who was the author of his prosperity. But gratitude is not to be satisfied in this manner. If the person to whom we owe many obligations is made happy without our assistance, though it pleases our love, it does not content our gratitude. Till we have recompensed him, till we ourselves have been instrumental in promoting his happiness, we feel ourselves still loaded with that debt which his past services have laid upon us. (p. 95)

The Opportunity to Reciprocate Created by the Presence of a Third Person. The opportunity to reciprocate need not involve direct exchange between recipient and donor, but may, under certain conditions, involve indirect exchange via a third party. The opportunity to reciprocate indirectly rests on the assumption that by helping the third person, the recipient is in effect benefiting the donor. This circumstance can occur in three ways. First, the recipient may not be in a position to aid the donor directly, whereas a third person may be. In this situation, the recipient can supply resources to the third person along with instructions to pass them on to the donor. Second, when the recipient does not possess resources needed by the donor, but the third person does, the recipient may benefit the third person and direct him to make repayment by helping the donor.

A third, and somewhat different, circumstance permitting the recipient to reciprocate indirectly could occur when the recipient is unable to aid the donor directly but is in a position to aid a third

person whose welfare is valued by the donor. The greater the importance that the recipient perceives the donor attaches to a third person's
welfare, the stronger is that person's candidacy as a substitute for the
original donor. Third persons capable of mediating reciprocity in this
way would include those with whom the donor is perceived to have
a close unit relationship, such as members of his family and close
friends. Evidence supporting this proposition is provided by Greenberg et al. (1974), who compared subjects' responses to the following
two questions: (1) "If you were indebted to someone, how indebted
would you still feel if you then helped someone with whom the help-
giver was not acquainted?" and (2) "If you were indebted to someone,
how indebted would you still feel if you helped someone close to the
help-giver such as a member of his/her family?" Identical 7-point
response scales were provided for each question, with alternatives
ranging from "Still feel indebted" (7) to "No longer feel indebted" (1).
Results indicated that subjects felt that they would feel less indebted
($p < .001$) after helping a member of the donor's family ($M = 4.25$)
than after helping a stranger ($M = 6.60$).

The above evidence indicates that the presence of a third person
can increase the recipient's opportunity to reciprocate, either because
the third person serves as the recipient's agent or because the third
person functions as a substitute for the original donor.

The substitute function of a third person can come about in yet
another way. If the recipient anticipates no opportunity to interact
further with the donor, he may be able to reduce his indebtedness by
helping someone who is *similar* to the donor but whose welfare is not
necessarily valued by the donor. The substitutability of a third person
for the original donor probably operates via stimulus generalization.
The greater the similarity between the donor and the third person on
relevant dimensions, the greater is the likelihood that the third person
will be an object of reciprocity. In choosing to help someone who
resembles the donor, the recipient increases his opportunity to reciprocate by broadening the width of the donor category. There is
suggestive empirical evidence for repayment to substitute donors.
Berkowitz and Friedman (1967), for example, found that recipients
who were prevented from helping the same person who had helped
them previously worked as hard to help a third person as did recipients
who were permitted to help the same person who had helped them.
Moreover, in a study by Greenglass (1969), subjects were either
hindered, not helped, or helped by a supposed other subject on the
first of two tasks. On the second task, subjects were paired with a
different other, who was made to appear either similar or dissimilar to

the person with whom they had worked on the first task. Data revealed a tendency for recipients of help to give more help to the similar other than to the dissimilar other ($p < .05$, one-tailed).

Cognitive Restructuring. The magnitude of indebtedness can also be assessed by measuring the strength of attempts to reduce it through cognitive restructuring, the cognitions at issue being those which determine the magnitude of indebtedness. Thus, the recipient can reexamine his original assessment of the situation and decide that: (a) the magnitude of his net benefits was not as great as he originally thought, (b) the donor incurred smaller net costs than he originally believed, (c) the locus of causality of the donor's actions was more external to the recipient than he perceived originally (this change in belief could involve a determination that chance factors or role obligations affected the donor's actions), (d) the donor's motives were not as altruistic as he thought formerly, and/or (e) he misperceived or misinterpreted the opinions of relevant others concerning the extent to which he was obligated to reciprocate.

The recipient can facilitate cognitive restructuring further by enlarging his past and future time perspective. By reassessing the donor's actions in terms of a more extended time dimension, the recipient can come to believe that the donor was merely repaying a past debt. Recognition of this would lead the recipient to reevaluate his beliefs about the locus of causality of the donor's action and the donor's motives for providing the benefit. By enlarging his future time perspective to include anticipated opportunities to reciprocate, the recipient may be able to convince himself that the indebtedness condition is only temporary. Gross and Latané (1974) have shown that although this cognition would not itself reduce the magnitude of indebtedness, it might at least reduce some of the discomfort and tension associated with this state.

Conditions Affecting Use of the Cognitive Restructuring Mode. In attempting to reduce the magnitude of indebtedness, it is assumed that recipients will prefer the least costly mode of reduction. The major cost involved in the use of cognitive restructuring derives from risks inherent in the distortion of reality. The realization that his cognitive structure is at variance with reality could cause the recipient to have doubts about his objectivity. Moreover, recognition by others, including the donor, that the recipient has distorted reality may result in the recipient's being the object of social disapproval. Accordingly, cognitive restructuring is likely to become the preferred mode of indebtedness reduction to the extent that (a) cognitions associated with the helping act are ambiguous, (b) there are few witnesses to the helping act, (c) further interaction with the donor and witnesses is not anticipated, and (d) the recipient perceives little or no opportunity to reciprocate. When cognitions are ambiguous, that is, when they are not clearly linked to objective reality, the recipient will find it somewhat easier to restructure his beliefs about the situation, since his beliefs are less subject to objective disconfirmation. Similarly, when there are few witnesses to the helping act, the recipient is less likely to encounter a social reality which contradicts his beliefs. In addition, when no further interaction with the donor or witnesses is anticipated, the recipient need not fear that his beliefs about the helping event will be challenged by these individuals. Finally, cognitive restructuring will be preferred when use of the reciprocity mode is unavailable or very costly. This can occur when the recipient believes that the donor will not accept his help, when he lacks the ability to help the donor, or when reciprocation involves expenditure of large amounts of time, energy, and/or money.

Because investigations have focused almost exclusively on the reciprocity mode of indebtedness reduction, evidence relevant to cognitive restructuring is almost entirely lacking. In one of the few studies designed to investigate the cognitive restructuring mode, Gergen, Morse, and Bode (1974) found that recipients who received more than they felt they deserved tended to minimize their net benefits by overestimating the magnitude of their costs. In comparison, subjects who received no more than they expected did not show such evidence of cognitive restructuring. In the absence of additional experimental evidence, propositions concerning cognitive restructuring must be regarded as speculative.

In this section on methods for assessing the magnitude of indebtedness, it has been shown that indebtedness can be inferred from self-reports as well as from the strength of attempts to reduce it. Regarding modes of indebtedness reduction, there is ample support for use of the reciprocity mode, whereas the empirical status of the cognitive restructuring mode remains to be determined.

Comparison between Indebtedness and Inequity

The antecedents and consequences of indebtedness having been explicated, an attempt will now be made to differentiate between indebtedness and inequity. Both can be viewed as forms of cognitive dissonance (Festinger, 1957) deriving from a discrepancy between what an individual receives from another and what he believes he ought to receive in the normative sense. Viewed from this perspective, indebtedness is similar to Adams's (1963, 1965) concept of inequity in that the recipient has a more favorable ratio of outcomes to inputs than the donor.

Yet, although indebtedness is similar to inequity, it differs in several important ways. First, equity motivation, as described by Adams (1963, 1965), is solely a function of the disproportionality between the donor's and recipient's outcomes and inputs. In comparison, indebtedness motivation considers not only the disproportionality but also the reasons for the disproportionality, namely, the locus of causality and the motives attributed to the donor. It is noteworthy that the locus of causality variable has been included in a recent reformulation of the equity model by Walster, Berscheid, and Walster (1973).

Second, indebtedness derives from the actions of only two parties—a donor and a recipient—whereas inequity can and often does involve a third party who is responsible for the allocation of rewards between two individuals. The presence of a third party creates interpretive problems for equity theory, since it is often not clear with whom the recipient is comparing his outcomes–inputs ratio—the co-recipient or the reward distributor. Adams and his associates (e.g., Adams & Jacobsen, 1964; Adams & Rosenbaum, 1962) view the high rate of performance of "overpaid" workers as an attempt to increase their inputs so as to achieve equity with their more qualified co-workers. In contrast, from an indebtedness perspective, the worker's high rate of productivity represents an attempt to repay a generous reward distributor by improving the latter's outcomes.

Third, not all the modes of reducing inequity are appropriate for reducing indebtedness. Whereas the recipient's *actual* alteration of his own outcomes–inputs ratio (as opposed to cognitive distortion of the ratio) may serve to reduce inequity, no reduction in the magnitude of indebtedness is expected by the use of this mechanism. That is, indebtedness is not reduced by the recipient's actually increasing his inputs or decreasing his outcomes. Rather, a reduction of indebtedness occurs when the recipient effects a change in the *donor's ratio* of outcomes to inputs, by increasing the donor's outcomes and/or helping him to reduce his inputs.

Fourth, unlike the reduction of inequity, indebtedness is not reduced when the recipient perceives that a third party is responsible for improving the donor's ratio outcomes to inputs. On the contrary, indebtedness theory predicts that such intervention by a third person may *increase* rather than *decrease* the recipient's discomfort, expecially when the recipient perceives that he has the resources to repay the donor. In order to reduce indebtedness, the recipient must perceive himself and not a third person as responsible for improving the donor's ratio of outcomes to inputs. As noted earlier, the recipient may employ a third party to repay the debt, but in this instance, the third party would be acting as the recipient's agent or instrument of reciprocity.

Cultural Variations

Gouldner (1960) described the norm of reciprocity and its attendant state of indebtedness as being "universal." Although this proposition awaits empirical confirmation, evidence has accumulated in recent years that indebtedness is not confined to a white, middle-class, American college population. In this section we will examine evidence for the presence of indebtedness motivation among diverse cultural groups. Unlike the experimental evidence cited in the previous sections, the evidence presented here derives primarily from field studies conducted by anthropologists and sociologists.

In his classic examination of gift exchange in archaic societies, Mauss (1954/1967) noted that gift exchange constituted "a total social fact" in that it fulfilled economic, religious, legal, and social functions. Citing evidence from numerous primitive societies, Mauss documented the existence of three obligations characteristic of such societies: the obligations to give, to receive, and to repay. With regard to the latter he observed that "the obligation of worthy return is imperative. Face is lost forever if it is not made. . . . The Haida say . . . that a girl's mother who gives a betrothal payment to the mother of a young chief 'puts a thread on him'" (p. 41).

Farb's (1968) examination of the Eskimo culture shows that the Eskimo was keenly aware of the obligation to repay a benefit and the discomfort felt by the debtor. This is reflected in the phrase, "With gifts you make slaves just as with whips you make dogs" (p. 43). The norm of reciprocity and the feelings of indebtedness engendered by it have important survival value in a society where one's fortune can vary easily from feast to famine. As Farb notes:

> an Eskimo knows that despite his plenty today, assuredly he will be in want tomorrow. He knows also that the best place for him to store his surplus is in someone else's stomach, because sooner or later he will want his gift repaid. (p. 43)

In addition to playing an important role in archaic societies, indebtedness has been found to affect the behavior of certain segments of the population in industrial societies such as the Philippines (Hollensteiner, 1964; Robolos, 1964) and Japan (Befu, 1966; Benedict, 1946/1967; Dore, 1959). Hollensteiner (1964), in her study of reciprocity behavior in the lowland communities of the Philippines, described a form of reciprocity known as *utang na loob*—"a debt inside oneself," or a "sense of gratitude." Accordingly, "every Filipino is expected to possess *utang na loob:* that is, he should be aware of his obligations to those from whom he receives favors and should repay them in an acceptable manner [usually with interest]" (p. 29). Hollensteiner reports further that there is an "uneasiness" about being indebted which serves to encourage repayment with interest when the opportunity presents itself. Failure to repay a debt with interest leads to *hiya*, or shame, except where close friends are concerned. In the latter case, each friend purportedly enjoys doing favors for the other, and neither is generally conscious of the interplay of the debt relationship. Similar to Whyte's (1955) description of street corner society mentioned earlier is Hollensteiner's report that only when there is a clearly one-sided relationship or when the friendship begins to dissolve do the two parties become aware of what each has done for the other. Hollensteiner concludes that "as the genuine desire to be closely bound to someone declines, there is a corresponding growth of uneasiness at being on the debtor side of an utang na loob relationship" (p. 41). Consistent with our earlier theorizing on the role of a third person in reducing indebtedness is Hollensteiner's further observation that reciprocation may be made to a third person, such as a member of the donor's family or ingroup.

The extent to which feelings of indebtedness are embedded in Philippine rural culture is further reflected in the folk-ritual system described by Robolos (1964). These folk rituals serve the function of acknowledging one's indebtedness to the spirits for providing the recipient with good fortune. It is believed that spirits control the quality and quantity of crop harvests, as well as the health of people and domestic animals. Thus, there exists the belief that

> when favors are granted and no troubles arise, rituals must be observed to express gratitude. Non-performance will earn the person or the community concerned punishment from the "spirits." Fear of the "spirits" wrath compels a person to submit to ritualism. (p. 100)

Of all the anthropological descriptions of indebtedness, those pertaining to Japan are perhaps the most detailed. In her classic description of Japanese prewar society, Benedict (1946/1967) described the various usages of the word *on*, meaning indebted or obligated:

> *On* is in all its uses a load, an indebtedness, a burden, which one carries as best one may. A man receives *on* from a superior and the act of accepting an *on* from any man not definitely one's superior or at least one's equal gives one an uncomfortable sense of inferiority. When they say, "I wear an

> *on* to him" they are saying, "I carry a load of obligations to him," and they
> call this creditor, this benefactor, their "on man." (pp. 99–100)

She further states:

> Casual favors from relative strangers are the ones most resented, for with
> neighbors and in old-established hierarchical relationships a man knows
> and has accepted the complications of an *on*. But with mere acquaintances
> and near-equals men chafe. They would prefer to avoid getting entangled
> in all the consequences of *on*. The passivity of a street crowd in Japan when
> an accident occurs is not just lack of initiative. It is a recognition that any
> non-official interference would make the recipient wear an *on*. (p. 104)

The Japanese distinguish between those debts that are limitless and
cannot be fully repaid (*gimu*), such as debts to one's parents and the
Emperor, and those debts which can and must be repaid with mathematical equivalence (*giri*). Considered as *giri* are those obligations
which result from receipt of gifts and favors from others. Benedict
describes the tension associated with *giri*, noting that "repaying *giri* is
full of malaise. The difficulties of being a debtor are at their maximum
in the 'circle of *giri*'" (p. 134).

Similar to Hollensteiner's description of indebtedness in the Philippines is Befu's (1966) report that in rural Japan, when the donor and
recipient are close friends, "the notion of reciprocity, of balance is
often lost. Such exacting formula and calculating attitude is considered
unworthy of friendship" (p. 172).

Finally, consistent with predictions derived from indebtedness
theory, Dore (1959) reports that Japanese recipients feel greater obligation to reciprocate when they believe the locus of causality resides
in themselves than when they believe it resides in the donor. Dore
describes an incident in which the recipient reasoned "that as A had
brought the gift of his own accord the return gift should be of slightly
less value than the original gift, but if she had asked A to get the
melon for her it would have had to be considerably more expensive"
(p. 261).

Examples such as those presented in the above paragraphs suggest
strongly that indebtedness motivation is found in diverse cultures and
that its potency in these cultures is no less than that found among
American college sophomores.

In conclusion, it has been argued here that under specifiable
conditions, receipt of a benefit generates feelings of indebtedness
which mediate subsequent cognitive and behavioral reactions. Although indebtedness is not an inevitable consequence of receiving a
benefit, we believe that it occurs with sufficient frequency to warrant
a cautionary note to would-be donors and would-be recipients. That
there are attendant risks for both parties is suggested by the material

presented in this paper. The donor, for example, may discover that his generosity is not reciprocated because the recipient has reduced his indebtedness via cognitive restructuring. On the other hand, the recipient's pleasure at receiving a benefit may turn to distress as he becomes aware of the burdens of obligation. In light of such risks, we would call to the attention of would-be donors the words of Bolitho (1929/1941): "You need more tact in the dangerous art of giving presents than in any other social action" (p. 150). And for the benefit of would-be recipients, we would amend the ancient adage, "Beware of Greeks bearing gifts," to read "Beware of anyone bearing gifts."

ACKNOWLEDGMENTS

The author would like to express his indebtedness to those individuals whose constructive comments contributed to the development of ideas expressed here. They are Carl Backman, Daniel Bar-Tal, Paul Chassey, Janelle Greenberg, Alan Gross, Eric Jackson, Randi Koeske, John Levine, and Charles Perfetti.

What Should Be Done with Equity Theory?

New Approaches to the Study of Fairness in Social Relationships

GERALD S. LEVENTHAL

INTRODUCTION

The Problem of Allocation

The distribution of rewards and resources is a universal phenomenon that occurs in social systems of all sizes, from small groups to whole societies (Parsons, 1951; Parsons, Shils, & Olds, 1951). All groups, organizations, and societies deal with the question of allocating rewards, punishments, and resources. The manner in which a social system deals with these issues has great impact on its effectiveness and on the satisfaction of its members. For these reasons, it is not surprising that social scientists from many disciplines—political scientists, economists, sociologists, and psychologists—have been concerned with the problem of allocation (e.g., Jones & Kaufman, 1974; Leventhal, 1976a; Pondy, 1970).

In social psychology and sociology, exchange theorists such as Thibaut and Kelley (1959), Homans (1974), and Blau (1964) have analyzed reward distribution and its effects. In addition, there has been considerable research on the perceived fairness of distributions

GERALD S. LEVENTHAL • Department of Psychology, Wayne State University, Detroit, Michigan 48202. Preparation of this chapter was supported by Grant GS-3171, from the National Science Foundation.

of reward and punishment, and on the effect of violating perceived fairness. Much of this research has been guided by equity theory. According to the theory, human beings believe that rewards and punishments should be distributed in accordance with recipients' inputs or contributions (Adams, 1963, 1965; Homans, 1974). From this simple conception, equity theory has generated several distinct lines of research (Adams & Freedman, 1976; Goodman & Friedman, 1971; Leventhal, 1976a; Pritchard, 1969; Walster, Berscheid, & Walster, 1973). However, for several reasons, the theory has outgrown its usefulness and should be replaced by a more comprehensive formulation. Accordingly, this paper sets forth in detail a clear alternative to the equity theory approach. In so doing, several problems with equity theory are discussed, and an attempt is made to answer the question: What should be done with equity theory?

Issues in Equity Theory

Three major problems with equity theory are considered. The first problem is that equity theory employs a unidimensional rather than a multidimensional conception of fairness. The theory conceptualizes perceived justice solely in terms of a merit principle. The second problem is that equity theory considers only the final distribution of reward. The procedures that generate that distribution are not examined. The focus is on fair distribution. Problems of fair procedure are ignored. The third problem is that equity theory tends to exaggerate the importance of fairness in social relationships. Concern for justice is only one motivational force among many that influence social perception and behavior, and it may often be a weaker force than others.

Other approaches to the study of fairness in social exchange share some of these problems with equity theory. No single approach has solved them all. However, because equity theory is so prominent, it is the focus of this critique.

A MULTIDIMENSIONAL APPROACH TO DISTRIBUTIVE FAIRNESS

The Unidimensional Approach of Equity Theory

Equity theory employs a unidimensional concept of justice. The theory assumes that an individual judges the fairness of his own or others' rewards solely in terms of a merit principle. Fairness exists when rewards are in proportion to contributions. Undoubtedly, the theory is correct in assuming that an individual's perception of fairness is affected strongly by a *contributions rule* which dictates that persons with greater contributions should receive higher outcomes. However, equity theory ignores the possible role of other standards of justice that influence perception of distributive fairness. In contrast, a number of theorists have recognized the need for a multidimensional concept of distributive fairness (e.g., Deutsch, 1975; Komorita & Chertkoff, 1973; Lerner, 1974a; Leventhal, 1976a,b; Pruitt, 1972; Sampson, 1969). For example, the multidimensional approach of the justice judgment model (Leventhal, 1976b) assumes that an individual's judgments of fairness may be based, not only on the contributions rule, but also on a *needs rule* which dictates that persons with greater need should receive higher outcomes, or an *equality rule* which dictates that everyone should receive similar outcomes regardless of needs or contributions.

Terminology

Before examining the multidimensional approach to perceived fairness, it is necessary to consider the definition of the term *equity*. Most equity theory researchers have equated the term with a type of justice based on merit or contributions. But this definition is much narrower than that employed in everyday language. *Webster's Third New International Dictionary* defines the term *equity* as "a free and reasonable conformity to accepted standards of natural right, law, and justice without prejudice, favoritism, or fraud and without rigor entailing undue hardship." This definition is much broader than that typically preferred by equity researchers. The dictionary definition of *equity* encompasses a whole panoply of justice standards, not just one. Only a few social psychologists (e.g., Pruitt, 1972) have favored such a broad use of the term. Close inspection of the writings of equity theorists suggests they do sometimes use the term in a broad sense, as well as the narrow. However, they do not differentiate between the two usages, and may slide casually from one to the other. Perhaps this tendency is not surprising, given the theory's use of a unidimensional concept of justice based on merit. In the present paper, because of this ambiguity, the practice shall be to avoid using the term *equity*. Instead, the terms *fairness* and *justice* are used to refer to equity in the general sense defined by *Webster's*. The term *contributions rule* refers to equity in the more narrow sense of justice that is based on a matching of rewards to contributions. The term *distributive fairness* is also used frequently in these pages. The phrase refers to judgments of fair distribution, irrespective of whether the criterion of justice is based on needs, equality, contributions, or a combination of these factors.

The Multidimensional Approach of Justice Judgment Theory

The justice judgment model (Leventhal, 1976b) employs a multi-dimensional conception of justice that poses a clear alternative to equity theory. Justice judgment theory assumes that an individual's perception of fairness is based on several rules rather than on a single rule as employed in equity theory. In the present paper, which presents a revised and expanded form of the theory, a *justice rule* is defined as an individual's belief that a distribution of outcomes, or procedure for distributing outcomes, is fair and appropriate when it satisfies certain criteria. This definition presupposes two categories of justice rules, namely, *distribution rules* and *procedural rules*. A *distribution rule* is defined as the individual's belief that it is fair and appropriate when rewards, punishments, or resources are distributed in accordance with certain criteria. A specific criterion might require the matching of rewards to contributions, or matching rewards to needs, or dividing rewards equally. Thus, a contributions rule, needs rule, and equality rule are among the major distributive rules that can influence an individual's perception of distributive fairness.

Procedural rules constitute the second category of justice rules. A *procedural rule* is defined as an individual's belief that allocative procedures which satisfy certain criteria are fair and appropriate. Unfortunately, there are few studies of the impact of procedural factors on perceived fairness. Relatively little is known about an individual's evaluation of procedural components of the social system that regulate the allocative process. Theoretical proposals about the specific criteria that define rules of fair procedure must, therefore, be quite speculative. Nevertheless, later in this paper, six rules of fair procedure will be proposed and discussed. For the moment, however, the problem of procedural fairness is set aside, and the issue of distributive fairness is the main concern.

Judgments of Distributive Fairness

A major tenet of the justice judgment model is that an individual applies distribution rules selectively and follows different rules at different times. Thus, the individual's basic criteria for evaluating fairness may change with circumstances. In some situations, he or she may believe that one distribution rule is more relevant than others, in which case that rule has greater impact on the evaluation of distributive fairness.

The model assumes a four-stage justice judgment sequence by

which an individual evaluates the fairness of his own or others' rewards and punishments. As described below, the four stages are weighting, preliminary estimation, rule combination, and outcome evaluation.

1. *Weighting.* In the weighting stage of the justice judgment sequence, the individual decides which distribution rules are applicable, and the relative importance of the rules. Rules of greater importance are assigned higher weight in the judgment sequence and have greater impact on the perception of fairness.

2. *Preliminary Estimation.* In the preliminary estimation stage, the individual estimates the amount and type of outcomes that receivers deserve based on each applicable rule. It is assumed that an individual uses a separate information-processing subroutine (Anderson, 1974) for each rule to estimate the receiver's deservingness based on that rule. Consequently, if several rules have been assigned high weight, several information-processing subroutines will operate in parallel. Except in young children, the perceptual-cognitive skills involved in such judgments are probably well-practiced and automatic. Consequently, an individual can make several nearly simultaneous estimates of deservingness, based on different distribution rules.

3. *Rule Combination.* In the rule-combination stage of the justice judgment sequence, the individual combines the several preliminary estimates to arrive at a final judgment of the receiver's deservingness. The events in this stage are summarized by the following rule-combination equation:

$$\text{Deserved outcomes} = w_c D_{\text{by contributions}} + w_n D_{\text{by needs}} +$$
$$w_e D_{\text{by equality}} + w_o D_{\text{by other rules}}$$

In this equation, the letter w stands for the word *weight,* and the letter D stands for the word *deservingness.* The terms w_c, w_n, w_e and w_o represent, respectively, the weights of the contributions rule, needs rule, equality rule, and any other distribution rule that may influence the individual's perception of a recipient's deservingness. The terms, $D_{\text{by contributions}}$, $D_{\text{by needs}}$, $D_{\text{by equality}}$, and $D_{\text{by other rules}}$ represent, respectively, an individual's preliminary estimates of recipients' deservingness based on the contributions rule, needs rule, equality rule, and any other distribution rules that influence his or her judgments of distributive fairness. The rule-combination equation states that the relative impact of each preliminary estimate on a perceiver's judgments of deservingness depends on the relative weight of the justice rules.

Distribution rules with similar weight may have contradictory implications. For example, the needs rule and contributions rule would dictate opposite distributions of reward in the case of a recipient with high need and low contributions. An individual usually deals with such contradictions by compromising between the opposed rules. A recipient with high need and low contributions may be evaluated as average in deservingness. Of course, distribution rules are not always contradictory. For example, the needs rule and contributions rule would dictate similar distributions of reward in the case of a recipient who is high in both contributions and need, or low in both respects.

A perceiver often evaluates the deservingness of several recipients at a time. In some cases, he or she may judge them collectively and estimate the deservingness of an entire group of persons. In other cases, the individual uses several parallel versions of the rule-combination equation, one for each recipient whose deservingness is under evaluation (Leventhal, 1976b).

4. *Outcome Evaluation.* In the outcome-evaluation stage, the final stage of the justice judgment sequence, the individual assesses the fairness of the receiver's outcomes. The individual has estimated what receivers ought to get and can now determine whether their actual (or potential) rewards and punishments are in line with what they deserve.

New Directions for Research

The justice judgment model suggests several new directions for research on distributive fairness. First, it calls for studies of factors that determine the relative weight of different distribution rules. The study of determinants of the relative weight of justice rules is one of the most important research questions posed by the multidimensional analysis of perceived fairness. Second, it calls for careful study of the attribution processes by which perceivers estimate deservingness based on each rule. An important question is whether the judgmental operations associated with one distribution rule differ in form from those associated with other distribution rules. Third, the model calls for studies that examine the role of additional distribution rules. The final term of the rule-combination equation, $w_o D_{by\ other\ rules}$, emphasizes that other justice rules besides the contributions, needs, and equality rules may have important effects on the perception of distributive fairness. The following section elaborates on what these other justice rules and their implications might be.

Other Justice Rules

At least five additional distribution rules have been identified that may affect an individual's perception of distributive fairness. First, it has been suggested there is a *rule of justified self-interest*, which dictates that, in appropriate circumstances, it is fair for an individual to take as much for himself as possible (Lerner, 1971, 1974a). Second, it has been suggested there is a *rule of adhering to commitments,* which dictates that fairness is violated unless persons receive that which has been promised to them (Leventhal, 1976a; Pruitt, 1971, 1972). Third, it has been suggested there is a *legality rule,* which dictates that fairness is violated if the distribution of reward or punishment is inconsistent with existing laws and regulations (Berkowitz & Walker, 1967; Kaufmann, 1970; Lerner, 1974a).

These suggestions call for two types of study. First, factors that affect the relative weight of these rules must be examined. For example, one might investigate conditions that lead an individual to disregard past promises or commitments and to evaluate distributive fairness in other terms. Second, it is important to examine the consequences of conflict between these distribution rules and others. For example, one might investigate the effect of conflict between the needs rule and the legality rule that occurs when existing laws prevent needy persons from improving their lot.

Two additional distribution rules remain to be discussed: the ownership rule and the status rule. It is assumed there is an *ownership rule* which dictates it is fair for individuals to continue to possess rewards and resources that already belong to them, and it is unfair to take these resources from them. This rule is exemplified by the concepts of *squatter's rights* and *private property.* The basic tenet of the ownership rule is that the owner has the right to decide when and how his property shall be used.

Of the distribution rules considered in this section, the status rule has probably received more explicit attention than the others. Both sociologists and social psychologists have discussed the operation of pressures toward status congruence, i.e., of a tendency to equilibrate people's rank on different dimensions of status (e.g., Berger, Zelditch, Anderson, & Cohen, 1972; Homans, 1974; Sampson, 1963, 1969). In the present framework, the *status rule* dictates it is fair when persons of high social rank receive higher outcomes than those of low social rank.

From the vantage point of equity theory, one might question the distinction between the status rule and the contributions rule. Equity theory treats characteristics such as sex, ethnicity, and social position as inputs that merit appropriate outcomes. Furthermore, it might be argued that an individual's perceived social rank is usually so highly correlated with perceived contributions that the distinction between the two rules has no significance. However, the actual correlation between perceived social status and perceived contributions is probably quite imperfect. Although persons of higher social position may

often be seen as having higher contributions, there are many exceptions. There are cases in which individuals of high social status make
low contributions (e.g., the prodigal son of a wealthy, established
family), and cases in which individuals of low social status have high
contributions (e.g., an uneducated immigrant who works hard and is
successful in business). In such instances, the status rule and contributions rule are in direct conflict, and it is meaningful to distinguish
between them.

Many questions remain unanswered about additional distribution
rules and their role in the perception of distributive fairness. Such
rules are an important aspect of multidimensional models of perceived
justice and require further study.

What Should Be Done with Equity Theory?

The preceding discussion answers a question posed at the beginning of this paper: What should be done about equity theory? The
answer is that equity theory should be incorporated into a more
comprehensive theoretical framework that takes a broader view of the
problem of perceived justice in social relationships. The justice judgment model which, by virtue of its multidimensional approach is more
comprehensive than equity theory, accomplishes this task by treating
the basic equity theory equation as one component of a multistage
sequence of interlocking and parallel judgments. The equation for
estimating $D_{by\ contributions}$, which is a slightly modified version of the
core equation of equity theory, is a component of the justice judgment
sequence.

THE PERCEPTION OF PROCEDURAL FAIRNESS

Procedural Fairness Defined

Every group, organization, or society has procedures that regulate
the distribution of rewards and resources. There is a network of
regulatory procedures that guides the allocative process. The distribution of reward or punishment is only the final step in a sequence of
events. However, equity theory and the concept of distributive fairness
restrict the analysis of perceived justice to this last step in the allocative
process. Perceived fairness is defined solely in terms of the distribution
of reward. The social system which generates that distribution is not
considered. No provision is made for an individual's internal concep-

tual representation of properties of the social system that regulate the allocative process. However, pioneering work by Thibaut, Walker, and their associates (Freidland, Thibaut, & Walker, 1973; Thibaut, Friedland, & Walker, 1974; Thibaut, Walker, LaTour, & Houlden, 1974; Walker, LaTour, Lind, & Thibaut, 1974), and philosophical analyses of the problem of justice (e.g., Rawls, 1971), indicate that procedural aspects of the allocative process are important determinants of perceived fairness.

The concept of *procedural fairness* refers to an individual's perception of the fairness of procedural components of the social system that regulate the allocative process. The concept focuses on the individual's cognitive map of events that precede the distribution of reward, and the evaluation of those events. Perhaps the best way to introduce the concept of procedural fairness is to relate an incident that occurred shortly before this paper was written. It involved a telephone call from a faculty member in another department whose request for a Faculty Research Award had just been turned down. He called me because I was the chairperson of the Behavioral-Social Sciences Subcommittee that had reviewed his proposal. This subcommittee was a part of a larger body, the Faculty Research Awards Committee, that evaluated approximately 150 proposals from faculty members requesting financial support for their research. The typical proposal requested four to five thousand dollars, and, since the committee had only $132,000 at its disposal, some difficult choices had to be made.

In my conversation with the person whose proposal was turned down, I answered all questions truthfully, but also tried to be friendly and supportive. At the outset, my caller spoke with an air of quiet anger and firmness. Who had chosen the members of the subcommittee, he asked, and why was there no one from his department on the committee, someone who might have understood his proposal more fully? I explained that I didn't know how the subcommittee members were chosen, but pointed out that they came from a wide range of schools and disciplines. I said that, in my judgment, an attempt had been made to include a broad and representative range of subcommittee members with diverse competencies and interests. I also emphasized that, in any one year, it was impossible to include on the subcommittee a representative from every one of the numerous departments that might have grant proposals reviewed by the Behavioral-Social Sciences Subcommittee.

In further remarks, I described the process by which our subcommittee had made its decisions. I noted that each of the six members had first made a private and independent evaluation of the 29 proposals we reviewed. We had held two meetings, and, in the second of them, pooled our judgments and collectively ranked the proposals. It was emphasized that the proposals were discussed carefully, and that the entire process was carried out with a concern for accuracy. I also noted that there was a high degree of unanimity in the ratings of proposals. I added that, in view of the fact that there wasn't enough money to fund all the proposals that deserved support, we had done the best job we could under difficult circumstances.

Up to this point, I had said little about the subcommittee's actual evaluation of my caller's application. I had not yet told him he ranked 21st in a field of 29 applicants, and that only the top eight had been funded. After communicating these facts, I gave a detailed explanation of our reaction to his proposal, and noted that, although the proposal was interesting, we were troubled by the absence of focused hypotheses, and the failure to describe the precise nature of the research to be conducted. In short, I said, the proposal received a low rating because it was vague and unclear. Wouldn't it have been possible, my caller asked, to have contacted him for further clarification? I stated that such a procedure would create serious difficulties, because we had to treat everyone alike. Whatever we would do for one would have to be done for the others. If we contacted him, we would have to contact all applicants and give everyone an opportunity for an interview. I indicated that such a procedure would involve the subcommittee members, all of whom were busy people, in an endless round of interviews and confrontations with applicants whose presonal concern and anxiety was so great that it would be difficult to maintain objectivity. At this point my caller seemed satisfied. Our conversation ended amicably and I urged him to call me again if he wished.

From a theoretical viewpoint, what does this story demonstrate? First, it shows there is often a complex network of events and procedures that precedes the final distribution of reward. Decision makers have to be selected, the structure of a group decision process has to be decided, and so on. Second, the story demonstrates that the decision makers who control the allocative process, and the individuals who receive reward, readily form cognitive maps of procedural components of the allocative process. Third, the story indicates that an individual readily evaluates the fairness of procedural components, and that such evaluations affect the perceived fairness of the final distribution of reward. If the procedures are seen as fair, then the final distribution is likely to be accepted as fair even though it may be disadvantageous. Fourth, the story suggests that an individual's judgments of fair procedure are influenced by personal self-interest. The receiver whose rewards are low is inclined to doubt the fairness of allocative procedures, and to search for flaws in the system that will justify claims for higher reward (cf. Patchen, 1961). Conversely, the decision maker who wants to back up his decisions and protect his position may strongly emphasize that existing procedures are fair.

With respect to the final point about a decision maker's seeking to strengthen his position, in thinking back over my phone conversation, it is clear that I attempted to persuade my caller that fair procedures had been used to evaluate his proposal. Without fully realizing it, I presented a series of persuasive messages that manipulated his perception of procedural fairness. But what were the major factors in this influence attempt? It seems there were two. First, I identified several procedural components of the allocative process. They ranged from the process of selecting members of the subcommittee, to the structure of the subcommittee's decision-making process. Next, without realizing it, I applied certain implicit standards or rules of fair procedure to these procedural components in order to prove they were fair. The method I chanced on for influencing my caller's perception of procedural fairness contains a simple theoretical paradigm. This paradigm for analyzing the perception of procedural fairness has two steps. First, the major procedural components in an individual's cognitive map of the allocative process are identified. Then, the justice rules used to evaluate procedural fairness are applied to those components. This paradigm is developed in the following sections.

Structural Components in Cognitive Maps of the Allocative Process

An individual develops cognitive maps of the interaction settings and social systems in which he functions. These internal representations of the social environment contain structural elements that correspond to important features of the allocative process. A perceiver may evaluate the fairness of any of these structural elements. The evaluation is based on rules of fair procedure that are discussed in a later section. The present section focuses on identifying and defining the procedural elements.

It is postulated that an individual may discriminate any of seven categories of procedural components, i.e., selection of agents, setting ground rules, gathering information, decision structure, appeals, safeguards, and change mechanisms. An individual may evaluate the fairness of any of these structural components in his or her cognitive map of the social environment. The perceived components of procedure are defined as follows:

1. *Selection of Agents.* The sequence of events begins with proce-

dures for choosing the persons or agents who serve as decision makers or information collectors in the allocative process. These individuals may be elected, or selected by higher authorities.

2. *Setting Ground Rules.* The sequence next involves procedures for informing potential receivers about the nature of available rewards, and what must be done to obtain them. Performance goals and evaluation criteria must be defined and communicated to the receivers.

3. *Gathering Information.* Next come procedures for gathering and utilizing information about the prospective receivers of reward. Before distributing reward, it is usually necessary to evaluate the recipients. For this purpose, reliable information about their behavior must be obtained. In addition, it may be necessary to develop criteria for deciding which types of information constitute usable evidence.

4. *Decision Structure.* The next set of procedures defines the structure of the final decision process by which reward or punishment is allocated. This factor is especially important in the case of collective allocation decisions, because the structure of a group decision process may be quite complex. A variety of procedural arrangements is possible when decisions are made by a group or committee, or by a succession of individuals located at progressively higher (or lower) levels in the social system.

5. *Appeals.* Social systems usually have some form of grievance or appeal procedures that give dissatisfied individuals, and their sympathizers, an opportunity to seek redress. They may attempt to modify either the distribution of reward itself, or actions taken at earlier stages in the allocative process. The appeal procedures may be highly structured and formal, or quite informal.

6. *Safeguards.* Some procedures serve as safeguards which ensure that agents who administer the allocative process are performing their responsibilities with honesty and integrity. Other procedures deter opportunistic individuals from obtaining rewards or resources by illicit means. In either case, the procedures involve monitoring behavior and applying sanctions when required.

7. *Change Mechanisms.* A final set of procedures involves methods for changing procedures that regulate the allocative process. The methods for changing procedures may profoundly affect both the stability of distribution policies over time and the possibility of correcting unfair situations.

The seven structural components listed above may be present in an individual's cognitive map of any interaction setting or social system in which rewards, punishments, or resources are distributed. The settings may range from courtrooms in which fines and jail sentences are dispensed, to classrooms in which students are tested and graded, to work situations in which promotions and pay raises are given, to university research award committees which allocate research funds to faculty members. In any of these situations, a perceiver may cognize any of the types of regulatory procedure that are listed above, and each procedural component in the perceiver's cognitive map may become the focus of a judgment process that evaluates the fairness of that procedure.

Justice Rules for Evaluating Procedural Fairness

An individual uses justice rules to evaluate the fairness of allocative procedures. In the study of procedural fairness, a *justice rule* is defined as a belief that allocative procedures are fair when they satisfy certain criteria. This type of justice rule is referred to as a *procedural rule*, to distinguish it from distribution rules that were discussed earlier. The criteria that define the rules of fair procedure can only be guessed at this time, because there have been few studies of procedural fairness. However, the view adopted here is that it is better to have speculative statements about such rules than none at all.

Six procedural justice rules are postulated that define criteria which allocative procedures must often satisfy to be perceived as fair. They are the consistency rule, bias-suppression rule, accuracy rule, correctability rule, representativeness rule, and ethicality rule. Because there are few relevant studies, descriptions of organizations by other commentators, and the author's own observations of groups and organizations, constitute the primary evidence for the theoretical proposals.

The following analysis assumes that an individual applies procedural rules selectively and follows different rules at different times. The basic criteria used to evaluate the fairness of procedures change with circumstances. In some situations, one procedural rule may be considered much more relevant than others, in which case judgments of procedural fairness may be dominated by that rule. In other situations, however, several procedural rules may be applicable. The influence of a rule on the individual's judgments of procedural fairness is defined as it *weight*. If one procedural rule has greater impact than others on judgments of procedural fairness, that rule is said to have greater weight. As with distribution rules, procedural rules may have contradictory implications, or may be fully compatible.

In the following analysis, six procedural rules are defined. For each rule, examples are presented which show how that rule is used to evaluate the fairness of the various components of allocative procedure that are listed above. In all, 42 possible combinations can be derived when the seven components of procedure are paired with the six justice rules that are presumed to govern the evaluation of procedural fairness.

1. *The Consistency Rule.* An individual's judgments of procedural fairness may be based on a consistency rule which dictates that allocative procedures should be consistent across persons and over time. Lack of consistency in procedure may lead an individual to believe that procedural fairness is being violated. When applied *across persons,* the consistency rule dictates that it is necessary to apply similar procedures to all potential recipients of reward, and to give special advantage to none. In this form, the rule is closely related to the notion of *equality of opportunity.*

The rule of consistency across persons may be applied to any of the seven procedural components of the allocative process. For example, in gathering information about job applicants, it would be considered unfair to give persons applying for the same position aptitude tests that differ in difficulty. The rule of consistency across persons also applies to setting ground rules, that is, to procedures that provide potential receivers with information about what must be done to obtain available rewards. For example, a high official of the Energy Research and Development Administration attempted recently to put to rest fears that "inside information" might bias the selection of a site for a new solar energy research institute. To preserve the impression that procedural fairness would be scrupulously maintained, he pledged that "no citizen or organization is allowed to have a preferred position, or even appear to have knowledge which would give an unfair advantage over any other organization or person. . . ." (Boffey, 1975).

When applied *over time,* the consistency rule dictates that it is necessary to keep procedures stable, at least over the short term. The rule of consistency over time may be applied to any procedural component. For example, it has obvious relevance to change mechanisms that are used to modify allocative procedures. If changes are made too frequently or too easily, the perceived fairness of the allocative process will be reduced. The rule also applies to setting ground rules for performance evaluation. Leaders of work groups must often set performance expectations and must specify in advance the criteria for evaluating performance (e.g., Fleishman, Harris & Burt, 1955; House & Dessler, 1974). The rule of consistency over time suggests that once such standards are established, a sudden or marked deviation from them will be perceived as a violation of fair procedure. Support for this suggestion is found in college students' comments about grading procedures, as revealed in preliminary interviews conducted by Philip Bock, Sheldon Alexander, and the author. A number of students stated that it was highly inappropriate for an instructor abruptly to change evaluation procedures that had been agreed upon at the beginning of the term. Further support for the suggestion is found in results from a study by Leventhal and Whiteside (1973), in which subjects awarded grades to hypothetical students. When the subjects believed that the students had been forewarned that a certain criterion would be used, the students applied that criterion more rigorously.

2. *The Bias-Suppression Rule*. An individual's judgments of procedural fairness may be based on a bias-suppression rule which dictates that personal self-interest and blind allegiance to narrow preconceptions should be prevented at all points in the allocative process. An individual is likely to believe that procedural fairness is violated when there is unrestrained self-interest, or devotion to doctrinaire views.

The role of the bias-suppression rule is evident in practices followed by study sections of the National Institutes of Health which evaluate research grant proposals. Grant applications submitted by persons who are members of a study section are never evaluated by that study section. In addition, study section members are required to absent themselves during debate and final vote when the proposal under review has been submitted by a person from their own institution (Gustafson, 1975). These practices involve application of the bias-suppression rule to the selection of agents who administer the allocative process. The procedures maintain fairness by separating decision-making roles from personal advocacy. More generally, failure to separate the judicial and adversary roles reduces perceived fairness. The bias-suppression rule dictates that one should not serve as a judge in one's own case. Similarly, many would doubt the fairness of a situation in which a school board locked in battle with striking teachers held hearings on the teachers' qualifications to teach, decided the teachers were unfit, and then fired them (Finkin, 1975).

3. *The Accuracy Rule*. An individual's judgments of procedural fairness may be based on an accuracy rule which dictates that it is necessary to base the allocative process on as much good information and informed opinion as possible. Information and opinion must be gathered and processed with a minimum of error.

The accuracy rule may be applied to any procedural component, but has especially clear relevance to methods of gathering information about potential receivers of reward. Procedural fairness is violated when performance is evaluated on the basis of inappropriate information, or information provided by incompetent observers (Miner, 1972). For example, students probably believe it is unfair to evaluate them with tests that are either too difficult or too easy. Similarly, students probably believe it would be unfair if essay tests were graded by an unqualified person. In industrial settings, most observers would consider it unfair to screen prospective employees with an employment test that did not predict future performance reliably. In the courts, the perceived fairness of the judicial process is probably enhanced by procedures that prohibit the introduction of evidence that is irrelevant and unreliable.

The accuracy rule also affects the perceived fairness of other components of allocative procedure. For example, when the selection of agents to administer the allocative process is determined by election, the perceived fairness of the electoral process is probably enhanced when accurate and relevant information about candidates' views and character is available. The accuracy rule is also of great importance with respect to safeguards that deter people from violating fair procedure. Some safeguards help assure that agents who administer the allocative process are performing their duties properly. In such cases, we may speak of *accountability* which has two aspects: monitoring and sanctions. The integrity of the allocative process is preserved by procedures that detect violations and punish them. Accordingly, the perceived level of fairness will be enhanced when monitoring is accurate and sanctions are effective.

Record keeping is one important method for accurate monitoring of the behavior of agents who control the allocative process. Often, detailed records are kept for inspection by concerned parties. The records may contain facts used as bases of evaluation, e.g., test scores, letters of recommendation, or supervisors' evaluations, or facts about the past distribution of reward that reveal how much was received by various persons. When such records are accurate and honest, they constitute an effective deterrent to wrongdoing, because they make it more difficult for violators to escape detection.

Other safeguards help prevent opportunistic persons from obtaining rewards and resources by illicit means such as deception or theft. Persons who want more than the social system can deliver may try to increase their rewards by circumventing normal operating procedures (Leventhal, 1976a). The procedural safeguards that detect and prevent such opportunistic garnering of rewards and resources are diverse, but in all cases, perceived fairness will be enhanced when accurate methods are used to detect violations. For example, during examinations, the presence of attentive proctors probably increases the level of perceived fairness. And, on busy streets, the use of parking meters to detect parking violations probably increases the perceived fairness of penalties.

4. *The Correctability Rule.* The correctability rule dictates that

opportunities must exist to modify and reverse decisions made at various points in the allocative process. Even the most well-intentioned and competent decision makers commit errors or oversights. Consequently, the perceived level of fairness will be increased by the presence of appeal procedures (both formal and informal) that allow for review and modification of decisions at various stages of the allocative process. A perceiver will attribute greater fairness to groups and organizations that provide legitimate avenues for challenging and overturning decisions.

A grievance or appeal procedure often comes into play after the distribution of reward or punishment has been decided. An attempt may be made to modify directly the distribution. However, appeals may also be launched at earlier stages in the allocative process. For example, an individual may wish to challenge the fairness of procedures for gathering information, even though the final distribution of rewards has not been decided. Thus, students often complain about the ambiguity of test items before an examination has been scored. Similarly, an individual may challenge the selection of persons who serve as decision makers. Such appeals can take the form of demands for a recount in an election, or complaints about the propriety of an appointment process.

Appeal procedures differ greatly, and the differences may have considerable impact on an individual's perception of procedural fairness. For example, the perceived level of fairness will be reduced when there are barriers that deter dissatisfied individuals from lodging complaints. To be fair, the procedures must be safe and easy to use. Plaintiffs must feel free to lodge an appeal without fear of punishment or retaliation. Procedures that involve long delays, or great expenditure of time, effort, and resources are perceived as less fair.

A final determinant of the perceived fairness of an appeal procedure involves a joint application of the bias-suppression rule and correctability rule. To preserve fairness, the actual processing of an appeal must be unbiased. For example, the appeal should not have to rely on a channel of communication that is dominated by the decision maker whose decision is under challenge. Such a communication channel confounds the judicial and adversary roles. Perceived fairness is reduced unless the original decision maker can be bypassed, and the final judgment rendered by decision makers at higher levels in the social system.

5. *The Representativeness Rule.* An individual's judgments of procedural fairness may be based on a representativeness rule which dictates that all phases of the allocative process must reflect the basic concerns, values, and outlook of important subgroups in the popula-

tion of individuals affected by the allocative process. The precise operationalization of this justice rule may vary greatly from one perceiver to the next, depending on which subgroups are considered important. A perceiver's judgments of a subgroup's importance may be determined by the subgroup's size, prestige, or by other factors.

The representativeness rule has obvious relevance for the selection of agents who decide the distribution of reward. The rule requires that decision-making bodies such as committees or legislatures should include representatives of important subgroups in the total population, perhaps in proportion to the subgroups' prestige and numerical size. The role of the representativeness rule in such cases is shown in Fox and Swazey's (1974) study of kidney dialysis units. The authors describe criteria that were to be used in selecting members of a committee that would draw up nonmedical criteria for deciding which kidney patients would have access to life-saving dialysis machines that were in short supply. One goal was to form a committee that would represent a broad socioeconomic spectrum of the community. In reality, the members chosen were quite homogeneous in socioeconomic background, a fact that ultimately generated considerable debate about the fairness of the procedures for deciding who would live and who would die.

The impact of the representativeness rule on the selection of decision makers can also be seen in attempts by federal agencies that award research grants to preserve an image of fairness by broadening the membership of peer-review committees. Representativeness has been increased by the importation of reviewers from adjacent disciplines, and reviewers not associated with elite universities (Greenberg, 1975). Another indication of the effort to ensure representativeness in the grant review process is the frequent practice of not reappointing reviewers (Gustafson, 1975). The National Institutes of Health policy of rapidly rotating individuals through decision-making positions reduces the likelihood that an unrepresentative clique will exercise control, and ensures that a broad range of individuals is recruited from the biomedical research community.

The application of the representativeness rule to the selection of agents is also involved in questions of *power sharing* and *participatory decision making*. Individuals probably assign greater weight to the rule when their own power is involved. They are likely to attribute greater fairness when they have greater control over the allocative process (Leventhal, 1976b). From an individual's own vantage point, such a situation is fairer because it gives greater representation to a very important individual, namely, himself. In accordance with this assumption, workers believe a pay system is fairer when they have greater control over it (Lawler, 1971). More generally, workers probably attribute greater fairness to allocative procedures when there is genuine participatory decision making and frequent consultation with management (cf. Vroom, 1969). Research on fairness of judicial proceedings is also consistent with this suggestion. Defendants attribute greater fairness to trial procedures which give them greater control over the introduction and interpretation of evidence (Thibaut, Walker, LaTour, & Houlden, 1974).

The representativeness rule is also relevant to the question of *censorship*. Censorship involves restriction on the flow of information. The restriction may occur in any phase of the allocative process, with the result that available information and opinion is no longer representative of the total array that is potentially available. It is proposed that, to the extent an individual believes there is censorship, perceived fairness is reduced.

Censorship may occur in gathering or disseminating information, or in formulating guidelines on the proper use of information as evidence. Certain facts and viewpoints may be suppressed. To the extent that an individual has knowledge of such suppression, the violation of the representativeness rule will reduce perceived fairness. This suggestion is consistent with a recent case in which the editors of a well-known magazine were criticized as unfair for their refusal to publish an article attacking resource allocation policies in the nuclear energy field (*Science*, 1976). Many other examples of alleged unfairness in the communications media can be found.

The representativeness rule also applies when censorship exists within the decision structure of a group of committee that decides the distribution of reward. In decision-making groups, there is often a rapid suppression of minority viewpoints, and of opinions that diverge from those of more powerful members. In addition, pressure for quick decisions often prevents exploration and consideration of a full range of alternatives (Hoffman, 1965; Steiner, 1976). Such tendencies produce a marked restriction in the availability of information and opinion in the group. Much that could be said and should be said is left unstated. Consequently, the range of opinion and information actually presented to the group is unrepresentative of that which is potentially available. In such situations, individuals who recognize that important points of view are being suppressed are likely to attribute lower fairness to the decision process which determines the distribution of reward.

6. *The Ethicality Rule*. An individual's judgments of procedural fairness may be based on an ethicality rule which dictates that allocative procedures must be compatible with the fundamental moral and ethical values accepted by that individual. Perceived fairness will be

reduced when allocative procedures violate personal standards of ethics and morality. When applied to gathering information about potential receivers, the ethicality rule may dictate that methods of observation that involve deception or that invade privacy are unfair. Similarly, procedures that involve bribery or spying are seen as unfair (Friedland, Thibaut, & Walker, 1973).

The postulation of an ethicality rule is based on the assumption that judgments of fairness and justice are related to a larger intrapsychic system of moral and ethical values and standards. Linkages between the components of this moral-ethical system are probably quite weak. However, the connections may often be strong enough for a violation of moral and ethical standards to affect the perception of procedural fairness. For example, an individual who believes that blind obedience to authority is wrong may attribute lower fairness to an allocative procedure that requires such obedience, regardless of the effect of the procedure on the final distribution of reward. Similarly, an individual who believes that deception and trickery are wrong may attribute lower fairness to an allocative procedure that involves such practices, even when the practices do not decrease the fairness of the final distribution of reward.

The Relative Weight of Procedural Rules

Six justice rules have been postulated that define criteria an individual may use to evaluate the fairness of allocative procedures. It is assumed that an individual applies procedural rules selectively, and follows different rules at different times. The relative weight of procedural rules may differ from one situation to the next, and one procedural component to the next. However, in the absence of research on the determinants of rule weight, only the most general statements can be made about the relative importance of different rules in different situations. For example, it is likely that individuals assign higher weight to procedural rules that favor their own interests. In addition, they probably assign higher weight to procedural rules that are followed by other persons, or are favored by legitimate authorities. Another probable determinant of the weight of procedural rules is the perceived level of *distributive* fairness. An individual who believes that existing distributions are fair is likely to support existing procedures, and give high weight to procedural rules that reaffirm the fairness of existing procedures. Conversely, an individual who believes existing distributions are unfair gives high weight to procedural rules that cast doubt on the fairness of existing procedures and support changing them. Thus, individuals who prefer certain distributions are likely to prefer procedures that generate those distributions, and assign weights to procedural rules on that basis.

The absence of research also makes it difficult to predict the outcome of situations in which several procedural rules receive high weight but have contradictory implications. For example, one can imagine situations in which, for a given individual, the dictates of the representativeness rule clash with the dictates of the accuracy rule. The individual might believe that a numerically important subgroup in the population ought to have direct representation in the decision-making process that controls the distribution of resources, but simultaneously believe that that subgroup contains few members qualified to make accurate judgments. To resolve this contradiction between procedural rules, the individual might be forced to choose between having no representatives or having representatives with modest qualifications. Until more research is available, little can be said about the manner in which an individual resolves such conflicts between procedural rules.

THE IMPACT OF PERCEIVED FAIRNESS ON BEHAVIOR

The Importance of Fairness

Equity theory tends to overstate the importance of perceived fairness as a determinant of behavior. Writings in the equity theory tradition convey the impression that an individual's perception of justice is a very powerful determinant of social behavior. In contrast, the position adopted in this paper is that an individual's concern about fairness is only one motivational force among many that affect perception and behavior, and that it is often a weaker force than others. In many situations, most individuals probably give little thought to questions of fairness (cf. Schwartz, 1968a,b). To be sure, an individual is usually capable of judging the fairness of distributions and allocative procedures. However, he or she is unlikely to make such judgments continuously, and when such judgments are made, they may not be thorough or precise.

Questions about the importance of perceived fairness necessitate a clearer definition of the theoretical boundaries of the analysis of fairness. An individual's concern for fairness and justice must be viewed as one component within the larger framework of the total pattern of social behavior. To move in this direction, two issues are considered in the following sections. The first focuses on situational factors that cause an individual to be concerned about fairness, or indifferent to it. The second issue focuses on the relative potency of concern for fairness as a determinant of behavior, once that concern is aroused.

Activation of the Justice Judgment Sequence

This section identifies factors that determine an individual's level of concern about fairness. Four types of determinants are examined. They are the individual's role, the importance of the individual's other goals, the perceived likelihood of rule violation, and the pluralism of normative standards within the social system.

The Effect of Role

An individual may be highly concerned about procedural or distributive fairness because he occupies a social role that has the task of maintaining fairness. The role may involve enforcing an existing set of rules, or proposing solutions to interpersonal disagreements. Such roles include that of judge or juror, sports referee, ombudsman, labor mediator, and others. For example, a judge or sports referee sees to it that fair procedures are followed during competitive interaction between adversaries. In court, or on the playing field, the contest is regulated by a comprehensive set of rules. It is the judge's or referee's duty to interpret and follow these rules, and to require the contestants to follow them. Consequently, when enacting their roles, judges, referees, and similar individuals evaluate fairness carefully. However, in other settings, they may display no greater concern about fairness than anyone else.

Importance of Other Goals

When preoccupied with goals of greater importance, an individual's concern about fairness is likely to be reduced. The justice judgment sequence may be suppressed because it interferes with more important goals. Such suppression can often be observed when an individual's primary concern is to control the behavior of other persons. One such case occurs when a supervisor is extremely concerned about maximizing workers' performance. When a supervisor's desire to elicit high performance is exceptionally great, considerations of distributive fairness may be ignored. The supervisor may resort to any strategy that is considered likely to prove effective. For example,

Greenberg and Leventhal (1976) placed subjects under strong pressure to motivate failing performers to do better work. The subjects responded by giving higher pay than was deserved based on performance. Furthermore, under some conditions the subjects completely violated the contributions rule. They gave higher reward to failing groups than to successful groups, and higher reward to lazy performers than to well-motivated performers. The subjects who followed this strategy did so because they believed it would maximize productivity. Concern about distributive fairness was completely overshadowed by the need to do what was necessary to elicit better work.

Concern about procedural fairness is often suppressed when an individual is anxious to control the behavior of persons who are believed dangerous. Such suppression of concern for procedural fairness is evident in public attitudes toward civil liberties. In the abstract, there is high public support for freedom of speech and expression, and other rights. However, many individuals favor setting aside these procedural rights in the case of Communists, atheists, or other groups that are considered dangerous to the self or social order. Procedural rights would be denied to such threatening groups (Erskine & Siegel, 1975; Sears, 1969; Zellman, 1975).

Concern about procedural fairness may also be minimal when an individual's personal involvement in the social system is low, and the system satisfies the few needs it is supposed to. For example, union members expect their union to bargain collectively for wages and protect them from abuse by supervisors. So long as the union performs these functions adequately, most members remain indifferent to the details of its operations (e.g., Lipset, Trow, & Coleman, 1956; Tannenbaum, 1965). They view the governance and internal functioning of the union as the province of the leadership, and if the leaders execute these tasks without bothering them, so much the better. This indifference to procedural matters may explain why many union members are willing to accept conditions that, from the viewpoint of other observers, appear to involve extensive violations of procedural fairness.

Probability of Violation

An individual is more likely to evaluate the fairness of distributions or allocative procedures when there is reason to suspect that justice rules have been violated. Suspicion of violation may increase when there are large or sudden changes in the distribution of reward, or allocative procedures. Such changes raise doubts that may activate the justice judgment sequence. Judgments of fairness may also be triggered by complaints or warnings from other persons that fairness is being violated. More generally, the prevailing social climate may create an atmosphere of distrust in social institutions and in the persons who occupy the decision-making roles that regulate the allocative process. Such distrust may be widespread when there have been major scandals in government, business, or politics. As Gustafson (1975) suggests, "in mistrustful times the good faith of all administrators is under suspicion" (p. 1064).

An individual's personal experience sometimes provides prima facie evidence of violation of distributive fairness. For example, his or her own rewards may be too low. Such perceived violations of distributive fairness may stimulate an intensive appraisal of the fairness of allocative procedures, especially when the individual is preparing to take corrective action. By finding flaws in procedure and faulting the system, the individual can justify an appeal for changing the distribution of reward. On the other side of the fence, analogous factors may heighten a decision maker's concern about procedural fairness. The knowledge that disgruntled recipients search for violations of fair procedure stimulates the decision maker to review carefully the fairness of his procedures for distributing rewards and resources. By locating potential violations in advance and correcting them, the administrator strengthens his position and protects against possible criticism. As Greenberg (1975) suggests, the appearance of fairness may be as important as actual fairness. By stressing fair procedure, the decision maker neutralizes adverse reactions to the final distribution of reward.

Monolithic versus Pluralist Social Systems

An individual's concern about fairness also depends on the extent to which the social system is monolithic and imposes consistent, stable rules of fair procedure and fair distribution. When leaders endorse and legitimize certain rules consistently, fairness will be defined in terms of these rules. More importantly, after a time, existing procedures and distributions are likely to be taken for granted. The fairness of existing arrangements may no longer be evaluated. Consequently, in a monolithic social system, the justice judgment sequence will be activated infrequently.

In a pluralist social system that lacks uniformity, and in which leaders do not require strict adherence to a consistent set of rules, questions of distributive and procedural fairness will be more salient. Competing standards of fairness will be present, and the justice judgment sequence is more likely to be activated. This is probably the case in labor unions that have a multiparty system of governance. In such pluralist systems, independent and well-established subgroups compete for the members' attention and votes (Lipset, Trow, & Coleman, 1956). Consequently, questions about the fairness of distributional and procedural policies may often be brought to members' attention. Uncritical acceptance of the leadership's views is less likely under these circumstances. In contrast, in monolithic unions which operate with a one-party system, questions about the fairness of union policies are less likely to be raised.

Under appropriate conditions, even when a social system imposes a monolithic view of the allocative process, some individuals may question the fairness of existing arrangements. This is likely when an individual has experience in other social settings that favor alternative standards of distributive and procedural fairness. For example, consider a family in which parents impose a stable and consistent set of rules. Their view of fairness will prevail, and the children will believe that existing procedures and distributions are fair, even though, from an external observer's viewpoint, one child may have more advantages than another (Ihinger, 1975). However, as a child's range of contacts expands, experience is gained in other social settings, and the conceptions of procedural and distributive fairness that prevail in those settings may be somewhat different from those at home. To the extent that the child internalizes these new rules, the justice judgment sequence is likely to be aroused when the child returns to the family. Procedures and distributions which, heretofore, were accepted uncritically may be subject to searching evaluation because they are inconsistent with standards newly acquired in other social settings.

Concern for Fairness and Other Causes of "Fair" Behavior

Another aspect to questions about the importance of perceived fairness must be considered. Even when the justice judgment sequence is activated, concern about fairness, in its own right, may often have relatively weak effects on behavior. Furthermore, actions that help maintain fairness often arise from motivational forces unrelated to concern for justice. Although a behavior helps contribute to the maintenance of perceived fairness, the concern for fairness may be only a secondary cause of that behavior (Leventhal, 1976a). Ostensibly fair behavior may be caused by motives unrelated to moral or ethical concerns. Consequently, the fairness-restoring effects of an action may be an epiphenomenon, or at least of secondary importance, in the overall pattern of behavior.

Studies of the behavior of decision makers who distribute rewards to others illustrate the preceding point. In such studies, it is often difficult to determine whether the decision maker's behavior is guided by a desire for fairness, a desire to control recipients' behavior, or both factors operating in tandem (Leventhal, 1976a). For example, an allocator who is interested in encouraging good performance usually follows the contributions rule. More is given to better performers. But is the allocator's goal to be fair, or to reward good performance because such a policy encourages high productivity? Similarly, in cohesive groups, allocators often divide rewards equally (Bales, 1950; Lerner, 1974b; Leventhal, Michaels, & Sanford, 1972). But is this because they want to be fair, or because they hope that equal allocations will preserve solidarity? Either or both factors could be involved. In past research, relatively few attempts have been made to separate those portions of an allocator's response which are caused by concern for fairness and justice from those portions which are caused by a desire to manipulate and control recipients' behavior.

The issue raised here is found in equity theory in latent form. In their examination of equity theory, Walster, Berscheid, and Walster (1973) suggest that motivational factors such as *retaliation distress* (conditioned anxiety) and *self-concept distress* may underlie the tendency to restore distributive fairness. However, these constructs are never brought into play on the theoretical chessboard. They are merely identified and left standing in place. Basically, the analysis treats the desire for distributive fairness as a motivational force in its own right, without regard to underlying motives that may energize it. The links between concern for fairness, on the one hand, and the self-concept and conditioned anxiety on the other, are not explored. Nor is the possibility raised, as in this paper, that concern for fairness may be aroused in parallel with and produce effects superficially similar to those generated by other motivational forces.

A Distinction between Fair and Quasi-Fair Behavior

In future research, it may be useful to distinguish *fair* behavior that is motivated by a concern for fairness from *quasi-fair* behavior that is superficially similar, but stems primarily from other motivational bases. Quasi-fair behavior resembles fair behavior, but is actually different, because only fair behavior arises from moral and ethical concerns.

Past research has often failed to distinguish between these two categories of behavior. However, appropriately designed studies will probably reveal important differences between them. One approach to this problem is suggested by studies of ingratiation (Jones, 1964) and

Machiavellianism (Christie & Geis, 1970). One can readily imagine a type of quasi-fair behavior that is part of a carefully orchestrated strategy for deceiving and manipulating others. Once the deception has been achieved, quasi-fair behavior might give way rapidly to blatant exploitation. Genuinely fair behavior would not. Another approach involves situations in which quasi-fair behavior proves ineffective for obtaining the goals it is designed to achieve. Since quasi-fair behavior is an instrumental rather than a moral response, it will be abandoned as readily as any other instrumental response that proves ineffective. In contrast, fair behavior, motivated by genuine concern for fairness and justice, will tend to persist even when more pragmatic goals are not achieved.

A word of caution is in order. It has not been the purpose of this section to suggest that an individual's concern for fairness and justice is trivial. The study of social motivation indicates that, under appropriate conditions, any cluster of ideas and beliefs, including beliefs about fairness, can become a major motivational force for the individual (McClelland, 1965; McClelland & Winter, 1969). At a given point in time, an individual may be very much concerned about fairness, and this concern may strongly influence behavior. Furthermore, some individuals may be very much concerned about fairness in a wide variety of social contexts. Concern about fairness and justice is not a mere epiphenomenon that can be stripped away or discarded by reduction to supposedly more basic motives. Nevertheless, concern for fairness may often be a less important motive than others. Other goals can override it, or, more subtly, can generate responses that superficially resemble responses that are stimulated by genuine concern for fairness and justice.

SUMMARY

Equity theory in its present form has serious limitations as a framework for studying perceived fairness in social relationships. The theory must be incorporated into a larger framework that takes account of problems that equity theory does not consider. This paper has proposed such a framework. It was suggested that the perception of fairness is governed by two types of justice rules—distribution rules and procedural rules. Distribution rules dictate that rewards, punishments, and resources should be allocated in accordance with certain criteria. The relative importance of distribution rules changes from one situation to the next. The weights assigned to them depend on the social setting, and the individual's role in that setting.

A multistage justice judgment sequence was postulated in which an individual assigns weights to distribution rules, then estimates recipients' deservingness based on each applicable rule, and then uses the rule-combination equation to combine the separate estimates into a final judgment of fair distribution. A separate information-processing subroutine is used for each rule to estimate deservingness based on that rule. In this model of the justice judgment process, the core equation of equity theory is used to describe the information-processing subroutine for judgments of fairness based on contributions.

An individual evaluates not only distributions of reward, but also the mechanisms in the social system that generate those distributions. A complex sequence of procedures often precedes the final distribution of reward, and an individual usually develops a cognitive map of the allocative process. Any component in this cognitive map may become the focus of a judgment sequence that evaluates procedural fairness. For example, an individual may evaluate the fairness of methods for selecting decision makers who control the allocative process; methods of gathering information about potential recipients of reward; or methods for changing existing procedures. The fairness of such practices is evaluated with procedural rules which dictate criteria that allocative procedures must satisfy to be fair. For example, fairness may be judged in terms of a procedure's consistency over time and across persons; its accuracy and prevention of personal bias; or its representativeness of the values, interests, and outlook of important subgroups in the population of persons affected by the allocative process. The relative importance of different procedural rules probably changes from one situation to the next. However, little is known about the determinants of the relative weight of procedural rules.

The conceptual analysis of procedural fairness remains speculative because most research has focused on the problem of fair distribution. However, the present analysis affords an opportunity to apply the concept of procedural fairness in laboratory and field studies of issues such as censorship, participatory decision making, equal opportunity, and the representativeness of social institutions.

An individual's concern for fairness and justice represents only one component in the total structure of behavior and personality. Consequently, he or she may often be unconcerned about fairness. The justice judgment sequence may not be activated because the individual is absorbed by more important goals, or for other reasons. Even when concern for justice is aroused, the perceived fairness of procedures and distributions may have modest impact on behavior. Moreover, behavior that helps preserve fairness is often stimulated by motivational forces unrelated to moral or ethical concerns. The behavior may be more an instrumental response motivated by pragmatic concerns than a moral response motivated by genuine concern for fairness and justice. However, although concern for fairness may have less impact on behavior than some other motives, such concern is not an epiphenomenon that is reducible to supposedly more basic motives. Concern for fairness and justice can be a powerful motivational force in its own right.

ACKNOWLEDGMENTS

The author is indebted to Jurgis Karuza and Sheldon Alexander for their many valuable comments.

3

The Search for Uniqueness and Valuation of Scarcity

Neglected Dimensions of Value in Exchange Theory*

HOWARD L. FROMKIN AND C. R. SNYDER

INTRODUCTION

The widespread pressure toward conformity in opinion and behavior in current society has captured the attention of many social scientists. Several recent attempts to integrate diverse perspectives and findings on conformity use social exchange theory (Blau, 1964; Homans, 1961, 1974; Nord, 1969b; Secord & Backman, 1964). While integrative, the social exchange view of conformity neglects some important motives, values, and costs. For instance, our research identifies a need for distinctiveness or "uniqueness," that is, a need to see oneself as different from one's peers, as a prevalent determinant of behavior. Thus, the outcomes of pressures to conform may depend upon the degree and nature of competing pressures for uniqueness. Alternatively, the act of conformity may arouse or augment pressure toward the foregone alternative of establishing or maintaining the self-perception of uniqueness. The present chapter develops the latter thesis by reviewing the theory and research on uniqueness and discussing implications for the social exchange view of conformity.

* This paper was prepared while the first author was a visiting professor in the Department of Psychology, Bar Ilan University, Ramat Gan, Israel.

HOWARD L. FROMKIN • Department of Psychology, York University, Downsview, Ontario M3J 1P3, Canada. C. R. SNYDER • Clinical Psychology Program, University of Kansas, Lawrence, Kansas 66045.

CONFORMITY AS SOCIAL EXCHANGE

Pressures toward uniformity in attitude and behavior are commonly present in any particular group. Group life requires consensus and interdependent action, not only to attain group goals, but also to meet a vast complex of individual needs such as prestige, status, affiliation, and achievement. As a result, anomalous behavior is often met with social disapproval and mistreatment.

Although there are many different conceptualizations of conformity, most definitions are operationally based on either (1) *congruence* or matching between observed behavior and some norm or normative ideal, or (2) *movement* or change in behavior due to the influence of another person or group which results in increased congruence (Allen, 1965; Willis, 1965). The latter definition, conformity as a change in congruence in response to immediate social pressure, is adopted throughout this chapter.

The conformity literature seems, at first glance, quite at home within the social exchange approach. Conformity is therein viewed as an instrumental response to attain rewards or to avoid costs. One of the most general social rewards is approval, and in a wide variety of contexts conformity is exchanged for social approval. Although social approval operates as a generalized reinforcer, it is often purchased only at some cost. One may have to deny oneself one activity to engage in another. A "profit" accrues from any single action when the benefits are greater than the costs, and presumably a person engages in activities which maximize the expected profit. For example, a person may derive greater psychological profit from owning a new sports car than from a vacation in Paris because the benefits derived from the car exceed the expectations from the foregone alternative, the vacation.

Homans (1961, p. 58) defined the cost in a given exchange as the value of the foregone alternative. This definition is illustrated by Homans's (1961, pp. 93–99) interpretation of some experimental findings by Gerard (1954). After reading a case on a union–management dispute, subjects were divided into three groups by levels of agreement about the probable outcome. A second manipulation divided each of these groups into two levels of attraction. After each of the resulting three-man groups completed a face-to-face discussion of the case, subjects again indicated their opinion about the probable outcome. About a week later, each subject met with an experimental confederate who took a position placing the subject between himself and the group. The two dependent variables were the percentages of subjects changing toward the confederate, and toward the group.

Homans identified social approval and dissonance reduction as two potential rewards for changing one's opinion toward the group. In addition, he proposed a third, competing motive—namely, "maintenance of his personal integrity achieved by sticking to his own independent and publicly expressed opinion on the issue of the case." That is, when subjects complied with the influence exerted by the group, they accepted the abandonment of their integrity as a cost in that immediate situation. The dynamics of a similar concept have received theoretical development and empirical support in a series of studies in our laboratories (cf. Fromkin, 1973).

UNIQUENESS STUDIES

According to our theory of uniqueness, the need to see oneself as different from other persons in our social environment is aroused and competes with other motives in situations which threaten the self-perception of uniqueness. The research demonstrates that the self-perception of uniqueness is threatened when a person perceives himself to be highly similar to a large number of other persons on a large number of attributes. Relative to subjects who received dissimilarity feedback, subjects who perceived that they were highly similar on a large number of their attitudes to large numbers of their college peers expressed greater unpleasant affect as measured by the Mood Adjective Checklist (Fromkin, 1972a); a greater number of unique uses as measured by Guilford's Unusual Uses Test (Fromkin, 1968); and, less assumed similarity to an unknown other subject as measured by a projective technique (Fromkin, 1968). Another series of experiments follows the Byrne (1971) similarity–attraction paradigm where subjects receive information about the degree of attitude similarity between themselves and an unknown peer and rate the attractiveness of the peer (Fromkin, Brandt, Dipboye, & Pyle, 1974). The findings demonstrate that the linear relationship between attitude similarity and attraction usually obtained by Byrne and his colleagues (Byrne, 1971) became curvilinear as the number of attitudes which were similar and the number of strangers who were similar increased beyond a single stranger or 30 similar attitudes. Last, a more recent series of experiments demonstrated that the positive correlation between similarity and self-esteem (Johnson, Gormly, & Gormly, 1973) becomes curvilinear as the number of similar persons and the number of similar attitudes increase beyond a single person and 30 attitudes (Ganster, McCuddy, & Fromkin, 1977). Under large numbers of similar strangers and large numbers of similar attitudes, there is unfavorable change in self-esteem. Although the findings of any one experiment can be challenged, the full portfolio of studies (described above and below) provides impressive support for uniqueness-theory contentions about the avoidance of excessive similarity.

All the above situations involve similarity as a threat to self-perceived uniqueness, but do not involve instrumental rewards for public distinctiveness. The dynamics of instrumental distinctiveness are demonstrated in an experiment by Dipboye and Fromkin (1972).

Under the guise of a study of first impressions, subjects were informed that an attractive or an unattractive female (the first independent variable) would select only *one* of them for a "coke-date" based upon their answers to her questions. The experimental paradigm was fashioned after the television program "The Dating Game," where the female can only hear the answers of her potential dates. Subjects participated in groups of two or five (the second independent variable). However, each subject was informed that he was either subject number 2 (in the two-subject condition), or subject number 5 (in the five-subject condition). The bogus responses of the "other subjects" were prerecorded and were unanimous. The questions asked by the female confederate were the items of the Social Desirability Scale (Crowne & Marlowe, 1964). The dependent variable was the magnitude of subject's deviations from the alleged group's response. As predicted, deviations from the group were greatest for the attractive female and the larger groups, and smallest for the unattractive female and the smaller groups. Presumably, the public expression of distinctive attitudes is instrumental to obtaining a valued outcome, i.e., being chosen for a date with an attractive female.

A more direct test of the idea of similarity and conformity as a threat to uniqueness is found in a dissertation by Duval (1972), who attempted to test a derivation of objective self-awareness theory. Duval predicted that the *proportion* of similar others on one set of opinions is inversely related to the tendency toward conformity on separate and unrelated opinions, and that this ratio effect would be enhanced by the arousal of objective self-awareness. In a procedure similar to Fromkin (1968, 1970, 1972a), 82 female subjects received similarity feedback which demonstrated that either 5%, 50%, or 95% of 10,000 college students agreed with their "ten most important attitudes," the first independent variable. Following this manipulation, subjects were asked to estimate the number of dots on each slide in ten pairs of slides. On the first slide in each pair, subjects estimated the number of dots without feedback. On the second slide in each pair, which was identical to the first, subjects heard confederates' estimates which were 150 to 200 dots greater than their own responses to the first slide, and then made estimates about the number of dots in the second slide (the dependent variable). For the objective self awareness manipulation (the second independent variable), one-half of the subjects viewed their own image on a TV monitor, and the remaining half were exposed only to a blank television screen. The ten trials were divided into two blocks of five, blocks being the third independent variable.

Two measures of conformity (amount and frequency of change) yielded only one significant main effect—conformity *decreased* as the proportion of similar others increased. The expected interaction between objective self-awareness and similarity was not obtained; objective self-awareness did not enhance the relationship between similarity and conformity.

In sum, it appears that when similarity or other relevant features of the immediate social environment do *not* threaten the self-perception of uniqueness, approval and uniqueness needs do not compete, and conformity is unchallenged. In contrast, when threats to uniqueness are present, e.g., high degrees of self-perceived similarity, approval and uniqueness may become competitive. Given the observable prevalence of conformity in our current culture, it seems reasonable to conclude that the immediate rewards of approval for conformity are a more powerful determinant of behavior in most situations.[1]

Uniqueness as a Neglected Cost

The apparent contradiction between the pervasive amount of conformity that we observe in everyday life and our advocation of a need for uniqueness is resolved rather simply in exchange theory— perhaps too simply. Exchange theory holds that we engage in activities or manifest behaviors which have the greatest payoff value or the greatest profit. For instance, in many situations, such as the socialization of new group members (cf. Schein, 1968; Ziller, 1964, 1965), the need for approval and affiliation-related needs may compete with the need to see oneself as distinct from other persons. Conformity prevails when the rewards for compliance are more valued than the immediate costs of the deprivation of self-perceived uniqueness. Yet, when a person elects to conform, the self-perception of uniqueness becomes a cost.

Exchange theories focus almost exclusively upon maximization of

[1] Behavior also depends on the degree to which the individual is predisposed to respond to threats to his uniqueness (cf. a review of uniqueness-scale construction by Lipshitz & Fromkin, 1976). Although exchange theories do not account for individual difference variables (cf. Nord, 1969b), their discussion is beyond the scope of the present paper.

profit only in the *immediate* situation. They neglect residual aspects of behavior which develop with the passage of time as a result of the exchange. What becomes of the costs or lost alternatives? Do we simply ignore or forget them? Can it be assumed that the costs of the return in any single exchange do not affect *subsequent* behavior? Most views of social exchange pay relatively little attention to the subsequent dynamics of costs, such as deprived motives which occur as an outcome of a trade between an individual and a group. One notable exception is Gergen (1969, pp. 89–91), who suggests that boredom and a need for novelty may be aroused as a result of conformity to social norms. After a transaction is concluded, the costs and dissatisfactions which accrue to the individual as a result of deprived motives do affect his behavior.

The process of profit maximization, however, *continues beyond* the immediate situation. In particular, when a person cannot secure opposing approval and uniqueness outcomes in the same situation, he is likely to seek other modes of gaining uniqueness for himself, while conforming to the norms which furnish him with protection, approval, and admission to groups. Some subtle methods of gratifying our uniqueness needs without loss of approval for conformity appear in many speculative accounts of our cultural organization. For instance, studies of group formation describe the many different roles which emerge among group members, e.g., tension reducer, dispute mediator, clarifier (Bales & Slater, 1955). Furthermore, since most persons are members of many different groups at the same time, the sum total of any individual's group identities is another basis upon which to confirm our self-perceptions of uniqueness. According to the French sociologist, George Simmel, the greater the number of our group affiliations and group roles, the more improbable it is that another individual will exhibit the same configuration of memberships. Each new group with which a person becomes affiliated "circumscribes him more exactly, more unambiguously, and more uniquely" (Simmel, 1955, p. 140). Ziller (1964) describes a similar process of interpersonal mapping by which the individual attempts to perceive himself as more differentiated from other persons in his environment—the greater the number of bits of information which are required by the individual to discriminate himself from persons around him, the more deindividuated he will perceive himself to be.

Similarly, community planners recognize the many personal satisfactions served by religious, ethnic, and regional diversity among neighbors, as in Levittown (Gans, 1967, p. 167–168). Dissatisfied with the smothering of creativity in the middle-class suburbs in the mid-1950s, Allen (1954) advocated social change to establish neighborhoods of people with a heterogeneous mixture of differences in racial, religious, age, and socioeconomic background, for a "community which includes a diversity of people, with different kinds and degrees of fortune, may be livelier and more productive than a standardized one." Rubin (1973, p. 154) recognizes the delicate balance between people's needs for similar and dissimilar other persons—"for a human being to adapt to a rapidly changing world, he needs the companionship and support of others with whom he may sometimes disagree, but nevertheless feels a fundamental kind of likemindedness." Gans (1967) also recognized the need to moderate differentness. He recommends that neighborhoods be designed with homogeneous subblocks of persons with similar age and economic backgrounds embedded in more heterogeneous larger communities. The larger community provides opportunities for diversity in less intimate social contacts, such as schools and other neighborhood facilities.

At a more macrolevel of analysis, Lemaine's studies in France reveal that merely a heightened awareness of other persons arouses a threat to self-differentiation. "The re-establishment of this identity is achieved by way of a search for differentness, difference, for *otherness*, by the creation and subsequent accentuation of heterogeneity" (Lemaine, 1974, p. 20). For instance, nationalism and the search for a distinct language which is not contaminated by outside influences is viewed as a collective search for differentiation (Fishman, 1972). Similarly, the "jive" or slang used by American blacks may be described as a declaration of independence and differentiation from the larger cultural group (Mezzrow & Wolfe, 1972). The creation of unique linguistics and distinctive behavior of the hippy movement represented a movement toward a more differentiated position and rejection of the uniformity among middle-class values and norms (Pitts, 1969).

In sum, the above discussion focuses upon interpretive accounts of uniqueness-seeking behaviors which appear to occur simultaneously with conformity. These descriptions of behavior suggest that the search for uniqueness, when in direct competition with pressures for conformity, may only be forgone temporarily, if at all. Indeed, it is more likely that pressures toward conformity may arouse uniqueness motivation which is gratified in other ways and in other situations. The following review of experimental literature demonstrates how attributes, such as our names, our clothing, our dates or mates, our beliefs, and our performance, can serve as socially acceptable ways of establishing and/or maintaining our uniqueness.

UNIQUENESS ATTRIBUTES

Earlier, we suggested that, in a society fraught with pressures toward deindividuation and conformity, individual needs for unique ·

ness are not forgone, but merely manifested in more subtle and practical ways. That is, in spite of the widely observed tendency toward public conformity and apparent preferences for anonymity, man wants to be different, and clings to anchors of his individuality (Fromkin, 1968, 1973). Such socially acceptable manifestations of uniqueness allow the individual to gain approval and retain membership in groups. For instance, we suggested that the possession of commodities (material or information) which are scarce or unavailable to other persons is a method of defining the self as distinct (Fromkin, 1968). Also, we identified a number of self-attributes (e.g., physical, material, informational, experiential) which help to define the person as different from members of the reference group, but which, at the same time, do not arouse the forces of rejection for deviancy. These attributes are referred to as *uniqueness attributes* (Fromkin, 1973, p. 68).

Although the identification of the payoff value of certain goods is central to predictions of exchange theory, the notion that scarcity and availability can increase or decrease the payoff values of commodities and the valuations of uniqueness attributes is overlooked in conceptualizations of conformity by exchange theories (cf. Nord, 1969b). The following discussion presents the theory and research surrounding these neglected dimensions of scarcity and uniqueness.

Scarcity

William James, whose seminal thinking set the stage for many contemporary self theories, defined the *material self* as:

> The total of all that he can call his, not only his body and his psychic powers, but his clothes and his house, his wife and his children, his ancestors and friends, his reputation and works, his lands and horses, his yacht and bank account. All these things give him the same emotions. (James, 1890, p. 291)

It follows that an expensive house and expensive automobile may define a "wealthy or successful self," canonical ornaments may define a "religious self," and objets d'art may define a "cultural self." The widely observed tendency to augment and horde material possessions may represent a manifestation of our search for separate identities. That is, it is also likely that the possession of commodities which are rare, scarce, or unavailable to other persons (i.e., uniqueness attributes) may define a *unique self*.

Brock (1968) ordered an impressive body of literature to a series of general propositions, *commodity theory*, which suggests that a commodity will be valued to the extent that it is perceived as unavailable.

Commodity theory, in contrast to economic theory (Fromkin, 1972b), is a psychological theory which suggests that individuals value unavailable commodities because of their perceived *scarcity*, in and of itself, even when there is no increased demand. A *commodity* is any object (e.g., informational, experiential, or material) which a potential possessor perceives as useful, and which is conveyable from person to person (Brock, 1968). The symbolic or informational value of a message is defined as its effectiveness in producing acceptance. Persuasive communications (Fromkin & Brock, 1971), simulated drug experiences (Fromkin, 1970), new products (Fromkin, 1971), leather boots (Fromkin, Olson, Dipboye, & Barnaby, 1971), ladies pant suits (Szybillo, 1973), and pornographic materials (Fromkin & Brock, 1973; Zellinger, Fromkin, Speller, & Kohn, 1975) were all found to be associated with greater valuation when they were perceived as scarce. Commodity theory contains a number of theoretical propositions describing situational variations, such as perception of scarcity, delay, and transmission restrictions, which may augment the perceived scarcity or unavailability of the object (Brock, 1968).

More recently, we suggested that the desire to see oneself as different from one's peers is a potential explanatory dynamic for the enhanced valuation which accompanies scarcity (Fromkin, 1970, 1973). We proposed that the tendency to prize scarce and unavailable commodities may be a symbolic representation of a desire for the self-perception of uniqueness. The economist Veblen (1931) also recognized a similar psychological meaning for the accumulation of possessions. We reasoned that the possession of scarce commodities is one *socially acceptable* way to redefine the self as different in a society which continually confronts the individual with pressures toward conformity and deindividuation. Some consensual validation for our ideas is found in the increased trends for several advertising campaigns to emphasize product scarcity and to imply a direct link between their product and social distinctiveness. For example, a major television manufacturer announced that only 2,000 television sets of a particular model were to be produced and marketed. A television commercial asked consumers to be patient in their search for their razor blades. Advertisements for a prominent cigarette suggested that not everybody will like their cigarette. Although the above examples represent different connotations of scarcity, they share the assumption of a perception that possession of a scarce product enhances one's sense of individuality.

In order to test the postulated link between scarcity and self-enhancement, we conducted a laboratory experiment in which we varied the degree of self-perceived similarity. Behavioroid measures assessed the degree of subjects' preferences for experiences which were unavailable to large numbers of other college students, and experiences which were available to large numbers of other students (Fromkin, 1968). Under conditions of low degrees of self-perceived similarity, subjects did not exhibit preferences for scarce experiences. However, as the degree of self-perceived similarity increased, subjects' preferences for scarce experiences increased significantly. Thus, it appears that confirmation of the self-attribute of uniqueness can arise as a result of possession of scarce commodities which are unavailable to large numbers of similar others. When these findings are taken in concert with other research, noted above, it seems reasonable to conclude that a society's value of scarce goods is enhanced in social climates which reward conformity and arouse feelings of undistinctiveness.

Names

Another potential uniqueness attribute is our own name, which may be the "most important anchorage of our self identity" (Allport, 1961, p. 117). The special significance of our name is revealed by the anger which is frequently observed when someone forgets, misspells, or mispronounces it. Furthermore, individuals tend to retain their *original initials* after they have changed, shortened, or discarded their original names (Strauss, 1959), and possessions often display the owners' initials. Yet, it is not the possession but the *person* who is personalized by his initials or name. Names do more than merely identify an individual. A direct link between our names and self-identity is found in a study by Bugental and Zelen (1949–1950), who examined subjects' self-perceptions by asking the question, "Who are you?" Content analyses of subjects' responses against 17 different dimensions revealed that names were the most frequent.

Names become intimately linked with our self-concept through various social mechanisms. For example, dimensions of our self-concept are often determined by the degree of status which is associated with our social and occupational positions (Brown & Ford, 1961). Similarly, our names are associated frequently with status and recognition. In schools and other organizations, achievements are often displayed by honor roles, trophies and certificates, news releases, and so on. Presumably, these avenues of recognition serve to distinguish us from others for the approval of significant persons such as parents, teachers, coaches, and supervisors. Eventually, names become autonomous from these instrumental utilities and acquire value, in and of themselves, through their prior association with social rewards. The psychological relationship between surnames and self-perceptions of uniqueness may be seen in reports of the harassment of women who retain their maiden names after marriage. A public-relations counselor describes the many embarrassments which she endured to retain her maiden name and her "separate sense of individuality" after her marriage (Krech, Crutchfield, & Ballachey, 1962, p. 417). The journalist, Ruth Hale, refused to concede to the social dictum that she adopt her husband's name after marriage. Among other instances of resistance, she insisted that both her maiden name and her husband's name be on their mailbox, and answered phone requests for *Mrs.* with the phone number of her husband's mother (*Ms.* Magazine, 1973). Where social interactions are characterized by pressures toward conformity and anonymity, our names may acquire greater value as symbols of our uniqueness.

Some indirect support for this conjecture is found in a survey of birth records in New York hospitals by Beadle (1973), which revealed a tendency for parents to select more uncommon or unusual names in the 1970s than in the 1930s. Perhaps this trend can be attributed, in part, to the rapidly expanding population growth and the increased need to distinguish ourselves from our fellow man.

Preliminary findings from experiments in our laboratories reveal the potential of names as symbols of our uniqueness (Fromkin, 1973). Subjects participated in an impression-formation study which required them to evaluate a written description of another college student. Pilot research established that the students in the descriptions were perceived as neutral in attractiveness. The independent variable was the degree of similarity between the names of the subject and the other. In the name-similarity conditions, subjects received a description of another student whose name was the same as the subject, but was spelled differently, e.g., Catherene became Catherine and Jeffery became Jeffrey. In the name-different conditions, subjects received a description of the other student whose name was different. Relative to controls, similar-name students were perceived as less attractive and more dissimilar than dissimilar-name students.

Nicknames, too, are identifying labels, often self-generated, that become part of the self-definitional process. The trend observed in the early 1970s away from profanity toward "nickname graffiti"—the endless repetition of names and street numbers on walls, posters, street signs, and the subways of New York and Philadelphia—is apparently a kind of identity phenomenon. It seems to reflect an enhancement of the identity and distinctiveness needs accompanying urban anonymity and the rapid population expansion of the 1960s.

Clothing

The intimate linkage between self-identity and clothing is recognized in many different disciplines. The sociologist Stone (1962) holds that the self is established, maintained, and altered in and through communication during social transactions. Stone identifies appearance as one important form of communication in symbolic interaction, and clothing is a primary dimension of appearance. For example, social announcements of the self are made by means of symbols such as uniforms or distinctive apparel (e.g., the pince-nez of Teddy Roosevelt). Indeed, "distinctive persistent dress may replace the name as well as establish it" (Stone, 1962, p. 95). The French sociologist, George Simmel (1956), observes how similarity in dress "unites" members of the same social class or group, and, at the same time, "segregates" them from a larger number of members of other social classes or groups.

Although there is a great deal of obvious conformity in clothing styles, the anxiety which is commonly anticipated when two women wear the identical dress or two men wear the identical tie to the same social event seems to confirm the important relationship between clothing and the self-perception of uniqueness. Three experiments demonstrate the enhanced valuation of clothing apparel that is unavailable to many other people. Subjects participated in alleged market research being conducted by a fictitious French hosiery company (Fromkin, Olson, Dipboye, & Barnaby, 1971). Female subjects perceived nylons as personally more desirable when available only to a few other persons than when available to many others.

In a doctoral dissertation by Szybillo (1973), subjects participated in an alleged consumer psychology study of advertising and marketing. Subjects viewed slides of ladies' pant suits which varied according to their price (e.g., low or $18.00; no price; high or $48.00), and the number of suits which were to be shipped to the local community (e.g., scarce or 26 suits; no information; plentiful or 182 suits). Subjects were also divided according to premeasures into two groups of high and low fashion-opinion leadership. The main dependent variables were subjects' ratings of the "overall desirability," "distinctiveness," "quality," and "likelihood of purchase" of each of the pant suits. Separate analysis of variance performed on each of these measures yielded four significant main effects: scarce pant suits were perceived as more desirable, more distinctive, of higher quality, and more likely to be purchased than plentiful pant suits. In addition, there was one significant interaction: preferences for scarce pant suits was greater for fashion-opinion leaders than nonleaders. Thus, there seems to be some link between the tendency to be an innovator of products and ideas and the valuation of commodities which are unavailable to other persons. Perhaps those individuals who can be identified as "innovators" are expressing, at least in part, socially acceptable manifestations of the desire to see themselves as different from their peers (Fromkin, 1971).

In a third experiment, by Fromkin, Williams, and Dipboye (in Fromkin, 1973), male and female subjects responded to 12 rating-scale items which seem to reflect a desire to see themselves as unique. Subjects who obtained high uniqueness scores exhibited greater preferences for leather boots which were perceived as available only to few others relative to boots that were perceived as available to large numbers of others. This preference was not shown by subjects who obtained low uniqueness scores.

The role of fashion and clothing as uniqueness attributes is also recognized by students of fashion and clothing merchandising. Studies by Daniels (1951) and Barber and Lobel (1952) find that distribution of large numbers of a particular garment may reduce their "individualistic" value, whereas a limited number of garments may enhance it. Although "original" or limited editions in fashion are often confounded with high prices and perceptions of high quality, both high price and high quality may also be used to differentiate the self from large numbers of other persons.

A more extreme response to the social structures which tend to dehumanize and deindividuate is "ego screaming," or

> the tendency to extremes in fads and fashions . . . generated by identity problems, prevalent in mass society, which frustrates the ego and makes it scream for attention. People are seeking audiences, trying to draw attention, rather like entertainers and celebrities. They choose styles—cosmetics, hairdos, beards, sandals, wigs, eyepatches, flamboyant costumes, much as an actor choosing a costume in a dressing room—with an eye to its impact on audiences, to catching attention with startling effects. (Klapp, 1969, p. 84)

Dates and Mates

"The cliché that men prefer hard-to-get women misses the point. Men really adore women who are hard for other men to get" conclude Walster, Piliavin, and Walster (1973, p. 80) from their findings in a series of experiments examining college men's perceptions of women. In the final experiment, scarcity was varied in three conditions: a female who was reluctant to date either the subject or the four other fictitious participants (uniformly hard-to-get); a female who was willing to date the subject or any of the four fictitious participants (uniformly easy-to-get); and a female who was willing to date the subject and reluctant to date the four fictitious participants (selectively hard-to-get). Almost all the subjects preferred the selectively hard-to-get female. "The reason for her popularity is evident. Men ascribe to her all the assets of the uniformly hard-to-get and the uniformly easy-to-get women, and none of their liabilities" (Walster, Walster, Piliavin, & Schmidt, 1973, p. 120).

However, there is another obvious explanation for the enhanced ratings of the *selectively* hard-to-get woman. Being selected relative to one's peers by a more discriminating person produces an increment in positive self-regard (cf. Aronson, 1969), which is associated with that person. In addition, subjects who were selectively chosen were potential possessors of a commodity (i.e., a date) which was unavailable to other persons. Thus, according to commodity theory, one would expect the hard-to-get woman to be more valued. Several of the findings, cited above, that support the enhanced valuation which accompanies perceived unavailability, are explained by the person's desire to see himself as different from his peers (Fromkin, 1973). In light of the findings of Walster and her colleagues, it is intriguing to speculate that dating and marrying women "who are hard for other men to get" may be in part a manifestation of a uniqueness motive.

Beliefs

In addition to scarce commodities, names, clothing, and mates or dates, there are a number of other attributes which fit the definition of uniqueness attributes. A survey by Fromkin and Demming (1967) found that college students perceived their attitudes, beliefs, and values as "most unique about themselves," and their behavior as "least unique about themselves." Apparently, individuals covet a small compendium of beliefs which they believe are highly idiosyncratic to themselves. Support for the idea of beliefs as uniqueness attributes may be derived from theories of attitudes which emphasize the different functions which attitudes perform for the individual. For example, Sarnoff (1960) suggests that attitudes derive from the reduction of tension arising from conflicting motives. Similarly, Katz (Katz, 1960; Katz & Stotland, 1959) suggests that an attitude can serve one of four general functions. According to the *value-expressive* function, "the individual derives satisfaction from expressing attitudes appropriate to his personal values and to his concept of himself" (Katz, 1960, p. 170).

The value-expressive function of attitudes has been largely ignored in the research of social psychologists. By contrast, it is central to the doctrines of ego psychology, which stress the importance of self-expression, self-importance, self-development, and self-realization. Katz (1960, p. 173) suggested that the relevant rewards are "not so much a matter of gaining social recognition or monetary rewards as of establishing his self identity and confirming his notion of the sort of person he sees himself to be." Furthermore, he specifies that such attitudes should be most salient when (1) there are appeals to the individual to reassert his self-image or (2) when there are ambiguities which threaten his self-concept. Threats to self and the attitudinal redefinition which accompany threats have been termed *social adjustment* by Smith, Bruner, and White (1956). Evidence regarding the self-defining function of attitudes is provided by the descriptive data collected by these authors, whose in-depth interviews with ten men found that each man's opinions were significant modes of affirming to himself and to others what he "was" socially. Subjects' responses during the interviews showed several different ways in which opinions become involved in the process of social adjustment.

A dissertation by Weir (1971) tests derivations from uniqueness theory (Fromkin, 1968), and provides convincing support for our notion that beliefs can serve as uniqueness attributes. Under the guise of studying the relationship between attitudes and aesthetic preferences, subjects completed a 30-item attitude questionnaire by rating (1) their own attitude position on each item, (2) their perception of the attitude position of the average college student at their university on each item, and (3) how important it was for them to maintain a difference between their own attitude and the position of the average college student on each item. On the basis of these ratings, subjects were cast into three experimental conditions. A basis for a *high* uniqueness-deprived condition was begun by selecting five attitudes which subjects rated as highly different from other college students. A *low* uniqueness-deprived manipulation was begun by selecting five attitudes which subjects rated as slightly different from other college students. A uniqueness-nondeprived manipulation was begun by selecting five attitudes which subjects rated as similar to other college students. During the second experimental session, each subject was led to believe that he was one of three subjects. The bogus responses of two confederate subjects were always identical to each other and always agreed with the subject's original attitude position. After hearing the two bogus responses, subjects stated again their own position on the attitude item. This procedure was repeated five times— once for each of the five attitude items. Subjects' change away from their original attitude position was the dependent variable.

The main findings of this experiment provide strong confirmation for the uniqueness hypotheses. Subjects who were deprived of an attitude position which they perceived to be different from other college students (high uniqueness-deprived condition) changed their attitude away from their original position significantly more than subjects whose original position was not coopted by the two confederate strangers. Furthermore, a significant trials-by-deprivation interaction also shows that attitude change away from the original position increased significantly as the number of coopted attitudes increased from one to five in the two uniqueness-deprived conditions.

The Weir (1971) procedure was used by Brandt and Fromkin (1975) in a survey of 200 male and 200 female college students at Purdue University. The questionnaire contained 200 items on beliefs in such categories as religious, political, sexual, academic, economic, social, and moral. Subjects responded to each item by rating their own attitude position, their perception of the attitude position of the average college student at Purdue, and the degree to which it was important to maintain any difference between their own and the attitude position of the average college student at Purdue.

The findings show that female subjects rated their sexual beliefs as most unique, and male subjects rated their religious beliefs as most unique. Surprisingly, there was very little variance among female responses to the sexual items, or male responses to the religious items. That is, attitude positions that subjects believed to be different were, in fact, not very different from their peers. F. H. Allport (1924) identified "pluralistic ignorance" as a state where each person mistakenly believes himself to have a set of nonconformist beliefs. One explanation for these findings is that females rarely discuss their sexual beliefs in public, and males rarely discuss their religious beliefs in public. It seems that females are responding to a real or imagined norm or stereotype which dictates that it is less acceptable for females to discuss sex openly. In turn, it seems that males are responding to a real or imagined norm or stereotype which dictates that it is less acceptable for the males to discuss religion openly.

Performance

Some hints about the potential for variations in performances to serve as uniqueness attributes is found in Brickman's studies of subjects' satisfactions with their task performance under conditions of high, average, and low scores which were either similar or dissimilar to the scores obtained by other subjects. In the first study, when subjects received their own scores and the scores of three other subjects (Brickman, 1972), performance satisfaction was lower when all four persons obtained the same average scores than when some persons obtained above average and other subjects obtained below average scores. Similarly, persons were more satisfied with their performance when they obtained one high and one low score than when they obtained two average scores (Goldberg, 1973). Perhaps people prefer to perceive their performance, and thereby themselves, as distinct or different over and above preferences for high performance.

In a more direct test of this explanation, Brickman (1973) designed an experiment in which the test scores of a subject and a confederate varied on four different tests so that subjects and confederates obtained high and low scores on the same *or* different tests. In *identical-equality* conditions, the subject and the confederate obtained high scores on tests A and B and low scores on tests C and D. In *unique-equality* conditions, subjects obtained high scores on tests A and B and low scores on tests C and D, whereas the confederate obtained high scores on tests C and D and low scores on tests A and B. In the *mixed-equality* conditions, subjects obtained high scores on tests A and B and low scores on tests C and D, whereas the confederate obtained high scores on tests B and C and low scores on tests A and D. Females preferred situations of mixed- or unique-equality or some degree of uniqueness, and males preferred conditions of identical-equality or similarity. All subjects perceived the tests as more fair when their scores were different from the confederate's. One interpretation of these results is that females have a greater concern for maintaining individual differences than males.

Alternatively, Brickman suggests that males may share a greater preference for the potential competition implied by similar test scores, and females tend to avoid competitive situations. Other research has demonstrated the power of situational states to affect performance (Brock, Edelman, Edwards, & Schuck, 1965). In particular, Breer and Locke (1965) have shown that "individuality" interacts with performance, so it is unfortunate that Brickman's subjects did not have an opportunity to perform some task after obtaining their test scores. The tenability of the "competition" interpretation would be reduced and that of the uniqueness interpretation enhanced if subjects were to adjust their task performance upward and downward to avoid excessive similarity.

DEINDIVIDUATION AND UNIQUENESS

The foregoing discussion reveals that names, clothing, beliefs, task performance, and the selection of dates may serve to define the person as different. However, there are a number of other kinds of self-defining responses to conformity pressures which do not fit neatly into the above definition of uniqueness attributes. These reactions are often antisocial, and are related to the phenomenon known as *deindividuation* which characterizes many of the social structures in current society (Fromkin, 1973).

Most conceptualizations of deindividuation refer to undistinctiveness of self, nonidentifiability of self to others, anonymity, and loss of self-consciousness. Experimental operationalizations have utilized some form of name tags and formal or customary clothing versus no name tags, lab coats, and large hoods or costumes to vary the person's identifiability from the victim or other group members (Cannavale, Scarr, & Pepitone, 1970; Festinger, Pepitone, & Newcomb, 1952; Singer, Brush, & Lublin, 1965; Watson, 1973; Zimbardo, 1970). Although there are many subtle points of divergence, most social scientists would agree that the principal precursor of deindividuation is an attack on ego identity, i.e., the *person's* "loss of self-consciousness," or the *subjective* feelings of nonidentifiability (cf. Duval & Wicklund, 1972). For instance, this "loss of identity can be conferred by being submerged in a crowd, disguised, masked, or dressed in a uniform like everyone else, or by darkness" (Zimbardo, 1970, p. 255).

Most conceptualizations of deindividuation contain at least two principal components—*uniformity* or similarity in appearance, and *anonymity* or nonidentifiability by observers (cf. Baron, 1970). It is likely that high degrees of interpersonal similarity which threaten self-perceived uniqueness are more closely allied with the uniformity component. The responses to similarity-induced threat, described above under Uniqueness Attributes, can usually be classified as socially acceptable modes of self-redefinition. However, when threats to uniqueness involve both uniformity and anonymity, the addition of the latter may release restraints, and responses will tend to be more asocial or antisocial. For example, the violence that erupted on the nation's college campuses during the decade of the 1950s has been linked to the impersonal modes of instruction and the resulting denial of uniqueness which accompany the rapid growth of modern universities (Keniston, 1970; Kristol, 1966, p. 8; Reich, 1970).

Deindividuation serves most clearly as a stimulus for the release of restraints when uniforms or dress standards prohibit distinctive clothing and thereby reduce the amount of identifying information conveyed to observers. For instance, under tense conditions of arousal and excitement, the relative anonymity of one uniformed policeman from another during the 1968 Democratic National Convention in Chicago, or one National Guardsman from another at Kent State University, may have reduced restraints against violent acts.

However, the picture of deindividuation has yet to be fully or clearly developed. Camus (1956, p. 45) described the rebellious nature of modern man as motivated by "the negation of everything that denies the individual and the glorification of everything that exalts and ministers to the individual." For Camus, violence, such as "killing in order to be unique," is retaliation against the success of deindividuation. Likewise, Milgram and Toch (1969) provide evidence that the group aggression which occurs during riots may not be only a release of restraints in crowds, but more a response to the chronic anonymity of ghetto life. A resident of the Watts district explains: "I don't believe in burning, stealing, or killing but I can see why the boys did what they did. They just wanted to be noticed, to let the world know the seriousness of their state in life" (Milgram & Toch, 1969, p. 576). Similarly, the substantial increase in the number of senseless and apparently motiveless acts of violence in major metropolitan areas has been attributed to the anonymity produced by rapid urbanization (Zimbardo, 1970).

SUMMARY

In sum, the major thesis of this chapter is that the study of social behavior as a single act of exchange has bred a benign neglect of a host of important variables and related processes. For example, when conformity is conceptualized in an exchange theory perspective, the act of exchange is often viewed as static. That is, it assumed that conformity is exchanged for approval because the immediate rewards for conformity are greater than the immediate rewards for nonconformity. However, the theory and research cited in this chapter suggest that compliance with group norms for approval and membership is only the beginning of a continuing process. The act of conformity can begin a process which involves the arousal of competing motives, such as the desire to see oneself as unique. Social exchange theories do not predict the resulting variation in the payoff values for scarce commodities and socially acceptable or deviant actions which are related to the redefinition of the self as unique among members of our reference groups.

4

Resource Theory

Interpersonal Behavior as Exchange

EDNA B. FOA AND URIEL G. FOA

INTRODUCTION

At the marketplace, interpersonal behavior has been traditionally conceptualized as exchange of resources. In a barter society commodities were literally exchanged for one another. Later on, one commodity—money—became standardized and widely accepted; the money–merchandise exchange was then born, and to this day it has maintained the pride of place in economic practice and thinking. But money is also exchanged with services when we pay the plumber for repairing the pipes and the gardener for improving the landscape. Information is exchanged with money when we buy a newspaper or register for a course. Only recently, economists have turned their attention to the exchange of money with services and with information. However, these areas of investigation are still regarded with suspicion, since they fail to lend themselves easily to the elegant formulations of the money–commodities exchange.

Although economists are still reluctant to include information and services in their theoretical notions, other social scientists have attempted to extend the economic model to incorporate all interpersonal transactions, including expressions of esteem and respect, friendship and love. In many occasions, goods, services, and information are indeed exchanged with expressions of gratitude, admiration, or affec-

EDNA B. FOA • Department of Psychiatry, Temple University Health Sciences Center, Eastern Pennsylvania Psychiatric Institute, Philadelphia, Pennsylvania 19129. URIEL G. FOA • Department of Psychology, Temple University, Philadelphia, Pennsylvania 19129.

tion, rather than with money. A further extension of the economic model, to include not only interpersonal transactions but also political exchanges, has been proposed by Easton (1965), and by Ilchman and Uphoff (1969).

Social scientists have been concerned with describing exchange processes and with the specification of equilibrium rules. The trend toward extension of the economic model to noneconomic exchanges was probably stimulated by the simple elegance of the economic conceptualization and by its success in predicting price fluctuations, at least in the ideal conditions of a free market. Another factor contributing to this "economic imperialism" (Boulding, 1973, p. 11) is the traditional indifference of learning theory toward attempts to classify various forms of behavior in terms other than their reinforcing or punishing properties. The assumption that all exchanges follow the economic rule of loss and gain fits well with the Skinnerian notion that any event which increases the frequency of emitting a given behavior is a reinforcement, and any event which decreases it is a punishment. The enquiry into *what* is exchanged was largely disregarded.

Let us try then to group the variety of interpersonal exchanges into classes in such a way that within each class the same rules will prevail. Further parsimony may be achieved if the classes can be ordered so that those closer to each other in the configuration will have more similar rules of exchange. To this task of defining classes and charting their pattern of similarities, we now turn. We shall then proceed to consider the development of these classes and its relationship to some of their properties. After presenting empirical findings in various areas of interpersonal behavior, we shall conclude with a discussion of the application of resource theory to problems in society.

We have limited ourselves here to the treatment of resource exchanges. A description of the cognitive mechanisms that underlie exchange, their development in childhood, cross-cultural differences, and pathology of exchange is provided in Foa and Foa (1974).

SIX RESOURCE CLASSES

Resource is anything transacted in an interpersonal situation. It encompasses, therefore, many different events: material objects such as a dress, a flower or a bottle of wine, money and equivalent forms of payment, a kiss, a medical or beauty treatment, a newspaper, a congratulatory handshake, a glance of admiration or reproach, a pat on the back, or a punch on the nose. In short, resource is any item, concrete or symbolic, which can become the object of exchange among people.

We have found it useful to group resources transacted through interpersonal encounters into six classes, labeled love, status, information, money, goods, and services. *Love* is defined as an expression of affectionate regard, warmth, or comfort; *status* is an expression of evaluative judgment which conveys high or low prestige, regard, or esteem; *information* includes advice, opinions, instruction, or enlightenment, but excludes those behaviors which could be classed as love or status; *money* is any coin, currency, or token which has some standard unit of exchange value; *goods* are tangible products, objects, or materials; and *services* involve activities on the body or belongings of a person which often constitute labor for another.

All six classes proposed here have appeared in the literature: economists have dealt with money, goods, and services and have considered the relations among these resources in terms of prices and wages; love is prominent in Freud's conception of human motivation; Adler has seen interpersonal relations as a struggle for the acquisition of status. More recently, information processing has been proposed as a central construct in the conception of human nature (e.g., Berlyne, 1960). Previous theories of interpersonal resources have emphasized one or more classes, but largely ignored the others. Our contribution consists of conceptualizing all classes of resources within a single framework that accommodates their differences as well as their similarities.

The following two attributes or coordinates were used for ordering the six classes: concreteness versus symbolism, and particularism versus universalism. Observation of interpersonal behavior shows that it varies from concrete to symbolic. Some behaviors, like giving an object or performing an activity upon the body or the belongings of another individual, are quite concrete. Some others are more symbolic: language, posture of the body, a smile, gesture, or facial expression. Another characteristic on which resources differ is the significance of the person who provides the resource. Changing the bank teller will not make much of a difference for the client wishing to cash a check. A change of doctor or lawyer is less likely to be accepted with indifference. One is even more particularistic with regard to a friend, a spouse, or a mother. Harlow and Suomi (1970) showed that when the facial features of a surrogate mother are altered, the baby monkey reacts with fear, refusing to accept the change. In some animal species certain communications are more target specific than others. Mating calls are more particularistic than status signals, and the latter are less general than distress or alarm signals (Johnsgard, 1967). In operant terminology, the particularism–universalism attribute may be thought of as the degree to which variables associate with the agent of reinforcement constitute discriminative stimuli affecting the salience of the reinforcer. It derives from the writings of Parsons (1951) and Longabaugh (1963), and is similar to Blau's (1964) notion of intrinsic and extrinsic rewards.

Each of the six resources can be classified on the basis of the two coordinates suggested: concrete-symbolic and particularistic-universal. On the first coordinate, concreteness, services, and goods involve the exchange of some overtly tangible activity or product, and are classed as concrete. Status and information, on the other hand, are typically conveyed by verbal or paralinguistic behaviors, and are thus more symbolic. Love and money are exchanged in both concrete and symbolic forms, and thus occupy intermediate positions on this coordinate.

The positions of love and money are extreme and opposite on the particularistic coordinate. It matters a great deal from whom we receive love, since its reinforcing effectiveness is closely tied to the stimulus person. Money, on the other hand, is the least particularistic resource, since, of all resources, it is most likely to retain the same value regardless of the relation between, or characteristics of, the reinforcing agent and recipient. Services and status are less particularistic than love, but more particularistic than goods and information.

The positions of the six resource classes plotted on the two coordinates is shown in Figure 1. For simplicity's sake, these six classes of resources have been represented by discrete points. It is more accurate to consider each class as occupying a range in the order, so that some of its elements will be nearer to one of the two neighboring classes than to the other. A verbal expression of love such as "I like you very much" is symbolic, and thus is more similar to status than to services. Conversely, fondling and kissing are concrete ways of expressing affection, closer to services than to status. Services to the

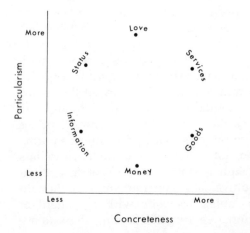

FIGURE 1. Configuration of the six resource classes plotted on the coordinates of concreteness and particularism. Copyright ©1971 by the American Association for the Advancement of Science.

body are proximal to love, whereas services to one's belongings are nearer to goods. Likewise, consumption goods are closer to services than durable goods. A credit card can be considered a kind of money, but it is more particularistic than currency; not every merchant will honor a credit card, and the card is not issued to everybody. This form of payment is also more symbolic than currency; although nothing concrete is given in a credit-card payment, currency actually changes hands. Thus, a credit card will be nearer to information than currency. In fact, the card provides information on the solvency of its holder.

At the interface between classes, the elements of one class merge into those of the other. Consequently, the structure determines only the ordinal distance among classes, whereas the cardinal distance depends on the particular sample of items chosen in each class. Thus, love is always closer to services than to goods and most distant from money, but the degree of similarity between any two given classes varies within these limits. The distance between love and service will be small for items such as fondling and massaging, and larger when love is expressed by saying, "I am happy to see you" and the service consists of changing a tire. In either case, however, the love item will be closer to services than to goods.

The structure depicted in Figure 1 shows essentially the relative similarity among the various resource classes on the two attributes of concreteness and particularism; the nearer any two classes are on a given coordinate, the more similar they are perceived on the corresponding attribute. Thus, for example, status and services are similar in particularisms, but differ in concreteness; status and information, on the other hand, are similar in symbolism, but they differ in particularism. It is possible, of course, to find other attributes which may lead to a different arrangement of the classes. The two attributes chosen by us are of interest only because the configuration they provide has received a good deal of empirical support, as we shall see later. In other words, similarity on given attributes is significant to the extent that it indicates similarity on other important behavioral properties, such as degree by which two resources are likely to be exchanged with, or substituted for, one another.

Relationship between Resource Exchange and Interpersonal Behavior

When interpersonal behavior is defined in terms of its meaning, it becomes almost synonymous with resource exchange. Most interpersonal encounters involve an exchange of resources and, conversely, resources are obtained mostly through interpersonal encounters. Indeed, economic resources are obtained by an interaction with those who control or own them. Love and status are produced mostly in interpersonal situations; therefore, their exchange requires interpersonal contact. The skill to perform a service and the knowledge to impart information are often controlled by persons and can be obtained through encounters with them.

Rarely, a single social act will transmit only one given resource. Usually two, and sometimes even more resources are involved in the same act. Resources, then, can be conceptualized as component elements of social behavior so that any given behavior can be described and analyzed in terms of the resources that compose it. In this sense, resources are like chemical elements: in nature, they seldom occur in a pure state, but they provide a basis for classifying and analyzing the compounds they form. On first sight, the lack of one-to-one correspondence between actions and resources may seem disadvantageous from a theoretical and practical point of view, as it complicates the model as well as the predictions derived from it. However, if each action would convey only one resource, no relationship among classes and, therefore, no structural pattern, would be found. The fact that certain resources are proximal in the structure (see Figure 1) and, therefore, are more related, indicates that they tend to occur jointly in the same action more often than do distal resources. For example, actions expressing both love and esteem (status) are more frequent in the behavioral repertoire of persons than are actions which provide status and goods. Indeed, love and status are proximal in the structure of resources, whereas goods are distant from status. If, however, love and status would *always* appear together, they could hardly constitute two distinct classes: each resource is sometimes transmitted alone. The process of differentiation among resources in childhood depends precisely on the emergence of psychomotoric and social conditions that permit the transmission of one resource at a time.

DIFFERENTIATION OF RESOURCES IN CHILDHOOD

In early infancy, the human being is exposed to an undifferentiated bundle of love and service; the flowing milk, the warmth and softness of his mother's body, and her care for him. The differentiation between love and services becomes possible after the child has acquired some psychomotoric skills sufficient for giving some services to himself—feeding himself, washing his hands, etc. At this time, his mother can give him love without services by requesting him to serve himself and, at the same time, encouraging him to do so. Successively to this first differentiation between love and services, goods are differentiated from services and status from love. Consumption goods, like food, are hard to differentiate from service, since they can be used only once. It is only when the child becomes interested in durable goods, such as toys which can be used again and again, that the differentiation between services and goods becomes feasible. The differentiation of status from love requires some acquisition of language, because most transactions of status ("Gee, you did it") are verbal. Later on, money is differentiated from goods, and information from status. Money is a promise of future goods, so that this differentiation requires some ability to delay rewards. At first, information is hardly distinguishable from status: parents praise their children for the new information they have acquired. When the child broadens his social world to contact with his peers, he has the opportunity to discover criteria for status, such as physical strength, which are different from information.

The developmental sequence described here is depicted in Figure 2. Examination of this figure reveals that the development of resource classes proceeds along the particularism–universalism dimension. Each

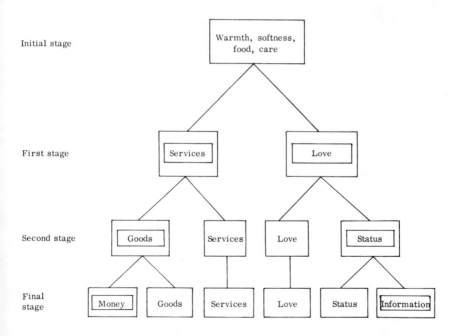

FIGURE 2. A schematic representation of the differentiation of resource classes, in which a newly differentiated class is indicated by a double frame. Copyright © 1974 by Charles C Thomas, Publisher.

stage consists of developing less particularistic resources, starting with love (the most particularistic) and services, through status and goods, to information and money (the least particularistic). However, a further differentiation takes place along the dimension of concreteness, resulting at each stage in the development of two classes.

Exigencies of representation on a flat surface place money and information on the two extremes in the last row of Figure 2. Because these two classes are similar in degree of particularism, the last row should be folded in order to achieve correct representation. When this is done, the same order appears in Figure 2 and in Figure 1. The identity of order suggests that the developmental sequence determines the structure of resource classes found in the adult. This sequence seems also to affect certain characteristics of resource classes to which we now turn for examination.

EXCHANGE OUTCOMES AND ENVIRONMENTAL INFLUENCES

Resource classes vary with respect to their exchange outcomes as well as to the environmental conditions that facilitate or hinder their exchange. These characteristics change systematically according to the position of each class on the particularistic dimension, so that love and money, being at opposite poles of this dimension, differ most on them. For the sake of brevity, then, the following description of these characteristics will refer mainly to love and to money; the other classes occupy intermediate positions between these two extremes: services and status are more similar to love than to money, and goods and information are closer to money.

The first two properties considered here refer to exchange outcomes, and the others are concerned with environmental conditions that facilitate specific exchanges.

Relationship between Self and Other

The relationship between giving the resource to the other and giving it to self is positive for love, but decreases and becomes negative as one moves from love toward money, its opposite in the order. This prediction is related to the intuitive notion that the ability to love others requires self-acceptance, and is supported by the repeated finding of a positive relationship between giving love to self and to others. Quite the opposite is true with regard to money, since one person's gain is another's loss. In consequence, an exchange of money can be a zero-sum game, but an exchange of love cannot.

Relationship between Giving and Taking

In love there is usually a certain degree of ambivalence even in normal individuals; giving love does not exclude the concurrent presence of some hostility, or the taking away of love. However, giving and taking away money are unlikely to occur in the same act.

Relationship between Interpersonal Situation and Exchange

Money does not require an interpersonal relationship in order to be transmitted or kept for future exchanges, and it can be sent conveniently through a third person. Love, on the other hand, can hardly be separated from the interpersonal situation, kept for a long time in the absence of actual exchange, or transmitted by an intermediary without incurring a loss.

Time for Processing Input

Giving and receiving love cannot be done in a hurry; it requires time. Money, to the contrary, can change hands very rapidly.

Delay of Reward

Love is a relatively long-term investment, with rewards being reaped only after several encounters; a friendship needs to be "cultivated", so that trust (that is, expectation that the exchange will be completed) is a necessary condition. On the other hand, an exchange of money with another resource can be completed in a single encounter.

Optimum Group Size

It has been noted (Carpenter, 1963) that in animal species living in groups, such as monkeys and apes, there is an optimal group size, presumably related to the input processing capacity of the species.

When this size is exceeded, aggressive behavior and other tendencies disruptive of group life increase greatly (Calhoun, 1962). In the human species, the optimal group size for an orderly exchange of resources may vary with the resource class, being smallest for love and largest for money. Lataneé and Darley (1969) have indeed found that the larger the number of bystanders, the less likely it is that any one of them will intervene in an emergency situation. Helping belongs to the class of services, a neighbor of love in the order, and the optimal group size of this resource appears to be small, according to the findings of Latané and Darley. On the other hand, large groups are involved in trading in a stock or commodities exchange, and access to a large market is considered advantageous by businessmen.

The relationship between order and properties of resource classes may originate in the sequence of cognitive development of these classes during socialization; the characteristics of each resource indeed appear to reflect the conditions that exist when it became a distinct cognitive class. Love develops early, in the small and relatively permanent family group, before the "self–other" and "giving–taking" differentiations have become firmly established (Foa & Foa, 1974). Money, on the other hand, acquires its meaning much later, after one has learned that "self" is not "other" and "giving" is not "taking," and, from the beginning, it is used mostly for exchanges outside the family. Thus, resources are best exchanged in conditions that resemble those under which they had been learned in the past.

EMPIRICAL SUPPORT FOR RESOURCE THEORY

We shall now turn to discuss empirical findings related to basic proportions of resource theory. This review will be narrative and informal; a more technical and complete presentation of data and methodology can be found in Foa and Foa (1974).

Homogeneity of Classes

The first question to be answered was whether our classification of resources into six classes would be used by naive subjects when given the task of categorizing them. Each of 11 subjects was provided with a deck of 18 cards. This deck contained three representative messages for each of the six resource classes, one message to each card. Examples of messages are: I feel affection for you (love); you do things very well (status); here is my opinion (information); here is some money for you (money); here is a package for you (goods); and I ran that errand for you (services). Subjects were told to sort the 18 cards into as many different categories as they thought appropriate. Only one subject used more than six categories in performing this task.

Similarity and Substitution

Next, we investigate the hypothesis that messages belonging to neighboring classes (see Figure 1) are perceived as more similar and more substitutable with one another than are messages belonging to distal classes. The message cards prepared for the previous study were used in another group of 37 subjects. This group received, in succession, a series of messages, and were asked to return, from the messages available to them, the one most similar as well as the one most dissimilar to the message just received. In the deck of messages provided to the subject, all classes were represented except the one to which the message received belonged, so that he was denied the option of returning a message from the same class.

The results supported the hypothesis; subjects were, indeed, more likely to substitute for the missing class a proximal, rather than a distal, message. When subjects were asked to choose the most dissimilar resource, the same order was obtained with the size of frequencies reversed, as expected. The highest frequency occurred in the class most distant from the one received, with a gradual decrease in frequency for less remote classes.

Structure

The results obtained in the similarity study provided support for the structural hypothesis by showing that classes which are closer to one another in the configuration depicted in Figure 1, elicit more similar responses. In a more direct test of this hypothesis, 120 subjects were presented with six hypothetical situations in which they had given a certain resource to a friend, and were instructed to indicate what they would prefer to receive in return. Preference scores were intercorrelated to find out whether resources closer in the order would elicit more similar responses. As expected, the correlations were higher the more proximal the resources. More important, this intercorrelation pattern remained invariant across different exchange situations, that is, when the resource given by the subject or the resource desired by him varied. Several other investigations, exploring further aspects of resource theory, supplied additional evidence for the structural hypothesis.

Exchange

A number of investigations were designed to test the proposition that, given the choice, people would prefer certain resources over certain others. More specifically, it was expected that exchanges with the same or proximal resources would be more frequent than transactions involving distal resources. Some of these investigations used questionnaires, and others involved experimental manipulations. Both exchanges of giving as well as exchanges of taking away, i.e., aggression–aggression sequences (Foa & Foa, 1974, pp. 220–238) were considered. In the questionnaire studies subjects were asked to imagine situations in which they had given a particular resource to another person, or in which they had been deprived of a resource by the other. Using paired comparisons, they were then requested to choose the preferred resources for reciprocation or for retaliation. In the experimental work, subjects were actually deprived of a resource by the experimenter's confederate, and were then given the opportunity to deprive him of a resource of their choice.

By and large, the hypothesis that exchanges between proximal resources are preferred over transactions of distal ones was supported. However, some additional factors influencing frequency of choice have emerged from the investigations:

1. Although love tends to be exchanged mainly with love, money is exchanged with a wider range of proximal resources, but seldom with money itself.

2. The resource chosen for reciprocation is influenced not only by the resource previously received, but also by the institutional setting in which the exchange takes place. Thus, not surprisingly, love is frequently used to reciprocate friends, and money is used in commercial transactions.

3. In negative exchanges (i.e., aggression), retaliation by denial of love is prevalent in hypothetical situations elicited by questionnaire responses. In actual experimental conditions, however, retaliation with a similar resource class is preferred.

On the whole, the results indicate that when no constraints are imposed on the availability of resources, certain exchanges are more likely to occur than certain others. However, such freedom of choice may not be that common in real life. It is, therefore, of practical interest to study the effects of unavailability of the resource most suitable for a given exchange.

Effect of Restrictions

It was hypothesized that restricting an exchange by denial of the most suitable resources will have two effects: (1.) The response will be more intense as if to substitute quantity for quality. (2.) In spite of such increased intensity, the exchange will be less effective and less satisfying than one that involves suitable resources.

Two experiments were designed to test these hypotheses. In the first experiment, subjects who had been deprived of a given resource could retaliate by using a resource that was predetermined by the experimental design; however, they were free to choose the intensity of retaliation. The result indicated that subjects who retaliated by depriving the confederate of money chose the strongest retaliation when the resource they had previously lost was love, the class most distal from money. Moving away from the class of love, the strength of the retaliation decreased progressively. This pattern was completely reversed when the subject was premitted to deprive the confederate of love. Furthermore, the results indicated that increased intensity of retaliation, occurring when the resource available was not appropriate, did not effectively reduce residual hostility in the resource of which one had been previously deprived (Donnenwerth & Foa, 1974).

In a second experiment, positive exchanges were studied. Subjects were induced to provide a stooge with a given predetermined resource. The stooge then reciprocated by giving a resource to the subject. In some cases, this resource was appropriate to the one previously given to her by the subject; in other groups the stooge reciprocated with a resource that was remote from the one she had received. Subjects were then asked to rate their degree of satisfaction with this interaction. It was predicted that those who reciprocated with an appropriate resource would be more satisfied than the others. This prediction was well supported for the less particular resources; appropriate exchanges of love and status, however, were less satisfying than expected. A possible explanation for this deviation is that the time allowed for particularlistic exchanges was too short; as noted earlier, these transactions require more time than do less particularistic ones. Indeed, when more time was later available, degree of satisfaction increased (Teichman & Foa, 1975).

Helping Behavior

Within resource-theory framework, helping somebody in an emergency is perceived as a particular type of exchange. The helper provides some resource, often services, and, more rarely, money or goods;

reciprocation consists most often in receiving expressions of gratitude (love) from the helped, and admiration (status) from bystanders— especially when helping involved some danger; on rarer occasions, reciprocation may involve money or a gift (goods). This analysis suggests that a person needing the resource expected in return for helping will be more likely to help than somebody who needs a resource different from the one expected. In the experiment designed to test this proposition, subjects who had been deprived of a given resource were then exposed to an emergency situation—hearing a person in a nearby room ostensibly falling from a chair on which he was standing. As predicted, subjects previously deprived of love were the quickest to respond, whereas those deprived of money were the slowest. Control subjects who were not deprived of any resource were the fastest to offer help. Apparently, poverty in any resource inhibits helping behavior, but less so when the act of helping provides an occasion for offsetting the shortage (Foa & Foa, 1974, pp. 199–203).

With few noted exceptions, all these studies provided further support for the structure of resource classes, since proximal classes assumed more similar values on the dependent variables than did distal ones.

RECENT DEVELOPMENTS

Although early research was concerned with basic hypotheses derived from resource theory, later investigations were directed to test specific interpersonal issues.

Differentiation of Resources in Hetero- and Homosexual Males

Informal observations suggest that homosexual liasons are more transitory than heterosexual ones, and, in general, do not require as much emotional involvement. The assumption that these behavioral differences would be reflected in cognition suggests the following hypothesis: Heterosexual males perceive a closer relationship between sexual behavior and love than do homosexuals. To test this hypothesis, subjects were provided with cards containing statements that pertain to sex, love, and services. They were instructed to sort them into two piles according to their similarity. As expected, heterosexual subjects combined love and sex statements into the same pile. Homosexual subjects, on the other hand, separated sex statements from both love and services; for them, the class of sexual behavior stands apart, differentiated from both love and services. These results may explain the differential courtship behavior in the two groups, and the difficulty in moving from one group to the other. It would be inappropriate for a homosexual pursued by another male to insist that sexual encounter between them should be postponed until emotional ties have been established. On the other hand, a straightforward sexual approach in heterosexual encounters may result in rejection, as being dissonant (Foa & Foa, 1974, pp. 140–150) with the expected relation between sex and love. Once this underlying difference has been identified, it can serve as a guideline in the clinical setting. Through behavioral rehearsal and training, the therapist can increase the match between the degree of cognitive differentiation that prevails in the group to which the client belongs and the behavioral practices to be adopted by him.

Asymmetry in Generalization

The issue of generalization among resources was also studied by investigating what happens when love accompanies the transmission of another resource. We were told by our parents and we tell our children that by "being nice" one facilitates social exchanges. Is this really true?

Sixth-grade students were taught material on the life of wolves by teachers who acted friendly and warm in one class and cold and distant (but not hostile) in the other class. Students of "nice" teachers not only liked them better, but also learned more. This latter effect was most pronounced when both teacher and students were females, and almost disappeared when both were males.

In another experiment, subjects who were deprived of money by a confederate expressed dislike for him. When the money was returned in full the hostility of the subject decreased somewhat. Return of expressed hostility to the low level which preceded deprivation occurred only when money restitution was accompanied by expression of liking and regret.

Both studies suggest that the effective transmission of a resource is enhanced by the simultaneous giving of affection: students who received love retained more of the information provided by their teachers; restitution of money became totally effective in reducing residual aggression only when accompanied by an expression of love. We also found that deprivation of money results in a deficit of love: subjects deprived of money expressed more hostility (aggression in love) than did controls; high residual hostility was also expressed by subjects after being engaged in mutual deprivation of money with a confederate (Foa & Foa, 1974, p. 197). If provision or deprivation of a given resource affects the balance of other resources, then: (a) provision of any given resource (e.g., money) should increase the amount of love possessed by the recipient; (b) deprivation of love should produce a deficit in other resources as well. The evidence, however, contradicts these suggestions: money restitution by the harm-doer did not reduce dislike for him; it seems, then, that provision of money does not affect love. On the other hand, personal rejection (loss of love) did not increase the tendency to deprive the rejector of money (Foa & Foa, 1974).

Considered together, these various results suggest that generalization across resource classes is not symmetrical. When love is provided, there is a gain in other resources, but no love is gained when other resources are given. Conversely, deprivation in other resources results in a loss of love, although love deprivation does not produce a deficit in other resources. Consequently, the loss of love occurring when other resources are taken away is not offset by receiving these resources. By contrast, the gain in other resources when love is provided is not wiped out by deprivation of love. In the long run, the system seems to favor other resources over love; its loss following deprivation of other resources is not offset by their provision. To maintain equilibrium and avoid accumulation of hostility, it appears necessary that, in the long run, more love should be given than received.

Asymmetric processes such as the one described here have been found in other sciences: a classic example is the second law of thermodynamics. In a closed system, asymmetric processes result in progressive decay and only external intervention can maintain the system in a steady state. The evidence for the asymmetry discussed here suggests that it is impossible to achieve a self-regulating utopian society; intervention and purposeful changes will always be required in order to reduce tensions and preserve a viable equilibrium.

Further Results

Additional findings have been obtained more recently and are summarized here below:

1. Using an instrument called IWIR (Inventory of Wishes for Interpersonal Resources), devised to measure perceived need for each class of resources, it was found that:

    a. with increasing age, need for love reduces much more than need for money

b. need for love is lesser in those who more often changed residence in young age

c. married people reported less need for love than unmarried ones

d. prostitutes, drug addicts, and, to a lesser degree, alcoholics, have a need for love and status higher than normals, but do not, however, differ from normals in need for money and goods

2.   Experimental work has shown that anxiety about the threatened loss of one resource generalizes to other resources according to their position in the structure.

These latter findings serve well to illustrate the relevance of resource theory to problems of society, a topic taken up in the concluding portion of this chapter. In preparation for this discussion of applied aspects, it seem appropriate to summarize what has become known so far on the modalities of resource exchange.

RULES OF THE GAME

Resource exchanges can be likened to a game in which participants give and take resources from one another. Their respective gains and losses depend on the resource transacted, as well as on the conditions surrounding the exchange; this notion is implicit in much of the theoretical considerations and empirical findings discussed thus far. Stating it in explicit form has lead to the exchanges rules which follow:

1. The larger the amount of a resource possessed by a person, the more likely it is to be given to others.

2. The smaller the amount of a resource possessed by a person, the more he is likely to take it away from others.

3. The nearer two resources are (in the structure), the more likely they are to be exchanged with one another.

4. The nearer to love a resource is, the more likely it is to be exchanged with same resource. Love is exchanged for love, money is rarely exchanged with money.

5. The nearer to love a resource is, the narrower the range of resources with which it is likely to be exchanged.

6. For resources closer to money, the amount lost by the giver tends to approach the amount gained by the receiver (so that one's gain is the other's loss).

7. When a resource is not available for exchange, it is more likely

to be substituted by a less particularistic than by a more particularistic one.

    8. The simultaneous transmission of love and another resource increases the value of this other resource, or facilitates its transmission.

    9. Taking away any resource (other than love) produces a loss of love.

    10. The optimal range (neither too little nor too much) of a resource is narrowest for love, and increases progressively for resources closer to money.

    11. In absence of exchange, the decrease in amount of love possessed decreases, and is greater for resources closer to love.

    12. Other conditions being equal, the probability of occurrence of a given exchange is contingent upon the institutional setting in which it may take place.

    13. The probability of love exchange is higher in small groups. The opposite is true for money.

Such rules emphasize a main theme of the present chapter: resource classes are different from one another, yet systematically interrelated. Integration of their differences and similarities in a single framework offers a fresh viewpoint for examining problems in modern society.

Application to Problems of Society

There has been some progress in recognizing the close interplay of economic and social factors which characterizes problems of modern society, particularly those of metropolitan areas. Thus, an innovative economist, Kenneth Boulding (1973), has proposed that love and fear provide noneconomic reciprocation to economic grants, defined as one-way transfers of economic goods. Furthermore, the search for social indicators as indices of the quality of life has been spurred by the realization that economic indicators present only a partial picture of the state of society, because other factors, although less clearly identified, influence human happiness and well-being.

Resource theory provides the conceptual tools required for developing this line of thinking in a more specific and precise way. It offers, indeed, a unified framework that accommodates economic, as well as social, behavior. It spells out their diversities and, at the same time, reveals orderliness in their laws of exchange and the environmental conditions which influence the likelihood of specific transactions to occur.

II

Exchange Theory in Specialized Settings

INTRODUCTION

The first section of this volume was devoted primarily to a number of general theoretical extensions of the initial exchange formulation. The papers in this second section each take a more detailed look at several more specific domains—group leadership, organizational behavior, and romantic relationships. Each illustrates how the general exchange orientation can be heuristically applied within a selected problem area. Although these areas are richly diverse, reliance on a common perspective should aid the reader to trace important linkages among the various contexts. With each application, the implications of the shared perspective are broadened.

These applications are applied only in a relative sense. They do not spell out operational guides to action for professional practitioners or policymakers, nor do they provide direct personal advice on how to win friends and influence people. Rather, they constitute applications in the sense that each borrows the basic orientation of exchange theory and adapts it to some topic not emphasized in the initial formulations of Homans (1961), Thibaut and Kelley (1959), and Blau (1964). Although the concerns of these papers vary in specificity, the objective in all cases is to extend the basic theory to specific contexts, rather than to provide rules for coping with concrete problem situations. The goal is primarily to extend descriptive theory, not to make prescriptions.

SCARCITY OF PRESCRIPTIVE APPLICATIONS

One may wonder why no explicitly prescriptive case studies have been included in the present volume. It is because they rarely occur in the published literature. As revealed by recent reviews and surveys (Berkowitz & Walster, 1976; Chadwick-Jones, 1976; Emerson, 1976;

Walster, Walster, & Berscheid, 1978), the social-exchange literature consists entirely of research reports, descriptive theorizing and critiques thereof, and applications or adaptations similar to those in the present section. There are numerous reports of investigations conducted in applied field settings, but these are primarily validation studies related to the general exchange framework.

One possible reason for this scarcity is that journal editors and contributors often hold applied work in low esteem. Another is that exchange theory may in fact have very little potential for application. Although the first reason is undoubtedly valid, the second is not. Speaking of one member of the exchange-theory family, equity theory, Adams and Freedman (1976, p. 55) astutely note that a vast array of social conflicts are fundamentally problems of real or imagined inequity, and that the theory thus has great potential relevance to economic, legal, interpersonal, and intergroup relations. That is the good news. The bad news is that the theory, in their view, is weakly prepared at present to be applied effectively. In particular, a major reason for the poor level of applicability of contemporary equity theory is that it has not been formulated with sufficient quantitative precision. They write:

> There is a striking absence of attempts to quantify the magnitude of inputs and outcomes (commensurately), and thus of inequities. . . . The earliest studies focused on monetary exchanges principally because outcomes were thereby roughly quantifiable, as were inputs such as productivity. In retrospect, this was a tactical error because, by arousing curiosity in counter-intuitive payment phenomena, rapid expansion of research into more socially significant areas may have been inhibited. Be that as it may, the point is that as equity theory matures . . . more precise measurement of variables and parametric investigations appear desirable. (p. 52)

A first step toward quantifying equity theory, they continue, is the establishment of a unit of measurement common to both inputs and outcomes, perhaps by magnitude estimation or multivariate pair comparison procedures. In any case, subjects—not experimenters— would decide which entities are inputs and which are outcomes, for Tornow (1971) has demonstrated that the same thing may be perceived as an input by one observer and as an outcome by another. The second step in their proposal is to put to work the common unit of measurement, once established, and a suitable psychometric technology in the systematic determination of additivity functions—that is, of functions describing how component inputs and outcomes operate in combination in the production of experienced inequity.

It may seem at first glance that Adams and Freedman are suggesting a route—a "primrose path," even—similar to one taken in the domain of operations research, namely, concentrating only on those phenomena which can be measured and modeled precisely. However, their proposal calls not for confining attention to *easily* quantified variables such as money and productivity, but rather for vigorous programmatic efforts toward the expansion of the number and kind of important variables that can be handled quantitatively. On this account, one may applaud the spirit of their proposal. However, it may be far too optimistic.

It may be too optimistic insofar as it assumes that the determination of additivity functions are basically technical problems that can be solved through refinements in psychometric methodology alone. To us it appears that these problems have no hope of solution except through a broadly based attack combining methodological endeavors with searching conceptual analyses. Strong interdependencies between conceptual and operational questions are illustrated by recent proposals and counterproposals for modifying Adams's ratio definition of equity so that measurement is not restricted to inputs and outcomes of positive sign (Harris, 1976; Romer, 1977; Samuel, 1976a,b; Walster, 1976).

One basic conceptual question concerns when inputs and outcomes are compared and when they are not. Any "common unit" used by the experimenter to make comparisons that are not made by the subject will succeed only in misleading. When inputs and outcomes are qualitatively very different, the individual may resort to compartmentalization or other tactics for avoiding even the effort of comparing. Consider love and money. "Identical amounts" or "amounts of identical dollar or utile value," even providing the phrases in quotes can be given meaning, are not intersubstitutable. "Different amounts" are, *a fortiori*, not substitutable, and often not even roughly comparable. The classes of exchangeable resources used by Foa and Foa (Chapter 4, this volume, and elsewhere as referenced there), two of which are love and money, provide a promising approach to problems of noncomparability.

Even when inputs and outcomes can be quantified, each in their own units, one may be unable or unwilling to make comparisons. Human-life costs can be measured precisely either in units of fatalities or in years of life expectancy lost. In situations in which it is possible to estimate the expected dollar cost of saving a given number of lives, decision makers may strongly resist making the comparison, because they do not want to know the rate of exchange they are accepting (McKenzie & Tullock, 1975, pp. 160–162). Such decisions not to compare may be personally rational, even if not morally defensible, if the psychic costs of knowing are high enough. Beyond this, even if one is both able and willing to make comparisons, one may be quite unwilling to reveal this fact. Consider the executives of an American automobile company, who, some believe, knew quite well the rate of exchange they were accepting between human lives and the added expense of a safer fuel-tank design.

If Adams and Freedman's proposal is overly optimistic and ambitious regarding general solutions to measurement problems, it is, at the same time, too narrow. A more comprehensive plan of attack is needed. We have already spoken of the interplay between conceptual and measurement issues. There is also the crucial question of a sufficiently broad observational base, where observations include both research data and less formally obtained experience. Adams and Freedman note the need for practitioners—the "public"—to be familiar with theory, but it works both ways. Theorists need to be familiar with the activities of practitioners and policymakers. They should know, for example, what kinds of problems and decisions are faced, and under what conditions and constraints. They should understand the difference between successful and unsuccessful practitioners, and should know something about the interactions between individual differences and situational variables. In brief, they need to be sensitized to the full range of relevant factors in each specific context of interest.

Optimists and Pessimists

Application is a matter of proceeding from the general to the particular. Ideally, one's theory is sufficiently general to provide solutions for all the kinds of problems one encounters or accepts. Although less elegant, a collection of less general theories or heuristics, plus some scheme for knowing when to try which, may work almost as well. This is approximately the situation in management science. Several different theories, models, and techniques (decision theory, game theory, linear programming, dynamic programming, queuing theory, network theory, and Monte Carlo techniques, among others) are available. No one is applicable to all types of problems, but it is often possible to structure a given problem to fit one or another. In a field which is behavioral and predominantly descriptive, such as organizational behavior, neither the theories nor the guidelines suggesting when to use which ones are nearly as well explicated at present. Perhaps they never will be. It depends greatly on the boundaries defining the field—that is, on how many poorly structured problems are accepted. Beyond this, there are strong differences of opinion about the degree of theoretical generality that is possible in principle.

The radical optimists include advocates of General Systems Theory, who hold that physical, biological, and social systems share a number of basic principles that make it possible to say quite a lot about a system without knowing much about the special area or discipline in which it is encountered (Bertalanffy, 1968, 1975; Laszlo, 1972). The radical pessimists are not in evidence, having gravitated no doubt to fields outside science about which they feel more sanguine. Among social psychologists, a relatively pessimistic position is taken by Gergen (1973), who feels that, in his field at least, it is not possible to establish predictive principles that are truly independent of time, place, and circumstance. According to this view, social psychologists should strive to conduct themselves professionally more like historians and less like physical scientists. If the pessimists are the more nearly correct, then evidently the best that can be hoped for from behavioral theory is a set of heuristic sensitizing devices that require periodic updating in response to changing times. Contrasting positions have been taken by Schlenker (1974) and Triandis (1978), and most of the fall 1976 issue of the *Personality and Social Psychology Bulletin* was devoted to an exchange of arguments on both sides.

The pessimistic view has at least one very optimistic implication. It can serve as a powerful antidote to the burden, mentioned above, that a behavioral scientist might experience in attempting to apply theory. If one accepts the fact that a major function of behavioral theory in application is to sensitize, success does not hinge on predictive precision.

The Present Contribution

Having glimpsed several pressing problems in the utilization of exchange theory for predictive application, we can now consider the present array of chapters in which application takes the form of theoretical elaboration or extension.

In the first selection, Edwin Hollander looks at the development and maintenance of leadership in small groups. His chapter contains a synthesis of his extensive contributions to this area. One of the most significant of these is his elaboration of the concept of one's group credit rating. People do not, as the initial theories often assumed, attend only to the payoff structure at the moment of action. They also appear to respond to the pattern of previous payoffs, such that an individual may, through good works, acquire the credit to deviate in subsequent transactions. This emphasis on payoff history is fully congruent with the arguments of Levinger and Huesmann (Chapter 8, this volume) for historically sensitive analysis of exchange relations. In addition, Hollander's paper calls attention to the attribution process in followers' evaluations of either the leader's actions or motives. He thus joins a number of other exchange theorists who have explicitly incorporated elements of attributions into their models (e.g., Greenberg, Chapter 1, this volume). Also noteworthy is Hollander's conceptualization of leadership as an exchange between leader and followers. By stressing influence and transfers in both directions, he provides a more balanced view than the unilateral one. Leaders are given more latitude to deviate from general norms in exchange for compliance with the more specific and crucial requirements of their role. The most important of these role requirements relates to attaining group goals and treating followers fairly.

In Chapter 6, Walter Nord proposes a resource-exchange paradigm for examining exchanges within and between organizations and the impact of these exchanges on organizational structures and processes. This paradigm, which represents a hybrid of the microconcerns of exchange theorists and the macroconcerns of "resource" theorists, provides a set of concepts capable of integrating research at a variety of levels of organizational functioning. Although the framework developed by Nord can be applied to microlevel phenomena such as individual exchanges between organization members, the paper's major contribution is in providing a meaningful framework for integrating phenomena at the macrolevel, such as interorganization networks, exchange between organizations, and between organizational subunits such as departments and divisions. Although the unit of analysis is the organization or department and not the individual, one can see striking similarities between the processes affecting these macro and micro units. Particularly noteworthy is the interplay between strategic and normative components. The evidence reviewed by Nord illustrates further the limits of a strictly economic exchange analysis of organization transactions, and demonstrates the need for including specific resources such as status, trust, and approval. This point is directly related to the major thesis of Foa and Foa (Chapter 4, this volume).

Richard Willis and Irene Hanson Frieze, in Chapter 7, consider the effect of sex roles on exchange processes as these mediate romantic relationships. They outline a framework or model for interrelating pair formation, compatibility, and stability. Illustrating the heuristic use of this model, they derive a number of hypotheses and briefly report recent evidence in support of some of them. Initial pair formation is viewed as a global exchange process in which the rate of exchange is determined by psychological processes, social roles, and "economic" factors of supply and demand. More specific similarities and comple-

mentary differences contribute to subsequent compatibility, with both
the need and resource aspects of dispositional traits being taken into
account. Stability is viewed as jointly determined by intrinsic compatibility and by external conditions of supply and demand, in particular,
the numbers and kinds of "loners" available to provide alternative
relationships. Here again, as in the previous chapter by Nord, both
micro- and macrolevel variables are represented. It should be noted
that although this model clearly views even romantic relationships as
being influenced strongly by economic factors of supply and demand,
it in no way implies anything like direct exchanges of love and money.
The principles of economic exchange, as traditionally developed for
material commodities and impersonal services, are taken seriously but
not literally, so to speak, and have been modified substantially in their
application here.

Levinger and Huesmann's treatment of the love relationship
(Chapter 8) shifts the perspective from the general payoff structure in
the dyad as it is fashioned by the broad social context to the microlevel
of the relationship itself. In order to account for the shift in dyadic
relationships over time, the authors propose fundamental alternatives
in the traditional exchange perspective. The latter has almost exclusively been concerned with payoff structures as they are frozen at any
given juncture of a relationship. If changes in payoff patterns are
discussed, it is primarily in the context of exploring the effects of a
specific factor (e.g., causal attribution, order effects) on the change in
payoff value for a given outcome. Yet in the present chapter, Levinger
and Huesmann shift from a synchronic to a diachronic mode of
analysis, elucidating the dynamic, ever shifting, and multiplex alteration of the payoff structure over time. Although one can hardly view
the present treatment as a completed design for diachronic analysis, it
is a significant first step in a vital direction (Rosnow, 1978).

5

Leadership and Social Exchange Processes

Edwin P. Hollander

Introduction

No conception of leadership is complete without attention to followers. Give and take on both sides are vital, for, as Homans (1961, p. 286) has said, "Influence over others is purchased at the price of allowing one's self to be influenced by others." The leader receives approval in the form of status, esteem, and the potential for greater influence. The followers in turn receive the benefits of the leader's efforts, if successful, in the form of favorable group results. A lack of group success removes the major benefit provided by the leader, and thereby puts his or her position at risk (Jacobs, 1971).

Another feature of the exchange process is the individual's sense of being treated fairly. In any group or organization, there is bound to be concern with equity or justice in the achievement of collective goals—that is, with how people are treated along the way. Therefore, two types of exchange can be identified. One deals with *system progress*, which is a response to the question of "How are we doing?"; the other concerns individual enhancement and issues of *equity*, such as fairness and recognition.

Social exchange is an essential feature of the transactional approach to leadership developed here, which stresses two-way influence and

Edwin P. Hollander • Department of Psychology, State University of New York at Buffalo, Amherst, New York 14226. The preparation of this chapter was facilitated by the support provided by ONR Contract N00014–76–C–0754 from the Organizational Effectiveness Research Programs of the Office of Naval Research Psychological Sciences Division.

the relationship over time between leader and followers. This perspective is also oriented to the way that followers perceive and respond to the leader. In due course, we will return to the transactional approach, after briefly considering leadership as a field of study.

LEADERSHIP IN RETROSPECT

Leadership is a process, not a person, but traditionally the leader has been viewed as possessing unique and presumably inborn traits, as in the "great man" theory. This *trait approach* prevailed during the first half of this century. Stress was placed on such factors as height, weight, appearance, intelligence, self-confidence, and other variables that might be correlated with leadership. The most commonly reported findings, summarized by Stogdill (1948) and Mann (1959), were that leaders tend to be slightly above nonleaders in intelligence, followed by general adjustment, extroversion, and dominance. Even these tendencies are not very stable, so leaders are fundamentally similar to other group members.

The largest deficiency in the trait approach was its insistence upon looking for stable features of leaders across *many* situations. The recognition that different leadership functions are demanded in different situations was the basis for the *situational approach* which took hold in the 1950s, and which pointed to requirements growing out of the group's task or function, its structure, and other contextual features. Characteristics of the leader were *not* neglected, but rather were recognized as variably appropriate to circumstances.

"Naive situationism" ran the risk of overstatement, and also the omission of a concern with process. Often little attention was given to followers' responses to leaders over time, and problems of leaders' *maintaining* as well as *attaining* status were not much considered. The leader was typically viewed as someone who occupied a position in a relatively fixed sense. Clearly, a form of faddism took researchers from one extreme to another in little more than a decade (Hollander & Julian, 1969, pp. 388–389).

An extension and refinement of the situational approach occurred through two interrelated developments. One was the development of *contingency models* (Fiedler, 1965; House, 1971; Vroom & Yetton, 1973). The other was the emergence of a *transactional approach* to leader–follower relations seen as a process (Hollander, 1958, 1964, 1978).

Contingency models attempt to specify what leader attributes are appropriate for various contingencies in the situation. For example, in

one of these (Vroom & Yetton, 1973), the amount of follower participation in making decisions is viewed as a function of such contingencies as the amount of information possessed by the leader, the importance of decision quality, the followers' motivation to solve the
problem, how much their acceptance is necessary to implementation
of the solution, and the probability that the decision made by the
leader alone will be acceptable.

This particular contingency model stresses leader–follower relations and parallels the emphasis of the transactional approach, which
does not treat the leader and followers as categorically apart. We now
consider several distinctive features of this approach.

LEADERSHIP AS A TRANSACTIONAL INFLUENCE PROCESS

In the *transactional approach*, the leader and followers are seen as
active participants. The emphasis is much more on dynamic elements,
including interpersonal perception and the fulfillment of expectancies.
For instance, the leader's legitimacy—which is crucial to authority—is
not seen as a fixed, but rather as a dynamic attribute. Thus, the leader's
standing, or credits with followers, is a vital component of the relationship. The more traditional view has been to emphasize *stasis*,
which often means accepting the leader and follower relationship as
set. Yet, a reality in the day-to-day functioning of leadership is for the
leader to maintain legitimacy in the face of potential challenges to
authority from below, from equal-status peers, and from above.

Relatedly, the followers' ties to the leader depend on how they
construe the leader's actions and motives. Given the powerful consequences which flow from their perceptions, it is surprising how often
these perceptions have been neglected. More than two decades ago,
the late Fillmore Sanford (1950, p. 4) captured the essential point when
he noted that there is some justification for regarding the follower as
the most crucial factor in any leadership event, and argued that
research directed at the follower would yield handsome payoffs. Sanford was trying to go beyond the then dominant situational approach
by arguing that the followers were also vital to the leadership process,
in addition to the leader or the situation, which defines task demands.

The present-day emphasis on leader–follower relations as a transaction gives credence to the notion that each follower holds the
potential for being reacted to by the others as an influence source. It
is also particularly important to appreciate that changes may occur in
the parties as a result of their interaction over time. In that respect, my
use of the term *transaction* for this process is meant to indicate a more

active role for followers than the usual term "interaction" suggests. Among other things, a transaction includes the potential for counter-influence.

Regarding the two-way feature of the leader–follower transaction, Hollander and Julian (1969) assert that

> the person in the role of leader who fulfills expectations and achieves group goals provides rewards for others which are reciprocated in the form of status, esteem, and heightened influence. Because leadership embodies a two-way influence relationship, recipients of influence assertions may respond by asserting influence in return, that is, by making demands on the leader. The very sustenance of the relationship depends upon some yielding to influence on both sides. (p. 390)

The traditional view of the leader as the influence source leaves out this essential feature of counterinfluence. As noted before, the willingness of group members to accept the influence of a leader depends upon a process of exchange in which the leader gives something and gets something in return.

In a simple transactional view, the leader directs communications to followers, to which they may react in various ways. The leader attempts to take account of the perceptual-motivational states of followers, and they, in turn, evaluate the leader's, with particular regard to responsiveness to their needs. Especially pertinent are the followers' perceptions of the leader's effectiveness, and how they construe and evaluate the leader's actions and motives.

The leader is usually the central figure in moving the group toward its goals. Where the leader has the resources but routinely fails to deliver, there is bound to be dissatisfaction. If, for example, the leader appears to be deviating from the accepted standards, such nonconformity may be tolerated initially. This is a feature of the idiosyncrasy credit concept, to be discussed shortly, which emphasizes sources of earned status and the leader's related latitude for innovation (Hollander, 1958). However, when a leader's nonconformity seems to produce *unsuccessful* outcomes, the leader is more vulnerable to blame (Alvarez, 1968). It is as if the group said, "We expect good results from your actions. If you choose an unusual course, we will go along with you and give you some latitude. But you are responsible if the outcome is that the group fails to achieve its goals."

As noted earlier, the leader can be seen to be a group resource— ideally one who provides for the attainment of the group's goals. From the position itself, the leader derives certain benefits in status and heightened influence which serve as rewards. However, in acting as a leader, an individual necessarily *transacts* with followers who can evaluate his or her performance.

This approach is in keeping with the social exchange views found in Thibaut and Kelley (1959), Homans (1958, 1961, 1974), Blau (1964), and the newer work by Jacobs (1971). In these terms, the leader's demands upon the followers are reciprocated in their demands made upon the leader. Therefore, the integrity of the relationship depends upon some yielding to influence on both sides. In resource allocation terms, when common ends are being sought, it is expected that each person will do his or her share. But the leader provides a very special resource, which is consumed most clearly in activities directed toward the achievement of goals. The leader is also uniquely a *definer of reality* for the others, by setting goals, but also by communicating relevant information about progress, impediments, and needed redirections.

The leadership function of goal setting is of considerable importance, although not many studies have given it the attention it deserves. In one of those which do, Burke (1966) found with discussion groups that the leader's failure to provide the group with goal orientations provoked antagonism, tension, and absenteeism. In one way, this effect may be interpreted as a reaction to uncertainty. It also shows a failure of the leader–follower transaction, and was found to be most acute when the group had clearly agreed who was to act as the leader. Though expectations such as these are probably widespread in groups, their fulfillment or lack of it has been relatively neglected in studies of leadership.

One consistent weakness across many group and organizational settings is the failure to share information which will define the situation. Too often, giving orders substitutes for giving information. Up to a point this may be effective somewhat in reducing uncertainty, which is usually found to be disturbing. Eventually, though, the vacuum created by a lack of information will be filled by other voices, often less familiar with the prevailing circumstances. In practical terms, therefore, the leader's failure to provide a realistic *definition of the situation* is an invitation for others to do so. Indeed, giving perspective to events is what a large part of political life is about, and its broader significance for organizational leadership has long since been noted by Selznick (1957). Whether dealing with leadership, conformity, or attitude-change phenomena, the process of influence involves a transaction in which there is communication. Information is transmitted from a source to a recipient in the form of a message, which may be verbal, nonverbal, or both.

The source may be called a leader, or a propagandist, but the label is not as relevant as the structural properties of the relationship shaping the response of the receiver, who is not just a passive reactor to the influence assertions of the source. Bauer (1964) has emphasized this point in his statement of the transactional features of the communications process. The receiver is active in accepting or rejecting communications, Bauer says. Therefore, the relationship is shaped on a psychological level by perceptual and motivational factors at work within the receiver, who also perceives them within the source. This is associated, for example, with the element of *credibility* in work on persuasion. The credible source is usually seen as having expertise, and being trustworthy (Hovland, Janis, & Kelley, 1953). How the source is perceived by the audience matters considerably in the effects produced in persuasion, and in leadership phenomena.

Communication plays a significant role in the leadership process through *goal setting, implementation, evaluation,* and *feedback.* These are steps in a communication link between the leader and followers that give them the reward of a unified view of the group's common purpose. There are other interpersonal qualities associated with leadership effectiveness and exercising influence. However, influence is not sufficient by itself, but depends as well on the followers' perceptions of a leader's competence, fairness, and identification with the group and its goals. The content of these is judged in the particular circumstances that exist in a given situation.

For instance, Katz and Lazarsfeld (1955) have indicated the importance of an individual's group affiliations in screening influence assertions in their "two-step flow" of communication model. In other words, a person's attention and reaction to attempted persuasion depends upon a group-based judgment about the source.

Although the leader's action and verbal assertions are clearly in the nature of "communication" to the group, other qualities of the leader which are perceived, including loyalty to the group, constitute part of the leader's perceived attributes. It may be appropriate, therefore, for members to ask whether the individual seeking to exert influence over them is motivated by aspirations similar to their own. This recalls Brown's (1936) point concerning the need for leaders to show "member character" in the sense of being accepted as members of the group. Indeed, the process of making attributions is a significant one in determining influence effects, as Heider (1958), among others, has contended. Two examples are the attribution of ability, and that of trustworthiness—approximating "can" and "will" in Heider's terms. If the leader can do something, but seems unwilling to do so, there may be a crisis.

A crucial factor in the exchange between leaders and followers is that the leader be seen to be competent in producing results. Therefore, the effectiveness of the leadership process is bound to become a basis for judging whether an exchange is fair. After all, the organization and group members reward the leader more liberally than anyone else, and good results are expected. Although often subjective, judgments about "getting results," "showing ability," and other such qualities carry weight in followers' perceptions of the leader. This factor is also the main initial source of idiosyncrasy credit, which allows the leader latitude for influence and innovation. Another source is conformity to the group's norms, which is the basis at first for assessing the leader's loyalty to the group.

Leader Legitimacy and Social Exchange

Among the more substantial features of the leader's role is perceived legitimacy—how it is attained and maintained. As Read (1974) has put it:

> leader legitimacy cannot be considered a general disposition but involves a complex interaction of attitudes toward the leader and his source of authority, with the leader's actual behavior contributing substantially to his task influence and continuing legitimacy. (p. 203)

A social exchange conception provides one vehicle for understanding how the leader's role is legitimated. Such a conception fundamentally stresses rewards from others, in the conventional reinforcement paradigm. In particular, the process is one of gaining a response from others indicating the differentiation of status linked to influence. The effect of reinforcement is to signal the granting of legitimacy, which in turn opens the way for leader activity. This process has been demonstrated in various research settings.

In an early experiment by Pepinsky, Hemphill, and Shevitz (1958), students who were found to be low on leader activity were led to behave far more actively in that role by having the group show agreement with their suggestions. Other students, who were found to be high on leader activity, were affected in the reverse way by having the group show disagreement with their suggestions. These results may be interpreted to show that an exchange process occurred in which the group raised the reward and lowered the cost of leader activity for the first set of students, and did the opposite for the second.

In a related vein, Rudraswamy (1964) conducted an experiment where some members of a group were made conscious of their own higher status. They were found to attempt significantly more leader acts than others in their group, and even outdistanced subjects who had been given more relevant information about the task itself. Further work has shown that even the use of signal lights as reinforcers can have a significant effect on the target person's proportion of talking time and perceived leader status (Bavelas, Hastorf, Gross, & Kite, 1965; Zdep & Oakes, 1967). These lights not only produced a heightening of leader acts, but may have also created the impression of greater legitimacy and influence as well.

In short, when a reward is provided for exerting influence legitimately, individuals are inclined to behave as leaders. There may, however, still be individual differences in the tendency to act, even when the right conditions prevail. A study by Gordon and Medland (1965) with soldiers found that positive peer ratings on leadership in army squads was consistently related to a measure of "aspiration to lead."

In discussion groups, too, there are members who show a greater willingness to make contributions. Talking, especially regarding quantity of output, appears to place a person in a leader role, largely independent of quality (Regula & Julian, 1973). A recent experiment by Sorrentino and Boutillier (1975) indicated that the most vocal group members were usually seen as leaders without much regard to the merit of their suggestions. These investigators conclude that the quantity of a person's ouput indicates motivation, and quality indicates ability. Evidently quantity is what pays off, at least in the initial impression made in a discussion group.

IDIOSYNCRASY CREDIT AND INNOVATION

As already noted, the possibility of acting as a leader, and being perceived as one, depends upon some validation from other group members. This is the key element in the "idiosyncrasy credit" model (Hollander, 1958, 1960, 1961a,b, 1964), which deals with the impressions individuals have of one another that allow for innovative action in groups. The leader is most often the one from whom initiatives for change are expected, and who has the potential for taking innovative action in coping with new or altered demands.

The idiosyncrasy credit model emphasizes earned status. It starts with the apparent paradox that leaders are said to conform more to the group's norms, and yet are also likely to be influential in bringing about innovations. Actually, these elements can fit together when seen as a matter of sequence. In the early contact between the leader, or would-be leader, and followers, credits are gained by signs of a *contribution to the group's primary task* and *loyalty to the group's norms.* As summary terms, these two factors are referred to as "competence" and "conformity."

The role of leader carries the *potential* to take innovative action in coping with new or altered demands. But how successful the leader is in effecting change depends upon the perceptions followers have of the leader's actions and related motivations. Accordingly, when a leader's nonconformity seems to produce *unsuccessful* outcomes, the leader is more vulnerable to blame (Alvarez, 1968).

With a fund of credits, an individual's assertions of influence become more acceptable. Furthermore, there is the expectation that, once accumulated, credits will be used to take actions which are in the direction of needed innovation. A failure to do so may result in loss of credits. The leader who "sits" on his or her credits may be seen as not fulfilling role obligations. Although credits exist in the shared perceptions which group members gain of others over time, credits have operational significance in allowing later deviations which would otherwise be viewed negatively if a person did not have a sufficient balance upon which to draw. As a case in point, a newcomer to the group is poorly positioned to assert influence or take innovative action. However, a particular individual may bring derivative credit from another group, based on his or her reputation. The credit concept may, therefore, apply to appointed leaders as well as to elected ones, even though followers are not the major source of legitimacy for appointed leaders.

The credit concept assumes that a process of evaluation goes on. This means, for instance, that maintaining a leader role depends on showing results that can be judged. The process may vary considerably from situation to situation, but ordinarily there are validators who have some basis for judging the adequacy of the leader's performance. However, even if the judgment is negative, it may not be possible to displace the leader. For example, a term of office may be involved, or a contractual arrangement. Also, the validators responsible for the leader's original placement in the position are likely to be unwilling to admit error.

This reluctance is even seen with an elected leader whose validators are the followers or constituents. They may have a sense of investment in the leader which makes them feel a greater responsibility for the leader's performance. When it is poor, there may be at least an initial rallying around to support the leader (Hollander, Fallon, & Edwards, 1977). Deposing an elected leader can offer considerable hurdles, especially in the midst of a fixed term. The matter of a leader's legitimacy in the role is at stake, and this requires some additional comment shortly.

Some of the earliest experimentation with the idiosyncrasy credit model is reported by Hollander (1960, 1961a,b, 1964). In brief, this work indicated that early nonconformity by an otherwise competent group member blocks the acceptance of his influence, whereas later nonconformity is taken as the basis for alterations in the group's norms; and nonconformity to group norms is more readily accepted from someone already granted high accorded status than from someone who is low.

There are a number of experiments whose results do not entirely confirm the model, but do suggest some needed refinements. Among these is the experiment by Wiggins, Dill, and Schwartz (1965), which indicates that high-status group members have less latitude to deviate from particular role obligations. However, these members may deviate with less cost from norms applying to members in general. One reasonable inference is that leaders and other high-status members are given more latitude to deviate from general norms *in exchange for* adhering to the more crucial requirements of their roles. The basis for the exchange may be to compensate the incumbent for the extra costs levied by specific role requirements.

Wahrman and Pugh (1972) have found that subjects in all-male groups disliked and resented procedural norm violations from a member who had *not* first contributed competent behaviors and conformity. But, in contrast to previous findings (Hollander, 1960), this pattern did not lead to an apparent loss of influence; early nonconformity was found to be associated with greater influence.

This result is not necessarily at odds with the model, since nonconformity from a competent group member can in fact serve to call attention to the performer. Indeed, the point has been made that

> actions which call attention to a person may lead him to a position of influence because of favorable outcomes. Then, since his activity now becomes more crucial to the group's attainment of goals, his visibility is even further increased. (Hollander, 1964, p. 227)

Here we see an obvious parallel to the influence evidently generated by the quantity of talking in discussion groups. However, both these effects are no doubt limited, and a point may be reached where a person is rejected.

In another experiment, Wahrman and Pugh (1974) found that if the deviating member is not of the same sex as the other group members, credits are not earned for competence as in the all-male groups studied earlier, and early nonconformity does not yield influence. These results with a female nonconformer among males suggest that a member may not as readily deviate if a demarcation has been made that sets the individual apart, which is in keeping with a basic concept in labeling theory (see Lemert, 1972).

An experiment referred to earlier (Alvarez, 1968) found that in successful organizations the higher-status person lost credits at a slower rate than did one of lower status, for the same infractions of work rules. In unsuccessful organizations, the opposite was true; there the higher-status person lost credits faster as a consequence of greater blame for the unfavorable outcome. Jacobs (1971) has suggested that the apparently inappropriate behavior of the leader is likely to be disregarded when the group is successful, but that failure creates the sense of an unfair exchange and the group's withdrawal of support for the leader (p. 109).

A related concept of interest is Jones's (1964, 1965) ingratiation model. He, too, is interested in the effect of conformity or nonconformity in ongoing interaction. In his model, ingratiation is a tactic that may be applied especially where a person of lower status seeks to gain rewards from one of higher status in a relationship. In that case, the person may use flattery, call attention to one's favorable features, and show signs of compliance, to increase his or her value to the other.

Basic to both the idiosyncrasy credit and ingratiation models is the idea that conformity may be used as a reward in interaction. In his treatment of conformity as a feature of social exchange, Nord (1969a) has indicated that "conformity appears to be supplied for rewards in much the same way as other responses . . . a large number of studies have demonstrated that people conform to avoid a loss of status or approval" (pp. 192–193).

It is important to recognize, however, that both of these models are *non*normative, and describe a process rather than indicating what should be the case. Indeed, conceptions of conformity and nonconformity indicate a place for independence as a basis for achieving a favorable response from others in ongoing interaction (Hollander & Willis, 1964, 1967; Willis, 1963, 1965; Willis & Hollander, 1964a,b). Hollander and Marcia (1970), for instance, found with preadolescents that children chosen as leaders by their peers were among those most independent from both peer and adult pressures. There is still more to be said in behalf of independence as a source of influence, as I have indicated elsewhere (Hollander, 1975).

LEADER LEGITIMACY AND SYSTEM PROGRESS

Legitimacy is the base on which leaders can operate to exert influence in the direction of helping the group deal with the need for change. As suggested earlier, legitimacy may come through various sources, by appointment, election, or through the support of followers in a less formal way. The essential point about legitimacy is that it produces the belief that the leader has the authority to exert influence (Hollander, 1978, Chapter 3).

Credits contribute to legitimacy in the sense of followers validating the leader's status. In appointive leadership, the leader is validated less by followers than by superordinate authority, although followers' perceptions matter nevertheless. The elements in the validation process already noted include the impressions of the leader's competence and conformity. However, legitimacy can also be seen to depend on a cluster of impressions which followers gain of the leader, including his or her source of authority, what the leader is perceived to be doing in line with desired group ends, and, most significantly, the judged success or failure of those actions.

In a research program extending over a number of years, these processes have been studied through experiments on decision-making discussion groups with leaders who were either elected or appointed (Hollander & Julian, 1970, 1978). The leader's sense of legitimacy in taking innovative actions, especially in adopting an independent stand from the group's, has been one focus of attention. In one of these experiments, elected leaders were initially found to be more assertive than appointed leaders, and more willing to expend their "credits" by deviating from group judgments. The other side of this process is the group's reaction to these assertions by the leader. In that respect, elected leaders serving as group spokesmen have been found to be more vulnerable to rejection by the group for failure (Julian, Hollander, & Regula, 1969).

This set of findings suggests an intriguing balance: the feeling of investment in the elected leader was related to the leader's evident sense of having credit to deviate from the group's position; but that same factor could lead to the leader's being deposed. A clear inference therefore is that election or appointment create differing bases of perceived legitimacy, and thereby affect the reality within which the leader and followers operate (see Hollander, 1974; Read, 1974).

Returning to an earlier point, the leader can be construed to be a resource who provides an input to the group's activity. The leader also organizes the effort to apply other human and physical resources as inputs to achieve desired ends, or outputs. However, this process has variable psychological implications, depending upon whether the leader is appointed or elected, because of the differing character of the followers' investment.

Although much depends on the circumstances of appointment, election offers a contrast by evidently inducing a greater vested interest in the leader. It also seems to create higher expectations among followers. The leader who is "put in charge" by appointment from above is much less the responsibility of followers. In social exchange terms, their cost or investment is lower. Therefore, while the appointed leader may "underperform" with greater impunity, he or she also operates with less sense of group support.

There are some other noteworthy correlates of electing leaders which bear directly on the matter of influence. In a recent experiment by Hollander, Fallon, and Edwards (1977), it was found that under comparable conditions elected leaders were initially less influential than appointed leaders. But after the groups experienced apparent failure in their decision-making task, the result was reversed. For at least a time, elected leaders became more influential. This was construed to be due in part to a "rallying around" effect. That is, the leader was the beneficiary of the group's feeling of commitment, up to a point. When the groups were studied for still another phase, however, it was found that continued failure led to a willingness to depose the elected leader.

Especially interesting in this regard is the finding that before the groups knew how they were performing, there was one group member who was more influential than the elected leader. Subsequently, that member usually emerged as the group's choice for leader when a new election was held. The replacement therefore was "standing in the wings" awaiting a cue, after the crisis had run its course.

Leadership Effectiveness and a Fair Exchange

An entire system of relationships is involved in effective leadership. The typical conception of one person directing others is grossly misleading in describing leadership, because it neglects the interpersonal and task systems at work. A group or organization operates with a set of resources as "inputs" aimed at producing desired "outputs" (Katz & Kahn, 1966). Gaining such outputs is obviously facilitated by the directive functions centered in the leader, but the resources are not the leader's alone.

Effectiveness cannot be gauged only by the leader's ability to be influential, without asking further to what ends this process is turned. Furthermore, the leader's actual contribution to effectiveness may vary considerably, as a function of other conditions. The evidence indicates that the leader's perceived competence in facilitating the group's productive activities is one crucial element in affecting the followers' responsiveness, and leadership effectiveness. Another element is the leader's perceived motivation to be loyal to the group, its members and goals. But there is a need for further amplification of these elements and their impact.

For instance, one likely source for the divergent findings concerning qualities of the leader is the existence of differential expectations concerning the functions the leader is to perform. Clearly, there are various leadership roles, or components of them, and while the leader is one who often "initiates structure," as Hemphill (1961) put it, the leader also may be a "decision maker" or "advocate." And that by no means exhausts the list, or the various combinations of activity possible within it.

An example of the effects of distinguishing elements of a leader's role is shown by an experiment conducted with four-man groups by Anderson and Fiedler (1964). The leaders in half the groups were told to serve as a "chairman," in a participatory way, and in the others to serve as an "officer in charge," in a supervisory way. The results indicated that the participatory leaders were significantly more influential, and made more of a contribution to the group's performance. Furthermore, leader attributes, such as intelligence, related significantly to group performance for some tasks under the participatory condition, but not for any under the supervisory condition. The conclusion is inescapable that the characteristics of a leader, including intelligence, are made more salient and are more highly related to group achievement where the leader participates more, rather than standing in a formal position to the group.

One illustration of the system demands and constraints on the leader is found in Fiedler's "contingency model" (1965, 1967, 1974). He predicts differing levels of effectiveness for *different combinations* of leader and situational characteristics. There are three of the latter, i.e., the quality of leader–member liking, the degree of task structure, and the power of the leader. Depending upon the leader's orientation to co-workers, Fiedler finds distinct variations in leader effectiveness.

The leader's orientation is tapped by the LPC measure, for "Least Preferred Co-worker." It is said to measure a relationship versus a task-orientation. Leaders who are high on one or the other end do better in various circumstances. Basically, Fiedler (1974) indicates that the High LPC (relationship-oriented) leaders perform best in a relatively *uncertain* situation, that is, one where these situational factors are mixed or intermediate. By contrast, the Low LPC (task-oriented) leaders do best in the more *certain* extremes of either favorability or unfavorability.

Effectiveness in this case is largely seen as a matter of productivity, without reference to followers' perceptions. However, another way to look at effectiveness is with respect to individual member satisfaction with the return on the investment he or she feels has been made. The leader's behavior has a great deal to do with this sense of gratification and equity. How this is accomplished depends upon that much abused term "style."

Style is a set of qualities which affects others in a particular way in a particular situation. In the case of trustworthiness, for example, much is still not known about how it is transmitted and sustained, although it clearly is important in maintaining an equitable relationship.

The nature of the leader's role is such that he or she is likely to have many and varied relationships with others in the group (Graen, 1975). Furthermore, the quality of these relationships matters to the other individuals involved, particularly with regard to equity and justice concerns. Within the group the leader determines the distribution of rewards, and the leader's actions give signs of the "goodness" or "badness" of the performance of group members.

An important consideration therefore is the *perceived fairness* of the leader's actions. By rewarding the members whose activities contribute to the group's goals, and not rewarding those whose activities do not, the leader provides a basis for effecting desired ends, among which are productive relationships among group members.

A vital element in this process is the leader's *dependability*. In social interaction generally, regularity and predictability of behavior is rewarding. These qualities are even more significant for followers in their relationships with the leader. Where a leader's position is known, and can be counted on, uncertainty is reduced, and followers have a more stable situation within which to function. On the other hand, where the leader behaves impulsively or by the whim of the moment, instability and uncertainty are created.

The skills contributing to leadership effectiveness also include the ability to show *foresight* and *planning* in dealing with new conditions. Imagination and a sense of what might be are essential to this process. Training individuals in skills for leadership effectiveness is quite possible, even though some individuals can be identified who have greater potential to be effective as a result of capacity and experience. Maintaining the role of leader is another important aspect of effectiveness. It depends upon fulfilling expectations for performance, and being adaptable to changing requirements.

A significant function of leadership is to facilitate efforts for planned change. Some changes occur whether or not people initiate them, because of life circumstances. But change may be planned or resisted, or shaped, by the efforts of concerned individuals. Where a need is recognized, they take the initiative in seeking imaginative ways to meet new circumstances, and new leaders may arise.

The essential point of the social exchange emphasis is that leadership effectiveness cannot disregard how the follower fares in the group's activities. A fair exchange involves a climate in which the leader tries to provide equitable rewards. Basic to the exchange process is the belief that rewards, such as recognition, will be received for benefits given. However, it is difficult to accomplish this routinely. Even if it were done, the rewards would take on less value due to their frequency, since the scarce reward is usually valued more than the abundant one (Homans, 1961). But there is probably an optimal range for rewards, so that some attention to their contributions, even if not frequent, is necessary if people are to feel fairly treated. Furthermore, some followers may have a closer relationship with the leader than others. This can produce greater benefits for them, in part because of the resources the leader commands. However, there also can be higher costs because of the direct association with the leader (Graen, 1975). The actual "profit" of those close to the leader therefore may be no greater than for the other followers who receive less but who also have lower costs.

Summing up these points, the transaction between a leader and followers includes the two factors of *system progress* and *equity*. The first deals with attaining group goals, and the second with the followers' sense of being treated fairly along the way. Simply put, where they have a choice, followers require a sufficient feeling of being fairly rewarded to remain inside the group and participate. This sense of equity often depends upon a comparison with what others, of comparable characteristics and responsibility, are receiving relative to their inputs. However, the leader especially needs to be alert to perceived inequities, and will likely be blamed for them as a determiner of rewards. These perceptions are subjective judgments, since rewards and costs are always relative to the people involved and their particular needs.

The transactional approach also considers that followers need some latitude to exert counterinfluence, rather than being locked into a situation of great control by the leader. Leader–follower relationships may be made difficult by the leader's assertions of power, which exert a cost to the leader as well as to the followers. From a pragmatic standpoint, therefore, a desirable feature of the social-exchange perspective is to help check egoism and the abuse of power. In fact, it has been found that power can be diffused and shared in an organization, rather than being held tightly in one place (Tannenbaum, 1968). All of which is by way of encouraging the prospect for followers to have greater involvement in group, organizational, and societal functioning.

The Study of Organizations through a Resource–Exchange Paradigm

WALTER R. NORD

INTRODUCTION

Although not without its critics (e.g., Gouldner, 1970; Weick, 1974; Zaleznik, 1967), the open-systems model has been a major integrative perspective used by many contemporary students of organizations. The systems view is meaningful for many purposes, and indeed will be incorporated into what follows; however, the approach is often an empty one. Although providing an overview of entities which operate as systems, it often fails to provide a set of concepts which focus attention on specific processes which characterize any one set of systems.

One of the general processes is the flow of inputs between the open system and its environment. In organizations these input–output transactions take place at at least two levels. These correspond roughly to the division of the field between micro- and macroanalysis. The microtheorist tends to focus on the transactions between the individual and either other individuals or the organization. On the other hand, the macrotheorist focuses on transactions between the organization and its environment. In addition, the macrotheorist is concerned with the flow of resources between the organization and its constituent departments or formal groups.

In this paper I will explore the potential of a resource–exchange (R–E) paradigm to serve as a framework for facilitating a macro-micro integration. The R–E paradigm is a hybrid of two closely related

WALTER R. NORD • School of Business, Washington University, St. Louis, Missouri 63130.

approaches. The first is social exchange "theory."[1] Recent works using the exchange metaphor include Thibaut and Kelley's (1959) game-theoretic model, Homans's (1961, 1974) and Emerson's approaches which drew heavily upon operant psychology, Blau's (1964) "prolego-menon of a theory of social structure" (p. 2), and Coleman's (1966) description of emergent sociological processes. In addition, Ekeh (1974) discussed some elements of "collectivistic theory social exchange," found in the work of writers such as Lévi-Strauss. The above models differ in important ways—most notably in the varied stress given to cognitive processes, and the levels of social behavior which they take as problematic. Nevertheless, they all center on how various resources are affecting individual behavior, and, to greater or lesser degrees, the emergent processes of social systems.

The second strand of the R–E model has been developed in the work of Yuchtman and Seashore (1967), White (1974a,b), and a number of other writers, which has focused primarily on macroorganizational processes. This body of work is presently integrated mainly by the common use of resource flows as a major factor determining the structure and functioning of organizations.

Although these two strands are not directly equivalent to each other, I am suggesting that they have enough in common to be linked together. First, both approaches draw heavily on some common work—especially that of Emerson (1962), Blau (1964), and Coleman (1964a, 1966). Second, both approaches begin with resources as the primary stimulus for social interaction. Moreover, both conceptualize resources as economic, in that one can be obtained only by giving up another (Homan, Hart, & Sametz, 1958). Thus, a resource must be scarce (i.e., a greater quantity of it is needed to satisfy all wants for it than is now available), and it must be wanted by people in the relevant market (i.e., more of it is preferable to less of it). Third, both approaches are concerned with the conditions which affect the flows of resources. Finally, both approaches recognize and take as problematic the influence of resource flows on the elements of the system and the structure of the relationships among these elements. This recognition reflects an awareness that elements and their relationships are a function of resource exchange as well as factors which affect the flows.

However, despite these general similarities, there are also important differences. Although there is considerable overlap, the exchange

---

[1] I have put "theory" between quotation marks to reflect the fact that I agree with Emerson's (1972) observation that it is premature to label the exchange approach as a theory in the formal sense of the word.

theorists tend to study individuals and very small groups. Consequently, the resources they are concerned with are of the type discussed by Foa and Foa (Chapter 4, this volume): money, goods, information, love, status, and services. The resource theorists, since they are more interested in relationships among larger units, are more concerned with the resources listed by White (1974b): skills, knowledge, money, materials, equipment, customers, patients, and clients.

Similarly, the types of interrelationships among the social units overlap, but differ. Implicit in the exchange theorist's approach is the assumption that exchanges which occur within organizations are merely special cases of more general laws of human interaction. By contrast, the resource theorists consider the exchanges they study as unique properties of organized activity. This contrast, which is a correlate of the tendency to focus on units of different size, appears to represent a de facto divergence more than a theoretical incompatibility.

As a hybrid of these two approaches, the R–E paradigm assumes what is common to both approaches—a fundamental aspect of social interaction is the exchange of resources. Based on this assumption, the R–E view draws heavily upon the exchange theorist to discuss microlevel and interindividual processes, and more heavily on the resource theorist for discussing macrolevel and collective relationships. At intermediate levels, it is often helpful to use both approaches in more equal proportions. Thus, though the two approaches are not, as yet, fully interwoven within the paradigm, their common assumptions and complementary nature support their combination into a unified perspective.

Since I am assuming that the reader is familiar with the microlevel implications of exchange theory from other papers in this book, I will not deal with such topics as leadership, groups, and equity at great length. Subsequently I will discuss some of these topics briefly, but the major portion of the paper will be concerned with exploring organizational processes.

Although the conditions of the more strictly economic exchanges are taken as given, for the most part, I consider them to be quite important. In fact, I agree completely with Zald's (1970b) concern about the tendency of sociologists to ignore price theory, the theory of the firm, costs, and the analysis of supply and demand in their treatment or organizations. Such omissions are unfortunate, because it is these areas, as Zald observed, "that the impetus to organizational change, the resources for growing salaries and other 'minor' features of organizational life are found" (p. 235).

RESOURCE EXCHANGES IN ORGANIZATIONAL ANALYSIS

In this section I will consider the role of resource exchanges at the more macrolevels of organizational analysis. After a brief discussion of several of the more important foundation studies, I will review some of the recent developments which show the importance of resource exchanges in determining the quality of the relationships between organizations and various elements which comprise their environments.

Historical Development

For the most part, students of organization have limited their attention to events and processes which exist within the boundaries of a particular focal organization. Basically, this work has left organizational-environmental relationships to economists, political scientists, and anthropologists. However, a number of writers, including Thompson (1967), Lawrence and Lorsch (1969), Emery and Trist (1965), Evan (1966), and numerous others, have attempted to incorporate the study of environmental factors more fully into organizational theory. Some of the impetus undoubtedly is owing to the impact of general systems theory (Buckley, 1968; Katz & Kahn, 1966; Terreberry, 1968). The R–E paradigm is well suited for examining some of the processes through which the open systems we call organizations relate to their environments. The foundation for this view was developed a number of years ago by Barnard (1938) and March and Simon (1958).

Barnard (1938) observed that the availability of incentives to members of an organization depends on its effectiveness in coping with its environment. However, though he recognized the importance of organization–environment interaction as a constraint, much of Barnard's attention was directed to a discussion of individual incentives, rather than toward the more macrolevel analysis which concerns us here.

Following Barnard, March and Simon's (1958) organizational theory emphasized the role of incentives or inducements. Although they observed that little attention had been given to the role of incentives for groups other than employees (e.g., investors and consumers), they too tended to omit detailed study of such incentives; for the most part they confined their attention to the inducements–contributions postulate as a way to analyze the decisions of individual employees about participation in the organization. Earlier, however, Simon (1957) had linked internal incentives very explicitly to the effectiveness of the organization in dealing with its environment. He wrote:

> The contributions of one group are the source of inducements that the organization offers others. If the sum of the contributions is sufficient, in quantity and kind, to supply the necessary quantity and kinds of inducements, the organization survives and grows; otherwise it shrinks and ultimately disappears unless an equilibrium is reached. (p. 111)

Still, the work of Barnard, and March and Simon did not fully explore the organization's relationship with its environment. However, their analysis of incentives did provide a foundation from which others explored the issue in more depth.

One of the earliest papers to focus on this linkage was written by Clark and Wilson (1961). They emphasized the role of the incentive system as the principal variable affecting organizational behavior, and the deliberate alteration of the incentive system by the organization's executive to respond to change. They observed that the analysis of incentive systems

> makes it possible to relate environmental trends, personality factors, patterns of expectation, and organizational history to the behavior of organizations and perhaps to bridge the gap between the study of individual behavior and the study of organizational behavior. (p. 131)

In addition, Clark and Wilson developed the concept of resources further, and discussed how the organization's autonomy vis-à-vis its competitors can influence its ability to obtain the resources it needs from the environment, and hence affect its ability to maintain its incentives at an appropriate level.

In the same year, Levine and White (1961) published their famous paper on interorganizational exchange. Their work has special significance for us in several respects. First, they showed that the exchange model could be used to describe resource flows between health organizations other than just traditional economic transactions involving money and material goods. Second, they showed the applicability of a slightly revised version of Homans's exchange theory for viewing organizational relationships. Third, they described "domain consensus" as a truly social aspect of the interorganizational exchange process. Domain consensus refers to the degree of agreement among relevant parts of the system about the specific goals and functions a particular organization is to pursue. According to Levine and White, the achievement of domain consensus is a necessary condition for interorganizational exchange. In their words, "the flow of elements in the health system is contingent upon solving the problem of 'who gets what for what purpose'" (p. 599).

Yuchtman and Seashore (1967) developed a comprehensive view of organizational effectiveness by integrating these exchange views with the general systems perspective in what they termed "a system resource approach to organizational effectiveness." They began with the general systems model as a vehicle for conceptualizing the interaction processes between organizations as *entities* (i.e., "not as phenomena incidental to individual or nonentital functioning" [p. 897]) and their environments. The basic process which mediates this relationship is one of exchange. In their words:

> The interdependence between the organization and its environment takes the form of input–output transactions of various kinds relating to various things; furthermore, much of the stuff that is the object of these transactions falls into the category of *scarce and valued resources*. (p. 897)

Based on this premise, they suggested that the effectiveness of an organization can be defined in terms of its bargaining position, which is reflected in the ability of the organization to acquire scarce and valued resources. This definition of organizational effectiveness focuses attention on the "continuous and never ending processes of exchange and competition over scarce and valued resources" (pp. 898–899).

This framework led Yuchtman and Seashore to make two important distinctions. First, they observed that the transactions that organizations carry on with their environments vary in the extent to which they are competitive or are characterized by complementarity or exchange. Second, they distinguished among different characteristics of resources. They suggested that these distinctions could facilitate the analysis of organizational effectiveness by encouraging (a) the development of an inclusive taxonomy of resources, (b) the identification of different types of resources that are mutually relevant for particular organizations, and (c) the determination of relative positions of organizations through analysis of the amounts and kinds of resources available and the organization's efficiency in using these resources to get further resources. In short, Yuchtman and Seashore showed how an R–E model could be used to translate the broad perspective of general systems theory into the study of specific aspects of organizational-environmental relationships.

R–E Processes in Organization–Environment Relationships

Thompson (1967) noted that there are a number of strategies which organizations use to carry on effective transactions with their environments. Frequently these strategies and tactics have been more the subject matter of economics and political science than of organizational sociologists and organizational behaviorists.

The R–E model would seem to have considerable face validity as an approach linking the work of the sociologist and the organizational behaviorist to the work of these other disciplines for at least two reasons. First, an exchange process is at the root of economic analysis of the relationship between the firm and its environment. R–E theorists and economists share the same metaphor and the same fundamental concern with the flow of resources. Second, the R–E approach leads directly to the study of power and dependence, which are fundamental concerns of many political scientists, as well as some economists.

However, the R–E perspective would provide more than just a model of organizations which would be linked to these disciplines. It can provide a framework from which to derive, and through which to organize, insights into organization–environment interaction which are not well handled by any one discipline. Moreover, it can serve as a tool for understanding the nature of organizations' attempts to cope with their environments. In the following section I will review several studies which I believe demonstrate some of this potential, even though the studies themselves were often not based, at least explicitly, on an exchange approach.

Some R–E "Extra-Economic" Aspects of Interorganizational Relations

Two papers give clear support to the proposition that the R–E perspective may describe important processes which are omitted by economic theorists. First, in the previously cited paper by Levine and White (1961) the discussion of the concept of domain consensus and the nature of the transactions among health organizations clearly represents an important addition to conventional economic analysis. Economists usually deal with transactions in which domain consensus exists as a function of the values of society which legitimate competitive business activity. However, Levine and White's position suggests that this class of exchanges may just be a special case of interorganizational relationships. A complete understanding of organizational interrelations requires more comprehensive sociological analysis.

Macaulay (1963) provided additional evidence about the significance of social exchange processes in the transactions among organizations. Importantly, he was concerned only with business firms. Thus, his findings of the major role played by nonmaterial and nonlegalistic factors provide strong support for the additive nature of a social exchange view to the conventional economic perspective.

Macaulay found that many transactions were not neatly rationalized by those who engaged in them. Businessmen often preferred to rely on such things as a person's word in a brief letter, a handshake, or "common honesty and decency" even when risks were substantial. In addition, many business exchanges reflected a minimal amount of preplanning about the problems of defective performance. Instead, heavy reliance was placed upon good-faith settlements of disputes which might arise during the life of the exchange relationship. In fact, some businessmen felt that too much preplanning was undesirable, because it indicated a lack of trust. Moreover, any disputes which did occur were frequently settled without reference to the specific contract or to legal sanctions. The enforcement of these agreements was a product of a series of social processes including informal relationships among organizational participants at various levels, the concern for reputation, reciprocity, the adherence to certain norms, and the desire to continue relationships.

The R–E approach may complement economic models in yet another way by helping us to deal with such acts as corporate giving to charitable causes, which, at first glance, appear to violate basic economic assumptions. Certainly the exchange model would enable us to incorporate the personal benefits that corporate members get by using organizational resources to further certain causes. Jacobs (1974) has suggested that such behavior can be understood through the concept of indirect exchanges, which involve groups of organizations helping another organization because all members of the group want certain goals achieved. Of course, there are some writers such as McCall (1973) who argue that corporate giving is usually quite consistent with the profit interests of the firm. Thus, while conventional economic theory may require no help in explaining corporate charity, nevertheless it is possible that in much the same way that the study of individual "helping" behavior or "altruism" has been stimulated by comparison with assumptions about the profit-maximizing nature of individuals, the study of organizational altruism might lead to greater insights about certain decision processes which have yet to be incorporated fully into either economics or organization theory. The R–E paradigm may provide both a stimulus and framework for such inquiry.

Organizational Coping

An organization's ability to obtain needed resources from its environment influences the structure and behavior of the organization. Although a number of these effects can be treated most conveniently later in our discussion of intraorganizational processes, several aspects will be discussed here, because they deal more or less directly with how the organization relates to its environment.

Pfeffer's (1973) work showed that the composition of hospital boards of directors was related to organizational effectiveness. Building directly on Yuchtman and Seashore's (1967) analysis, Pfeffer studied 57 hospitals. His criteria of organizational effectiveness included the percentage increase of the hospital's budget, the percentage increase in the number of beds in the hospital, and measures of increases in the equipment and services during the last five years. These measures were used as indices of the organization's ability to obtain resources from its environment. In general, those organizations which were effective tended to have boards of directors whose members were particularly well-suited to obtain the resources in the given context. For example, the data provided clear support for the position that hospitals whose boards were selected for fund raising rather than for administration, and hospitals whose boards fit the environments where the organization derived its most important resources, were the more effective ones in obtaining needed resources.

A study by Staw and Szwajkowski (1975) demonstrated the relationship between the resource position of organizations and their tendency to violate the law. Based on data from very large organizations (i.e., firms from the *Fortune* 500), they found clear support for their hypothesis of a relationship between munificence and illegal acts. Looking at the 105 firms which had been cited in 1968–1972 for illegal trade practices, Staw and Szwajkowski found that for the five years prior to being cited for illegal acts, the financial performance of these firms was significantly lower than that of the other firms in the *Fortune* 500. Moreover, the performance of other firms of the same industry as the cited firms was also below that of firms from other industries. Since, within industries, the performance of the cited firms did not differ from that of the firms which were not cited, the authors concluded that environmental security affecting the industry was more important in contributing to the violations than were intraorganizational factors. Apparently, such actions as price fixing, mergers, and reciprocity between firms are a response to their need to extract additional resources from their environments.

Interorganizational Networks

Exchange analysis seems to be well suited to dealing with one other facet of organizations' relationships with their environments—namely, the formation and functioning of macroorganizations and organization networks. Although little study has been reported on such relationships, Metcalfe (1974) has suggested that macroorganizations are a new type of phenomenon. According to Metcalfe, these macroorganizations represent adaptive behavior at a system level as opposed to the organizational level. He argued that political science provides the most promising source of ideas for analyzing these structures, which are not coordinated through the price system but rather are integrated through the *"political* processes of exchange and bargaining among the component organizations" (p. 651). Although I am not suggesting that a resource–exchange perspective will be fully adequate for understanding the intricacies of these processes, it does seem capable of providing a useful place to start. For example, consider Benson's (1975) discussion of organizational networks.

Benson used a political-economic perspective to describe interorganizational relations. He suggested that the emergent networks of relations among organizations must be taken as objects of analysis themselves, rather than taken merely as environmental elements which affect a particular focal organization. Basing his analysis on empirical study of relationships among human service agencies, and drawing on Yuchtman and Seashore's (1967) system–resource view, Benson argued that interorganizational networks can be understood by analyzing the operation of two basic resources—money and power. He explicated a number of dimensions which describe variations in the distribution of money and power resources among organizations and between organization networks and their environments.

Benson's analysis is significant for this paper in several ways. First, it shows the potential value of the resource-based approach for the study of organizational networks, not merely interorganizational relationships. Second, it highlights the interaction of money and power resources. In particular, he noted that a certain minimum degree of power by each party was a necessary condition for cooperative exchanges. Moreover, he suggested that the use of disruptive strategies (i.e., behavior which threatens the resource-generating capacity of a target agency) was a function of the degree of power imbalance between the parties and the nature of the resource channels. Third, he suggested that changes in the supply of resources in the environment of an interorganizational network operates to change the network itself. For example, alterations in the flow of resources can force out marginal members or cause members to readjust their priorities.

Overall, resources appear to be a major determinant of the character of the interaction of organizations with elements in their environment. Recent theoretical and empirical efforts have given strong support to this proposition, and have provided insights into the nature of these transactions which are often excluded by conventional economic analysis. These results support the R–E paradigm as a viable candidate for integrating existing knowledge within the field of organizational behavior. They also suggest the value of the R–E paradigm as a tool to link the treatment of organizations by economists, sociologists, and social psychologists. Moreover, the R–E paradigm seems well-suited to stimulate research in directions facilitating rapprochement with political science. In particular, it can stimulate analysis of extra-normative resource flows such as side payments, bribes, political payoffs, and other deviant acts which, judging by news accounts of the last few years, play a far more important role than is reflected in modern organizational theory.[2] Moreover, the R–E paradigm centers study on the processes of power, which, as most behavioral scientists agree, have been given too little attention.

Power and Dependence

The R–E perspective has been important in the emergence of organizational power and dependence as major topics for study by investigators of organization–environment interaction. Mindlin and Aldrich (1975) observed that as we have come to view organizations as open systems, we have given greater attention to the role of constraints and contingencies which lie outside the bounds of the organization. One result has been the emergence of "a resource-dependence model of organization–environment interaction" (p. 382), which views as a crucial factor the dependence of an organization upon other organizations that control resources and markets.

The foundation for this perspective has been built mainly from ideas provided by Emerson (1962) and Blau (1964). Emerson developed an approach to social power based on the premise that the power of Person over Other is based on Other's dependency on Person for things that Other values. This framework permitted him to describe a number of processes which could change power relationships. Many of these processes resemble factors which affect the supply and demand functions in economics, including reduction of costs to one party in

---

[2] To date most of what we know about the role of nonnormative exchanges within organizations comes from journalistic accounts, from critics of organizations, and from our own everyday experiences. Although Cyert and March (1963) and Thompson (1967) did discuss some of these issues briefly, scholarly investigation of such exchanges has been sparse.

meeting the demands of another, a change in the motivational investment the parties attach to certain outcomes, and changes in the availability of alternative sources of outcomes. Blau (1964) reformulated Emerson's approach to focus more directly on how power imbalances are derived from exchange processes, but basically his discussion of mechanisms which affected power-dependence relationships differed little from Emerson's, except in his introduction of coercion as a form of influence.

More recently, Jacobs (1974) has combined a reformulation of Emerson's discussion, Blau's exchange theory, and the concept of an ecological niche, into an analysis of the nature of the dependency of organizations on components of their environment. Jacobs specified five points at which organizations are dependent upon elements in their environment: (1) input acquisition, (2) output disposal, (3) capital acquisition, (4) acquisition of production factors, and (5) acquisition of a labor force. He suggested that the degree of an organization's dependency is a function of the essentiality of the given resource, the degree to which substitutes for the resource can be found, and the existence of alternative suppliers. Likewise, the dependency of a particular organization's buyers on that organization vary as a function of similar factors. From this analysis Jacobs developed several hypotheses. First, organizations are controlled by those parties who comprise or control the organization's most problematic contingencies. He argued that "organizational behavior can be represented in part as a rank-weighted average of the organization's five areas of dependence on its environment" (p. 55). Second, the more fractionated and dispersed are a group of buyers, the less control they will be able to exercise over the organization from which they purchase. Third, attempts at coercive control are influenced by the disparities in values between the organization and those environmental actors upon which the organization is *most* and *least* dependent. The greater these disparities, the more likely to use coercive tactics are those actors upon which the organization is least dependent.

In sum, the resource–exchange paradigm has played an important part in the development of the analysis of organization–environment interaction. However, it should be clear that so far I have discussed mainly some applications of the approach to the study of the behavior of organizations as a whole. Obviously, if the paradigm is to act as a truly integrative one, it must be useful in analyzing intraorganizational resource transactions, and be capable of describing how these intraorganizational processes are related to the more macrolevel resource flows.

IMPLICATIONS OF THE R–E PARADIGM FOR INTRAORGANIZATIONAL PROCESSES

The influence of the flow of resources between organizations and their environments upon the internal functioning of organizations has received growing empirical and theoretical attention. Many of these investigations have explicitly employed a resource-flow or an exchange framework. Papers by Georgiou (1973) and White (1974b) are particularly important in establishing the linkage between studies of organization–environment resource flows and intraorganizational resource exchanges which influence the distribution of power and other aspects of interindividual, interdepartmental, and individual–organizational relationships. A brief review of the work of Georgiou and White will provide a convenient starting point.

Georgiou and White agreed on some fundamental points. Both writers maintained that analysis of the exchange processes which occurs within organizations provides a better starting point for organizational analysis than does the concept of organizational goals. Both argued that organizations themselves are mechanisms through which individuals satisfy their own needs. Moreover, they shared the view that (1) goals, rules, and other forms of collective agreement among members arise out of and are modified by the continuous exchange process through which individual members pursue their own goals, and that (2) owing to a limited supply of resources, conflict and tension arise over their allocation.

Given these underlying similarities, the divergences of White and Georgiou are instructive. Georgiou built upon Barnard (1938) and Clark and Wilson (1961). He took the individual as the major unit for analysis, and sought to explain the emergence of organizations' structures and processes. He treated the organization as "a marketplace in which incentives are exchanged" (p. 306). Moreover, he argued that a focus on the organization as a unit for analysis is arbitrary and limiting, because the "basic strategic factor in organization is the individual" (p. 305). Consequently, the concept of organizational goals is misleading, because what appear to be goals of the collectivity are really the product of individual actors pursuing diverse goals and exchanging a variety of incentives. In short, Georgiou used the exchange model to build up from the individual: "understanding behavior in the complex of relationships called 'organization' can only be based on ascertaining the rewards which various individuals pursue through the organization" (pp. 305–306).

In contrast to Georgiou, White (1974b) drew heavily on the work of Coleman (1964a, 1966). Coleman (1966) was explicitly concerned with collective action, which, in his view, could not be accounted for through the "individualistically" oriented exchange models of Thibaut and Kelley, Homans, and Blau. White extended Coleman's collective decision model by viewing the organization as "a mechanism or tool which individuals utilize under constraints to realize their individual goals" (p. 377). Thus, though he assumed that individual goals are important factors, White modified or even abandoned the metaphor of organizations as marketplaces, in favor of a model which emphasized that the nature of the available resources and competition among organizational participants to use the same resources to achieve their particular goals act as constraints upon the use of the resources by each individual member.

The actual allocation of resources depends on decisions made by individuals seeking to advance their own goals. However, the competition inherent in this process does not prohibit collective action, since over time there are a number of allocation decisions about a number of resources. Individuals are differentially interested in these various decisions, and hence are able to modify each others' control over resources. Consequently, the distribution of resources is effected through a process in which individuals make agreements and trade-offs to obtain influence on the decisions of most interest to them. These agreements, according to White, are honored because each individual operates on the premise that he will be better off by "adhering to rules that he expects others to honor over the long run" (p. 372).

White added two important observations. First, certain resources are controlled by the collectivity (e.g., community swimming pools), and second, other resources can only be used by a collectivity (e.g., a complex technology requiring a division of labor). Thus, to the degree that exchange models are based on the assumption that individuals control and use resources as individuals, they are quite far removed from the actual state of affairs in many organizations. In White's view, collective behavior is more than the sum of exchange relations.

Thus, despite their agreement on the fundamental role played by individual goals, the work of Georgiou and White point in different directions. Georgiou leads us toward microanalysis, whereas White leads us more to a macroperspective. However, these approaches are much more complementary than mutually exclusive. For example, although White was attempting to explain collective behavior, and explicitly reserved the term *exchange* to describe processes within dyads, he did assume that motivation was explained by the pursuit of goals by individuals. Thus, as with Coleman's work, because the major thrust of White's analysis was upon collective behavior, it can be viewed as additive to the work of Homans. However, White's analysis of collective behavior seems readily reducible to psychological propositions, through the same type of reasoning that Homans (1971) applied to Coleman's work.

Internal Processes—Some Macrolevel Studies

The resource–exchange approach seems well-suited as a framework for integrating a number of theoretical and empirical studies which have been concerned with the behavior of collectivities within organizations. Zald's (1970a,b) work may be a useful starting point. His political economy perspective recognizes the importance of dealing with the basic exchange processes which affect the behavior of organizational participants and of organizations themselves. In addition, however, his analysis directs attention to the political context in which these exchanges occur. Zald (1970b) argued that no internal economy of an organization operates according to pure market processes. Rather, traditional rules of thumb, bargaining, and hierarchical assignments all affect the allocation of people and other resources. Consequently, it is necessary to study a number of aspects of an organization, including: (1) organizational constitutions; (2) the operating political economy (i.e., the power system by which decisions are made); and (3) such aspects of the internal political economy as the distribution of power, the division of labor, incentive allocations, and information and control systems.

A number of these factors, particularly those dealing with power, were included by Hickson, Hinings, Lee, Schneck, and Pennings (1971) in their strategic-contingencies theory of organizational power. Taking Emerson's (1962) view of power, they argued that the power of any particular subunit is a function of that unit's ability to help other subunits cope with uncertainty. Drawing directly upon Blau (1964), they wrote, "subunits can be seen to be exchanging control of strategic contingencies one for the other under normative regulation of an encompassing social system, and acquiring power in the system through the exchange" (p. 222). In a more recent exploratory project, Hinings, Hickson, Pennings and Schneck (1974) reported general support for their basic theory. In the seven organizations they studied, the power of a given subunit was likely to be strong if it (1) helped other subunits to deal effectively with uncertainties, (2) had immediate and severe effects on the final outputs of the organization, (3) provided services for which the organization cannot find substitutes, and (4) was closely linked to the work flow of other subunits. In short, the power of a subunit was a function of the value of the resources it provided to other organization units.

Similarly, the work of Salancik and Pfeffer (1974) revealed that the ability of subunits to obtain scarce resources from the environment is related to intraorganizational power and to the patterns of exchanges within a university. Their measures of subunit power were highly correlated both with the ability of the subunits to bring in outside grants and contrasts, and with the internal allocation to subunits of scarce and critical resources. Moreover, "power is more highly correlated with the allocation of the resources which are more critical and more scarce" (p. 469). Interestingly, they found a negative correlation between the allocation of less critical resources and power. They suggested that this outcome would be attributed to the costs of using power.

A recent study by Lourenco and Glidewell (1975) also found a relationship between success and power in *vertically* related subunits. One factor leading to a growth in autonomy of the subordinate unit was an apparent decrease in the ability of the superordinate unit to contribute to the success of the organization. The authors noted that many of the particulars of this process were consistent with Blau's (1964) theory. Lourenco and Glidewell may be said to have added a new dimension to the strategic-contingencies view of social power.

Finally, the resource–exchange model directs attention to a study of the process through which resources are allocated within organizations. As Pondy (1970) and Pfeffer and Salancik (1974) have observed, social scientists have given little attention to the problem of resource allocation within organizations.

Pondy (1970) argued that the allocation of resources by organizational participants is not completely bound by the impact of external markets, but that participants have access to certain discretionary resources which they can use to advance their personal and/or departmental special interests. As a result, the actual use of resources is influenced by a political process involving bargaining, joint agreements, and the exchange of information about each department's costs. As in any such competitive process, the information exchanged may be biased, and, further, there is a need to enforce the agreements, because it is often to the advantage of an individual party to "welch." Pondy described the dynamics of this process as similar to a form of the prisoner's dilemma situation, but with special characteristics arising from the use of hierarchical authority.

In addition to control by authority, Pondy suggested that an internal price adjustment system (e.g., overhead charges) may be used.

This induces more voluntary coordination, makes welching less likely, and replaces bargaining between departments with bargaining between each department and an authority figure over price. For many purposes the process can be studied meaningfully in its own right without resorting to the psychological level in which the department's behavior is analysed in terms of the rewards and costs of each departmental member. Of course, such microanalysis is not precluded, but, as with the other work we have reviewed in this section, it is not necessary either.

Building on Pondy's conceptual analysis, Pfeffer and Salancik (1974) studied the resource allocation process within a university, finding that departmental power played a significant role. In general, the more powerful departments received more discretionary resources from the university, regardless of their work loads. Their findings demonstrate that if departments are used as units for analysis, without resorting to psychological reduction, the conclusions may be generally consistent with an exchange framework.

However, these results do not necessarily imply that the R–E perspective is the best for understanding all the political processes which characterize an organization. Not all resource flows, either within or between organizations, are qualitatively the same. In this regard, papers by Ekeh (1974) and Boulding (1973) provide some important thoughts. Stimulated by what Lévi-Strauss called "univocal reciprocity," Ekeh advanced the concept of *generalized exchange*. In generalized exchanges, in contrast to mutual or reciprocal exchanges, resource flows are not limited to mutual transactions between individuals. For example, Person might give a valuable resource to Other, Other similarly benefits Third Man, and Third Man benefits Person. In addition, Person and all other individuals who compose a group may carry on exchanges with the rest of the group as a whole. Such patterns are, of course, extremely frequent in organizations; organizations institutionalize such exchanges and depend on such patterns for their success. In fact, one reason that formal organizations are useful tools to accomplish so many things is that they make it possible to design and conduct predictable, stable social relationships in a short period of time. The feasibility of such arrangements is aided greatly by the willingness of individuals to engage in such generalized exchanges.

Boulding (1973) noted that sometimes resources flow only in one direction. In one-way flows, which Boulding called grants, resources are given by Person to Other, and Other does not (nor is he expected to) return exchangeable resources to Person. One possible outcome is that a social system is more integrated in the sense of community than is a system based on purely exchange relations. Boulding argued that grants are a particularly important item in understanding the dynamics of intraorganizational processes, since many resource flows within organizations do not consist of mutual exchanges of material resources.

Internal Processes—Some Micro-Considerations

In some ways the development of modern individualistic exchange theory appears rooted in the efforts of Blau and Homans to understand the various forces which accounted for individual and small group behavior in organizations. Moreover, some of the more severe critics of the contemporary exchange theory have acknowledged the value of the approach for the study of the behavior of individuals in organizations. For example, Berkowitz (1972) observed:

> Organizational conditions might well promote, in many people at least, the kinds of concerns stressed by exchange analyses. The required work is often routine and uninteresting; it is carried out not for intrinsic values but for extrinsic benefits. . . . Organizations, furthermore, generally emphasize status considerations, and ideas of status congruence and distributive justice. (p. 105)

As a result of the more obvious linkages between organizational processes at microlevels and exchange theory, for present purposes I will devote relatively little attention to it. However, a few points deserve mention.

First, one major area of convergence between the macro- and microlevel approaches appears to lie in the study of the use of discretionary resources, as Pondy's (1970) and Pfeffer and Salancik's (1974) papers discussed in the previous section demonstrated. In addition, Williamson's (1964) work provides additional support for the importance of the study of discretionary resources in stimulating such a convergence.

Williamson examined the influence of individual preferences upon the use of discretionary resources. Although the nature of Williamson's study dictates that only tentative conclusions can be drawn, he did find considerable evidence to support his assertion that "where discretion in the decision-making units exists, this will ordinarily be exercised in a fashion that reflects the individual interests of the decision makers" (p. 55). Certainly, an interesting problem for study is the process through which the preferences of individuals are linked to and expressed in departmental decisions about resource allocations. This is the type of problem which can provide a clear linkage between the micro- and macrolevels of analysis. Moreover, it is a problem which the models of Homans and Blau may be very useful in exploring.

Second, microlevel exchange analysis, particularly if it is modified to deal more adequately with cognitive and other internal psychological processes,[3] may be linked closely to other models which have dealt with individual behavior in organizations. In particular, data generated by the expectancy theories of such writers as Vroom (1964) and Porter and Lawler (1968), and path–goal approaches following Georgopoulus, Mahoney, and Jones (1957), can be used readily to relate individual behavior to organizational contingencies. Similarly, the work of such individuals as Nord (1969a), Jablonsky and DeVries (1972), Luthans and Kreitner (1975), Hamner (1974), Schneier (1974), and others who have sought to analyze organizational processes through an operant-conditioning perspective can be easily incorporated. An important practical advantage of such an approach is that it can be translated easily into terms that managers and administrators relate to easily.

Third, the exchange model has been a fruitful stimulus to a growing amount of research on microlevel organizational processes. In addition to the seminal work of Homans and Blau, in the last few years a number of studies have used the exchange model as a framework for the study of leadership (cf. Hollander, Chapter 5 this volume). Some of this work has been reported by Jacobs (1971), Hinton and Barrow (1975), Organ (1974), and Dansereau, Graen, and Haga (1975). Moreover, other recent work, including that of Evans (1970), Greene (1975), and Hammer and Dachler (1975), has yielded results which are consistent generally with exchange predictions, although the studies themselves came from different paradigms.

Fourth, the exchange model has rather obvious appeal for dealing with other topics of concern at the microlevel of organizational analysis. Pay and other reward systems are two such topics. In addition, many studies about equity and justice have their roots in exchange theory. Other topics about which exchange theory has already been a stimulus to thought, or has clear potential as a guide to future work, include group behavior, decision making, social change, and training. Finally, as the work of Blau (1964) and Emerson (1972b) has shown so convincingly, the exchange model forces attention to be focused directly on a topic which has been ignored and inadequately conceptualized by students of organizations—social power.

---

[3] The A–R–D model presented by Staats (1975) may provide a useful paradigm for such a modification.

CONCLUSIONS

In this paper I have explored the potential of the R–E model as a source for the development of a comprehensive theory of organizations. It forces us to look at all rewards and costs in a situation—not just easily measured ones like economic and/or material rewards—and can lead to more adequate theory and practice. The perspective seems to be useful for integrating research on both micro- and macrolevel topics, and, because the R–E paradigm helps to conceptualize resource flows and directs attention to the interaction of exchanges of resources and organizational structures and processes, it is more useful for analysis of a number of specific processes relevant to organizations than is general systems theory. In addition, I have suggested that the R–E framework provides a perspective for approaching at least some of the means by which macrolevel forces are translated into behavior of people which is observed at more microlevels of analysis.

However, it is at this macro-micro interface that some problems occur. As Ekeh (1974) pointed out, individualistic exchanges can lead to qualitatively different social relationships than do generalized or collectivistic exchanges. Similarly, Coleman (1964a, 1966) pointed to certain discontinuities between predictions derived from individualistic exchange models and collective behavior.

Organizations involve collective endeavors. These collective endeavors are of a particular type in the sense that often they are influenced by formal rules, procedures, and structures. Moreover, they may be nonmutual and even one-way. Although the effects of these factors may be reduced to the psychological level to account for individual behavior, such efforts may cause us to overlook factors which are more properly synergistic or organic in nature. As Buckley (1967) observed, the explanation of so-called "composition effects" does not require any changes in the basic exchange propositions, but rather it requires that some propositions have to be *added*. Even though Homans (1974), Blau (1964), and others have sought to link their arguments to sociological levels of discourse, there is still the danger that users of the exchange approach will come to overlook more holistic processes which need analysis in and of themselves. This danger seems particularly great with the exchange approach which has been developed and is frequently employed post facto, and which, unless carefully used, becomes circular and all-encompassing (see Abrahamsson, 1970). Overall, however, if we are constantly on guard against such errors, the R–E model appears to have great potential for the student of organizations. It provides a set of concepts which can be used fruitfully at all levels of organizational functioning. Moreover, these concepts seem capable of linking the findings of a number of important studies about a variety of aspects of organizations into a common framework which is both general in the sense of being encompassing, and specific in focusing on the central causes, consequences, and substances of the flow of resources within organizations, between organizations, and between organizations and the larger systems in which they are embedded.

ACKNOWLEDGMENT

The helpful comments of Craig Pinder on earlier drafts of this paper are gratefully acknowledged.

Sex Roles, Social Exchange, and Couples

RICHARD H. WILLIS AND IRENE HANSON FRIEZE

INTRODUCTION

Romantic relationships have long been a focus of attention by novelists, poets, and other observers of human nature. On a more practical level, finding a spouse is one of the major concerns of young adults in our society. The success of such relationships is of interest, not only to the individuals themselves and to their families and friends, but also to society at large, because of the importance of the family as a primary institution for stabilizing adult personalities and socializing children.

This chapter attempts to integrate certain aspects of role theory and social-exchange theory within an analysis of the formation and stability of couple relations. Of special concern will be male and female expectations about one another. Although there is a large and rapidly growing literature on sex roles, to date exchange theory has made sparse use of gender as a variable. This chapter takes a step aimed toward changing this.

Many aspects of our analysis are given numerical form, and it is convenient to refer to our "model," yet our so-called model is really more of an illustration of an approach to generating interrelated hypotheses. As a consequence, this chapter has a decidedly speculative tone. Furthermore, this tone is accentuated by the absence of the customary introduction reviewing relevant literature. Such a section was written, rewritten, and rewritten again, but eventually the conclusion was forced upon us that any review of the several germane areas that conformed to space limitations would necessarily be quite super-

RICHARD H. WILLIS AND IRENE HANSON FRIEZE • Department of Psychology, University of Pittsburgh, Pittsburgh, Pennsylvania 15260.

ficial—hence our decision to assume a rather broadly knowledgeable reader. We believe that it will be apparent to such a reader that we have gone to considerable effort to base our analysis on assumptions that are compatible with available evidence.[1] Beyond this, research support for some aspects of the model have become available recently, and is reported briefly near the end of the chapter.

The main reason for introducing numerical values for the model variables is that this permits suggesting how they might be computed from more elemental measures, and, once computed, how they might be interrelated further at the next stage in the logical sequence. Although we have endeavored to choose intuitively plausible numerical values, we are of course *not* hypothesizing these particular values, but rather the more general underlying logic which they illustrate.

ROLE EXPECTATIONS

Ascribed and Achieved Status

A classic distinction in role theory is that between ascribed and achieved status (Linton, 1945). *Ascribed status* is associated with a position that a person assumes involuntarily, as, for example, by accident of birth. *Achieved status* is associated with a position that the person attains by virtue of his efforts and accomplishments. Standard examples of ascribed positions are sex, age, kinship by birth, and caste. Examples of achieved positions are occupation, husband or wife, college graduate, Olympic gold medalist, and Nobel prize laureate. The distinction is often fuzzy in practice, and is better considered as a continuum than a sharp dichotomy.

Sex Ascription and Sex Role Achievement

Gender is an excellent example of an ascribed position or status, for most individuals are born clearly belonging to one sex or the other. In contrast, to become accepted as an adequate adult of either sex is an achievement. It is not enough merely to survive until one becomes of age. One must also enact the appropriate sex role successfully, and the ability to do this is the product of an extended period of maturation

---

[1] Recent reviews and comprehensive sources include Berscheid and Walster (1978), Byrne (1971), Huston (1974), Kerckhoff (1974), Murstein (1971, 1976), Rausch, Barry, Hertel, and Swain (1974), Walster, Walster, and Berscheid (1978), and Whitley (1979b).

and socialization. At the same time, if one is already an adult, role expectations specific to one's own sex will be closer to the ascribed or required end of the ascribed-achieved dimension.

Behavior associated with the ascribed role of the *other* sex may be perceived either as (1) an optional achievement, or (2) a failure to meet one's own ascribed sex role requirements. If virtues, they will be optional; if shortcomings or vices, they will be disapproved. Some traits can change from vices to virtues or conversely under certain conditions. A professional football player such as Roosevelt "Rosie" Grier can make a virtue out of dexterity at needlepoint, but a man whose credentials as a virile male are less firmly established might run the risk of being judged effeminate if he publicly displayed the same skill. As fascinating as these evaluative reversals are, we shall sidestep the task of analyzing them, assuming hereafter that any trait can be categorized as either a strength or a shortcoming, independently of the context.

We assume further that any shortcoming can be reversed in interpretation, and so converted into a strength. This leaves but four ideal trait types: (1) those required for all adults, (2) those optional for all adults, (3) those required for women and optional for men, and (4) those required for men and optional for women. These ideal types clearly correspond respectively to general risks, general opportunities, risks for women but opportunities for men, and risks for men but opportunities for women.

Normative and Predictive Expectations

In our discussion so far we have been concerned with normative or evaluative expectations. Unfortunately the term *expectation* is also used, often without distinction, in a descriptive or nonevaluative sense to refer to subjective probabilities. In other words, an expectation can be either what is proper and good, or what probably is or will be. Worse yet, there is even a third meaning: mathematical expectation is the product of a probability and an evaluative magnitude, or the sum of such products. We are concerned with the first two meanings, and to distinguish them we shall refer to normative and predictive expectations.

Normative and predictive expectations are in fact often highly correlated, and the apparent correlation is enhanced by the inclination of people to conceal socially unacceptable actions. Over and above such actual or perceived correlations, the two kinds of expectations may have similar consequences for the evaluation of success and failure. Sarbin and Allen (1968, p. 552) assert that social disapproval follows failure to enact ascribed roles properly, but not achieved roles, and, by contrast, social approval is awarded success in enacting achieved roles, but not ascribed roles. Thus, to the extent that a behavior is normatively expected, its enactment is more or less assumed by society—with the result that expected nonfailure is ignored, but failure is punished; whereas, to the extent that aspiration to the role is voluntary, its attainment is not assumed—with the result that success is rewarded, and nonsuccess is ignored. These relationships are diagramed in idealized form in Figure 1.

The diagramed effects of normative expectations on the use of social sanctions are similar to those of predictive expectations of success on the value of task achievement (Atkinson, 1964, Chap. 9). For a very easy task, success has little or no reward value to the actor, but failure is punishing, whereas for a very difficult task, success is highly rewarding, but failure normally has little or no punishment value. Success on an easy task is credited to the nature of the task rather than to personal factors, whereas failure on such a task is often attributed to lack of ability or effort. Failure at a difficult task is again attributed to the task, but success may be perceived as the result of personal effort and ability (Frieze & Weiner, 1971). Similar attributional patterns may exist for success and failure at ascribed and achieved role tasks. Failure to perform an ascribed role may be especially punished, since it is likely to be attributed to lack of effort.

In brief, we hypothesize that normative and predictive expectations will have similar consequences for the evaluation of success and failure—partly because of empirical congruence, and partly because of

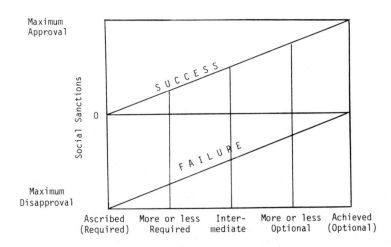

FIGURE 1.   Hypothetical social sanctions as a function of role optionality and performance (success/failure).

similar underlying processes of attribution. Thus, the common failure to distinguish consistently between kinds of expectation will not always lead one seriously astray. On the other hand, the higher the covariation, the more surprising any large discrepancy, and the greater its impact. Both the general level of congruence and the patterning of discrepancies are therefore theoretically important. Although we attempt no solution to the problem of specific discrepancies, the general level of congruence will be taken into some account in our analysis. Immediately below we consider differentiation of expectations between sexes, with congruence assumed within either sex. Later, in connection with differentiation of behavior between the sexes (role differentiation), we compare levels of congruence.

Evaluation of Male and Female Role Occupants

Assume that differences among individuals in their desirability as partners can be approximated satisfactorily by designating one of two levels on each of two variables. These variables, X and Y, are global, each representing a combination of more specific attributes and dispositions which are sufficiently correlated or similar in their consequences that they can be grouped in a first approximation. Both are virtues, and the higher level of each is the more desirable. X represents masculine virtues, and Y represents feminine virtues. The stereotypic male role entails a normative expectation of the higher level of X but allows either level of Y, and the stereotypic female role entails a normative expectation of the higher level of Y but allows either level of X. In other words, high X implies a relatively ascribed status for males and an optional achievement for females, and high Y implies a relatively ascribed status for females and an optional achievement for males.

If Talcott Parsons's (1955) view of sex-role functions were accepted, X and Y would be interpretable as instrumental or task competence, and expressive or socioemotional capacity, respectively. We prefer to interpret X and Y more broadly, along the following lines:

X = all instrumental competences, socioemotional and expressive capacities, and other traits and resources that are more or less required of men but optional for women;

Y = all instrumental competences, socioemotional and expressive capacities, and other traits and resources that are more or less required of women but optional for men.

In terms of the four ideal trait types outlined earlier, X is basically a cluster of risks for men and opportunities for women, and Y is basically a cluster of risks for women and opportunities for men. General risks and opportunities are not introduced explicitly, and are assumed to be treatable as if constant.

Each individual can be assigned a social desirability value, or a Social Value (SV) for short, according to role or gender and levels of X and Y. Table I shows hypothetical contributions to SV of each trait at each level for each role. The contributions made by success and failure on the optional or role-peripheral trait are assigned arbitrary values of 1 and 0, thus defining a unit and zero point. That is, a high X level for females and a high Y level for males have cell entries of +1, and a low X level for females and a low Y level for males have cell entries of 0.

The role-central traits are assumed to differ from the role-peripheral ones in three ways. First, by definition they are *more required*, and so are further to the left in Figure 1. Second, for a given level of subjective difficulty, success will be subjectively *more probable*. Finally, other things being equal, the role-central trait will be *more important*, in that success/failure will make a bigger difference in SV than it will for the peripheral trait. In brief, expectation effects in combination will *reduce the sum* of the cell entries for high and low levels, whereas the importance effect will increase the difference.

If the expectation effects reduce *each* cell entry (not just the sum), and the importance effect also influences *each* cell entry (not just the difference), then the central trait contributions for success SV_S and for failure SV_F can be expressed as follows:

$$SV_S = 1 - \text{expectation decrement} + \text{importance increment}$$

$$SV_F = 0 - \text{expectation decrement} - \text{importance decrement}$$

If the expectation effects and the importance effect are each set equal to one-half, they cancel under success and combine to −1 under failure,

TABLE I
Social Evaluation Matrices for Males
and Females

Cluster of virtues	Males		Females	
	Low	High	Low	High
X	−1	+1	0	+1
Y	0	+1	−1	+1

producing the entries in Table I for levels of X and Y for males and females. Although these magnitudes have been selected to yield a simple pattern, and are otherwise rather arbitrary, the resulting pattern is both intuitively plausible and empirically supported by preliminary research reported briefly in a later section.

Simply put, Table I says that an individual gets equal credit for possessing either virtue, is penalized for lacking the ascribed or role-central virtue, and is evaluated neutrally for failing to achieve or possess the optional virtue.

Partner Markets and Initial Formation

Couples are assumed to be formed by some mode of SV-matching among the participants of a partner market. A partner market involves both *fields of availables* and *fields of eligibles* (Kerchhoff, 1974). The field of potential partners for a particular unattached individual is the intersection of these two fields—that is, those of the opposite sex that he or she knows or can get to know, who at the same time meet certain social requirements such as similarity of age, socioeconomic class, religion, educational level, and race. Obviously, such fields are not in reality sharply bounded, but we make the simplifying assumption that they are. We also assume that a group of market participants of one sex all have the same field of potential partners, and that they in turn comprise the field of potential partners for the first. The two such mutually interrelated sets of participants then define a partner market. Excluded, of course, are all individuals preferring not to have any partner of the opposite sex.

The number of participants in the two groups need not be equal. Pronounced local imbalances can be produced by any number of factors, such as, for example, the young men of a community leaving in greater numbers than the young women. There will often be tendencies for these local imbalances to be corrected over time as the market system seeks equilibrium, but this equilibration process will not necessarily operate quickly enough to find partners for all participants. If the market is viewed over a relatively short interval, during which few participants leave or enter, then the major conditions of supply and demand will be (1) the relative numbers of males and females, and (2) the prevailing preferences for partners within each group.

Consider first equal numbers of males and females who are similarly distributed across all SV levels. What will happen if members of each group are *SV-strivers* that prefer partners at the highest possible

SV level? Those at the top of each group will promptly choose each other, after which those at the next level down will chose one another, and so on down until those at the bottom are left to one another. The net result is perfect SV-matching of partners. Still assuming equal numbers, what happens if all participants are *SV-matchers* who prefer partners as closely matched to themselves on SV as possible? Clearly, the net result will again be perfect SV-matching. Thus, it makes no difference whether participants are all SV-strivers or all SV-matchers.

Now let one group be larger than the other. The preference structure will now make a difference, and this difference will be seen most clearly in *the loner pattern*, the distribution of those from the larger group left without partners. For SV-strivers, the loners will be recruited from the lower SV strata. For SV-matchers, however, the loners will be recruited equally from all SV strata. Some of the "best" people will be left out, but, on the bright side, everyone finding a partner will find one as strongly preferred as any. This is not true for the SV-strivers market, where members of the larger group finding partners must sometimes settle for partners who are "beneath" them. In fact, even with equal numbers, the SV-strivers market provides most-preferred partners only to those near enough to the top of each group. The level of mutual preferences between partners decreases directly with their shared SV level.

If preferences are some combination of SV-striving and SV-matching, and if groups are of unequal size, the observed distribution of loners will allow one to infer the relative importance of the preference components. A more formal and detailed analysis of the SV-strivers partner market, and a comparison with the classical model of perfect economic competition, is to be found in Willis and Olson (1978).

Let us return for the time being to equal-sized groups, and consider further the implications of SV as a function of trait levels and gender, as given earlier in Table I. In particular, we now wish to look beyond the global SV values of partners, into the patterning of trait levels in combination as this relates to compatibility and stability.

INTRINSIC COMPATIBILITY

If the pairing process always matches partners on SV, a certain number of pair types will occur; if formation is not constrained by SV-matching, the number of pair types that can occur will be considerably larger. It can be seen from Table I that an individual can have one of four SV scores (2, 1, 0, or −1). Under strict SV-matching, four pair types can be formed. Otherwise, as many as 16 different types of pairs are possible.

In any event, for any given degree of goodness of SV-matching, there will be differences in the extent to which the "fine-grained" patterning on specific traits will facilitate a harmonious and mutually rewarding relationship. The degree to which a relationship is harmonious and mutually rewarding can be said to define the level of compatibility. If factors outside the relationship can be disregarded, one can speak of the *intrinsic* compatibility of the partners. Other things being equal, the higher the intrinsic compatibility, the greater the stability of the relationship. For the present we consider only intrinsic compatibility; later we look at some external influences on stability.

Components of Compatibility

Specific Patterns

In order to assess overall compatibility, it is necessary to consider a greater variety of patterns than simple similarity and simple complementarity, the two patterns that are usually considered. Even with only two dimensions (X and Y), both dichotomous, and with compatibility considered dichotomously, there are 16 possible patterns a component can exhibit (not to be confused with the 16 pair types mentioned above). That is, if we consider only one score per partner, the possibilities can be represented as a 2×2 table, and if signs are entered into its four cells—plus for compatible, minus for incompatible—the signs can exhibit 16 possible patterns. We confine our discussion to six of these 16. All six appear to be important for any realistic analysis; some of the remaining ten may also be. After a discussion of these patterns, we will then relate them to individual and overall SV values.

For each of the 2×2 matrices in Table II, rows indicate attribute (X or Y) levels for one partner, and columns indicate those for the other. All patterns are symmetrical with respect to gender, so it makes no difference whose levels go with rows and whose with columns. For a particular interpretation of any given pattern, rows and columns may refer to levels of the same attribute (both X or both Y), or to different attributes (one X and the other Y). The sign entries inside each matrix indicate whether or not the combination of trait levels contributes to overall compatibility. The first pattern, for example, diagrams cases in which compatibility is facilitated if partners have the same level, but not otherwise.

It is important to recognize that compatibility contributions (the matrix cell signs) depend not only on the levels of both X and Y, but

TABLE II
Some Possible Patterns of Component Compatibility Contributions[a]

Pattern				Example

Correlative

1. Similarity

	−	+
+	−	+	Attitudes, beliefs, interests
−	+	−	Shared goals

2. Complementarity

	−	+
+	+	−	Dominance/Submission
−	−	+	Jack Spratt situation

Disjunctive

3. Compensatory

	−	+
+	+	+	Bread winning
−	−	+	Homemaking

4. Distributive

	−	+
+	+	−	Verbal drive
−	+	+	Give and take

Conjunctive

5. Double Hurdle

	−	+
+	−	+	Affection
−	−	−	Fidelity

6. Double Jeopardy

	−	+
+	−	−	Internal competition
−	+	−	Internal quid pro quo

[a] The rows of each 2 × 2 table correspond to levels of a trait for one partner, and the columns correspond to levels of a trait for the other partner. Rows and columns of a particular table can refer to the same trait or to different traits. The signs within each 2 × 2 table refer to the contribution that each combination of levels makes to the compatibility of the couple; a + indicates that compatibility is enhanced, while a − indicates that it is not.

also on the extent to which X and Y are manifested as *needs* or *resources* in each partner. This model thus conceptualizes compatibility quite differently from the need-complementarity notion of Winch (1958). The need/resource quality of a dispositional attribute depends on the ease and degree of adaptability with which its level can be changed over a wide range in response to changes in the requirements of the momentary situation. The greater the rigidity, the more needlike the disposition; the greater the flexibility, the more resourcelike. Possessing a dispositional trait with both need and resource aspects is in some ways analogous to having a response-producing machine that can be made to run faster or slower than some natural rate, within limits, but only at an increase in cost. If even small rate changes are expensive, the trait is needlike; if the rate can be adaptively increased or decreased over a wide range with little or no increase in costs, it is resourcelike.

The six patterns of Table II consist of three general types, each with two subtypes. In *Correlative* patterns (Similarity and Complementarity), compatible combinations of levels are either directly or inversely correlated.[2] In *Disjunctive* patterns (Compensatory and Distributive), the presence of *either* attribute at a specified level, either high or low, is a sufficient condition for compatibility facilitation. In the *Conjunctive* patterns (Double Hurdle and Double Jeopardy), the presence of *both* attributes at a specified level is necessary for a contribution to compatibility. Conjunctive patterns are thus the most demanding, disjunctive ones the least, and correlative ones intermediate.

Two examples are provided for each pattern to clarify their actual operation. Although the model in the form presented is confined to traits X and Y, our illustrations necessarily draw on a rather large variety of personal characteristics.

Examples of Similarity are (1) similar attitudes and beliefs, and (2) shared interests and goals. Agreement, or similarity, on almost any significant attitude, issue, or belief can make a contribution to compatibility, and obviously common interests and goal communality critically affect the internal harmony of a couple relationship.

With regard to Complementarity, dominance/submission is often given as an example (e.g., Carson, 1969, Chap. 4; Leary, 1957; Winch, 1958), for the more dominant one partner, the more submissive the other must be for friction to be avoided; and if the submissiveness of the one reflects a need to be dominated, then ideally it will be offset by a corresponding need of the other to dominate. In addition, any "Jack Spratt and wife" situation, in which contrasting preferences prevent competition or allow cooperation, implies complementarity.

Pattern 3, the Compensatory, is exemplified under certain conditions by the two basic family functions of "bread winning" and homemaking. Although somebody must go out and earn some money, both partners can contribute to the family income. Sex roles and wage differentials may dictate which partner should or best can assume the

[2] Kelley and Thibaut (1978, pp. 66–67) say that similarity and complementarity are formally indistinguishable, but psychologically different. They state further that relationships cannot be characterized in terms of similarity versus complementarity if the partners' behavioral choices are not the same. These assertions are made within the context of their outcome-matrix framework, and are apparently intended to apply only within that context.

major responsibility in a given area, but, from a strictly interpersonal perspective, it may make little or no difference. Only if neither one is willing or able to assume the responsibility for necessary tasks is there trouble.

The other disjunctive pattern, the Distributive, applies to any situation in which turns must be taken, that is, to any situation in which time or some other mutually valued commodity must be shared or distributed. If both partners insist on talking most of the time, an area of incompatibility is created. No other combination of levels of verbal drive leads to any particular trouble. If both are comfortable in saying very little and speak only when something needs saying, for example, this just means that more time will be left over for activities other than talking and listening. More generally, many kinds of give-and-take situations are likely to fit Pattern 4. If both insist on doing most of the taking, or most of the giving for that matter, a problem is created quite analogous to that of too much talking.

An example of the Double Hurdle pattern is affection, or its expression. Even assuming that each cares deeply for the other, it is necessary that each be sufficiently expressive to make this clear to the other. Traditional fidelity provides another example. Excluding the possibility of a mutually accepted double standard, it is necessary for each partner to give a credible demonstration of an exclusive commitment to the other.

The last pattern, Double Jeopardy, is rather unusual, insofar as only the simultaneous absence of both virtues leads to a beneficial effect. Many such situations involve attributes which are virtues with respect to external activities, but become vices or shortcomings when manifested internally within the dyad without appropriate modification. Thus, career ambition—whether one's chosen career is that of a homemaker or something else—is fine as long as it is directed toward the career itself. If it should be directed toward the partner, and so becomes transformed into internal competitiveness, it may take a destructive form. Internal competitiveness can be indirect as well as direct. The breadwinner and the homemaker may each strive to best the other through superior performances in his and her own respective areas. Although such indirect competition can be beneficial, and is no doubt less risky than direct competition, it too can obviously be overdone.

The quid pro quo example of the last pattern appears to have a special significance. In external dealings with third parties, it is often quite functional to adopt a more or less "show me" attitude. In business and other kinds of relations with those one does not know well and with which one has no strong personal bonds, it is no more than common sense to do so. Such commonsense prudence to the same degree is not appropriate in a personal relationship involving strong mutual positive sentiments. Prudence easily becomes transformed into distrust. If such distrust is not initially justified, it may well become so, for excessive suspiciousness has a destructive, self-fulfilling aspect to it.[3]

General Comments on Compatibility Components

Looking at all six patterns together, some more general observations can be made. First, the applicable pattern will be contingent on task, situation, and external environment, as well as the trait levels of the partners. Earning family income was used as an example of the Compensatory pattern, but if the economic environment is such that neither partner alone is able to earn enough, then clearly the Double Hurdle pattern will apply. Attitudes and interest served nicely above to illustrate the Similarity pattern, but in certain situations consensus conforms to the Complementarity pattern. This would occur when attitudes and interests influence preferences among the set of tasks confronting the couple, and when the task set includes many tasks that are acceptable to one or the other, but not both partners. The situation is then similar to that of Jack Spratt and his wife, but the Complementarity pattern now concerns work or production, rather than consumption.

This last example illustrates a second general point. *Resource* complementarity—which will strongly influence task specialization, both directly through abilities and indirectly through preferences—will often be more important than *need* complementarity. Clinical reports of poorly adjusted couples first suggested that need comple-

---

[3] We conjecture that strict quid pro quo is replaced by a kind of hypothetical equity for strong positive-sentiment relations. One party will then often be willing to reward the other even if he does not anticipate reciprocity, provided he believes the other would do the same for him if roles were reversed. Evidence that successful marriage partners may, in effect, adopt such a "Who's counting?" rule to a greater extent than do less successful ones has been reported by Gottman, Notarious, Markman, Bank, Yoppi, & Rubin (1976). They found more positive interpersonal behaviors generally in the more successful marriages, but little evidence of more positive or less negative *reciprocity*. They suggest that imperfect or even low reciprocity may contribute to compatibility. The same role-reversal test may also operate in many strong negative-sentiment relationships. In such cases the rule becomes, "Do unto him before he does unto me."

mentarity is less often a barrier to mutual satisfaction between normally healthy, flexible partners than between neurotic ones. At the same time, complementarity of neurotic needs may possibly be the basis of stability of neurotic couples more frequently than complementarity of resources. In this connection it is important to bear in mind that compatibility does not necessarily imply harmony in any absolute sense. In fact, for many couples a certain amount of uncertainty and even friction may be necessary to keep things from getting monotonous, and to keep each partner from taking the other's behavior for granted. If so, then one kind of stable neurotic couple would be partners matched on the need for a high level of turbulence in their relationship. Such a couple could remain "happily miserable" together to the very end. Although not harmonious, their relationship is high on *relative* compatibility, for they get along better with one another than either would with most other partners.

Most of the examples given above were *intra*trait patterns, which brings us to a third and final general point. Compatibility can be influenced by the joint effects of levels of either the same or different traits. With two traits, four joint effects must be considered—the intratrait effects XX and YY and the intertrait effects XY and YX. Furthermore, it is quite likely that these two-way contributions depend on the levels of the remaining two variables. The XX contribution, for example, may be different for different combinations of the two Y levels. However, taking all four levels into account at once leads to formidable complexity, and so we assume provisionally that levels can be considered just two at a time without introducing serious error.[4]

Overall Compatibility

The assumption that trait levels can be considered two at a time implies that an index of overall compatibility can be formed by taking the number of components out of the four that have a positive sign. This can be done only after each component has been assigned a pattern. It seems reasonable to assign Pattern 2, Complementarity, to

---

[4] Even if the processes and conditions determining it are highly complex, compatibility can sometimes be predicted successfully from simple global measures. Howard and Dawes (1976), for example,, found self-reports of marital satisfaction to be predictable from the reported frequency of sexual relations minus the reported frequency of arguments.

the XX component, at least to the extent that a high level of X implies not only an ability but also a need to be the instrumental task leader, for to that extent two potential task leaders will fight between themselves to see who will be *the* task leader. Pattern 3, Compensatory, appears most reasonable for the YY component, assuming that a high Y reflects primarily a resource rather than a need. Things will work out all right so long as someone, either the task leader or the follower, can supply the interpersonal sensitivity and flexibility to lubricate the interaction. With regard to the intertrait components, we have already seen that the only positive patterning of levels is the high/high one. Thus, for the XY and YX components Pattern 5, Double Hurdle, is assumed to apply.

These assignments of patterns to components mean collectively that—at any given time—the couple should contain *one and only one* person acting as a highly instrumental leader, *at least one* person acting as a highly socioemotionally skilled member, and, if there is only one of the latter, it should not be the same one who is highly instrumental.

All these arguments are based on the assumption that X has more need qualities than Y. If X were less a need and more a pure resource, then high XX couples might be quite effective in working together to solve task issues. Conversely, if Y were more a need, then a high YY relationship would suffer from an overemphasis on interpersonal feelings and difficulties, perhaps resulting in too little attention to more objective task requirements. With either change in assumptions, compatibility values would differ numerically from those used below.

Presumably the intrinsic compatibility level of two partners will exert its full impact on their reward levels only over a period of time. At the beginning, rewards will be largely anticipatory, and thus closely related to the pre-pairing strengths of preference of each for the other. Later, after the partners have had a chance to sample adequately their day-to-day interaction sequences—including many mundane and trivial ones, presumably—their experienced and anticipated reward levels will both be more closely related to their intrinsic compatibility. Satisfactions with the relationship will very likely be related to *changes* in reward levels, as well as to absolute levels. If so, then imperfect SV-matching between partners means that one partner may become disappointed, or more pleasantly surprised, than the other. Furthermore, there are any number of other reasons why partners may be unequally satisfied with their relationship in the long run. Generally, however, levels of partner satisfaction are highly correlated, and in this preliminary model we assume satisfaction to be symmetrical, and representable by the symmetrical compatibility index proposed above.

Relations among Formation, Compatibility, and Stability

Pair Types and Their Distributions

Table III shows, for each pair type, the SV score for each partner, the SV-matching index M, the sign values of each of the four components of compatibility, and the overall compatibility index C. The goodness of SV-matching is given by $M = 3 - (|SV_M - SV_F|)$. Overall compatibility C is equal to the number of plus signs in the preceding four columns. C ranges only between 0 and 3, for it is not possible for all four signs to be plus at once. Before these M and C values for each

TABLE III
Pair Types, SV-Matching, and Compatibility

Pair type	Participant trait levels				Social values		SV-matching	Compatibility				
	M		F		M	F		Components				Overall
								Intra-trait		Inter-trait		
	X	Y	X	Y	SV_M	SV_F	M^a	XX	YY	XY	YX	C^b
1	H	H	H	H	2	2	3	−	+	+	+	3
2	H	H	H	L	2	0	1	−	+	−	+	2
3	H	H	L	H	2	1	2	+	+	+	−	3
4	H	H	L	L	2	−1	0	+	+	−	−	2
5	H	L	H	H	1	2	2	−	+	+	−	2
6	H	L	H	L	1	0	2	−	−	−	−	0
7	H	L	L	H	1	1	3	+	+	+	−	3
8	H	L	L	L	1	−1	1	+	−	−	−	1
9	L	H	H	H	0	2	1	+	+	−	+	3
10	L	H	H	L	0	0	3	+	+	−	+	3
11	L	H	L	H	0	1	2	−	+	−	−	1
12	L	H	L	L	0	−1	2	−	+	−	−	1
13	L	L	H	H	−1	2	0	−	+	−	−	1
14	L	L	H	L	−1	0	2	+	−	−	−	1
15	L	L	L	H	−1	1	1	−	−	−	−	0
16	L	L	L	L	−1	−1	3	−	−	−	−	0

[a] $M = 3 - (|SV_M - SV_F|)$.
[b] C = Number of positive components. Component signs are based on the following component patterns from Table II: XX, Pattern 2; YY, Pattern 3; XY and YX, Pattern 5.

pair type can be interrelated, we need to know how the pair types are distributed.

Rather than presenting another complicated table giving the distribution of pair types under each of several conditions, we shall instead outline the procedure whereby these distributions were generated and used in the construction of Table IV, which shows matching and compatibility means for each distinct distribution.

Conditions considered combined two levels of market efficiency (random or "perfect," i.e., by preferences), two preference structures (SV-matchers and SV-strivers), two relative group sizes (equal and twice as many males), and two levels of role differentiation (none and high). These 16 combinations yield only eight distinct distributions, corresponding to the eight conditions in Table IV.

Under random pairing, any member of one group has an equal probability of being paired with any individual from the other group. If one group is larger, each member of the larger group has an equal probability of remaining a loner.

Under perfect market conditions, the pairing process is governed entirely by the preference structure. For equal sized groups, as we have seen, both preference structures will produce perfect partner matching. With unequal sized groups, partner matching is attenuated for the SV-strivers structure only.

No role differentiation is defined by equal and independent probabilities of one-half that any person, male or female, is high on X or high on Y. High role differentiation means that, within each gender, each person has independent probabilities of high levels on the required and optional traits of .75 and .25, respectively. Define four types of individuals: Winners (HH), Conformers (HL for males, LH for

TABLE IV
Mean SV-Matching of Partners and Mean
Intrinsic Compatibility

Conditions	Role differentiation			
	None		High	
	$\overline{M}$	$\overline{C}$	$\overline{M}$	$\overline{C}$
Random pairing	1.75	1.62	2.00	1.88
SV-matchers	3.00	2.25	3.00	2.44
SV-strivers: $N_M = M_F$	3.00	2.25	3.00	2.44
SV-Strivers: $N_M = 2M_F$	2.25	1.75	2.38	2.44

females), Deviates (LH for males, HL for females), and Losers (LL). Percentages of each type within either group are:

Type	SV	Role Differentiation	
		None	High
Winners	2	25	18.75
Conformers	1	25	56.25
Deviates	0	25	6.25
Losers	−1	25	18.75

Table I and the SV scores derived from it concerns differential role *evaluation*. Here it is differential role *enactment* that is involved. If the evaluations of Table I are assumed, then high role (enactment) differentiation implies a high level of congruence between behaviors and thus predictive expectations on the one hand, and normative expectations on the other. An absence of role differentiation implies only a baseline level of normative/prediction congruence. Role differentiation can be viewed as task or resource specialization. Other things being equal, the greater the differentiation of resources, the greater the complementarity of needs. Thus, the greater the level of role differentiation, the better off most people will be with the right partner, but also perhaps the less well equipped to get along on their own (Bem, 1975).

Market Characteristics and Mean Compatibility

For each of the eight distinct distributions of pair types occurring among the combinations of levels of the four market variables defined above, mean partner matching and mean compatibility values were computed, as shown in Table IV. The compatibility means are of greater long-run importance, while the matching levels help to relate compatibility to the pairing process.

There are two completely general effects of market variables on compatibility. First, as one would surely expect, random pairing produces substantially lower compatibility on the average than does pairing by either of the preference structures. Second, role differentiation enhances compatibility consistently, presumably because of the closer agreement between normative and predictive expectations.

Considering only pairing by preferences, or perfect markets, there are three more specific or interaction effects. First, close partner matching facilitates compatibility more under conditions of high role differentiation. Second, unequal group sizes reduces compatibility only without role differentiation. Third, the SV-strivers preference structure reduces compatibility only for unequal sized groups, without role differentiation. These three relationships can be summarized in part by stating that, for perfect markets, role differentiation is neither a necessary nor a sufficient condition for perfect partner matching, but it is a sufficient condition for high mean compatibility.

Effects of Loners on Stability

So far we have considered only the intrinsic compatibility of pairs that actually form, and relative group size has played a rather minor role. However, the difference in group size determines the number of loners, and the presence of a sizable loner group can be an external source of instability. The larger the number of loners, the less dependent on their partners will be members of the smaller group, generally, and especially during the earlier stages of the relationship before a firm, mutual commitment has developed. In the terminology of Thibaut and Kelley (1959), their mean comparison level for alternatives, CL_{alt}, will be higher than if there were no loners. As for more specific effects, we need not waste much time on the random pairing case. The presence of loners may decrease stability, but so long as re-pairing is random, the expected distribution of pair types will not change over time.

More detailed illustrative predictions of the influence of loners on stability under perfect market conditions can be made from Tables V and VI, which assume twice the number of males as females. Table V shows the theoretical distribution of loners for the SV-matchers and the SV-strivers preference structures, by levels of role differentiation. At a global level, the most important thing to observe is the very

TABLE V
Distributions of Loners under Perfect Market Conditions, for
$N_M = 2 N_F$[a]

Loner Type	SV	SV-matchers		SV-strivers	
		No RD	High RD	No RD	High RD
Winner	2	25	18.75	0	0
Conformer	1	25	56.25	0	50
Deviate	0	25	6.25	50	12.5
Loser	−1	25	18.75	50	37.5

[a] Because the male group is the larger and pairing is nonrandom, all loners are male.

strong interaction between preference structures and role differentiation in their effects on loner distributions.

Table VI reflects the perspectives of the females, the smaller group. For each preference structure, all occurring pair types are listed. SQ is the Status Quo reward level for females; the *early* SQ level applies immediately after the pair is formed, and the *later* level is approached over time. Early SQ is taken to equal the initial expectations of a female as represented by her strength of preference for her type of partner. For all SV-matchers this is M = 3. For the SV-strivers, the Early SQ is the male SV score, 3 for Winners and 2 for Conformers. Later—after the honeymoon, so to speak—the SQ reward level corresponds to day-to-day compatibility, C. Some females are disappointed, but most are not.

The CL_{alt} entries in Table VI are determined from Table V. For SV-matchers, CL_{alt} is taken to be the level of SV-matching between the female type in question and her most-preferred type of loner, and this M is 3 in all cases. For SV-strivers, CL_{alt} is taken to be the highest SV score among the loner types; this is either 0 or 1, depending on the level of role differentiation.

If the logic of Table VI is granted for illustrative purposes, vulnerable pair types can be spotted easily. Among the SV-matchers, only the Loser–Loser type becomes vulnerable, but extremely so. The prediction is that couples of this one type will almost certainly break up, although this is no catastrophe in and of itself, for the partners are intrinsically quite incompatible.

TABLE VI

Status Quo and Alternative Levels of Reward for Females after Choosing Partners, and Shifts over Time of SQ Reward Levels

Preferences	Male and female partner types	SQ		CL_{alt}	
		Early	Later	No RD	High RD
SV-Matchers	Winner–Winner	3	3	3	3
	Conformer–Conformer	3	3	3	3
	Deviate–Deviate	3	3	3	3
	Loser–Loser	3	0	3	3
SV-Strivers	Winner–Winner	3	3	0	1
	Winner–Conformer	3	3	0	1
	Conformer–Conformer	2	3	—	1
	Conformer–Deviate	2	0	0	1
	Conformer–Loser	2	1	0	1

[a] Early SQ reward level equals female's strength of preference for her partner; later it equals the intrinsic compatibility of the relationship. CL_{alt} equals female's strength of preference for the most preferred loner type present.

Among the SV-strivers, two types of females will eventually become disappointed with their Conformer partners—the Deviates and the Losers. However, under no role differentiation $CL_{alt} = 0$ for all females, so the presence of the loners adds little or nothing to the instability arising from intrinsic incompatibility. With high role differentiation, the Conformer–Deviate pair type becomes somewhat vulnerable, for SQ approaches 0 and $CL_{alt} = 1$.

Preliminary Research Support

This concludes our illustration, from which a number of interrelated hypotheses emerged. Two studies designed to test certain of these hypotheses have been conducted recently, and both have obtained supportive results. The first study, conducted by Bernard Whitley (1979a), attempted to confirm the relationship between role centrality and social approval shown in Table I. Male and female judges rated each of several desirable traits along a dimension of requiredness versus optionality with respect to the role of adult male. Another group of male and female subjects indicated, for each trait, amounts of approval accorded to males possessing the trait, the amounts of disapproval accorded those not possessing it. The obtained pattern displayed a distinct similarity to that obtained by interpolation from the male cell entries in Table I. Mean ratings of approval for success are high for all levels of requiredness or role centrality, although somewhat higher for high levels of requiredness. Mean approval ratings for failure are highly negative (strong disapproval) for the most role-required traits, and increase linearly almost up to zero (neutrality) for the most role-optional traits. This pattern was obtained for both the male and the female rater groups.

A second study, conducted by the first author and his students, employed an experimental simulation designed in part to test hypotheses about the distributions of loners under the SV-strivers and the SV-matchers preference structures.[5] The hypothetical distributions can be seen in Table V under the No Role Differentiation condition. The correspondence with the experimental conditions is increased by combining the top two types (Winner and Conformer) into an Above Average category, and by combining the bottom two types (Deviate and Loser) into a Below Average category.

[5] These students were Sue Clay, Joe Coyle, Kim Duncan, Connie Jacobs, Jan Lillie, Elaine Morrow, Marc Schwartz, and Bruce Stephen. A number of very helpful suggestions were made by Professor Josephine E. Olson.

Six groups of about 15 subjects each, all with about twice as many members of one sex as the other, simulated the pairing off into mixed doubles tennis teams under each of two conditions designed to induce the contrasting preferences. Results are strongly supportive of both hypotheses. For the total larger group, hypothetical experimenter-assigned SV-values (tennis skill) were equally often above and below average, and in each preference condition there were 25 loners either above or below average. In the SV-matchers condition, where loners were predicted to come about equally often from high and low levels, the loner distribution was 12 high and 13 low. In the SV-strivers condition, where loners were predicted to come mostly from the lower levels, the loner distribution was two high and 23 low.

SUMMARY

The object of this chapter has been to integrate certain basic ideas from role theory and social exchange theory as these relate to the formation, compatibility, and stability of opposite-sex couples. A preliminary model was presented from which a set of interrelated hypotheses emerged. The following points were incorporated into the model. The combined effects of normative and predictive expectations lead to role evaluations of males and females (Figure 1 and Table I); differential role enactment, or simply role differentiation, was represented by different probabilities of possessing role-required and role-optional traits.

The principle of equity, or fair rate of exchange, is built into the model at the global level by assuming that pairing tends to be by matching of partners on social evaluation (SV scores). Deviations from perfect partner matching arise from market inefficiency (randomicity) and also from such supply and demand conditions as relative group size and partner preference structures. Thus, the going rate of exchange, in SV currency, is sometimes quite different from the fair rate of exchange as defined by equal social value. Such discrepancies are assumed to contribute to instability by further attenuating the positive but imperfect correlation between the frequency with which a pair type is formed and its level of intrinsic compatibility.

Systematic changes in relationships as they develop are represented within the model by an assumed shift in the levels of reward over time from the strengths of partner preferences to the shared level of compatibility arising from patterns of day-to-day interactions. The general level of long-run intrinsic instability is determined by the mean compatibility of all pairs formed. External sources of instability are represented in the model by the number of loners of each type that serve as potential alternative partners. As illustrated under perfect market conditions, the model predicts that all loners will belong to the larger group. Had the illustration been extended to imperfect markets in which pairs are formed in part by preferences and in part by chance, some loners would belong to each group.

This last point exemplifies a general feature of the model. It has been presented in numerical terms primarily for the sake of illustrative concreteness, not predictive precision. The emergent hypotheses are more nearly embodied in the general approach than in the particular numerical values.

Preliminary research support is reported for the hypothesized joint effects of expectations and performance on role evaluation (Table I), and for the influence of preference structures on the distribution of loner types (Table V).

An 'Incremental Exchange' Perspective on the Pair Relationship

Interpersonal Reward and Level of Involvement

GEORGE LEVINGER AND L. ROWELL HUESMANN

INTRODUCTION

Until recently, models of social exchange have portrayed the reward structure of relationships as constant over time. In a previous paper (Huesmann & Levinger, 1976) we described a new model, based on a framework we called incremental exchange theory, which incorporates such temporal changes in the reward structure. This model was applied to altruistic behavior, self-disclosure, attraction, and romatic involvement.

The purpose of this paper is to suggest some revisions in our model, and to illustrate the revised model by applying it to romantic involvement. Central to the revisions is the meaning of "social reward," and the distinction between state of pair interaction and level of pair involvment. Before considering these matters, let us briefly review our earlier model.

EXCHANGE THEORY IN A SEQUENTIAL PERSPECTIVE

Imagine that a boy and a girl meet in a corridor, and that each has two response options, either ignoring the other or saying "hello." This

GEORGE LEVINGER • Department of Psychology, University of Massachusetts, Amherst, Massachusetts. L. ROWELL HUESMANN • Department of Psychology, University of Illinois, Chicago, Illinois.
 Work on this paper was supported in part by Grant GS–33641 from the National Science Foundation.

situation is depicted in Figure 1 by a dyadic outcome matrix of the kind used by Thibaut and Kelley (1959). Both are assumed to receive zero payoff from ignoring the other; each receives a small positive payoff (+1) if the other reciprocates a hello, but feels slightly bothered (−1) if the other fails to respond.

Figure 2a depicts the format of the more general outcome matrix for n behaviors, employed by Thibaut and Kelley. Their matrix has been used typically as though behavior options and payoffs remain stationary. In laboratory research, for example, two partners make choices within the same matrix repeatedly. This situation differs from interaction in everyday life, where each interactor's options change over time, and the relationship is modified by each successive interaction.

Incremental Exchange Theory

Systematic changes over time can be modeled, however, by use of a multiple, sequentially arranged set of interaction matrices as shown in Figure 2b. Here the interaction between Person and Other can move from one situation to another, and interactive situations may differ in the nature, the number, and the payoff consequences of the behavior options. The outcome of any given situation, then, may lead to the expansion or the contraction of the partners' behavior options, and to increments or decrements in prospective payoffs. Such patterns of "incremental" exchanges can be modeled through incremental exchange theory.

In Figure 1, if both boy and girl ignore one another, there is a zero

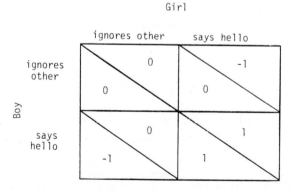

FIGURE 1.   An elementary dyadic outcome matrix.

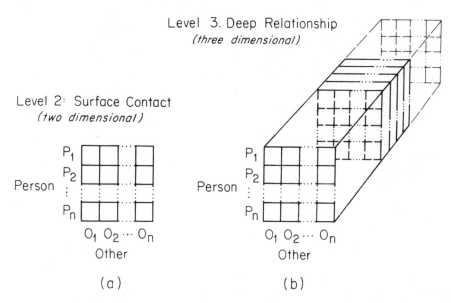

Level 3. Deep Relationship
(three dimensional)

Level 2: Surface Contact
(two dimensional)

(a)   (b)

FIGURE 2.   Dyadic outcome matrices for (a) the static model and (b) the incremental exchange model. (Adapted from Levinger, 1974.)

probability that the two will have a conversation. But if both were to exclaim a warm hello, the pair's interaction would perhaps transit into a conversation that is rewarding or costly for one or both interactants. In other words, outcomes in one situation determine the future of the encounter in general, and the occurrence of new situations in particular. If current interaction is satisfying, it often leads to more intensive interaction; conversely, if it fails to satisfy either partner, it tends to be terminated, or is moved toward greater distance. In everyday life, one partner's failure to reciprocate may lead the other to become less interdependent, or to break off the relationship entirely.

A fundamental assumption of incremental exchange theory, confined thus far to the pair relationship, is that deeper states of mutual involvement have greater expected values for each partner. (We use the term *expected value* in its mathematical sense.) Increasing expected values result from increases in payoffs, from decreases in costs, and from changes in behavioral probabilities. A deepening relationship is one in which expected rewards have become increasingly probable relative to anticipated costs; in contrast, a deteriorating relationship is one where anticipated rewards have become less attractive relative to the costs. Homans (1976) has criticized this fundamental assumption: "I do not think that the assumption, if I understand it aright, holds good generally. If it did, I believe, for instance, that there would be fewer divorces"(p. 233). However, Homans misunderstands the definitional character of this assumption. We *define* current depth of involvement as the current level of expected rewards for a relationship. Thus, if a married couple now receives lower mutual rewards than it did as a dating couple, the married couple is now at a lesser level of involvement. A pair contemplating divorce has usually become unable to derive adequate reward from its interaction relative to its previously established levels. Thus, the couple's involvement has decreased (Levinger, 1976).

THE RELATE MODEL

To provide a framework in which incremental exchange theory can be applied to particular social interactions, we constructed a computer simulation model called RELATE. In this model, a pair moves through different states of involvement over the course of its relationship. Each state is represented by a single set of behavior options, an accompanying payoff matrix, and a transition matrix which determines movement to a future state. We do not propose that persons process information in precisely the way that the model does, but we do believe that the model can predict dyadic behavior, and is useful for examining exchange theory.

Let us now summarize the structure of the RELATE model, which is described more fully in the earlier paper (Huesmann & Levinger, 1976). RELATE is a finite-state process model, based on the assumption that a pair's current interpersonal state is determined solely by the pair's previous state and by the actors' behaviors while in that previous state. For example, if a couple enters a state of heated argument, the model says that this state is predictable from the couple's immediately preceding state and their behavior in that state (e.g., a state of "discovering disagreement" and both partners' efforts to change the other's opinion). The influence of actions prior to that state is captured in the structure and values of the state-defining variables. Each interpersonal state is defined in terms of five essential characteristics:

1. The *behaviors* available in the state. Each actor has a set of mutually exclusive behavior options, which may either be the same or be quite different from the other's set.

2. The *cost* of each behavior independent of its payoff.[1]

---

[1] This concept of "cost" refers only to the negative utility of any particular behavior for the actor in that particular situation. This concept is somewhat different from the costs defined by Thibaut and Kelley (1959).

3. The *payoff matrix* for each actor. If Actor 1 selects behavior i and Actor 2 selects behavior j, Actor's 1's payoff is in row i and column j of his payoff matrix. Actor 2's payoff is in row j and column i of his matrix.

4. Each actor's *initial estimate of the probability* that his co-actor will choose any given behavior. A probability estimate of zero indicates that one is unaware that the co-actor has that option, or believes there is no change that he will use it. Estimates in any state are permitted to change during the course of interaction.

5. A *state transition matrix* which specifies what state follows each behavior outcome. Transitions are not probabilistic; if Actor 1 selects behavior i and Actor 2 behavior j, the next state will definitely be the state specified in row i and column j of the matrix. This next state may be either the same state, a state of deeper involvement, or a state of lesser involvement (Huesmann & Levinger, 1976, p. 198).

a. *Depth of search.* Current behavior often depends on assessment of a relationship's future. The distance that an actor looks ahead is called his "depth of search." This variable specifies the number of possible future states examined before choosing an action. An actor's minimal depth of search is 1, in which case he considers only the present situation. If his depth of search is 2, he considers also the value of every possible *second* or next state which can follow the present situation. This look-ahead process is analogous to searching all the branches of a tree, a tree whose size increases exponentially with the depth of search.

For example, a simple incremental 2×2 game with a depth of search of only 3 would require the consideration of 2^6 (or 64) potential outcome sequences at every step of the game. If a more complex interaction is modeled, in which each actor has available, say, four behaviors in every state, each look-ahead of five decision steps implies a decision tree with 4^{10} (over 1,000,000) possible sequences.

This look-ahead feature is important for bridging the gap between short-range "self interest" and long-range "altruism" (Huesmann & Levinger, 1976, pp. 205–214). For instance, Huesmann and Levinger showed that the competitive behavior which occurs in a mixed-motive game such as the Prisoner's Dilemma can be transformed into stable cooperation if both actors look forward into a series of such matrices with successive increments in the average payoff.

b. *Discount.* Immediate outcomes are often considered more important than possible future outcomes. Accordingly, the RELATE model permits actors to discount the weight of future payoffs in computing the expected values of behavior choices.

c. *Selecting a behavior.* The model assumes than an actor always selects the behavior that maximizes the sum of his expected payoffs over the number of steps ahead (depth of search) that he considers.[2] Of course, his behavior may have different consequences than the actor anticipated, depending upon what the co-actor does.

These, then, are the basic features of the RELATE model: An interconnected set of interactive states is traveled by two partners according to RELATE's rules and operations. For further details, the interested reader may turn to our formal treatment of the model (Huesmann & Levinger, 1976), or can consult our description of the computer program (Huesmann, Long, & Levinger, 1975). We will now describe one application of the RELATE model before considering some critical problems for exchange theory that the model illuminates.

Simulation of a Romantic Involvement

To illustrate the functioning of the RELATE model, we describe a simulation of a romantic involvement between two imaginary individuals, John and Susan. The following simulation was carried out by John Goldin (Goldin, Levinger, & Huesmann, 1975).

Incremental exchange theory is only a general paradigm. To model romantic involvement, one must have a specific scheme which conforms to the premises of this paradigm and which details the potential states, payoffs, behaviors, and transitions that may occur in a romantic involvement.

Suggestions of Levinger and Snoek (1972) were used to specify a set of situations attainable by John and Susan. Eleven potential states of involvement were mapped. Table I shows the behavior options.

To provide data inputs for the simulation depicted in Figure 3, a scaling study was performed with the help of several informants who took the role of either John or Susan after receiving a brief personality description of each partner. Each informant estimated the value of each partner's assumed payoff from each possible outcome; later, state-to-state transitions were arrived at for every outcome.

A fuller account and interpretation of the John-and-Susan simulation is offered elsewhere (Goldin, Levinger, & Huesmann, 1975; Huesmann & Levinger, 1976). Here we consider it merely as an example of the model's operation. Whereas John and Susan's relationship quickly proceeds toward "Testing Disclosure," as Figure 3 illustrates,

---

[2] Huesmann and Levinger (1976) assume that in deeper relationships an actor tends to consider his co-actor's payoffs in addition to his own.

Table I
States and Behaviors in the Simulation of Romantic Involvement[a]

State	Behavior options (for either person)
1. Meeting	1. Initiates a friendly interaction with other
	2. Responds warmly (adopts a warm stance toward other person)
	3. Responds coolly (adopts a cool stance toward other)
2. Request	1. Asks for a date
	2. Takes a warm stance toward other; says yes if other asks for a date
	3. Seems cool toward other; says no if other asks for a date
3. Begin dating	1. Actively communicates liking for the other person
	2. Nonverbally (i.e., nonexplicitly) communicates liking for the other person
	3. Nonverbally communicates disliking for the other person
4. Disclosure	1. Makes very intimate disclosures; shows great interest in hearing other's disclosures
	2. Makes only moderately intimate disclosures
	3. Does not volunteer personal self-disclosure and expresses only polite interest in other's disclosures
	4. Expresses clear disinterest in either making or hearing disclosures
5. Romance	1. Actively tries for deepening involvement; wants to see the other more often
	2. Takes a positive stance toward other; responds warmly
	3. Accepts present involvement but does not want any deepening of romantic involvement
	4. Dislikes present involvement; expresses rejection of the other person
6. Sex	1. Initiates sexual behavior more intimate than one's own usual standard
	2. Accepts sexual behavior more intimate than usual standard, if it is proposed
	3. Restricts sexual behavior to usual standard for the situation
	4. Restricts sexual behavior to less than usual standard
7. Harmony	1. Yields completely to the other's wishes
	2. Emphasizes compromise rather than conflict
	3. Negotiates and bargains; emphasizes formal agreement
8. Future	1. Proposes plans that involve the other person in the future (e.g., 6 months from present)

(continued)

TABLE I (*continued*)

State	Behavior options (for either person)
	2. Adopts an accepting stance toward future plans (though status of future is not made explicit)
	3. Rejects future planning
9. Commitment	1. Openly declares against romantic involvement with others by either partner
	2. Expresses disinterest in other romantic prospects
	3. Expresses interest in other romantic prospects
	4. Declares that self and other should maintain interest in other romantic contacts
10. Permanence	1. Initiates "semipublic" action that implies permanency
	2. Adopts a positive stance toward actions implying permanency
	3. Rejects only actions that imply permanency without rejecting the current relationship with the other person
11. Proposal	1. Suggests marriage
	2. Accepts suggestion of marriage, if it is made
	3. Rejects marriage at this time, without implying rejection of the other person
	4. Rejects other person and, therefore, marriage to that person

^a From Huesmann and Levinger, 1976, pp. 224–225.

the partners must interact there for a while before they progress to another plateau concerning a "Plan for Future." The two partners then must resolve their ambivalences about the relationship before it can proceed any deeper; when at last they do so, the relationship moves into a state of permanence, but it stops short of a marriage commitment. Throughout the simulation, each partner's payoffs continually change; new states of interaction bring forth new payoff matrices, and new experiences cause John and Susan to change their expectations (i.e., probability estimates) about the other's future actions. If an important stressor should hit the couple, the harmony of the relationship could be damaged, and it could deteriorate or break up.

The John–Susan simulation illustrates the difficulty of such simulations. It is hard—both for the investigator and for the informant in a scaling study—to arrive at a meaningful set of interpersonal states, payoffs, transitions, and initial probability estimates. Nevertheless, this simulation shows in principle how a *longitudinal* exchange process would operate.

Our 1976 paper contains several other applications of the RELATE model. In the present paper, we turn to examine two salient issues regarding exchange models: (1) the meaning of reward in the outcome matrix, and (2) the meaning of interpersonal involvement.

THE MEANING OF "REWARD" IN DYADIC INTERACTION

Incremental exchange theory, as described thus far, has expanded the applicability of the exchange matrix for considering dyadic inter-action, but it has not resolved some basic difficulties. A fundamental problem is specifying the utility of actors' outcomes. In order to predict actors' behaviors, one must be able to measure actors' utilities; but utilities can usually be determined only after behaviors have been observed. Such measurement problems of exchange theory have been noted previously (Huston, 1974; Simpson, 1972). They were also found in our simulation of romantic involvement, where it was difficult for informants to estimate the utility of each separate possible interactive event.

Less widely noted has been the restriction placed upon conceptions of reward. In the dyadic payoff matrix, a separate reward (or cost) is attached to each intersection of two actors' *behaviors*. This conception

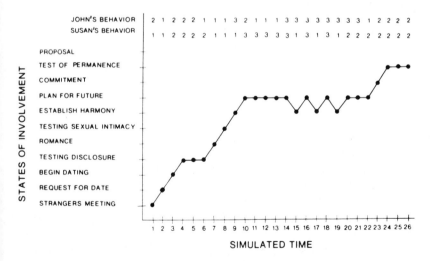

FIGURE 3. The progression of John and Susan's simulated relationship. John and Susan's behaviors are noted at the top and described in Table I. (From Huesmann & Levinger, 1976.)

of payoff, however, does not represent all the rewards that people obtain from their social relationships and we wish here to expand the meaning of reward.

Dimensions of Reward

Needs that may be fulfilled through interaction range from basic physiological needs to higher needs for self-actualization, achievement, or affiliation. Foa and Foa (1974; and Chapter 4, this volume) have recently proposed that human needs vary from the concrete to the symbolic, and from the impersonal to the highly personal.

Exchange theorists have been aware of the varied rewards that satisfy differing needs, but their focus has emphasized only behavioral outcomes. For instance, Homans (1961) has described a reward as any thing or activity someone receives which is valuable—e.g., one receives approval or one gets help. Thibaut and Kelley (1959) also emphasize behavioral outcomes; thus Simpson (1972) interprets their concept of reward as "satisfaction a person receives from performing an activity" (p. 10).

Yet, higher social rewards frequently result simply from a state of *being*, rather than of behaving; one feels rewarded merely from being competent, being accepted, worthwhile, or secure. Within the constraints of an exchange matrix, in which rows and columns represent simple behaviors or behavior sets, it is difficult to represent purely symbolic social rewards. This difficulty can be ameliorated, however, by extending the reward concept to include payoffs from a pair's current state of being. Let us, therefore, introduce a distinction between behavioral and relational rewards.

Behavioral versus Relational Rewards

Behavioral rewards refer to the immediate rewards that result directly from the behavior choices of each actor. For example, if a dating boy and girl attend a good movie together, their enjoyment from seeing the movie is a behavioral reward. Other behavioral rewards may derive from the partner's compliments, from physical contact, and so forth. These rewards can be readily represented within the exchange matrix, where each pair of behaviors leads to a discrete outcome for the actors.

Relational rewards, on the other hand, do not depend on specific behaviors, but are pegged to the actors' level of relational involvement.

Unlike behavioral rewards, which are received in discrete quanta, relational rewards are received *continuously* as long as the level of the relationship remains unchanged. In the case of the couple attending the movie, either member may receive a relational reward from being on a date, or from merely being seen in the other's company. (One may also derive relational rewards or costs from the connections one's relationship has to third parties, such as parents or peers.)

Relational rewards can be either positive or negative. For example, one might enjoy the relation of being unmarried; or one might find being unmarried so unrewarding that any marriage relationship would be acceptable. The crucial characteristic of a relational reward or cost is that it depends upon an interpersonal relation which continues over a considerable time span, and not upon any single behavioral event. (A relational reward is under the partner's "contact control"; see Jones & Gerard, 1967.) A relational reward may be activated by a specific event (e.g., being seen in public), but it derives from the state of the relationship rather than from the event.

Relational rewards cannot be represented in specific cells of outcome matrices, but they can be incorporated easily into incremental exchange theory. To do so, one associates with every level of involvement a corresponding magnitude of relational reward, which is obtained continuously as long as the actor remains there. Thus, two dating partners who attend a movie receive discrete behavioral rewards associated with particular outcomes, and they also receive a continuous reward associated with their level of involvement.

Other Dimensions of Reward

Additional distinctions are also important for classifying various aspects of reward. Incremental exchange theory, for example, distinguishes among rewards in temporal terms. Current rewards tend to be perceived differently from future potential rewards; actors may discount the value of the less immediate rewards.

Thibaut and Kelley (1959) proposed that rewards differ as to whether they derive mainly from exogenous or from endogenous determinants, whether they come from factors external to the relationship—the individual actor's own skills or actions which are transferable from one relationship to another—or whether they arise only inside the relationship itself. An associated distinction would classify rewards in regard to their *co-actor dependency;* some rewards are entirely independent of who is the co-actor, other rewards depend very much on their source. If a couple attends a movie together, one's behavioral reward from seeing a good film can be co-actor independent, but the reward from the other's physical touch is co-actor dependent. A relational reward from going steady together has many components that are co-actor dependent, but also some that are co-actor independent. This distinction is orthogonal to the behavioral versus relational distinction. Note that only co-actor independent rewards can be measured outside a pair's own interaction context and be used to predict behavior in general.

Rewards people obtain from their actions or their relationships are either *direct* or *attributional*. A direct reward consists of an immediate pleasure, as when one eats a delicious morsel, succeeds on a difficult task, or is kissed by a desirable other. Attributional rewards arise from one's own or others' interpretation of what has happened. For example, consuming a delicacy is not only pleasing in itself; it also implies that one is a gourmet. A student who receives the top grade in an exam receives immediate satisfaction from this success; he also may interpret this as confirmation that he can succeed in the future. Or, if a boy is kissed by a girl, the kiss is not only directly enjoyable; it implies that she likes him, and such acceptance is itself rewarding. Whereas direct rewards often depend on only a single interaction or event, attributional rewards may require a lengthy sequence of behaviors and outcomes. The attributional component is a large part of relational rewards; furthermore, it tends to be much more difficult to measure than the direct component.

Adaptation Levels, Comparison Levels, and Gradients

Exchange theorists have long recognized the importance of the *relative* magnitude of social rewards. For example, Thibaut and Kelley (1959) postulated the comparison level as "the standard against which the member evaluates the 'attractiveness' of the relationship" (p. 21). Subjective states such as *relative deprivation* are explained by assuming that the utility of a reward depends on its magnitude relative to the actor's comparison level—or, more generally, his adaptation level (Helson, 1964). Comparison levels vary as a function of previously experienced rewards. An earlier sequence of negative outcomes can lower one's comparison level and enhance the relative value of later positive outcomes.

Two contrasting views of this adaptation process may be suggested. A pessimistic view is that people are condemned "to live on a hedonic treadmill, to seek new levels of stimulation merely to maintain old levels of subjective pleasure" (Brickman & Campbell, 1971, p. 289).

A more optimistic alternative is that, even if permanent satisfaction is unreachable, and no matter how badly off one is, one can often be made happy with a little improvement.

To model an actor's adaptation, one must permit comparison levels to vary as a function of reward. Variations in comparison levels were not incorporated into our original formulation, but they can be introduced into the RELATE model by a program which modifies each actor's comparison level for each state on the basis of his recent payoffs. Also relevant here is the perceived slope of anticipated payoffs.

Slope of Anticipated Rewards

The emphasis of exchange theories on static behavioral rewards has obscured another process affecting the value of rewards. An actor's happiness with his current pair involvement (i.e., his current relational reward) may depend upon his perception of the *slope* of his reward function, not merely its magnitude.

For example, an employee may leave a relationship with one boss for that with another, even if the immediate salary and working conditions seem worse in the new relationship. Even if the payoff of the present job is immediately more attractive, he may prefer an increasing reward function of the alternative job to a declining or static reward function of the present job. In other words, actors may use the perceived slope of reward functions as an index of future satisfaction.

Some actors may even consider the slope of the cumulative reward function to be a reinforcer in itself. The activity of achieving or gaining is itself sometimes valued more than its associated outcome. An achievement-oriented actor may be more satisfied by low behavioral rewards that appear to increase sharply than by higher rewards with a lesser slope of gain; this permits him, perhaps, to see himself as able and self-confident.

This conception would explain the "grass is greener" phenomenon. For example, a boy may find the process of renewed "falling in love" (with a steep positive reward) more satisfying than "being in love" (with a flat slope). He may leave a reasonably satisfying relationship for one that looks as if it might become better. Actors who do not search deeply into the future may be particularly prone to believe that things will continue to get better, even in the absence of current evidence.

Exchange models need to incorporate gradient functions if they are to improve their ability to predict choices. Such functions would weight the slope of reward sequences and combine their value with the magnitude of current rewards.

THE MEANING OF INVOLVEMENT

The classification of rewards into relational or behavioral, immediate or future, co-actor dependent or independent, or into their direct
and attributional components does not resolve how to determine
payoffs; nor does a consideration of the slope of the reward function.
The recognition of these many aspects of reward does suggest that a
sequence of simple payoff matrices will not alone adequately model
different levels of pair involvement. It seems necessary to specify
relational and behavioral rewards separately, and to model gradient
effects. To do that appropriately, though, we must eliminate the
model's earlier one-to-one correspondence between level of pair involvement and state of interaction.

In our previous version of the RELATE model, every state of
interaction was represented by a single payoff matrix, which implied
a different level of mutual involvement. Each interaction was followed
by a transition to a state which was either more, less, or equally
involving (e.g., Table I, Figure 3). Depth of involvement was defined
by a state's expected reward magnitude.

For example, the state of Romance (Figure 3) had a higher expected
reward than Testing Disclosure, and thus was defined as more involving. Thus, payoff matrix and level of involvement were interwoven.

The earlier RELATE model has difficulty in accounting for longitudinal stepwise changes in relational rewards, and it does not recognize
the multiplicity of alternative interactions that can occur at the same
level of involvement. A more realistic version of the model must
account for the following sorts of complexity in the dating process:

> Couples . . . simultaneously [can become] intimate in several different
> sectors through several different channels, . . . intimacy often develops
> along these different routes in parallel, so that increasing self-disclosure
> tends to be related to increasing love, and both are related to increasing
> sexual intimacy. But this parallelism does not always hold. Sometimes a
> move toward intimacy in one channel is immediately offset by a move
> backward in another. . . . To capture these complexities, an adequate model
> of the development of intimacy will have to include more than one
> dimension. (Rubin, 1974, p. 10)

Toward a Revised Model

To help account for such complexities, we propose to separate *state*
of interaction from *level* of involvement. In our new RELATE model,
each level of involvement would contain many different potential states
of interaction. Thus, one can visualize the development of a relation-

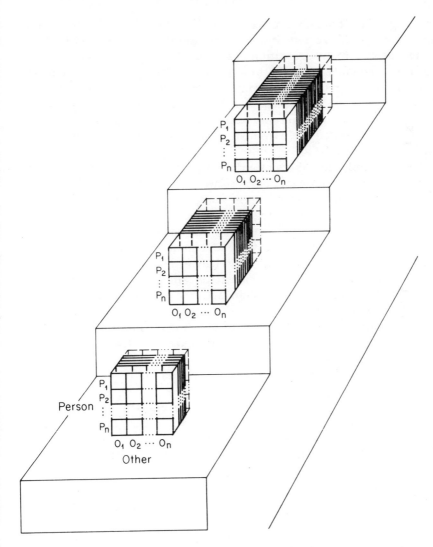

FIGURE 4. Varying distributions of interaction states and different levels of involvement in the revised RELATE model.

ship as shown in Figure 4, where levels of involvement are steps on which a variety of potential situations may be encountered. To progress from one level to the next, some minimal set of satisfactory outcomes must be obtained in the constituent situations of the first level.

In this revised model, each involvement level, or step, in Figure 4 is associated with some degree of relational reward. Within each level, specific situations are represented by payoff matrices of behavioral rewards. Movement between situations within a level is determined as before by transition matrices. Movement between levels, however, depends upon the total pattern of outcomes that occur in a level. A list of required outcomes, behaviors, or rewards must be defined for movement to each other level. When the requisite outcomes have occurred, movement will occur. A pair may stay within any one level—moving indefinitely from situation to situation—or it may move rapidly across levels.

For example, members of a dating couple may find themselves at a level which provides moderate relational rewards for both. Here, a variety of potential interactions is available—e.g., mutual disclosure, dancing together, or some degree of sexual interplay. Each such state has a payoff matrix which specifies the behavioral reward for each possible outcome. Within any involvement level, a couple's initial interaction depends somewhat on chance. Having searched into the future, and having balanced current payoffs against potential future payoffs, the actors engage in an activity which yields each some immediate behavioral payoffs. If the consequent outcome completes the appropriate prerequisite, a corresponding attributional reward will occur. If the outcome completes the prerequisites for movement to a new level, there will be such a movement to either a deeper or a shallower level. Otherwise, the transition will be to another situation within the same level.

Within this revised model, a separate gradient and adaptation function would be specified for each actor. The gradient function would determine to what extent the actor is influenced by the perceived slope of the reward function, and the adaptation function would change the value of potential rewards, depending on the receipt of recent rewards.

RECONSIDERING THE SIMULATION OF INTERPERSONAL INVOLVEMENT

In order to illustrate such revisions of the RELATE model, let us see how one might construct a new simulation of a romantic involvement. (Here we will merely indicate how a simulation would be conceived; it has not actually been attempted.) In contrast to the John–Susan simulation illustrated in Table I, let us consider two other imaginary individuals: Keith and Terry. Instead of John and Susan's eleven possible states, which represented eleven different levels of emotional involvement, we here postulate the existence of fewer involvement levels, within each of which can occur a variety of interactive situations.

Differing Levels of Involvement

Levinger and Snoek (1972) suggested that the relation between any two persons may vary in its level of contact. To begin with, there is no contact at all, no acquaintance whatsoever. The level of Unilateral Awareness refers to one individual merely having knowledge of the other, without necessarily any interaction. The level of Surface Contact refers to minimal interaction between two persons who know each other superficially. At a deeper level, two partners may build Mutuality, where they will have sizable behavioral interdependence or affective involvement. Between Surface Contact and Mutuality, then, lies a continuum of increasing involvement.

Although the meaning of progressive, interpersonal involvement differs widely across different cultures or subcultures, we here label some representative levels on the continuum between surface and depth. We may consider (see Figure 5) a plausible network of a pair's progression from superficial acquaintance to either close friendship or exclusive mateship. The various relational levels would include:[3]

A. *Surface Contact.* At this level, two strangers meet for the first time. Available behaviors consist of the usual platitudes exchanged in superficial encounters. For example, two persons may exchange polite conversation, give each other simple information, or they may work together on a joint task. Strangers may also ask questions about public matters, as when they ask the time or how to find a place.

B. *Casual Acquaintance.* A repeated encounter with another leads to casual acquaintance. Such acquaintance allows one to assess the other's desirability as a role partner. The behaviors here are not necessarily different from those at Level A, but one expects a larger variety and more predictable responses.

Beyond casual acquaintance lie two distinct paths for heterosexual attachments. One path (C) leads toward gradually increasing nonexclusive friendship; the other (D) leads toward romantic absorption and exclusiveness. We have, then, diverging possibilities; at each point

---

[3] Stambul (1975), in a doctoral dissertation that we did not see until after writing this paper, obtained empirical evidence which confirms an analogous set of "stages of courtship" from casual dating, to serious dating, to engagement, to marriage. Those four stages were the most frequently noted ones among the couples in Stambul's sample, although other labels and other sorts of progression also occurred.

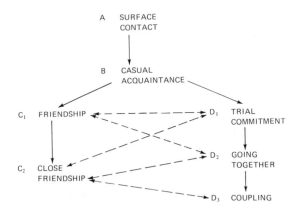

FIGURE 5. Paths of possible transition in a heterosexual relationship. Solid paths are more normative than broken paths; all paths refer to changes in levels of pair involvement.

there is some possibility of crossover between the two main categories of attachment.

C_1. *Friendship*. The development of reciprocated liking and respect leads toward friendship. Participants tend to be drawn into a friendship gradually, not even discovering its progression until after the relationship has developed. Although romantic involvement frequently entails a certain exclusiveness that requires decisions or step-by-step discrimination, the obligations of friendship are generally nonexclusive.

C_2. *Close Friendship*. Close friendship has some of the qualities of romantic coupling, but it also differs in important respects (Douvan, 1977; Rossi, 1974). Since close friendship usually makes less demands on the partner than mateship, it thereby may free the other to be entirely open. Furthermore, friendship is usually devoid of explicit sexuality, and thus allows friends to concentrate on other aspects of their emotional and instrumental interaction. Its emphasis on common concerns outside the relationship usually makes a close friendship extremely rewarding. Heterosexual pairs, however, may find it difficult to achieve extremely close friendship in which sexuality is absent.

Consider now the path toward romantic involvement. This path may lead through Trial Commitment to Going Together to Coupling.

D_1. *Trial Commitment*. In a romantic twosome, a first date is a limited commitment for a limited time. Each partner wants both to enjoy the other's company and to ascertain the other's suitability for a more extended involvement. Participants engage in more interdependent activities than during mere acquaintance, as well as more enjoyable and revealing ones. A first date may include physical closeness, the disclosure of fairly intimate information, and other actions that hold personal meaning.

D_2. *Going Together.* At some point a relationship becomes routinized; coming together and departing become part of an interpersonal cycle of continuing contact. Behaviors become part of repeated routines. They include many of the interactions possible above, but Going Together implies greater interdependency and mutual investment. Communication is frequent and revealing. Payoffs from desirable outcomes are greater and less uncertain.

D_3. *Coupling.* At its fantasied extreme, romantic coupling implies the disappearance of interpersonal boundaries, and the belief that self and partner share everything. A more tenable posture includes self–other differentiation in which two partners are deeply sensitive to each other, but expect alternation between distance and closeness, rather than a merging of their personalities (Karpel, 1976).

Toward a Revised Simulation of a Heterosexual Relationship

To incorporate the ideas suggested in Figures 4 and 5, we constructed a new set of interactive states.

Table II presents a set of interactional situations which is different from those in Table I. Let us examine the differences between the eleven states created for John and Susan, and the nineteen potential situations made available to Keith and Terry.

Varying Relational Rewards

First note that each level of relational involvement is here accorded its own relational reward. These rewards vary from zero (for Surface Contact and for Casual Acquaintance) to progressively greater for deeper levels of pair involvement. It is not necessary to assume that relational rewards are the same for all pairs of acquaintances or friends, or even that Keith's rewards must all equal Terry's. The relational rewards listed here are merely suggestive of this rarely considered property of dyadic payoffs.

Situations Appropriate at Each Level

Second, the interpersonal states and behavior options proposed for the Keith–Terry simulation are not unique to each single level of involvement, as they were for John and Susan. Most states may recur

TABLE II
Behaviors Available for Keith–Terry Simulation

Level (relational reward) States that are fairly likely	Behavior options for either person
A. Surface Contact (RR = 0)	
1. Meeting in corridor	1. Ignores other 2. Looks at other noncommittally 3. Smiles warmly
2. Seat neighbors	1. Ignores other 2. Becomes aware of other 3. Attempts to converse

3. Co-visitors at same
     semipublic affair (dance,
     party)
	1. Remains unaware of other
	2. Shows nonverbal interest
	3. Shows clear interest in other
	4. Responds warmly

4. Co-workers on a larger project	1. Works quite independently and apart 2. Indicates ability to assist 3. Actually helps other (or asks for help)

B.   Casual Acquaintance (RR = 0)
   1. Meeting in public place
   2. Seat neighbors
   3. Covisitors
   4. Co-workers
	Same behavior options as in States 1–4
	above: probabilities of positive
	behaviors have increased

5. Discussion of common
     experience or attitude
	1. Asserts opinion which is different
	   from other's
	2. Finds some overlap with other's
	   ideas
	3. Finds close correspondence between
	   own and other's ideas
	4. Stimulates fresh idea in other (or is
	   stimulated by other)

6. Disclosure of feeling	1. Ignores other's expression 2. Reacts noncommittally 3. Reacts acceptantly 4. Responds warmly and fully
7. Request to work with other	1. Refuses request 2. Evades an immediate reply 3. Implies acceptance 4. Shows enthusiasm
8. Request for a date or other trial	1. Acts coolly or negatively 2. Acts positively, but passively 3. Acts warmly and enthusiastically

Table II (*continued*)

Level (relational reward) States that are fairly likely	Behavior options for either person
9. Pair goes out together	1. Communicates distance (or dislike) 2. Communicates moderate liking 3. Communicates strong liking
10. Testing disclosure	1. Expresses clear disinterest in own or other's personal disclosures 2. Expresses interest in other's disclosures, but fails to reveal much for self 3. Makes moderately intimate disclosures 4. Makes very intimate disclosures
C_1. Friendship (RR = moderate) States 1–10	
11. Joint discussion	1. Talks coolly and factually 2. Talks warmly 3. Is enthusiastic and supportive
12. Joint recreation	1. Engages in game rather offhandedly 2. Emphasizes reciprocity 3. Helps partner improve game
C_2. Close Friendship (RR = high) States 1–12	Close Friendship may not contain any new interactive states, but its positive options are more probable, and its negative options are less probable than in lesser friendship
D_1. Trial Commitment (RR = moderate) States 1–12	
13. Considering romance	1. Shows disinterest in current trial relationship 2. Accepts present level of relationship, but shows reluctance to move further 3. Accepts present relationship 4. Shows receptivity to further involvement 5. Presses for deeper romantic involvement
14. Test of sexual intimacy	1. Shows disinterest in sexual contact (avoids touch, etc.) 2. Accepts normative sexual interchange 3. Shows receptiveness to sexual behavior beyond the usual standard 4. Initiates more intimate sexual behavior
D_2. Going Together (RR = high) States 1–14	

(*continued*)

TABLE II (continued)

Level (relational reward) States that are fairly likely	Behavior options for either person
15. Establishment of harmony	1. Retains personal independence without yielding to pair goals 2. Attempts to bridge between personal and pair goals by compromise 3. Gives more weight to pair's rather than to personal goals
16. Planning pair's future	1. Rejects planning for the future 2. Evades definite discussions about future 3. Is receptive, but uninitiating 4. Proposes future plans of greater pairing
17. Commitment to continuation	1. Declares that self and other remain free to maintain alternative relationships 2. Shows occasional interest in alternative relationships 3. Never shows alternative interests 4. Overtly declares disinterest in other partners 5. Supports a mutual commitment to the pair and against competing relationships
C₃. Coupling (RR = very high) States 1–15	
18. Test of permanence	1. Rejects permanence 2. Evades permanent commitment, but not conclusively so 3. Accepts thoughts of permanence 4. Warmly encourages commitment toward permanence
19. Test of unity	1. Emphasizes continued autonomy 2. Permits considerable interdependence 3. Encourages the full merging of possessions, ideas, or identities

repeatedly at different levels, although some interactive situations are, of course, inappropriate for the more superficial relationships.

Levels of involvement do differ in the probabilities of particular behaviors. As a relationship deepens, positively associative behaviors tend to become increasingly expected; dissociative behaviors become less expected. Thus, payoffs become increasingly predictable; established partners usually know how to coordinate their behaviors effectively.

Friendship versus Romantic Coupling

Third, the levels and states proposed in Table II imply a difference between the meaning of friendship and coupling. Table II does not suggest the criteria by which Keith or Terry decide whether or not their relationship becomes romantic, nor the prerequisites for moving the relationship from one involvement level to another. These specifications are beyond the scope of this paper, but do bear mentioning. For example, most persons would require that their partner engage in intimate self-disclosure before deciding to "go together," but it is hard to specify how much disclosure or precisely what sort. Nor is it possible to consider here how the partners' agreement or disagreement about interactive goals affects the nature of their relationship.

CONCLUSIONS

This paper has tried to extend our incremental exchange paradigm for understanding the development of close relationships. A basic premise is that persons act to maximize rewards, and that increasing interpersonal involvement offers the possibility of increasing reward. Partners who discover high payoff correspondence are likely to move forward to deeper involvement.

Essential to this formulation is the concept of reward in social interaction. This paper has proposed a major distinction between two sorts of reward—"behavioral rewards," associated with the outcomes of joint behaviors, and "relational rewards," associated with varying levels of involvement. Also, it was suggested that the perceived slope of an actor's reward function is sometimes important. This paper has further distinguished between a pair's momentary state of interaction and its current level of involvement. Differences between our present and our previous conception of the incremental exchange process are illustrated by comparing the earlier John-and-Susan simulation with a proposed Keith-and-Terry interaction structure.

Implications for Exchange Theory

Our incremental exchange paradigm is an attempt to move beyond certain limitations of earlier exchange theories. In trying to build our formal model, though, we notice that some of these limitations may be inescapable. Exchange theory functions well as an analogy or metaphor; it functions poorly as a precision tool. The present exercise has been no exception.

We reexamined the meaning of two central concepts—social reward and interpersonal involvement. Reward is the centerpiece of any hedonistic theory, but continued exploration of the concept shows that it is a many-splendored thing. It is unlikely that all its facets will be captured within a single formal theory.

Another sort of limitation has not been acknowledged so far. In our attempt at precision we have had to restrict our perspective to the interaction of only two social actors. Our focus has been limited to the pair in a rather neutral context; relations to third parties or to the wider social network have been relegated to their resultant effects on the actors' comparison levels. Although this limited focus is applicable to many purposes, the consequences of this restrictiveness have been considered recently in Ekeh's (1974) comparison of the *individualistic* and the *collectivistic* traditions in social exchange theory. The former orientation considers exchange in terms of reciprocities entirely within the dyad. In contrast, a collectivistic conception sees pair interaction as part of a larger picture of generalized exchange. It is not possible here to link the dyadic focus to a wider societal perspective, but this connection needs to be treated in a more complete social exchange theory.

ACKNOWLEDGMENTS

We have received helpful suggestions regarding an earlier draft from Ted Huston, Zick Rubin, and Alice Eagly.

Critical Analysis

INTRODUCTION

As the papers in this volume have shown, the social exchange approach provides an integrative framework for studying a broad array of social phenomena, such as leadership, interpersonal attraction, justice in interpersonal relations, indebtedness, political behavior, and interorganizational relations. Since the exchange approach has been used as a conceptual tool for studying a diverse number of problems in laboratory and field settings, it is not surprising that the theory has been subjected to critical scrutiny by scientists in a number of disciplines. In the years following publication of Homan's (1961) and Thibaut and Kelley's (1959) initial works, an increasing number of critics have focused their attention on evaluating the adequacy of the exchange approach as well as the individual theories that comprise this approach. Among the more detailed examinations are those by Chadwick-Jones (1976), Ekeh (1974), Emerson (1976), and Heath (1976). Controversies that have emerged from these and previous analyses center around the definition and measurement of key terms, the logical adequacy of the approach, and the issue of psychological reductionism.

DEFINITION AND MEASUREMENT OF KEY TERMS

Exchange theorists have been criticized for defining their terms in an often vague, imprecise, and tautological fashion (Abrahamsson, 1970; Davis, 1962; Deutsch, 1964; Deutsch & Krauss, 1965; Mulkay, 1971; Shaw & Costanzo, 1970). Abrahamsson, and Deutsch and Krauss, argue that such key concepts as *rewards*, *costs*, and *outcomes* are tautologically defined. Homans, in particular, has been criticized for his circular definition of the term *value*, defining it as that which is valued (Deutsch, 1964). Shaw and Costanzo (1970) comment:

> In order that Homans' well-stated and concise hypotheses be subject to empirical test, the terms and concepts upon which these hypotheses are

based need to be more precisely defined and linked to experimental operations. Removing the vagueness and indefiniteness from Homans' terms would undoubtedly decrease their conceptual generalizability, but it would at the same time increase their functional utility as experimental variables. (p. 81)

In his defense, Homans (1964) argues that tautologies serve a useful function in science in that they facilitate the integration and accumulation of empirical knowledge. He states:

> The classic example is that of force in mechanics as it appears in the equation: $f = ma$. In the interpretation of this equation, force is not defined independently of mass (m) and acceleration (a). Yet, force plays a useful part in the theory of mechanics, if only because a number of different force-functions, such as that of gravitation, may be substituted for f, and the deductive systems that contain these new equations can explain a wide variety of empirical propositions. (pp. 953–954)

Liska (1969) further articulates the constructive role of tautologies in science. By distinguishing between two types of tautology, empirical-contentual and theoretical-relational, Liska notes that the latter form is "basic to some of the most successful theoretical systems in physics and psychology" (p. 445). When the constructive functions of tautologies are made salient, the criticism that exchange theory contains an abundance of tautological definitions loses its edge (Chadwick-Jones, 1976).

Related to the problem of definition is the problem of measurement. Exchange theorists have been accused of not clearly specifying how rewards and costs are reducible to a single psychological scale (Chadwick-Jones, 1976; Deutsch, 1964). Although Thibaut and Kelley (1959) acknowledge this limitation, noting that "such a scaling operation would be a very ambitious enterprise and would present a number of technical difficulties," they defend their position by stating that their interest is in the "theoretical consequences of such an operation . . . rather than in its technical properties or even its feasibility" (p. 13). In contrast, Homans's (1964) response appears to miss the point:

> What my theory does imply—and all that it implies—is that a man faced with the possibility of emitting two alternative activities leading to two alternative rewards is apt to emit the activity that will bring him the reward of higher value . . . and it does not in the least require the assumption that a man must evaluate all his rewards consistently or on a single dimension. (pp. 221–222)

As Chadwick-Jones (1976) concludes, "this is a problem which is really left unresolved" (p. 47).

LOGICAL ADEQUACY OF EXCHANGE THEORY

Several critics have called attention to logical deficiencies in the exchange approach. Blau and Thibaut and Kelley have generally been immune to such challenges, since their approach is "pretheoretical," that is, they claim only to be working toward a possible theory. Homans, on the other hand, presents a more inviting target, since his claim—a deductive theory complete with a set of interrelated propositions and derivative corollaries—is less modest. Shortly after the appearance of *Social Behavior: Its Elementary Forms*, Davis (1962) noted the existence of *"ad hoc* assumptions, [and] rather spectacular leaps to conclusion" (p. 456). Several years later, Abrahamsson (1970) commented on the theory's "absence of inductive and deductive clarity" (p. 284). The most detailed critique of the logical adequacy of Homans's theory was made by Maris (1970), who, after examining Homans's propositions by applying rules of elementary logic, concluded that "major premises and conclusions are presented without an indication as to how the two are related. The book abounds in suppressed premises and incomplete arguments (which is not to say they cannot be supplied)" (p. 1075). Maris, in turn, was taken to task by Turner (1971), Gray (1971), and Price (1971), for several errors in his attempt to apply rules of formal logic to Homans's theory. They note that Homans's propositions are not translated adequately by Maris's symbolic statements, nor is Maris clear about which set of logical rules he is applying. Moreover, they contend that his use of temporal conditions to escape logical inconsistencies only serves to confuse the issue. Chadwick-Jones (1976) points out that though Maris is correct in his claim that Homans has not *formally* spelled out all the deductive steps, upon closer examination the necessary corollaries can be found in Homans's exposition.

PSYCHOLOGICAL REDUCTIONISM

A continuing controversy involving supporters as well as critics of exchange theory concerns the extent to which social interaction can be explained solely by principles derived from individual psychology. The two leading protagonists in this debate are Homans and Blau. Homans (1970) adheres to a philosophy of "methological individualism" which holds that "sociological propositions, propositions about the characteristics of social groups or aggregates, can in principle be derived from, reduced to, propositions about the behavior of individuals" (p. 325). Homans's attempt to derive a theory of social behavior based on pyschological and economic principles has drawn criticism from several quarters. Some, like Boulding (1962a) and Deutsch (1964), criticize Homans for borrowing insufficiently and unwisely from these disciplines. As Deutsch phrased it: ·

> Surely, Homans is too sophisticated to have thrown away the methodology and findings of Skinner to be left only with the odd notion that the behavior of laboratory-reared, isolated, semistarved, nonverbal pigeons in a drastically impoverished environment is an adequate model for the understanding of man's social behavior. (p. 165)

Others, like Blau (1964, 1970) and Emerson (1970) question the wisdom of the whole enterprise of trying to explain social interaction only in terms of psychological principles. Although Blau (1964) agrees that social exchange is rooted in "primitive psychological processes" (p. 4), he contends that as the number of interacting individuals increases, emergent properties appear (e.g., status or structural factors) which could not be explained or predicted from psychological principles. It is the familiar argument of the whole being more than the sum of the parts. In Blau's (1970) words:

> A basic assumption I make is that the behavior of organized aggregates follows its own principles, and the discovery of these explanatory principles does not require detailed knowledge of the principles that govern the behavior of sub-units. (p. 338)

The issues involved in this controversy are complex, and the positions deeply rooted. Neither side shows any sign of wavering, and the debate over the appropriate level of analysis is likely to continue for some time. A more complete treatment of the issues can be found in Chadwick-Jones (1976, pp. 360–390), who also provides a fitting conclusion to the present discussion:

> At its utmost, Homans' argument that social behavior is ultimately explained by psychological propositions is a declaration of faith, at a moment when, "in the social sciences a kind of sketchy logic is as much as we can ask and more than we usually get" (Homans, 1970, p. 314). (1976, p. 386)

FURTHER INQUIRY

In addition to the three controversies just cited, several book-length treatises present detailed discussion of other issues. These volumes provide constructive appraisals of the exchange approach, and suggest new directions for further research. One of the most comprehensive of these critical examinations is Anthony Heath's *Ra-*

tional Choice and Social Exchange: A Critique of Exchange Theory. The
volume contains many incisive observations, too numerous to review
in these pages. Important for our purposes is his argument that the
various theories of social exchange differ in a number of fundamental
ways, particularly in terms of their differential reliance on a rational-
choice model favored by economists, and in terms of the extent to
which they utilize a model of risky, as opposed to riskless, choice.
With regard to the latter, he notes that, excepting Homans (1967, 1974),
exchange theorists tend to employ a model of riskless choice. Whereas
the riskless-choice model assumes that an individual ranks his choices
in terms of subjective value and then chooses the highest, the model
of risky choice assumes that individuals attempt to maximize *expected
utility*, which is a function of the expected value of an outcome
weighted by the probability of its occurrence. In a subsequent chapter,
Heath succinctly differentiates between the rational choice versions of
Thibaut and Kelley and that of Homans, noting that the model of
human functioning utilized by Thibaut and Kelley assumes that individuals are forward-looking maximizers. In contrast, the model employed by Homans "is not a forward-looking maximizer endowed with
sophisticated reasoning powers but a practical creature who learns
from experience, avoiding what has proved painful in the past and
seeking out what has proved rewarding" (p. 171). In summing up the
positions of Homans and Thibaut and Kelley, Heath leaves no doubt
about his preference for the Thibaut and Kelley model.

Another significant critical analysis of social exchange theory is
provided by Peter Ekeh in *Social Exchange Theory: The Two Traditions.*
His central thesis is that two distinct traditions in sociology underlie
two separate types of social exchange theory: the French "collectivistic
orientation" which shaped the thinking of Lévi-Strauss (1949), and the
British "individualistic orientation" characterized by the work of
Homans and Blau. Ekeh contends that "the two traditions exist in non-
marriagable terms—only joined by the virulence of the polemics
against each other's tradition of thought" (p. 5). And it is this polemic
between the two orientations that has contributed to the development
of exchange theory. He contends further that the individualistic orientation as represented by the work of Homans attempts unsuccessfully
to reconcile the incompatible strands of Skinnerian operant conditioning and economic behavior. Ekeh views the basic incompatibility as
existing between the Skinnerian emphasis on maximizing benefits in
the *here and now,* and the economist's emphasis on maximizing *future*
benefits, which often involves the present toleration of costs and pains.

Ekeh's most telling remarks are contained in his criticism of the
individualistic orientations of Blau and Homans, whom he scores for

their reliance on a *restricted* social exchange model, as opposed to the collectivistic usage of a *generalized* exchange model. Ekeh's comparisons between the two types of exchange, and his delineation of the various forms of generalized social exchange, represent a distinct contribution to the exchange literature. Research on "exchange networks," discussed by Emerson (1976), exemplifies one direction such research might take. We agree with Heath (1976), however, that the claim for the superiority of the generalized exchange model in promoting group solidarity, though intuitively reasonable, is in need of further empirical demonstration (see Heath, 1976, p. 166).

The most ambitious attempt to evaluate the status of exchange theory can be found in John Chadwick-Jones's (1976) *Social Exchange Theory: Its Structure and Influence in Social Psychology.* In this truly monumental work, Chadwick-Jones reviews the theoretical and empirical status of the exchange approaches of Homans, Thibaut and Kelley, and Blau. The large body of empirical literature reviewed by Chadwick-Jones demonstrates that, despite the controversies surrounding exchange theory, many social scientists have found it to be an extremely useful conceptual framework for studying social interaction. In reviewing the individual approaches, Chadwick-Jones is least positive in his evaluation of the Thibaut and Kelley approach, noting that, by relying almost exclusively on the payoff matrix, they may be placing "too severe a restriction on the methods that can be used to test their model" (p. 65). He points out, however, that, despite these restrictions on the application of the model, it has proved useful in the study of dyadic negotiation, bargaining, cooperation, power, and social comparison.

PRESENT DEBATE

The four papers in this final section further extend the spirit of critical inquiry concerning the present and future development of exchange theory. The first paper, by Harumi Befu, an anthropologist, calls attention to the need for an interdisciplinary perspective toward social exchange. He contends that anthropologists and social psychologists take divergent perspectives in their study of social exchange processes, and that both perspectives are necessary for a comprehensive analysis of exchange behavior. Using as analytic tools the concepts of (1) culture-specific rules of exchange, (2) cultural frames of reference, and (3) individual strategies of exchange, the paper illustrates how anthropologists tend to focus on the first two concepts, whereas social psychologists have been interested primarily in individual strategies of exchange. Labeling the approach taken by anthropologists as the "structural" approach and the one taken by psychologists as the "motivational" approach, Befu notes that each takes for granted what the other regards as the central problem. Clearly, the efforts of both disciplines to understand social exchange behavior would be enriched if each took into account the perspective of the other. By considering the motivational approach, anthropologists might better account for differential rates of compliance with norms in a given culture. Likewise, psychologists who study individual strategies of social exchange could profit from a better recognition of the cultural context in which their subjects behave.

The second paper in this section represents a collaborative effort by an economist and an anthropologist. Frederick Pryor and Nelson Graburn present data which challenge anthropologists' assumptions that exhange in primitive or peasant societies is primarily reciprocal. Their data are based on extensive observation of exchanges between household members and members of other households in the Eskimo village of Sugluk, located in northern Canada. Data on three different kinds of exchange transactions were collected: (1) material goods exchanged, (2) services exchanged, and (3) length of visit. A regression analysis conducted on the data revealed a startling discrepancy between verbalizations about balanced exchange and the actual behavior of the villagers. Whereas villagers expressed the belief that exchange accounts were balanced among those equal in prestige, their data revealed that these accounts were indeed *not* balanced. This report questions the central assumption of reciprocity in exchange theory, and indicates that far more critical attention must be applied to arguments such as those of Gouldner (1973) and Boulding (1973), who contend that it is often functional for societies to make provisions for imbalanced exchanges. As they suggest, societies may create various mechanisms, such as normative sanctioning of one-way giving (e.g., Berkowitz's "norm of social responsibility" and Gouldner's "norm of beneficence"). In the present case, the myth that exchange accounts are roughly balanced between social equals allows less careful monitoring of these accounts, thereby permitting unbalanced accounts to be maintained without rancor. This is a highly provocative idea, since it calls attention to the paradoxical way in which ideology may be maintained in the face of contradictory behavior patterns.

The issue of the generalizability of findings across species is the primary subject of Barry Schwartz's contribution to this section. Schwartz reviews a number of recent empirical and theoretical developments in the field of operant conditioning which question the legitimacy of generalizing from the behavior of pigeons in the operant conditioning chamber to other organisms in other environments. Schwartz argues that the tautological definitions upon which operant conditioning rests can be circumvented empirically. Citing Meehl (1950), Schwartz contends that the demonstration of transsituational generality of the principles of conditioning "will save the system from tautologous vacuity." He then shows that recent findings cast doubt on the transituationality of operant conditioning research. Specifically, he points out that research in the areas of instinctive drift, taste-aversion learning, and autoshaping show that generality of conditioning principles is constrained by species-specific behavior and by features unique to the Skinner Box. The paper is particularly important in that it serves as a warning to investigators who uncritically apply the principles and findings of operant behavior to the domain of human social exchange.

In the final contribution to this section, Kenneth Gergen evaluates social exchange theory in terms of its transhistorical potential. His main line of contention as stated elsewhere (Gergen, 1973) is that because of shifts in historical circumstance and because of "enlightenment effects" produced in the population to whom social theories are supposed to apply, social theories are historically contingent. In one sense, Gergen's position is similar to that advanced by Schwartz in his contribution. Whereas Schwartz argues for the limited generalizability of principles and findings from operant behavior because of features unique to a particular species (i.e., the pigeon) and the circumstances under which the learning takes place (i.e., the Skinner Box), Gergen contends that the transhistorical generalizability of social exchange theory is likewise constrained by "the tide of changing events." Concluding that exchange theory (as well as other social theories) is of limited predictive value, he advances six additional criteria for evaluating the worth of a theory. Relative to other behavioral theories, social exchange theory fares very high on these criteria. In particular, he views social exchange theory "as one of the most significant theories of the era" in terms of its capacity to integrate apparently disconnected branches of science. Gergen's argument is well illustrated by the various papers presented in this volume.

In conclusion, the four papers in this section represent a sober and penetrating assessment of the virtues as well as the deficiencies of contemporary social exchange theory. Such criticism we believe to be particularly important in firing continued debate. Any theoretical orientation of the magnitude and intellectual impact of exchange theory requires such debate. In this way one remains continuously cognizant of the inherent descrepancy between theory and experience, and the search for more adequate conceptualization is maintained.

Structural and Motivational Approaches to Social Exchange

Harumi Befu

Introduction

In our daily life, we constantly encounter situations where we are giving favor and assistance in return for something else received in the past, or in anticipation of receiving something else in the future. This may be as simple as a smile in exchange for a smile, or morning's greetings for morning's greetings, or it may be a dinner invitation for a favor done. The notion of exchange, or reciprocity (see below for a conceptual distinction between these two terms), is so pervasive in our everyday life that we generally assume its operation without stopping to think about it. As we assume reciprocal behavior in our own daily life, in ethnographic reports of other peoples, too, anthropologists generally accept the same assumption. When they describe, for example, payment of cattle for a bride in East Africa, offering a gift in India to earn spiritual merit, exchanging favors between compadres in Middle America, giving a ceremonial necklace in return for an arm shell in the Trobriand kula ring, and potlatching each other by Kwakiutl chiefs, ethnographers are assuming the operation of some reciprocal principle. It is, in fact, probably safe to assume that in every society some form of reciprocal principle is operating, and that for every individual some of his behavior is governed by some such principle. Becker's designation of man as *Homo reciprocus* (1956) is quite apt, and

Harumi Befu • Department of Anthropology, Stanford University, Stanford, California 94305. The research on which the present paper is based was supported by a grant from the National Science Foundation (GS–2370).

197

points to the presumption that reciprocity in man is as old as human history.

Whereas for ages men have been reciprocating with one another, and for generations ethnographers have assumed the operation of social exchange and used the notion without analyzing or defining it carefully, recognition of the theoretical importance of reciprocity, or exchange, is a relatively recent phenomenon. Mauss's essay on the gift, probably the first really significant theoretical contribution in this field and now ranked among the classics in anthropology, did not appear until 1925, and its English translation until some 30 years later (Mauss, 1925; 1954). And Mauss's 1925 essay was not followed by another work of importance until 1949, when Lévi-Strauss published his monumental *Les Structures Elémentaires de la Parenté*. These two remained isolated works in the field of social exchange until around 1960—save perhaps Malinowski's less theoretical treatment of the subject (1922). Since around 1960, however, there has been an almost sudden upsurge in the interest in social exchange.

This recent upsurge is in part a result of the realization that, in Selby's words (1970) "We have mined out traditional constructs in social anthropology about as thoroughly as we profitably can, and . . . we must make an effort to reconceptualize the central subject matter of our discipline" (p. 45). For accuracy's sake, however, it should be added immediately that Selby does not discuss exchange theory as one such "effort" in the paper cited here. Whitten and Whitten (1972) also see "a shifting emphasis in anthropology from concern with social or cultural rules to an interest in adaptive strategies of human aggregates" (p. 247) in the past 20 years, and, moreover, they view exchange research as one of the fields representing this shifting emphasis.

The theoretical significance of social exchange as a conceptual field is summarized succinctly in the following quotation from Bennett's recent essay (1970):

> The social context of adjustive behavior is currently conceptualized by most anthropologists as *social exchange*. This concept focuses on transactions of human beings in which the actors attempted to realize their goals, receive their payoffs, and balance gain and loss. The concept provides for a point of union, as it were, of the dimensions of resources, power, status, manipulatory behavior, goal-directed behavior, and affect. The exchange situation also provides a focused frame for the observation of innovation and creative response. Exchange contexts are endlessly varied, and include economic phenomena, services, symbols, and prestige. They can be spontaneous or highly stylized or ritualized. They provide a means for simultaneously handling both cultural-level phenomena (i.e., relatively stable precedents and sanctioned responses), and individual innovative and manipulative responses to culture. (p. 240).

In the perspective of the sociology of knowledge, it is interesting to note that the anthropologist's realization of the importance of exchange has developed largely independently of the psychologist's interest in the topic. This is evident, for example, when one peruses the literature on social exchange in the two disciplines. One notes the virtual absence of reference by anthropologists to psychological contributions, and a similar inattention by psychologists to anthropological works in this area. Historians of science will long ponder over the reasons for this mutual disregard, when means of communication between them are readily available through publications, correspondence, and direct contact.

This phenomenon is all the more curious when one realizes that scholars of both disciplines are not only interested in the same topic, but also their approaches share at least some of the fundamental assumptions about exchange process. However, a close examination will reveal that, beyond sharing certain basic assumptions, interests of anthropologists and those of psychologists diverge, reflecting differences in the long-standing interests of the respective disciplines. In this paper, I wish first to examine the assumptions about social exchange made by anthropologists and psychologists alike. Then, in preparation for discussing divergent orientations of the two disciplines, I wish to develop the concepts of *exchange rule, exchange strategy,* and *cultural frame of reference.* Next, using these concepts, I wish to distinguish between what I will call the "structural" approach, primarily followed by anthropologists, and the "motivational" approach, largely pursued by psychologists, illustrating the two approaches by comparing relevant works of Claude Lévi-Strauss and George C. Homans.

The shared assumptions of anthropologists and psychologists concerning operations of social exchange have been discussed at length and most adequately by Alvin Gouldner and Marcel Mauss. It is fitting, then, to analyze these assumptions as discussed by Gouldner and Mauss.

The Norm of Reciprocity and Normative Values

It was Gouldner (1960) who stated explicitly the basic assumption of social exchange approach in terms of the norm of reciprocity:

> I suggest that a norm of reciprocity, in its universal form, makes two interrelated, minimal demands: (1) people should help those who have helped them, and (2) people should not injure those who have helped them. Generically, the norm of reciprocity may be conceived of as a dimension to be found in all value systems and, in particular, as one among

a number of "Principal Components" universally present in moral codes.
(p. 171)

Gouldner (1960) put the significance of this assumption in proper perspective when he noted that "a norm of reciprocity is, I suspect, no less universal and important an element of culture than the incest taboo" (p. 171).

First of all, it is important to note that this assumption is a normative one; *it has to do with moral compulsion.* For most participants of a culture, under most circumstances, to reciprocate or not to reciprocate is not a question which requires agonizing decision making. For the society has already provided the answer in positive form, that one must; and society has successfully inculcated this norm in most of its members. Second, Gouldner is pointing to a generalized, *universal norm* that one reciprocates; how this norm is applied at a particular place and at a specific time remains an empirical question.

Each culture has a set of *normative values,* in varying degrees of explicitness, which exhorts its members to give if they want return, and to return when given. The concept of fairness in American culture involves just this sense of reciprocity. In the Philippines the Tagalog concept of *utang na loob* implies a moral compulsion to return a favor (Kaut 1961). The Japanese terms of *on* and *giri* are also moral concepts implying a normative necessity of one who has received a favor to give an appropriate return (Befu, 1971 pp. 166–169; Lebra, 1969). These may be regarded as explicitly institutionalized expressions of the universal norm of reciprocity in a specific space–time coordinate. I do not imply that particular cultural manifestations of this norm are always explicit or institutionalized. The norm may be widespread in a population merely as an attitude or expectation.

Another extremely important process identified by Gouldner (1960) is what he calls a "starting mechanism." He offers this concept in answering the question of why people, strangers to each other, may be motivated to initiate interaction. That is, if we simply assume a utilitarian basis for social exchange, i.e., a person gives resources to the extent that he benefits from receiving other resources in return, then initiating an exchange relationship with a stranger becomes problematic, since both sides, not having benefited from each other, are suspicious of one another. He states:

> The norm of reciprocity may serve as a starting mechanism in such circumstances by preventing or enabling the parties to break out of this impasse. When internalized in both parties the norm *obliges* the one who has first received a benefit to repay it at some time; it thus provides some realistic grounds for confidence, in the one who first parts with valuables, that he will be repaid. Consequently, there may be less hesitancy in being

the first and a greater facility with which the exchange and social relation can get under way. (p. 177)

MAUSS AND GOULDNER COMPARED

At this juncture, a comparison of Mauss's theory of gift giving with Gouldner's concept of the norm of reciprocity recommends itself, for there is much that is similar, as well as much that is fundamentally different, between these two contributions to the field of social exchange. In his essay, *The Gift*, Mauss analyzes the nature of gift giving in primitive or "archaic" societies, and recognizes moral obligations to give, to receive, and to return. In speaking of these moral obligations, Mauss's analysis manifests antecedents to Gouldner's concept of the norm of reciprocity.

Although both Mauss and Gouldner maintain that reciprocity is "obligatory," that it is a "normative" concept, and that it is universal, there is some subtle difference between Mauss's and Gouldner's theories which should be pointed out. First of all, Gouldner's conception of the norm of reciprocity applies to (1) helping those who help a person, and (2) more passively, at least not injuring them. Mauss, on the other hand, spells out three *active* obligations, namely (1) to give gifts, (2) to receive them when offered, and (3) to repay for gifts received. Thus, Gouldner's norm of reciprocity only concerns Mauss's third obligation.

For Gouldner, giving as such is not an independent moral prescription, as it is for Mauss. For Gouldner, instead, giving is motivated by anticipation of reciprocation, an anticipation which is firmly anchored in the internalized norm of reciprocity, thus providing realistic grounds for having confidence in receiving benefits for whatever one gives. For Mauss, the obligation to give is not contingent on anticipation of a return, but is morally obligatory in itself, and "because the recipient has a sort of proprietary right over everything which belongs to the donor" (1954, p. 11).

Mauss's second obligation, namely to receive a gift, is again not explicitly considered by Gouldner. But since Gouldner's conception is based on a utilitarian model (though rooted in moral grounds), in which each party to a reciprocal transaction stands to benefit, a utilitarian motive would suffice to explain receiving of a gift or a benefit, making a moral component to it unnecessary. We do not deny the importance of the normative aspect in Gouldner's theory; but it is still couched in functionalist terms, i.e., the norm of reciprocity is conceived of as a moral underpinning for the "real" utilitarian business of the society. For Mauss, however, both giving and receiving are moral constraints. They are part of a moral system, together with returning; although not entirely divorced from utilitarian considerations, as H. K. Schneider (1974, p. 101) points out, it exists somewhat independently of it. Therefore, the moral and not utilitarian basis for receiving is necessary in Mauss's theory. This in turn is not to preclude utilitarian considerations from Mauss's theory, however. On the first page of his essay, he argues that economic or self-interest is at the basis of what seem like voluntary, disinterested and spontaneous prestations. Later on, he reiterates the same idea in pointing out that what Malinowski classified as "pure gifts" are, in his analysis, "calculated payments" (Mauss, 1954, p. 71). All this, however, is not to minimize Mauss's primary concern with gift giving as a moral system. Mauss does not mention not doing harm to those who help you—the second of Gouldner's assumptions. It is probably safe to assume that this assumption is implied in Mauss's obligation to repay. For if one is obligated to repay for gifts received, how can the society condone harming those to whom one is obligated to give gifts?

Another difference between Mauss and Gouldner is that Mauss is concerned primarily with reciprocity in "archaic" societies, whereas Gouldner's contention is that his norm is unequivocally universal, applicable to all societies, primitive or modern. Mauss (1954) contends that the same principles of exchange "are at work, *albeit less noticeable,* in our own society" (italics added) and intends to draw "conclusions of a moral nature about some of the problems confronting us in our present economic crisis" (p. 2). But his examples are mostly drawn from primitive societies which "have not yet reached the stage of pure individual contract, money market, sale proper, fixed price, and weighed coined money" (p. 45).[1] Thus, although Mauss's theory is in principle universally valid for all societies, empirical manifestations of his "obligations" apparently diminish to the extent that a society is governed by certain moral and economic principles such as pure individual contract, money market, etc.

RULES OF EXCHANGE

At this juncture I would like to introduce the concept of *rule of exchange* in contradistinction to the *norm of reciprocity.* Rule of exchange

[1] Mauss here perhaps foreshadows Polanyi's well-known tripartite classification of economic behavior into "reciprocal," "redistributive," and "market," the first being manifest most clearly in primitive (archaic) societies, and the last in modern Western societies.

refers to specific cultural rules governing particular manners of giving and receiving. This is analogous to saying that, though the incest taboo as such is universal, to which kinsmen it applies is a matter varying from culture to culture. A culturally specified amount of brideprice in Africa, or culturally prescribed types of gifts to gods to earn merit in Burma or Thailand, may be regarded as examples of the cultural rule of exchange. Rule of exchange as defined here differs from the norm of reciprocity in that the latter refers to a generalized expectation to reciprocate, irrespective of what is being given or returned, whereas rules of exchange vary precisely on the basis of the nature of what is to be exchanged. At the same time, rules are dependent on the norm, since it is the norm which supports and reinforces execution of rules of exchange.

It should be noted that cultural rules often do not specify the exact kind and amount of goods or other resources to be given or returned. Rather, a broad range of acceptable kinds and quantities of resources is often prescribed by the culture, giving rise to "strategies of exchange," to be taken up below. Thus, a Kwakiutl chief holding a potlatch is not obliged to give away a specific number of blankets or dried salmon. An American couple returning a dinner invitation has a wide range of recipes to follow in cooking a dinner which would be appropriate as a return for the dinner they had been invited to previously. And this range of acceptable exchange behavior varies from one circumstance to another. Existence of cultural limits is more noticeable when one steps out of bounds than when one stays within them. When a rule is violated, a normal, enculturated individual would immediately and intuitively sense the violation, and if he does not, others would make him aware by censuring him. Hogbin (1971, p. 37) recounts a headman in Ontong, Java who became an object of ridicule by the villagers because he stepped out of bounds and was too ostentatious in giving a betrothal gift for his daughter. In fact, to take a different kind of example, such English expressions as "flattery," "apple polishing," and "buttering up" indicate prestations over and beyond what is called for by cultural rules.

STRATEGIES OF EXCHANGE

These considerations give rise to the third concept of exchange, in addition to norm of reciprocity and rule of exchange, namely, *strategies of exchange*. Where culture sets perimeters of appropriate forms or amounts of giving or returning, or where culture prescribes no rule, individuals are free to exercise their discretion so as to maximize their opportunities.[2] Maximization of opportunities here does not necessarily refer to maximum material return; the return sought may be of intangible nature, such as receiving respect or being highly thought of. Also, to maximize one's opportunities, one need not give the maximum limit of a culturally prescribed range. To a receiver considered to be a "bad risk," for example, giving as much as one can would not be maximizing opportunities.

In short, an individual normally plays his strategy for a maximum return within the bounds set by the cultural rules and within the framework of a given culture (to be discussed below). It is important to distinguish between cultural rules and strategy. One refers to prescribed conventions, which are, for participants of a culture, by and large given; the other refers to the operation of an individual's motivations, depending on which cultural rules are variably utilized.

Cultural Frame of Reference

In addition to the universal norm of reciprocity, culture-specific rules of exchange, and individual strategies of exchange, it is important to recognize the cultural frame of reference, or framework within which exchange behavior takes place. Cultural frame sets the background before which the norm, rules, and strategies operate. In this sense, cultural frame is different from rules of exchange. This difference may be illustrated with the give and take between higher and lower castes in the Jajmani system. In Kolenda's words (1963), the Jajmani system is "a system of distribution in Indian villages whereby high-caste land owning families called jajmans are provided services and products by various lower-castes" (p. 11). In return, those of lower castes receive material compensations as culturally prescribed, i.e., according to cultural rules, in our terminology. However, it is quite obvious that this system of exchange operates within the context of Indian culture, that is to say, only when we assume such beliefs and institutions as inequality in caste ranking, the lower-castes' capacity to absorb pollution, economic superiority of Brahmans, paternalistic relationship

---

[2] This is not to imply that social exchange follows the pattern of the two-person zero-sum game, in which loss of one automatically implies gain for the other and that the amount of loss for one is a function of the gain of the other. As Kenneth Boulding has indicated to me (personal communication), social exchange is a positive-sum game. "Both parties to an exchange value what they get more than what they give up, otherwise the exchange would not take place." Elaboration of this point, however, would take us deep into the issues of evaluation of resources and balancing mechanisms in exchange theory, which are outside the scope of this paper.

obtaining between particular jajman and their kamins, and cultural ascriptions of hereditary occupations to various castes, do reciprocal operations of the jajmani system begin to make sense.

In short, cultural frame of reference refers to the overall cultural background, or context, which makes operations of rules and strategies possible. As such, it refers to factors exogenous to an exchange system, factors which are not recognized as variables affecting the outcome of exchange transactions in a given exchange system. These factors, nonetheless, vary from system to system, from culture to culture, accounting in part for cross-cultural differences in exchange systems.

To take an example from experience familiar to us, when an American observes cultural rules of exchanging Christmas gifts with his close relatives, he is operating within the context of the American kinship system, which defines, among other things, who are and who are not relatives. In other words, the system defines who on kinship basis should and who need not receive Christmas gifts. The American kinship system attaches no special significance to one's mother's brother (as against father's brother), as do matrilineal societies. It is thus that American society does not require one to give one's maternal uncle a gift any different from that given to one's paternal uncle. If one does, it is not because of a rule derived from the kinship system, but because of the idiosyncrasy of the individual situation. Kinship system, then, is part of the cultural frame within which rules as to who should receive gifts and what sort of gifts would apply.

The distinction made here among cultural rules, strategies, and cultural frame of reference parallels (although they are not identical to) that made by Buchler and Nutini (1969, pp. 7–8) among "ground rules," "strategy rules," and "cultural framework." According to them, ground rules are said to structure the cultural framework within which decision making occurs, and strategy rules are supposed to guide choices among the options which the cultural framework allows. Buchler and Nutini point out that the anthropologist often ignores strategy rules at the expense of concentrating his attention on ground rules, while the game theorist concerns himself with strategy rules, forgetting about ground rules.

One can easily make a parallel statement in exchange theory regarding the status of cultural rules and strategies of exchange. Namely, anthropologists concerned with exchange, by and large, have focused their attention on cultural rules of exchange, whereas psychologists interested in exchange have shown interest primarily in the strategy of exchange, ignoring cultural rules and frame of reference. Also, psychologists of exchange theory often work in areas where explicit cultural rules are absent and individuals operate on the basis of the norm of reciprocity. It is important to know, however, that even here the overall cultural frame of reference places constraint on behavior, so that principles of exchange behavior deduced cannot be immediately interpreted to have universal applications. On the other hand, anthropologists tend to paint a picture of exchange systems consisting of cultural rules and norms, and lacking in live human beings, who base their action on other factors in addition to rules and norms. For example, in East African societies it is often reported that cattle are given in exchange for a bride, which is a statement of a cultural rule. But the specific number of cattle to be transferred is seldom fixed; instead, it varies depending on situational factors. Decision as to how many cattle are to be given, then, is a function of how the giver perceives these factors, and what weighting he attaches to them. These are, in short, motivational considerations, and they are more often than not ignored or slighted by anthropologists, whose primary interest is in describing a society in terms of its norms and rules.

STRUCTURAL VERSUS MOTIVATIONAL APPROACHES

This contrastive characterization between those exchange theorists interested in cultural rules and those interested in strategies sets the stage for a further analysis of these two approaches, with actual examples from anthropological and psychological literature.

Introduction

In the structural approach, concern is primarily with what prescribed rules of exchange there are, and how they operate in relationship to each other; cultural frame of reference is brought into analysis from time to time, though not systematically. Individual strategies are generally ignored, or at best merely mentioned as a variable, perhaps with a few choice examples; and the process whereby individuals involve themselves in decision making or maximizing their opportunities is not analyzed carefully. The primary focus of this approach is in delineating exchange as a cultural system, as a system of norms and values.

In the motivational approach, in contrast, the concern is first and foremost with individual strategies, with how an individual decides, consciously or unconsciously, to enter into or maintain an exchange relation with another individual or other individuals on the basis of the choices allowed within a given cultural framework and within the limits set by cultural rules. In this approach, cultural frame and cultural rules are often only implicitly assumed, and not brought out into the open for explicit consideration. They are sometimes completely ignored, and individuals are assumed to be free agents, for whom cultural constraints are not explicitly recognized as delimiting their exchange behavior.

The structural approach is most common in anthropology, whereas the motivational approach is by and large followed in sociology and social psychology. It is a curious accident in the history of exchange research that the two approaches have developed in their relatively extreme forms with little attempt to synthesize them. In fact, as we shall see, in some formulations of these approaches the two are regarded as mutually exclusive. A major position taken in this paper is that the two approaches can and should be synthesized for a comprehensive analysis of exchange behavior. However, first let us review some of the specific and more prominent examples of the two approaches.

The Structural Approach

No one has presented a more comprehensive structural argument for social exchange than Lévi-Strauss in his *Les Structures Elémentaires de la Parenté* (1949), translated into English in 1969, in which he expounds a theory as to why societies practicing marriage of a man with his mother's brother's daughter are more prevalent than those practicing other forms of cousin marriage. The amount of scholarly energy this single work has generated in the anthropological profession is equaled by few others. Much of the controversy, to be sure, has to do with various facets of cross-cousin marriage, such as the meaning of prescription versus preference, empirical workability of the various combinations of residence rules and descent rules, and accuracy of interpretation and analysis of specific empirical cases. As such, they do not concern us in assessing the basic structure of exchange in Lévi-Strauss's theory. We shall, therefore, make no attempt to review his entire theory of cross-cousin marriage. Rather, only those aspects of his theory which are relevant for understanding what we have called the structural approach to exchange will be briefly outlined.

It is safe to say Lévi-Strauss has inherited the French sociological tradition, exemplified by Durkheim and Mauss in particular. From Durkheim, Lévi-Strauss has inherited the approach which sees the social group, or the society, as having its own raison d'être, sees the rationale for the existence of individual members of a society in the continuance of the society, sees "social facts" as having an existence apart from, and logically, though of course not empirically, prior to individual members, and sees society as creating external constraints on individuals. Norms and values, rules of descent, and residence are just such social facts. Lévi-Strauss's preference for the mechanical model (Lévi-Strauss, 1953), which consists of stated laws, rules, and values, over the statistical model, which analyzes actual behavior frequencies, has its intellectual debt in this element of Durkheimian sociology. It is this mechanical model which is used in Lévi-Strauss's analysis of cross-cousin marriage. (This concept of "mechanical" is of course not to be confused with Durkheim's "mechanical" solidarity of primitive societies, in which groups of a like form are organized into a society.)

Mauss has contributed to Lévi-Strauss's theory more directly in relation to social exchange. It is Mauss's notion of "total prestation" which Lévi-Strauss calls into operation in explaining cross-cousin marriage. Mauss (1954) states:

> In the systems of the past we do not find simple exchange of goods, wealth and produce through markets established among individuals. For it is groups, and not individuals, which carry on exchange, make contracts, and are bound by obligations; the persons represented in the contracts are moral persons—clans, tribes, and families; the groups, or the chiefs as intermediaries for the groups, confront and oppose each other. Further, what they exchange is not exclusively goods and wealth, real and personal property, and things of economic value. They exchange rather courtesies, entertainments, ritual, military assistance, women, children, dances and fests; and fairs in which the market is but one element and the circulation of wealth but one part of a wide and enduring contract. Finally, although the prestations and counter-prestations take place under a voluntary guise they are in essence strictly obligatory, and their sanction is private or open warfare. We propose to call this the system of *total prestations*. (p. 3)

Mauss here echoes Durkheim's notion of primacy of groups and his notion of moral constraints inherent in obligatory contracts and in moral persons (not free-willed individuals)—which are all incorporated in Lévi-Strauss's theory. Mauss, moreover, refers to exchanging, not of a particular commodity, but of all kinds of things, between groups:

> Food, women, children, possessions, charms, land, labor, services, religious offices, rank—everything is stuff to be given away and repaid. In perpetual exchange of what we may call a spiritual matter, comprising men and things, these elements pass and repass between clans and individuals, ranks, sexes, and their generations. (pp. 11–12)

Lévi-Strauss (1969) practically reiterates the above quotation when he says:

> Exchange, as a total phenomenon, is from the first a total exchange, comprising food, manufactured objects, and that most precious category of goods, women. (pp. 60–61)

Lévi-Strauss weaves these strands of the French intellectual tradition into a grand tapestry of marriage alliance. Lévi-Strauss's special contribution, among others, consists in singling out women as a special category of gifts in an exchange system, rather than considering women simply as one among numerous kinds of gifts as Mauss has done, and in considering its significance for creating social solidarity. In fact, Lévi-Strauss's emphasis on exchange of women is so great that he almost exclusively concerns himself with implications of marriage at the expense of other commodities and resources being exchanged between intermarrying groups. One problem arising from this over-emphasis on circulation of women is that the nature of balancing give and take between wife givers and wife takers at times becomes unclear; for we are not always told what, if anything, constitutes an adequate return for a wife. In short, Mauss's third element in exchange system, i.e., to return, is not considered adequately in Lévi-Strauss's analysis.

In placing Lévi-Strauss's analysis in the context of comparative exchange systems, it is important to note that his system is based on a mechanical, rather than a statistical, model, and that, epistemologically, the structure of marriage alliance created on this model is deductively arrived at from a small number of premises, rather than derived inductively through amassing of ethnographic data. These premises, such as women as the most valued gifts, the universal incest taboo, rules of residence, and rules of descent constitute the cultural framework within which exchange through marriage takes place. Cultural rules of exchange here have to do with rules of marriage—with patrilateral cross cousin, matrilateral parallel cousin, etc.

Other workers have formulated models of exchange in the tradition established by Lévi-Strauss but treating different subject matters. Rosman and Rubel have generally taken Lévi-Strauss's position in examining what they have called the "potlatch type" society (Rosman & Rubel, 1972a,b; Rubel & Rosman, 1970, 1971). Like Lévi-Strauss, Rosman and Rubel acknowledge their debt to Mauss as "the most significant of theorists" (1972a, p. 1). Potlatching as exchange serves at once to define groups of givers and receivers, and to create relationships between them. Whereas Lévi-Strauss's *Elementary Structures* centers around the function of marriage (at least as an immediate concern, whatever the ultimate purpose of the treatise might be), Rosman and Rubel concern themselves with the function of potlatch, and correlate variations in the forms of potlatch to variations in social structure, Nonetheless, Rosman and Rubel utilize the same basic

structure of argument as Lévi-Strauss: in both cases a logically constructed model of social structure is verified by a specific type of
exchange phenomenon, whether it be marriage or potlatch. In Lévi-
Strauss's theory, specific marriage rules result in exchange of women
either directly between two groups back and forth or indirectly group
A giving a woman in marriage to group B, B giving to C, etc., and
finally Z to A, in a "circulating connubium." In Rosman and Rubel,
exchanging of gifts through a series of potlatches between affinely
related groups serves "as *rites de passage* for society, providing a
ceremonial occasion for the affirmation of rearrangement of the rank
system" (Rubel & Rosman, 1970, p. 733). Rosman and Rubel do not
neglect the competitive and rivalrous side of potlatch for which Northwest Coast societies have been reputed. But they temper it with its
function of creating alliance between the very rivals, seeing alliance
and rivalry as two inseparable sides of the same coin.

Another interesting variation is Eric Schwimmer's (1974) analysis
of Orokaiva exchange behavior. Schwimmer acknowledges his debt to
Lévi-Strauss for his overall theoretical orientation, and constructs a
series of models of "cycles of exchange" which characterize man's
relations to land, handling of taro and pigs, and Orokaiva system of
marriage, etc. Schwimmer's model of Orokaiva exchange has four
elements: two objects of exchange (exchange partners), and two mediating elements standing between the two parties to exchange, one
element (gift, etc.) going from one party to the other, and the other
element going in the opposite direction. Schwimmer is able to account
for a great deal of his Orokaiva data by constructing one model after
another having the same basic structure. Schwimmer clearly recognizes
the role of cultural frame of reference, principally in terms of cultural
ideologies governing or defining the meaning of the mediating elements.

The Motivational Approach

In contrast to the above structural approach to exchange, which is
pursued mostly by anthropologists and which emphasizes cultural
rules and frames of reference, the motivational approach is by and
large associated with psychologists, and focuses on individual strategies of exchange. Since emphasis is on what motivates individuals to
enter into and maintain an exchange relationship, sentiment, approval,
conformity, attraction, and liking, which are qualities not uniformly
distributed over the population, but varying from one individual to
another, receive focal attention in this approach. For it is these

psychological qualities which are assumed to be the stuff underlying processes of social exchange. A problem in the motivational approach, then, is to locate causal factors which would manipulate motivational variables so that a varying exchange relationship can be predicted. There is considerably more research on exchange from this point of view than from the structural point of view. The number of publications with problems explicitly addressed to motivational questions of exchange is much greater than those dealing with structural treatment of the topic. To be sure, as we have said earlier, there are numerous ethnographic reports which in one way or another touch on, refer to, or assume an exchange frame of reference; but in comparison with psychologists' efforts, explicit treatment of structural problems is not as numerous.

To anthropologists, Homans's work is probably the best known, if only because of his authorship with Schneider of *Marriage, Authority and Final Cause: A Study of Unilateral Cross-Cousin Marriage*, a volume arguing for a motivational explanation of cross-cousin marriage. Homans's theoretical position on social exchange, however, is best developed in his *Social Behavior: Its Elementary Forms* (1961). It is probably more than a coincidence that both Lévi-Strauss and Homans claim in the titles of their books to be getting at *elementary* aspects of social phenomena. Both works present systematic treatment of social phenomena, building up their arguments from a small number of basic assumptions. One fundamental difference between them is that Homans begins his analysis from individual *behavior*, whereas Lévi-Strauss begins his from *social structure*. For Homans, it is observation of interactional behavior that supplies the data for his theory. As such, his theory is firmly grounded in empirical data, whereas Lévi-Strauss's theory is analytically formulated, and its relation to empirical data is not always clear.

Another major difference, remarked upon by many, has to do with the fact that Lévi-Strauss's concern is to provide an explanation of social phenomena (cross-cousin marriage, in his case) in terms of the phenomena's contribution to the maintenance of social structure. In Lévi-Strauss's theory, motivation is assumed to develop in such a way as to support social structure, and individual strategies for maximizing one's advantages are ignored. In Homans's theory, in contrast, social structure ("institution" in Homans's term) results from patterning of exchange behavior, properly reinforced by self-interested motivations. That is, once certain behavior patterns become rewarding and a degree of consensus is achieved over them, the consensus becomes an institutionalized norm. Homans does not assume, however, that the relationship between institution and behavior is one to one. When formerly rewarding behavior patterns no longer bring about satisfaction, behavior patterns would change in a direction which is more rewarding; until the new patterns of behavior crystallize into a consensus, and thus bring about institutional change, behavior and institution will remain discrepant.

Thus, we see that in logical construction, the social structure with attendant cultural framework and rules is prior to behavior for Lévi-Strauss, whereas behavior is prior to social structure for Homans. Very loosely put, for Homans individuals behave the way they do because of, and only because of, the psychological satisfaction they derive from being rewarded. Exchange, then, is a matter of rewarding those who reward you by continuing to emit the kind of activity which produced rewards in the past. For Homans, exchange is between *individuals*, whereas for Lévi-Strauss, exchange is between *groups*.

Other psychologists who have contributed toward exchange theory may be mentioned more briefly below. Nord (1969a) constructs a psychological model of social exchange, much like Homans, in which social conformity and approval are regarded as the "currency" of social exchange. In fact, he reinterprets much of psychological literature on conformity and approval in the light of an exchange model. Many others, such as Blau (1964), Foa (1971), and Gergen (1969), have made contributions to motivational processes of exchange behavior, details of which need not concern us in this paper. One point about the psychological approach is worth reiterating: namely, that psychologists are interested in discovering universal processes of exchange behavior which purportedly hold true of all cultures, and their writings betray this assumption. There is a danger here of ignoring or only implicitly assuming the cultural frame of reference within which psychologists observe exchange behavior. The danger is that of not recognizing the possibility that certain propositions regarding exchange behavior may hold true only because they are made in the context of a particular culture.

Methodologically, hypotheses dealing with universal, culture-free processes is suspect, for practically all the data on which such hypotheses are made are derived from the West, particularly the United States. Experimental data using American college students serving as subjects provide much of the basis of psychological formulations. In such experiments, the particular cultural background of the subjects, that is, the variables of cultural frame of reference, cultural values, and rules which they have internalized in the context of American culture, are generally not called into question. These variables may well have affected the outcome of the experiments, so that if the same experiment were executed in another culture, results might be different.

The extent to which structural and motivational approaches, or, if Homans and Schneider's terms are to be used, "final-cause" and "efficient-cause" approaches to social exchange have developed without notice to each other is perhaps understandable in light of the fundamental differences in the assumptions of the two approaches. As we have seen in our analysis of Lévi-Strauss and Homans, the primary foci of the two approaches are entirely different: each approach takes for granted what the other regards as the central problem. In the structural approach, individual variations—behavior resulting from differential motivation and what I have called individual strategies— are either ignored or assumed more or less automatically to result from structural arrangement of the society. The central problem here is in interpreting the relationship between groups as exhibiting exchange processes which contribute ultimately to the maintenance of the entire social system. In the motivational approach, on the other hand, relationship between groups and the question of societal integration is either taken for granted or ignored. Focus here is placed upon strategies of individuals as operating within the structural framework already assumed. What is needed at this juncture of our exchange research is integration of the two approaches, formulation of a theoretical scheme which considers both group relations and interpersonal relations as legitimate, and, moreover, interrelated problems of exchange.

Summary

Although not every single act by man is analyzable in the framework of social exchange theory, it is probably safe to assume that all human beings and all human groups of societies over the world engage in exchange acts through a good portion of their life career. Social exchange is in this sense a universal phenomenon. Its pervasiveness recommends and even demands its analysis. Yet, with notable exceptions, social scientists' attention was not turned to it until quite recently. Due to the recency of theoretical development, systematic integration of concepts and constructs in the exchange field is still at its infancy. As an effort at systematization in the field, the present paper has attempted to pull together some of the major contributions in the field in order to make explicit some of its basic assumptions.

The norm of reciprocity, rules and strategy of exchange, and cultural frame of reference are all intricately interrelated and organized into a system. The universal norm of reciprocity provides a premise, namely, that in all societies men are obliged to reciprocate benefits to one another. Rules of exchange are derivatives of this norm as manifested in a given space and time. To the extent that these rules allow certain latitudes of interpretation by individual actors, actors are free to apply them in ways which they consider most advantageous. These rules and strategies, however, do not make much sense unless they are seen against the background of the cultural frame of reference. Seen thus, the dichotomy between the structural and the motivational approaches becomes a false one. Both are needed for an integrated theory of social exchange.

ACKNOWLEDGMENT

Much of the writing of the paper was done during the tenure of the John Simon Guggenheim fellowship and the Japan Foundation fellowship. I wish to acknowledge my gratitude to these institutions. In writing this final draft, I benefited from comments supplied by Kenneth E. Boulding, George Dalton, Theodor Downing, Bridget O'Laughlin, and Michelle Rosaldo.

10

The Myth of Reciprocity

FREDERIC L. PRYOR AND NELSON H. H. GRABURN

INTRODUCTION

In anthropology, the concept of reciprocity has received great analytic stress. In part, this is because many analysts have placed a high ethical value on reciprocity, and have felt it worthwhile to study this phenomenon. In part, this is because reciprocity has been tied to certain notions about social stability. For instance, Marcel Mauss (1925) argued that various types of reciprocal exchange serve not only as a cohesive force internally, but also as a substitute or a replacement for war externally. Curiously, most anthropological analyses of reciprocity have focused on rather vague ethnographic impressions, rather than any type of quantitative evidence (a major exception is Henry, 1951). And few of the theoretical discussions about reciprocity have been accompanied by empirical evidence which permits any type of rigorous hypothesis testing. In this essay we hope to take steps in remedying this situation.

After surveying briefly several of the major approaches toward reciprocity which one finds in the anthropology literature, we turn to an empirical analysis of distribution in an Eskimo village, to determine whether or not any of the hypotheses about reciprocity can explain the data which we have collected. By and large, we find that the exchange accounts not only of individuals but also of collections of similar individuals (e.g., all men, or all people from wealthy families, or all people with political power) are quite out of balance. We explore the imbalances with the aid of a regression analysis, and the results permit us not only to isolate a number of important causal variables, but also

FREDERIC L. PRYOR • Department of Economics, Swarthmore College, Swarthmore, Pennsylvania. NELSON H. H. GRABURN • Department of Anthropology, University of California, Berkeley, California. This essay was partially financed by a grant from the Center for International Studies of the University of California at Berkeley.

to show that social invisibles such as prestige or status play a relatively small or even negligible role. We then examine a number of common hypotheses about the nature of reciprocity, and show their inadequacies in explaining the Eskimo data. Finally, we discuss whether reciprocity is a myth—not only to the natives, but also to the anthropologists—and the social role such a myth might play.

ANTHROPOLOGICAL APPROACHES TOWARD RECIPROCITY AND SOME HYPOTHESES

By *reciprocity theory*, we mean the attempt to use the concept of reciprocity as an analytic tool, rather than as an ex post facto rationalization of some exotic native custom. The custom of reciprocity has too rich an intellectual history in anthropology, and too many ramifications, to be discussed in full in a few pages. We wish only to consider a few of the most important approaches toward the nature of reciprocity, and a few of the most interesting hypotheses.

In his well-known essay on the gift, Marcel Mauss (1925) first raised the concept of reciprocity to a central place in anthropology. Although he discussed several different types of transfer (i.e., one-way gifts), he focused his analytic energies on an examination of the importance of reciprocity in primitive and peasant societies, delimited by the simple rules of the obligation to give, the obligation to receive ("One does not have the right to refuse a gift or a potlatch. To do so would show fear of having to repay and of being abused in default." p. 39), and the obligation to repay ("[This] is imperative. Face is lost forever if [a worthy return] is not made or if equivalent value is not destroyed." p. 41). Mauss's attempted systematization of the nature of reciprocity was based on a number of ethnographic accounts, two of which—those of Thurnwald on the Buin and of Malinowski on the Trobriand *kula*—focus on reciprocity as a key to the economic life of the peoples studied. In a later study, Malinowski (1926) elevated the concept of reciprocity to a central position in his analysis of the social organization on the Trobriand Islands. He declared that the principle of give and take pervades all tribal life, that it is the basis of the social structure, and that

> the whole division into totemic clans, into subclans of a local nature and into village communities, is characterized by a system of reciprocal services and duties, in which the groups play a game of give and take. . . . Reciprocity, the give-and-take principle, reigns supreme also within the clan, nay within the nearest group of kinsmen. (p. 47)

In the past few decades, the analysis of reciprocity has taken several divergent paths in anthropological theory. Most importantly, in the field of social structure known as *alliance theory* analysts have developed Maussian notions of reciprocity as the foundation of human social structure and as the fundamental quality of the human/social mind. In Claude Lévi-Strauss's most famous exposition (1949), this axiom is shown to act: (1) through the necessity for family groups to exchange women in particular patterns; (2) as the mainspring for the particular type of marital exchanges that are deemed necessary to produce a *balanced* reciprocity so essential for a stable social structure. This argument is based on an additional assumption, namely that there is a hierarchy of "things" to be exchanged among groups, with women the most valuable, followed by goods and services. Lévi-Strauss further argues that the natives may not be consciously aware of the kind of reciprocities involved, and may not actually calculate or consciously balance the accounts of women, goods, or services.

A second path was blazed by Edmund Leach (1951) in a reply to Lévi-Strauss. Leach agreed with the latter's ideas on the essential reciprocal nature of exchange, but disagreed that women are necessarily "the highest good," or, indeed, that the transactions needed to be balanced in tangibles such as women or men, the labor of women or men, consumer goods and money, capital goods, or ritual objects. Rather, he argued, part of the balance may be in intangibles, such as rights of a territorial and political nature, or relative status or prestige. (These terms, he noted, cannot be defined except in terms of the cultural situation; prestige may be derived from murder in one society, philanthropy in a second, success in a third.) Turning away from marital exchange, a number of anthropologists have since analyzed imbalances in the exchange of goods and services in terms of counter-flows of prestige, the most extensive being a book-length monograph of festive and ritual giving in a Maya community (Cancian, 1965).

A final path is that followed by anthropologists of the *substantivist* persuasion, based on many of the ideas of Karl Polyani. Of these, Marshall Sahlins (1972) has presented the most sophisticated attempt to analyze reciprocity and other modes of distribution, and has propounded a number of interesting propositions. He argues that transfer transactions of an altruistic nature (labeled *generalized reciprocity*) characterize the transactions between kinsmen. Among kin there is an obligation to give, but the obligation to receive, and, more importantly, to return are considerably more vague. Reckoning is not overt (in contradistinction to the approach of Mauss and Malinowski). Often, there is a sustained transfer, with goods moving toward one person (often a "have-not") for a very long period. According to Leach, this would be balanced by the flows of intangibles in the opposite direction, but Sahlins makes no such assertion. Sahlins also argues that transactions between strangers or enemies are characterized often by transfers of a malevolent nature (which he labels *negative reciprocity*). That is, the participants attempt to get something for less than its value by haggling, chicanery, theft, or other means, and, as a result, the transaction is often unbalanced. Finally, Sahlins argues that transactions between those whose social distance is somewhere between kin and enemies is characterized by reciprocal exchange (which he labels *balanced reciprocity*). He emphasizes that the exchange accounts may not be balanced at any point in time, but that in the long run the accounts are balanced.

If we can somehow calculate transaction accounts between individuals, we can test some of these ideas. If Mauss is basically correct, we should find relatively balanced transaction accounts; if Leach is correct, we may find unbalanced transactions, but the imbalances will be counterbalanced by a flow of social invisibles (Leach only considers "good" invisibles, such as prestige; however, "bad" invisibles, such as force can also be included); if Sahlins is correct, we may find unbalanced transactions, but the imbalances can be explained by the social distance between the transactors. These are the key hypotheses for which evidence is needed.

THE ETHNOGRAPHIC SETTING OF THE STUDY

The Society

The quantitative analysis was carried out on the Eskimo village of Sugluk, which is a settlement on the southwest side of the Hudson Strait, connecting Hudson Bay to the Atlantic Ocean. The 254 inhabitants of the village belong to the Takamiut Eskimo, and have been the subject of extensive ethnographic analysis (Graburn, 1964, 1969a,b, 1971).

The shores of Sugluk Inlet have been inhabited by the winter and summer camps of the Takamiut for many centuries. Sporadic contact with the whites began in the second half of the nineteenth century with the establishment of trade relations with distant posts: the Eskimos traded fox, seal, and caribou skins for metal implements, especially knives, guns, and powder, and more recently for textiles and flour. The first permanent trading post at Sugluk was established in

1916, and resident missionaries arrived after World War II. Until recently, however, the Eskimos lived by hunting and trapping, and followed a nomadic life in kin-based camp groups. Major changes came about in the late 1950s with increasing involvement of the Canadian government in the form of a local administrator. A generator was installed, a day school started, and by the end of the decade an extensive building program was begun, which aimed to move all the Eskimos into prefabricated houses in settlements.

By 1959, the time of the investigation, the Sugluk residents (called *Sallumiut*) lived in their settlement throughout the fall and winter, apart from all-male trapping expeditions. They formed smaller camp groups in the spring and summer for hunting and fishing, but increasing numbers stayed in the settlement the whole year, especially as more wage-labor positions became available as a consequence of various governmental building and educational programs. Many adults also carved soapstone sculpture for sale for cash income, since permanent wage jobs were confined to less than ten percent of the adults, and since seasonal wage employment was irregular, and only for the most physically fit. Economically, therefore, Sugluk was a mixed community; nearly all Eskimos hunted, fished, and trapped when they could and when they did not have other employment. Furthermore, all desired and attempted to live from native foods, although they also ate bannock (panfried bread) and tea in quantity.

The sociopolitical organization of 1959 reflected in part the traditional Eskimo economy, and in part economic and technological changes (particularly in the use of motorized boats) introduced in recent years. Larger than any traditional Eskimo community, the Sallumiut divided themselves residentially and economically into five kin-based groups, or bands. The cores of these groups were sibling groups which ran and co-owned (or hoped to do so) large motorized hunting vessels, the Peterhead boats. These kin-based groups had originally been independent, mobile camp groups from different areas of the Hudson Strait coast which were attracted to Sugluk by the physical amenities and the presence of white agencies. Each group had a traditional leadership pattern vested in the senior effective male, and all but one group was exogamous. Like all Eskimo groups, the bands had a bilateral kin structure (i.e., no unilineal kin groups) and ambilocal residence pattern (i.e., the initial postmarital residence was with the kin of the wife, but after the birth of the first child or two, the couple lived with the kin of the husband). Thus, band members were close kin and affines, but not all close kin were members of one's own band; for instance, young newly married men and older married women were members of bands apart from their patrikinsmen.

In brief, the major production units were the band and the smaller hunting groups which were usually composed of band members. The major consumption units were the households, which were usually composed of a nuclear family or a small extended family, but which might sometimes be composed of several families who chose to live together.

The community-wide sociopolitical structure in 1959 appeared to be a weak and artificially superimposed layer depending for the most part on white agencies: the Anglican Church had a senior and other catechists; the Canadian government had an Eskimo clerk with some power, and it encouraged the election and maintenance of an almost powerless community council; and the Hudson's Bay Company had an Eskimo assistant manager who enjoyed considerable community power because of his economic influence and his interpreting abilities. In actuality, the key elements in the community-wide layer were the various white personnel, but this layer was not of great importance to the Sallumiut *qua* community in 1959.

Data Gathering

The data on distributional transactions were gathered between July and September, 1959. Some of the men of the village were away for the first part of the period, engaged in wage labor in other settlements. Other men were doing some unskilled labor in the settlement. Most of the men were engaged in typical activities for the season: hunting by boat for seals and walrus, and by foot and boat for migrating wildfowl, and fishing. One or two government ships came into the settlement bringing back families and taking others to work as janitors at meteorological stations. Many families were building wooden winter houses for the first time, so that probably fewer families were out at hunting camps than in any previous year in history. The six-week period represents a typical time slice in Eskimo life, as further research showed that the exchange patterns in the spring and fall months were quite similar. In the winter time the exchange system began to break down, and in years previous many groups would leave the camp for better hunting areas.

In Sugluk it was permissible to visit any residence at any time. The ethnographer (Nelson Graburn) undertook a systematic series of visits to every household in the community to determine who was visiting whom and what was being exchanged. He made slightly over three hundred visits, and recorded 1,250 instances of different types of exchange (or nonexchange, if no other visitors appeared in the residence).

Ideally, the ethnographer would have visited each household the same number of times, and at the same time throughout the day. The fieldwork conditions and original intentions of the research precluded absolute perfection in sampling, and, therefore, the data had to be adjusted so that the data used in the analysis would reflect ideal sampling conditions. This proved, however, to be an easy matter (the details are described in Pryor, 1978).

Data on three different kinds of exchange transactions were collected: length of visit, material goods exchanged, and services exchanged. The ethnographer made a record of each visitor who came into the residence where he was, which person or persons he was visiting (the "visit unit" was allocated two-thirds to the prime visitee and one-third to the secondary visitee; if there was no secondary visitee, then the entire visit unit was attributed to the prime visitee), how long the visit lasted, what exchange of material goods or services occurred, what the apparent purpose of the visit was, and in what kinship relation the visitor stood with the prime visitee. The authors ended up with giant matrices recording these various transactions of every person with every other person in the village. The analytic problem of this chapter is to relate imbalances in the transaction flows to certain key socioeconomic variables.

To this end, a census was also made, so that age, marital status, occupation, family income, individual income, social status of the family, individual prestige, relative space of house, family wealth, political status, and other variables could be calculated. The classification of individuals and families in this census according to such socioeconomic factors was performed independently of, and before, the examination of the distribution accounts; thus the possibility of biasing the analyses with ex post rationalizations does not arise. In addition, it must be stressed that most of the classifications are on native categories, and were derived from native informants long before this quantitative analysis was conceived.

The Methods of Handling the Data

Distributional transactions that were recorded included the following three exchanges:

1. *Exchange between villagers taking place within the dwellings.* The Eskimos spent most of their leisure time either visiting or being visited, and thus exchange of hospitality was an important type of exchange. A great deal of exchange of food accompanied this hospitality, so much so that a considerable proportion of most people's diet obtained in households other than their own.

2. *Exchange between people within the village but outside the dwell-ings.* Such transactions included some of the borrowing of dogs, sleds, boats, gasoline, and ammunition; gambling and prostitution; and exchanges with white men (trading furs, sale of carvings, wage labor, welfare, etc.). Borrowing, gambling and prostitution were not record-ed; however, exchange occurring during gambling or prostitution (other than the acts themselves) were very minor. Exchanges with white men were recorded separately, and are not included in the analysis of intra-Eskimo exchange; however, the results of such ex-change are taken into consideration when classifying the various individuals according to money income, family wealth, size of dwell-ing, and so forth.

3. *Exchanges of women and children (through marriage, wife ex-change, and adoption).* These were recorded, but not included directly in the analysis of exchange transactions. However, many aspects of such exchanges are included, when they were components of such census categories as marital status, numbers of children, and prestige.

In short, we focus our quantitative attention on the exchanges that occurred within the residences. However, we try to take other types of exchange into account in a qualitative manner in the analysis of the results at a later stage.

A problem arose in the analysis on how the individuals in the community should be grouped, especially since exchange activities of Eskimos of diverse ages are quite different. Various experiments with the data suggested that the quantitative results are most meaningful when the society is divided into two groups: children and unmarried youth (boys, ca. 5–19; girls, ca. 5–18) and married youths, adults, and old persons. For analysis of visiting and gift transactions, we found it illuminating to consider two separate exchange universes: transactions between all members of the society except babies (designated below as Universe A), and transactions only between married youth, adults, and old persons (designated below as Universe B). Transactions only between children and unmarried youth are discussed in Pryor (1978). Several other problems deserve brief consideration.

First is the problem of what should be included in the exchange transactions. We have, of course, included all types of material ex-change. In addition, we have also treated the visit itself as a type of exchange, and have separated material gifts from such visiting. Al-though in our culture it is not necessarily clear what is being exchanged in a visit *per se*, among the Sallumiut the hosting of a visit was considered an act of giving. For this reason, we include a separate analysis of visit exchange.

Second is the problem of weight. How should visits of a certain length be converted so that they are comparable with visits of another length? How should one type of gift be compared with another? These problems could prove quite intractable, unless quite sophisticated techniques of economic analysis were applied; fortunately, this did not prove to be the case. Indeed, the results we obtained were relatively insensitive to several different "reasonable" weighting schemes that we tried. Full details of the weighting scheme chosen and its justification are given in Pryor (1978).

Third is the problem of divising an overall index for the balance of the exchange accounts. The following simple formulae were used:

$$\text{Net account index of visits} = \frac{\text{Weighted visits to others} - \text{weighted visits by others}}{\text{Weighted visits to others} + \text{weighted visits by others}}$$

$$\text{Net account index of gifts} = \frac{\text{Weighted gifts received} - \text{weighted gifts given}}{\text{Weighted gifts received} + \text{weighted gifts given}}$$

If a person only visited others or received gifts from others (i.e., received their hospitality or gifts), his net account index is 1.00; if a person is only visited or only gave gifts, his net account index is −1.00; and if a person received as many visitors or gifts as he gave, his net account index is 0.00. Or, more simply, hosts and gift givers have negative net account indices, and visitors and gift receivers have positive net account indices.[1] The definition of the net account indices introduces a certain statistical bias into the regression results presented below, but this should not make much difference.[2]

We can now turn to the empirical evidence to see whether the net account indices of the Sallumiut are balanced. The most simple aggregative measure of the variation of these net exchange indicates around the mean (which, for the society as a whole, is zero, since the amount of giving is equal to the amount of receiving) is the standard deviation

[1] It would have been desirable to analyze the degree to which every person's accounts were balanced with every other member of society; unfortunately, there were not enough data for this and, therefore, we focus on the analysis on the aggregate balance of each individual's accounts. Such a procedure obliterates the existence of those transfers described as *generalized exchange* (where A gives x to B, who gives x to C, who gives x to A), but the ethnographer did not feel that such types of chain occurred to any significant degree in the society.

[2] The bias occurs because the dependent variable is bounded between +1.00 and −1.00, whereas the regression model assumes no such upper and lower limits. The effect on the statistical calculation is to make the absolute values of the calculated coefficients somewhat less than what they really are. We do not believe, however, that such a bias is quantitatively of such importance that special statistical techniques (such as probit analysis) must be employed to sidestep such problems.

of these indices for the various individuals in the society (i.e., the net exchange index of each individual is used to calculate this statistic). Such standard deviations show that roughly one-third of the Sallumiut have net exchange indices which are greater than +.70 or less than −.70. These results do not immediately disprove Mauss's theory about strict reciprocity, since they may reflect more temporary imbalances. To test properly any of the hypotheses discussed, more sophisticated statistical techniques are required.

TESTING VARIOUS RECIPROCITY THEORIES

The Regression Analysis and Its Implications

If we assume, for the moment, that exchange in Sugluk was truly reciprocal, then there should be no particular pattern of the exchange imbalances. That is, the imbalances should be quite random, and reflect merely accidental circumstances occurring during the period of observation. If, on the other hand, there were certain structural features of the society which underlie these imbalances, then we should be able to isolate them through some type of multivariate analysis.

In the calculations presented below, we have assumed that the imbalances can be traced to a series of social, political, and economic variables in an additive fashion, so that a multiple-regression technique can be applied. We started our experiments with some thirty variables which the ethnographer felt might be related to such imbalances, and quickly culled from this list those variables which appeared most promising. The results which are presented in Table I reflect the final culling of possible explanatory variables. Each calculated regression coefficient indicates the impact of that particular variable on the net account indices, with all other variables held constant. In the parentheses below, each calculated regression coefficient is the standard error so that a test of statistical significance can be performed. In order to ease the burden on the reader, all calculated coefficients that are statistically significant at the .05 level are marked with an asterisk.

In all four cases, the explanatory variables contained in the linear regressions explain between one-quarter and one-half of the variance of the net exchange indices. (The exact explanatory power is measured by the coefficient of determination, which is the square of the coefficient of multiple correlation.) The conclusion to be drawn from such results is simple and powerful: the exchange imbalances are patterned,

TABLE I

Regression Analyses of the Net Exchange Indices (Explained Variable)[a]

	Universe A		Universe B	
	All members of society except babies		Married youth, adults, and old people among each other	
Explanatory variables	Visit index	Gift index	Visit index	Gift index
Constant	.766	1.442	1.053	1.924
Sex (Male = 0; Female = 12)	−.036*	−.021*	−.059*	−.029*
	(.007)	(.008)	(.010)	(.013)
Marital status	−.035*	−.023*	−.039*	−.023
(0 = single, divorced, widowed; 12 married)	(.009)	(.010)	(.010)	(.012)
Physical disability	.040*	.020	.057*	.013
(0 = totally disabled; 12 = able bodied)	(.018)	(.020)	(.018)	(.023)
Individual presence in community	−.006	−.022	.014	−.012
(0 = absent; 6 = absent part of time; 12 = always present)	(.023)	(.026)	(.026)	(.032)
Individual income	−.032	−.051*	−.063*	−.062*
(0 = lowest; 12 = highest)	(.016)	(.019)	(.020)	(.025)
Average family wealth	−.051*	−.033	−.051*	−.032
(0 = lowest; 12 = highest)	(.019)	(.022)	(.024)	(.030)
Size of house	−.038	−.090*	−.064*	−.127*
(0 = smallest house; 12 = largest house)	(.020)	(.023)	(.024)	(.030)
Relation to band leader	−.012	−.001	−.021	−.044
(no or distant relative = 0; children or sibling = 4; wife = 8; identity = 12)	(.017)	(.020)	(.017)	(.022)
Belong to band 1 (0 if no;	−.030*	−.029*	−.043*	−.055*
12 if yes)	(.009)	(.011)	(.011)	(.014)
Belong to band 2 (0 if no;	−.001	−.001	−.013	−.011
12 if yes)	(.009)	(.011)	(.011)	(.014)
Belong to band 5 (0 if no;	.002	−.026*	−.002	−.040*
12 if yes)	(.011)	(.013)	(.013)	(.017)
Size of sample (N)	182	182	112	112
Coefficient of determination	.3824	.2767	.4558	.3212

[a] A dash indicates that no gifts were given or received. All people who did not receive or give at least one visit in the universe under examination were eliminated from the analysis. If a person made or received visits, but neither gave nor received any gifts, his net gift index was calculated as 0.000. The numbers in the top part of the table are the calculated regression coefficients for each variable, and the numbers in parentheses are their standard errors. An asterisk denotes statistical significance at the .05 level.

and the strict reciprocity which we infer from the writings of Mauss do not seem to occur.

Another important conclusion can be drawn from these results: the kind of exchanges which are balanced by a reverse flow of "invisibles," as argued by Leach, also did not seem important, for none of the variables indicating relative prestige, family status, political power, or other social invisibles which the ethnographer felt relevant show any relationship to these exchange imbalances. Although it can be argued that income, average family wealth, and size of house reflect prestige or status and our conclusion is invalid, this interpretation must be rejected for two reasons. First, these variables are not highly correlated with the direct measures of prestige and status. Second, since the direct measures of prestige and status are not related to the net account indices, the aspects of income, wealth, etc., which are related to the net account indices are not proxies for prestige or status, but rather reflect other facets of Eskimo life. It must also be added that in this village there are no unilineal descent groups, preferred cross-cousin marriages, bride wealths or dowries, social classes or castes, or other sociological features which might place into question our interpretation of the regression results.[3]

Aside from these important results, there are also a number of interesting results which are seen by inspection of the regression coefficients. For instance, males are net receivers, and females are net givers (a phenomenon which does not appear related to courting customs of the society); single people are net receivers, and married people are net givers; high-income people are net givers, and low-income people are net receivers; the disabled are net receivers of visits (but *not* gifts), and the ablebodied are net givers of visits (but not gifts). It is fascinating to consider in greater detail the ethnographic significance of some of these causal variables; or the differences in results between universes (especially the universe of children, which is not included here); and the relative importance of economic, social, and political (especially the band connections) variables. However, since these issues are discussed elsewhere (Pryor, 1978) and are not germane to the theoretical issues of this essay, they are not pursued in greater detail below. The most important result to bear in mind is that

---

[3] Those readers who for mystical reasons believe that all interpersonal transactions must be balanced, will undoubtedly be able to find social invisibles which we have not discussed which will balance the transactions; similarly, those who for mystical reasons believe that all interpersonal transactions must be unbalanced, will undoubtedly be able to find still more social invisibles which will make the transaction accounts unbalanced again. Such foolish games can be played indefinitely.

exchange among the Eskimos is *not* balanced, and that the imbalances are related systematically to the variables which are shown in Table I. Rather than concentrate on such ethnographic details, we would like to focus on several more central concerns, namely, the meaning of the regression in the light of the nonincluded transactions, the importance of the time period when the data were gathered, and the differences in the results between visits and gift giving.

The most important types of intra-Eskimo transactions not included in our data are those within family groups sharing the same residence, and those taking place between the time of the kill and the return home from the hunt. When large game (sea mammals or large land animals) or large amounts of small game were killed, the products of the hunt were divided among the party of hunters present, according to who was responsible for the kill, and who assisted (Graburn, 1971, pp. 108–109). Some of the game might have been cached away from the settlement, and thus did not appear in our gift transactions at all. The successful hunter brought back significant quantities of game to his household, and then invited others to feast and carry away gifts. Such transactions form a considerable part of our gift-giving data, but by no means the whole, for visitors to Eskimo households were permitted to partake of any food they might see, even if it was not procured in large quantities. The distribution of game both within and outside the household was usually supervised by the band or group leader, who might also have reserved some of the best parts for his own household's consumption.

The exact impact of these nonincluded transactions on the regression results presented in Table I is difficult to determine. A qualitative examination of their effects (Pryor, 1978) suggests that they do not have a very great effect on the analysis of transactions which we have presented, and that this omission was quite unimportant.

We believe further that the results are not specifically an artifact of the six-week period during which data were collected numerically. The community was also under intensive observation during the months before and after this period, and during various times of the year in 1964, and again in 1968. It was not until 1968 that major changes in community structure, hospitality and generosity patterns, and, above all, the distribution of family income, were observed. If we had numerical data for the entire year of 1959–1960, it would probably show that sex, marital status, physical disability, individual income, average family wealth, space in house, and relation to band leader would still be the determinants of imbalanced exchange (and perhaps, also, belonging to the various bands). We must also stress that the period of observation was neither a feast nor a famine period, and that though some fortunate families were able to cache foods and build up credit at the store, they did so in a way that was *not* significantly different from other periods of observation. The concept of building up "social credit" by being more generous and hospitable than one feels like in order to draw upon it in time of famine or starvation is foreign to Eskimo ideology and practice, and two circumstances of Eskimo life contribute to this situation. First, there was a great deal of mobility in and out of the village, so that there was a high probability that long-term social creditors might never be able to locate their debtors to collect. Second, in times of famine or starvation, everyone is badly off and, as a matter of fact, the rules of generosity and reciprocity break down (Graburn, 1969a, pp. 72–76).

The differences in the regression results between gift giving (mostly food) and visits raise some interesting issues, especially to anthropologists. Here, we have two quite different types of interaction of which the Eskimos claim they take account. In both universes we are able to explain a higher percentage of the variation of the net exchange indices of visits than of gift giving, and this seems curious, for in our own culture, we would think that visiting would be more random than gift giving. One possible explanation for the Eskimo results is suggested in Sahlins's (1972) discussion of the special role of food exchanges vis-à-vis other types of exchange: "Staple foodstuffs cannot always be handled just like anything else" (p. 215). Food has a special element of sociability, so that more of it is given away without expectation of return than are other types of exchange media. According to this approach, net exchange indices in food exchanges would be more unbalanced than exchanges of other goods and services, and, furthermore, food exchanges would be, in a sense, less structured, since the rational, calculating element in individual decision making would play a less important role.

One way to test these ideas is to look at the variations in the net exchange indices of food gifts (which constitute all our gift-exchange index) and other gifts (visits) to see if the former is more unbalanced. In statistical terms this would mean that the standard deviation of the individual net exchange indices for gifts would be greater than for visits.

The data show that in both cases the standard deviation of the next exchange indices of gift giving is larger than of visiting, although the differences are not quite statistically significant at the .05 level when an F test is performed. The results, therefore, provide only a suggestion of positive evidence for the first part of Sahlins's hypothesis—that exchange accounts are more unbalanced for food than for other goods or services. The possible correctness of the first part of the hypothesis provides plausibility for the second part—that food exchange is less structured—and thus our results appear less paradoxical.

Although food and visit exchanges have certain differences, their similarities should not be overlooked. They share a number of the same explanatory variables, and, equally important, are not explained by a large number of the same variables. Concerning certain variables (e.g., the different role of physical disability in visiting and gift giving) a reasonable explanation can be given for the differences. Although transactions of food gifts and visits may be accounted in different psychological ledgers, as Sahlins suggests, the causal factors underlying the net exchange indices appear sufficiently similar that for many analytic purposes the two kinds of transactions could be combined into a single index without a great loss of information.

For both visits and gifts the regression analysis shows that there are patterned imbalances in the distributional transactions which cannot be explained by the inclusion of social invisibles in the analysis. These results place into serious question the approaches toward reciprocity of Mauss and Leach.

Reciprocity and Kinship Distance

As we discussed above, Sahlins (1972) has argued that distributional transactions between close kin should be characterized by transfers; that distributional transactions between strangers or enemies should also be characterized by transfers; and that distributional transactions between covillagers who are not kin or enemies should be characterized by reciprocity. Since Sugluk is a relatively small and closed community, we cannot test Sahlins's ideas about exchange between strangers or enemies, but we can examine the other parts of his hypothesis. And since there was no community leader in Sugluk in the sense of a person who pooled food and redistributed it (the band leaders sometimes assigned parts of large sea mammals caught by other community members, but this activity was less a redistribution function than an assignment function), we do not have a formal organization of reciprocities in a redistribution arrangement to complicate the analysis. We can, in other words, make a relatively clean test of Sahlins's approach.

In presenting his propositions about reciprocity and kinship distance, Sahlins noted that such distance may be reckoned in two ways: either by segmentary distance (group membership in clans or bands) or by genealogical distance and interpersonal kinship status. These two groups may or may not coincide, so that is is necessary to test his proposition using both approaches.

There are two ways in which we can examine the balance of exchange within and between bands. The simplest method is to calculate net exchange indices of each individual for these two groups, and then see whether the former have greater imbalances. Since the imbalances can be either positive or negative, the easiest way to make the comparison is to calculate standard deviations of the net exchange indices. The more unbalanced the exchange accounts, the higher the standard deviations.

One problem with such an attempt to test Sahlins's proposition is to hold other factors constant, such as sex, marital status, size of house, and other explanatory variables discussed in conjunction with Table I. The easiest way to hold all factors constant is to take the regressions presented in Table I and examine the residuals, that is, the differences between the actual values of the net exchange indices and the predicted values. According to Sahlins, we would expect greater imbalances (regression residuals) for those individuals who carry out most of their transactions within their band, than for those individuals who carry out most of their transactions with other bands.

For such an analysis, the first step is to calculate an index (Q) indicating the relative amount of transactions (both positive and negative) within the band (X) and with other bands (Y). The formula used is

$$Q = \frac{X-Y}{X+Y}$$

which is equal to $+1.0$ if the person only visited and received visits from his fellow bandmembers, and is equal to -1.0 if a person only visited and received visits from non-bandmembers. A similar index was used for gifts given and received. The people in each universe were then arranged according to the increasing value of Q for visits and for gifts. Standard deviations of the residuals (indicating imbalances other than those expected from the regression equation) were calculated for three groups of people according to their Q value. According to Sahlins, we would expect the standard deviations to increase as the Q index increases. Relevant data are given in Table II.

Universe B gives exactly the results predicted; and Universe A gives the predicted results with one exception (there is a decline in the standard deviation between the second and third group in the gift index). However, when an F test is performed, in most cases the

TABLE II

Standard Deviations From the Regression Line of Estimated
Net Exchange Indices According to Degree to Which
Transactions Are Made With Band Members[a]

Group	Universe A		Universe B	
	Visits	Gifts	Visits	Gifts
Group, $Q = -1.00$ to $-.40$[b]	.490	.554	.449	.565
Group, $Q = -.41$ to $+.40$[c]	.508	.633	.497	.628
Group, $Q = .41$ to 1.00[d]	.569	.577	.535	.662

[a] The samples used in the calculation are the same as in Table I. All transactions of "band 5" (which is actually a collection of bandless individuals) are classified as extraband. If a person has no transactions with a particular group (with extraband members), his net exchange ratio is defined as zero. In this calculation, secondary hosts and gift givers are not included, and the entire visit or gift is attributed to the prime host. Universes A and B are defined in Table I.
[b] Visits or gifts primarily with members of other bands.
[c] Visits or gifts primarily balanced between bandmembers and members of other bands.
[d] Visits or gifts primarily with bandmembers.

differences between standard deviations from group to group are not statistically significant. Therefore, we must conclude that, although the results give a suggestion that Sahlins's hypothesis is correct, they do not offer completely convincing evidence.

If we measure kinship distance by genealogical distance, then we can examine the data in a similar manner, comparing the standard deviations of the individual accounts with nonkin, distant kin, and close kin. Such an analysis raises some additional difficulties; and before plowing through our results, the reader should be warned that Sahlins's approach is not validated by our results, which turn out to be quite inconclusive.

For the purpose of this particular analysis, *close kin* are defined as those within two links (consanguineal or affinal) of Ego; this includes all those who are or were members of one's own nuclear family household or the nuclear family household of one's parents, one's siblings, one's spouse, or one's children. *Distant kinsmen* are defined as all others recognized as relatives by the Sallumiut, but *not* including those between whom only the ethnographer was able to trace relationships, or those to whom the Eskimos could trace a relationship, but one which was not dignified by a kinship term. *Nonkin* are all those whom a speaker would not address by a kinship term on a genealogical basis.

The first step is to devise an index to measure the relative importance of transactions with the three groups. We weighted the percentage of visits (both to and from) with nonkin by −1.00; the percentage of visits (both to and from) with far kin by 0.00; and the percentage of visits (both to and from) with near kin by +1.00; divided the total by 100; and ended up with an index ranging from −1.00 (if all visits were with nonkin) to +1.00 (if all visits were with near kin). If all visits were with far kin or if all visits were evenly balanced between nonkin or near kin, the index is 0.00. Such an index (designated below as the kin-distance index, KDI) corresponds to the index devised for the visits within and outside the band.[4]

The second step is to examine the standard deviations of the regression residuals of the individuals with different KDIs. If Sahlins is correct, we should expect that the standard deviations of the residuals increase with a raising KDI. Relevant data are presented in Table III.

The data do not support the hypothesis; out of fourteen pairs for which comparisons can be made, seven pairs show the predicted direction of differences in the standard deviations, and seven pairs show just the opposite. Two explanations for this failure can be given.

First, the bonds of band membership seem stronger than the bonds of kinship, probably because band membership was centered around much closer economic cooperation. Thus, kin who were not in the band received treatment more like that of other non-bandmembers than that of equivalent kin who were within the band.

TABLE III

Standard Deviations from the Regression Line of Estimated Net Exchange Indices According to the Degree to Which Transactions Are Made with Kin

	Universe A		Universe B	
Group	Visits	Gifts	Visits	Gifts
Group, KDI = −1.00 to −.40[a]	.542	.562	.552	.521
Group, KDI = − .41 to +.40[b]	.515	.611	.430	.609
Group, KDI = .41 to 1.00[c]	.429	.597	.480	.719

[a] Visits or gifts primarily with nonkin.
[b] Visits or gifts primarily with far kin.
[c] Visits or gifts primarily with near kin.

[4] We are assuming a linearity in the changes of the standard deviations, such that the standard deviations of regression residuals of people dealing with a balanced mix of near kin and nonkin are roughly the same as those of a person dealing just with distant kin.

Second, reciprocal kinship duties were quite highly structured, and reflected imbalances that would not be completely explained by the factors listed in Table I. These imbalances can be seen clearly by aggregating all exchanges occurring between people standing in a reciprocal kinship relation and then grouping these data according to kin distance. Such an exercise was carried out elsewhere (Pryor, 1978).

The statistical exercises presented in Tables II and III suggest that there is some merit in Sahlin's approach, if kinship is defined in terms of segmentary distance, rather than genealogical distance. Nevertheless, even the results of the analysis of distribution using the segmentary distance approach do not validate Sahlin's hypothesis, since the differences in standard deviations are not statistically significant at the .05 level.

Native Interpretations versus Our Interpretations of Exchange Transactions

Before we end this study, two last questions must be posed: To what extent are the categories used for this analysis significant to the Eskimos at Sugluk? And to what extent are our results consistent with native understanding of the exchange process?

The Sallumiut concept of reciprocity is the same as that used in this analysis, namely, balance of goods and services exchanged between gross status equals (Graburn, 1971, pp. 108–109). Thus, our interpretation of the net account indices would be similar to that of the Sallumiut. Moreover, it is important to note that most of the categories chosen for quantification are those used in the community. The villagers recognized the importance of factors such as sex, age, and marital status in social transactions. Further, native criteria were used in rating each individual according to prestige, and each family according to its social status. But, in addition, we have introduced a number of categories which we felt were important for analysis, but which the natives would not recognize, or, if they did, would believe to be irrelevant. The purpose of the regression analysis is to determine the actual determinants of Eskimo exchange behavior, not the ideology rationalizing such behavior. Indeed, by comparing our regression results with how the natives might explain or justify the pattern of transactions, we can determine the gap between the two, and obtain a clearer view of the relation between native theory and native practice.

In explaining the pattern of transactions and the net exchange indices, the natives of Sugluk would use the following model, which is an ideal used as a mental guide for action, and also which is the way the Sugluk villagers believe reality is structured. In the economic sphere, prestige was derived by being a successful hunter and conspicuously distributing the game according to the ideal. After the rules of the division during the hunt were followed (before the animal is brought to the village), one had the duty to share with members of the following social groups: one's own family and household, one's parents, one's restricted *ilagiit* (bilaterally reckoned relatives), one's band, and, lastly, the whole community, either as individuals or as an invited group. In addition, one was expected to visit and render services to these groups in the same order. Naturally, without significant hunting productivity or other useful skills, one could fulfill little of the overall model of generosity. The prescribed sharing patterns ensured that amounts of game totaling approximately three hundred pounds and up, and brought into the community, would be shared among others besides one's household and close relatives, and that truly large kills would be celebrated by feasts to which the host and hostess might invite all the men and women in the community to eat and carry away bags of meat. To host such an occasion was the epitome of Eskimo success. On a more mundane level, household members and all visitors were supposed to be able to partake of any food or drink that was available in a household without asking; a good host did, however, offer, and might even make available, comestibles that were not in sight.

Thus, like many American anthropologists and social psychologists, the Sallumiut argued that generosity and prestige were correlated, and that between those equal in prestige, exchange accounts were roughly balanced. Both aspects of this proposition deserve further analysis, especially because exchange accounts are highly unbalanced in this egalitarian society, and because prestige is not related to net generosity when other factors are taken into account. In short, the Sallumiut did not fully perceive the discrepancies between their model and their behavior, nor did the ethnographer, until we performed the regression analysis.

The Sallumiut perceptions of the relationships between generosity and prestige were maintained because they had many tautological elements. These relationships were so powerfully held that aspects might be violated without shaking their beliefs. For instance, we found that many people of low social status were very generous in their gift transactions, and yet they continued to be labeled as low-status individuals, in part because their members broke some of the other moral rules, but mainly because most of the Sallumiut hardly ever visited them, and were, therefore, able to accuse them of lack of hospitality. On the other hand, some of the most productive families were only irregularly generous, but were able to maintain their high prestige by occasional conspicuous giveaways on a scale that those who were physically unable or who were poor in hunting equipment were unable to maintain. Furthermore, conspicuous giveaways of successful families were long remembered, and what people said about the rules of sharing sometimes counted for more than what people did: for instance, the high-prestige persons always vehemently upheld the ethics of the system and the necessity of total generosity, whereas some of the poorest questioned the need to continue a distribution system that had been functional among much smaller traditional social groups. Yet, as our analysis indicates, some of the former were net takers (even after the giveaways had been taken into account), and some of the latter, net donors! In short, high-prestige people could maintain their position by a manipulation of the symbols of generosity, rather than by their actual behavior.

The notion that social equals had roughly balanced exchange transactions had a similar ideological reinforcement, and, in addition, did not make it necessary for the natives of Sugluk to keep an exact mental accounting. Thus, again, there was no confrontation between the facts of social behavior and the ideology of exchange.

One other factor influencing differences between the reality and ideology of exchange deserves brief mention. Most individual Sallumiut were more attracted to modern conveniences as opposed to traditional values than they liked to admit; thus, wealth in terms of modern material possessions significantly affected the net exchange indices (see Table I), although conveniences had no place in their traditional ideology.

An extremely important general hypothesis can be drawn from this discussion: the myth that exchange accounts are roughly balanced between social equals allows unbalanced accounts to be maintained without rancor; and a society with the ideology that everyone is trying to cheat everyone else might, for an analogous reason, show much more balanced net account indices. That is, the myth of reciprocity or nonreciprocity may be the most important causal factor in bringing the reverse situation in actual behavior.

SUMMARY AND CONCLUSIONS

This is an empirical study designed to test a series of hypotheses about the nature of reciprocity which are found in the anthropology literature, particularly in the writings of Mauss, Leach, and Sahlins. Our data from an Eskimo village show that there are great imbalances of exchange, and, furthermore, a certain patterning of these imbalances can be detected. We are not denying that reciprocal exchange took place. But, in addition to such balanced exchange, there are also extremely important unilateral transfers which can be traced to the action of certain economic, social, and political variables which we have isolated. Thus, the views of Mauss and others who believe that exchange in precapitalist societies is essentially reciprocal is belied by our results. Further, the Eskimos in our village who believed in the reality of strict reciprocity between social equals were also incorrect.

By including in our calculations a number of considerations of social invisibles such as prestige and status, we tried to test the notion that exchange may be balanced by the counterflow of such invisibles. Our regression experiments showed that these did not seem to play a sufficiently important role to yield statistically significant results. It is always a dangerous procedure for analysts to invoke the use of counterbalancing social invisibles to "explain" one-way transfers, and, in the ethnographic case under consideration, such a procedure seems clearly wrong. Thus, the views of Leach and his followers appear incorrect.

We have found the views of Sahlins more promising, although in this case as well, we provide evidence that he is only partially correct. In addition to the net exchange indices being influenced by the economic, social, and political factors which we isolated, we found that kin distance—defined in terms of membership in certain bands— also appeared to influence the results. However, this influence does not appear completely certain, since the statistical tests did not yield significant results.

It must finally be emphasized that the native belief that reciprocity does or does not occur does not necessarily reflect the reality of the situation, even as a rough approximation, since the existence of such a belief may bring about a reality which is exactly the opposite. That is, a belief in the occurrence of reciprocity makes it unnecessary for close attention to be paid to the exact balance of transactions, and, as a result, balanced exchange may never be achieved; conversely, a belief that reciprocal exchange seldom occurs may make participants in any type of exchange extremely sensitive about any types of imbalance which may occur, so that, as a result, transactions are generally balanced.

In short, the common assumption of anthropologists and others that exchange in primitive or peasant societies is primarily balanced, where balance can either include or exclude the flow of certain invisibles, needs reexamination in several ways. On a theoretical level, such an assumption leads often to vacuous tautologies, i.e., because transactions are not balanced, a social invisible is invented which balances the transaction at the analytic cost of obscuring the importance of transfer elements. On an empirical level, such an assumption does not lead to very useful predictions in case studies such as this where most of the necessary data for such an analysis are available.

The concept of reciprocity has certain mythic qualities to both Western social scientists and natives. Although myths are important social entities and, as such, deserve to be studied, this does not mean that we, as scholars, need believe them.

ACKNOWLEDGMENT

We would like to thank members of seminars at the University of California and also at Swarthmore College for their helpful remarks on an earlier draft of this study.

11

New Developments in Operant Conditioning and Their Implications

BARRY SCHWARTZ

INTRODUCTION

From the very beginning, the area of psychology known as the experimental analysis of behavior, or operant conditioning, has looked beyond itself for extension and application of its basic principles to complex situations. B. F. Skinner, the person most responsible for the development of operant-conditioning research, was at work on an account of language at the same time that his seminal *Behavior of Organisms* (1938) was published. The account of language was twenty years in the making (Skinner, 1957), but the important point is that it began at the same time that the laboratory discipline was beginning; it began when there were almost no basic principles to apply. This orientation toward extension of laboratory principles has characterized Skinner's work ever since (e.g., Skinner, 1948, 1953, 1968, 1971).

During the period in which Skinner's account of language came to fruition, George Homans (1961) used the principles of operant conditioning then available to develop a theory of social behavior. Of the five basic principles of social behavior proposed by Homans, three are simply statements, in the vocabulary of human affairs, of the operant conditioning principles that:

BARRY SCHWARTZ • Department of Psychology, Swarthmore College, Swarthmore, Pennsylvania 19081. Support for preparation of this paper was provided by NSF grants BMS73–01403 BNS–78–15461 to the author.

1. Rewards strengthen behavior.
2. Behavior is strengthened in proportion to the magnitude and frequency of reward.
3. Repeated experience of the same reward leads to satiation.

Homans's theory spawned an enormous amount of interesting and productive work in the area now known as social exchange, work to which this volume bears witness. Social exchange theory has developed on its own, largely unaffected by developments in the operant-conditioning laboratory. Though it continues to rest upon principles like the ones initially formulated by Homans—formulated when the "science of behavior" was more a promise than a realization—it has neither capitalized upon nor incorporated behavior principles which have emerged from the laboratory as the analysis of behavior has developed. The promise of a science of behavior was apparently sufficient to launch social exchange theory as an independent area of inquiry.

It is the purpose of this chapter to elucidate several significant developments in the field of operant conditioning as they relate to the exchange formulation. Unfortunately, my major argument is not simply that the analysis of behavior has uncovered principles of conditioning which an adequate theory of social behavior cannot overlook, though this is indeed the case. Rather, my major point is that recent empirical and theoretical developments threaten the most fundamental assumptions on which the study of operant conditioning rests.

What is at stake, as we shall see, is the legitimacy of generalizing from the behavior of pigeons in the operant-conditioning chamber to other organisms in other environments. As a result, these new developments are of particular relevance to extensions of operant conditioning like social exchange theory.

In order to describe and discuss these new developments, it is first necessary to discuss the theoretical and methodological assumptions which guide the experimental analysis of behavior. Thus, we will begin with a detailed look at the assumptions and definitions on which Skinner depended when he created the methods of operant conditioning research some forty years ago. In doing so, we will emphasize those aspects of Skinner's early formulations which are of particular importance to social exchange theory. With Skinner's key assumptions clearly identified, we can move on to a discussion of the recent developments that challenge these assumptions, to an evaluation of the significance of the challenge, and to some speculations about where the challenge leaves the analysis of behavior, especially in terms of extensions and applications.

The Experimental Analysis of Behavior: Methods and Assumptions

The Behavior of Organisms (1938) is a work of genius. It was written at a time when students of learning viewed learning as the development of stimulus–response (S–R) connections. The responses which were connected to stimuli were individual muscle movements. Thus, even a simple bit of behavior, like running down an alley for food, was conceived as a host of S–R connections chained together. It was difficult, under the influence of Pavlov and Thorndike, to view learning in any other way. However, to view learning in this molecular, S–R fashion, was almost to admit defeat at the start. The difficulty involved in specifying the stimulus members of S–R units and in identifying individual responses made explanations of the simplest learned behaviors woefully complex. In addition, it seemed clear that many behaviors which occurred were not triggered by an antecedent stimulus at all, and that organisms did not learn specific muscle movements, but whole classes of them. The rat trained to press the lever with its left paw would also press with its right paw; the rat trained to run down an alley would also swim down the alley.

Skinner was mindful of these inevitable difficulties even before research and theoretical debate made them apparent. As a result, he developed an alternative framework which flourished and grew while S–R connectionism was mired in a long series of theoretical challenges and crucial experiments which resolved little and confused much. The central orientation of Skinner's approach was functional. Instead of trying to analyze the individual movements of an organism, he defined a behavior functionally, in terms of its effects on the environment; instead of trying to specify stimuli which triggered responses by reference to an organism's sensory capacity, he specified them functionally, in terms of their demonstrable power to control behavior; instead of trying to define rewards in an absolute manner, by reference to the biological needs of an organism, he defined them functionally, in terms of their ability to control behavior. Skinner's framework, in broad outline, was nothing more than a strategy of approaching the identification of the key constituents of operant conditioning—stimulus, response, and reinforcer—with a functional orientation. Let us now examine these functional definitions more closely.

What is a stimulus? It is defined *in terms of the control it exerts over behavior*. If a pigeon is trained to peck at a green triangle, and subsequently is tested with a green circle and a white triangle, and it pecks only the green circle, then the stimulus is *green* and not *green triangle*.

The definition of reward or reinforcement parallels the definition of a stimulus. An event is reinforcing if and only if it increases the frequency of the behavior which precedes it. Reinforcers are defined in terms of *the control they exert over behavior*. Skinner was happy to leave a general theory of reward to the physiologist. His own definition allowed one to determine, for any particular event, whether it had reinforcing properties; simply present it contingent on a response, and note whether the frequency of the response increases. Precisely the same strategy applies to punishment.

Finally, what is a response? It is in this domain that Skinner's ingenuity is most apparent. If a rat learns to press a lever for food, should presses with the left paw be distinguished from presses with the right paw? Should forceful presses be distinguished from weak ones? In general, how molecular should we get in specifying the behavior which the animal is learning? Skinner's answer to this question is that we should not get molecular at all. Instead of dealing with molecular responses, we define an *operant*, a class of responses. The members of this class may be as different from one another as paw movements and tail flicks. All that is required for membership in the class is that the response satisfy the defining characteristic. And what is the defining characteristic? It is just that characteristic on which reinforcement depends. Thus, lever presses are movements of the organism which operate a switch connected to the lever. Any movement at all which meets this criterion is a lever press, and all lever presses, no matter how variable in topography they may be, are treated as identical instances of the operant. Thus, for Skinner, the response, or operant, is defined in terms of its consequences—in terms of the reinforcement contingency.

This approach to defining responses gives the investigator enormous freedom in setting up an experimental procedure. There are, after all, an indefinitely large number of properties of behavior which can be used as defining characteristics of an operant. What one chooses should be dictated by convenience. In Skinner's case, he was convinced that the soundest dependent variable available to the analysis of behavior was the frequency of occurrence of an operant. To this end, he needed to measure a behavior which could be repeated again and again without the intervention of the experimenter and without danger of fatiguing the subject. Lever pressing (in rats) and key pecking (in pigeons) were ideal in this regard; they suited Skinner's objectives admirably. In addition to convenience, there was one other criterion which influenced the choice of an operant. One's definition was good if manipulation of variables like deprivation, reinforcement frequency, or reinforcement magnitude, produced smooth and orderly changes in response rate. One's definition was bad if manipulation of these variables did not result in smooth and orderly functions.

This, then, is the simple and elegant set of definitions with which Skinner developed the methods which now dominate the study of operant conditioning. The careful reader may at this point be wondering whether "simple" and "elegant" are the appropriate adjectives. One might be tempted to substitute for them the words "tautological" and "vacuous," as some have (Chomsky, 1959). To see how the definitions risk tautology and how this problem may be solved, we must look at them a bit more closely.

Each of the three terms—stimulus, reinforcer, and operant—is defined in terms of the others. An event is a stimulus if it controls behavior; a class of responses is an operant if it is controlled by reinforcement. This network of interdependent definitions rests upon the premise that behavior is influenced in an orderly way by stimuli and reinforcers; it assumes the principle which many would argue is most in need of empirical verification: that contingencies of reinforcement shape and control behavior. If one presents a stimulus contingent on a response and the response does not increase in frequency, one concludes not that the principle of reinforcement is disconfirmed, but that the stimulus was not a reinforcer, or that the response was poorly defined (see Meehl, 1950). In essence, the problem of tautology amounts to a problem of determining whether the network of terms established by Skinner can ever do more than describe or interpret what has already been observed, that is, does the system have any predictive power at all? In his critique of Skinner's account of language, Chomsky (1959) called attention to the problem by reference to the behavior of a person in an art museum. The person stares at a painting. What is the stimulus which controls the person's behavior? If the person murmurs "red," it is presumably color which is controlling his behavior. If the person says "pastoral," it is presumably details of the scene depicted which are controlling his behavior. If the person says "impressionism," it is presumably both the painting and the observer's past history which are controlling his behavior. The point is that one cannot specify in advance what the controlling stimulus is. If this is an inevitable characteristic of the system, then the value of the system is dubious indeed.

Meehl (1950) saw that the logical problem of tautology could be circumvented empirically. If an event increases the frequency of a behavior which precedes it, then that event is tautologously identified as a reinforcer. However, one can then predict that the same event will be a reinforcer in a new and different situation. If it is, the tautology is broken. In short, it is the transsituational generality of the principles of conditioning which will save the system from tautologous vacuity.

The importance of transsituationality goes beyond the logical problem of definition of terms. It is significant for at least two other reasons. First, consider the intended scope of Skinner's system in comparison to the data on which it is based. Skinner's aim was to uncover functional relations which described the *behavior* of *organisms*. To do so, he studied the *lever pressing of rats* and the *key pecking of pigeons*. Even if powerful principles of behavior emerged from these investigations, what reason would there be to believe that these principles applied to organisms other than rats and pigeons in situations other than Skinner boxes? Unlike some of his empiricist predecessors, Skinner was sensitive from the beginning to the fact that species differ from one another in ways which influence their behavior significantly (1966). Many species specific behavior patterns exist, and their importance grows as one moves down the phylogenetic scale. This being the case, if one is interested in principles of behavior which transcend species boundaries, one must be sure that one's experimental situation is uncontaminated by species-specific influences. One must create an experimental environment which neutralizes whatever biological predispositions may exist. Skinner's methods were an explicit attempt to attain this goal. There is no doubt that what is a stimulus, what is a reinforcer, and what is a learnable response are all species dependent. The important thing, however, is to insure that relations between stimuli, responses, and reinforcers are not. Said another way, it is important that there be no intrinsic relation between pecking and food for the pigeon; that there be no intrinsic relation between tones and shocks for the rat. The relation between stimuli, behaviors, and reinforcers must be transsituational. An effective stimulus, defined in one situation, must serve as an effective stimulus in all situations; a reinforcer in one situation must be a reinforcer in all situations; a response class which is orderly in one situation must be orderly in all situations. One must be able to combine any effective stimulus with any effective response and any effective reinforcer without significantly affecting the outcome of one's experiment. Only if this condition is satisfied, at least approximately, is there justification for discussing the behavior of organisms based upon the key pecking of pigeons.

Thus, transsituationality is important both for logical reasons (the definitions) and for reasons of maximizing the generality of one's findings. In addition, transsituationality is particularly important when principles of conditioning are extended to human affairs. The experimental analysis of animal behavior cannot tell us what an effective stimulus, reinforcer, and response will be in studies of human behavior. It can provide clues and suggest possibilities, but reliable identification of these terms must result from direct investigation of human behavior. One's temptation is to find one good (orderly, convenient) experimental situation, and use it almost exclusively in studying human behavior. One assumes that since conditioning principles obtained from animals are general, they will be similarly general with people. But what if conditioning phenomena observed with pigeons and rats are not transsituational? How is one to assess the generality of findings with people? Since the only justification for studying the control of human behavior in a limited set of situations is the general power of similar strategies employed with animals, any threat to the generality of animal-conditioning studies has direct implications for one's interpretation of human research. For this reason, students of social exchange theory must be mindful of challenges to the presumption of transsituationality in research with animals. And in the last few years, these challenges, backed by an accumulation of impressive evidence, have been made. The challenges are of two general types, and we will discuss them separately.

The first type of challenge concedes that Skinner's methods succeed in creating a biologically neutral or unbiased environment. However, the claim is that learning in nature is not biologically neutral; that both the substance of the information acquired and the process by which learning occurs are critically dependent upon the biological makeup of a species. Thus, Skinnerian methods, if successful, create a phenomenon (unbiased learning) rather than analyzing one.

The second type of challenge largely concedes that organisms do learn in unbiased fashion, i.e., that not all of what an organism learns is species dependent. The claim is that Skinnerian methods fail to eliminate species-specific contributions to the determination of behavior. Thus, on this view, the problem is not that the goal of the analysis of behavior is misdirected, but that the methods used fail to achieve the goal. We can restate these two concerns concisely as:

1. Is learning in nature biologically neutral?
2. Is learning in the Skinner box biologically neutral?

We will take up each of these concerns separately.

Is Learning in Nature Biologically Neutral? The Ethological View

The view that the modification of behavior by experience is sharply constrained by the biological makeup of the species; that learning in nature, far from being unbiased, is finely tuned and constrained by an organism's genetic character, has long been a central tenet of the branch of biology known as ethology. It has perhaps been most clearly and boldly stated by Lorenz (1965):

> Whatever else learning may be, it certainly is an adaptive modification of behavior, and its adaptiveness, that is, its ability to adapt behavior, needs a causal explanation. There is an infinitesimally small chance that modification, as such, is adaptive to the particular environmental influence that happened to bring it about. Indeed, this chance is not greater than that of a mutation being adaptive. Geneticists rate this likelihood at about 10^{-8}. Whenever we do find a clearly adaptive *range of modifiability* . . . we know that these achievements of adaptation are not exclusively due to environmental influences, but just as much to a very *specialized range of modifiability which has been selected for in the pre-history of the species.*
>
> The more complicated an adapted process, the less chance there is that a random change will improve its adaptedness. There are no life processes more complicated than those which take place in the central nervous system and control behavior. Random change must, with an overpowering probability, result in their disintegration. . . .
>
> To anyone tolerably versed in biological thought, it is a matter of course that learning, like any function of comparably high differentiation and survival value, must necessarily be performed by a very special mechanism built into the organic system in the course of its evolution. (pp. 11–13; italics added)

It seems clear from this view that an ethological approach to the study of behavior disputes the most basic assumptions which underlie Skinnerian methods. If different species have evolved specialized learning mechanisms which are tuned to normal conditions in the natural environment, then the phenomena one observes in the artifical confines of the operant conditioning chamber will not reveal any of these specialized learning abilities. Instead of providing an analysis of behavior, operant methods will provide a synthesis of behavior: they will create phenomena which are characteristic of only artificial and biologically neutral situations.

The ethological approach has been around for some time. Until recently, ethology and learning theory have coexisted, despite the radical differences in their respective orientations, by ignoring each other. In recent years, particularly dramatic research findings have led an increasing number of learning researchers to a serious consideration of the ethological position. I will discuss just two of them here.

Instinctive Drift

In 1961, Marion and Keller Breland published a paper called "The Misbehavior of Organisms." The Brelands had been students of operant conditioning with Skinner, and had chosen to employ their knowledge of conditioning commercially. They trained animals to engage in a variety of novel and entertaining behavior sequences—sometimes as part of advertising campaigns, and sometimes as part of shows for paying customers. The Brelands were successful in training a wide variety of complex and intricate behaviors, all maintained by food reinforcement. Occasionally, and inexplicably, however, the Brelands would lose control of a bit of behavior. Behavior which had been well maintained by food reinforcement for some time would suddenly deteriorate. For example, chickens trained to "play baseball" by pulling a loop of string which moved a bat which knocked a ping pong ball off a pedestal toward an "outfield" destination behind a wire mesh screen, came reliably to pull the string. One day, the wire screen was removed so that the animals could be photographed. The chickens pecked the bat which then hit the ball. Then, instead of moving to the feeder to obtain their reward, they left their perches and frantically pursued the ball, pecking and scratching at it and ignoring their food.

After observing a number of such amusing and mysterious events, the Brelands came to see a common thread which underlay them all. The loss of control of behavior by reinforcement was the result of the intrusion of parts of species-specific consummatory repertoires; behaviors which were not controlled or modified by their consequences, but were built into the organism. Thus, chickens, which ordinarily peck and scratch for food in the barnyard, were pecking and scratching at the ping pong ball. Why? Presumably it was because the ball had been paired with food, and because the chickens were food deprived. This intrusion of species-specific behavior patterns into what seemed to be wholly artificial situations the Brelands labeled "instinctive drift." They suggested that whenever a situation allowed for the occurrence of these behaviors, they would occur, and when they occurred, they would successfully wrest control of the animals' activity away from the reinforcement contingency. If these behaviors were so powerfully determined that they occurred even under less than ideal conditions when they cost a hungry animal its food, it seemed reasonable to claim that any situation which prevented such behaviors from occurring would seriously distort the nature of behavior control in the natural environment. Thus the over-simple environment of the operant-conditioning chamber yielded principles which suggested that behavior could be perfectly controlled by contingencies of reinforcement just because other potential behavioral influences were prevented from intruding. According to the Brelands, if one used the standard methods of the analysis of behavior, one could not help but arrive at a distorted picture of the significance of the law of effect.

Somehow, the Brelands' findings, though widely acknowledged, had little influence on the course of research on the analysis of behavior. It was another phenomenon—one which had been around for years but only came to the attention of students of learning in the late 1960's—which compelled researchers to reexamine the assumptions on which their discipline rested. This was the phenomenon of taste-aversion learning.

Taste-Aversion Learning

If a rat is allowed access to a flavored solution, and some time later, the rat is given a sublethal dose of poison which produces extreme gastrointestinal upset, the rat will avoid the substance which it previously ingested. This phenomenon is known as taste-aversion learning (see Revusky & Garcia, 1970; Rozin & Kalat, 1971; Seligman & Hager, 1972). The rat associates a taste with stomach distress, and subsequently avoids the taste. As described, there is nothing especially surprising or intriguing about the phenomenon. It fits nicely into more familiar phenomena observed in conditioning laboratories as an instance of either Pavlovian (classical) conditioning, or an instance of discriminated avoidance learning. However, the phenomenon is intriguing and surprising for the following reasons:

1. Rats can learn the association even when taste and illness are separated by as much as 12 *hours*. This fact contrasts sharply with other studies of Pavlovian conditioning (e.g., eye blink, salivation), where the optimum interval between conditioned and unconditioned stimuli is 0.5 sec, and intervals much beyond 30 sec do not reliably result in conditioning.

2. The special nature of taste-aversion learning depends neither on the nature of the unconditioned stimulus (poison), nor on the nature of the conditioned stimulus (taste). Rather, it depends upon the *combination* of taste and illness. If a flashing light is substituted for the taste, conditioned responses to the light are acquired with great difficulty, if at all. If a shock is substituted for poison, conditioned responses to the taste do not develop. It is only when taste and poison are combined that rapid and impressive acquisition of conditioned aversion occurs (Garcia & Koelling, 1966). In short, taste and illness *belong* together. Just as people seem to attribute stomach upset to something they ate, and especially something novel they ate, so also rats associate stomach illness with something they ate, and, like people, especially if the substance they ingested was novel (Kalat & Rozin, 1970).

Thus, the phenomenon of taste-aversion learning seems to challenge the most basic assumptions of the analysis of behavior. All members of the class stimulus are not interchangeable; all members of the class reinforcer or unconditioned stimulus are not interchangeable.

It is a particular relation between a member of the class of stimuli and a member of the class of unconditioned stimuli which is responsible for taste-aversion learning. If this special relation is a commonplace of learning in nature, then the research tradition of learning theory is difficult to defend.

Is it a commonplace? Evidence which would permit an answer to this question is not presently available. What can be said at the least, however, is that "belongingness" is not unique to rats, tastes, and poisons. Wilcoxin, Dragoin and Kral (1971) did an important study of conditioned aversion in quail. They reasoned that, while rats depend upon taste to identify food in nature, quail and other birds depend upon vision. For quail, it is the visual properties of objects which mark them as food. This being the case, one might expect belongingness in the quail to promote associations of color and poison, rather than taste and poison. And indeed, when quail are poisoned after ingesting a solution which has a distinctive taste and a distinctive color, they selectively associate color, and not taste, with poison. Thus, one is tempted to make the generalization that organisms are built to associate stimuli of the sort they use to identify food with gastrointestinal changes, and that the ability to make this kind of association is special—built into the species, and governed by laws which are different from the laws of biologically neutral associations. A number of important and influential papers (Rozin & Kalat, 1971; Seligman, 1970; Shettleworth, 1972) have made this claim, and viewed taste aversion as merely a single instance of what are many adaptive specializations of learning. These papers have attempted to push the analysis of behavior in an ethological direction.

What is one to make of phenomena like instinctive drift and taste-aversion learning, among others? Do they threaten the very foundations of the analysis of behavior? Do they raise serious questions about the traditional methods of the field? On the contrary, I think that, rather than vitiating the methods and assumptions of the analysis of behavior, these new phenomena provide an eloquent and dramatic justification of those methods. What these phenomena reveal are (1) that biologically specialized learning abilities and sources of behavior control exist, and (2) that given the opportunity, these species-charac-teristic mechanisms will show themselves, and exert control over behavior. All that this means, however, is that if one is interested in uncovering *general principles* of behavior control, one must be sure to create a method which eliminates or neutralizes species-typical influ-ences. And this, of course, was precisely what Skinner was after in developing the methods of the analysis of behavior (see Schwartz, 1974).

The ethologists' most likely response to this claim is that *all* modification of behavior by experience is of a specialized form of the sort which characterizes taste-aversion learning, so that the quest for general principles of behavior control is misguided. However, this seems unlikely. It is by now a truism that organismal flexibility increases with phylogenetic complexity and with development. Simpler organisms profit less from experience than more complex ones. Similarly, infantile behavior is more rigid than adult behavior. What this suggests is that the significance of specialized learning mechanisms may vary with the species and the developmental stage of the organism under investigation. It seems clear that most of the learning done by human adults is of precisely the unbiased nature which characterizes learning in the conditioning chamber. Learning to swim, or drive a car, or play bridge or chess, or do statistics, hardly seems closely related to any specialized biological mechanisms. Therefore, it may be that the learning of associations among arbitrary events is characteristic of relatively adult, complex organisms (see Rozin, 1976). Furthermore, rats and pigeons placed in the artificial environment of the conditioning chamber do learn. Does not this very fact imply that not all learning mechanisms are specialized.? As Skinner (1969) has stated in criticizing the ethological view that the laboratory is not like real life:

> In any case, behavior in a natural habitat would have no special claim to genuineness. What an organism does is a fact about that organism regardless of the conditions under which it does it. A behavioral process is nonetheless real for being exhibted in an arbitrary setting. (p. 191)

In summary, while it seems clear from recent research that specialized learning mechanisms exist, it is not clear that this implies that all learning is specialized. The quest for principles of learning in biologically neutral situations may have special value in application to human behavior. This suggests that our main concern should be focused on a question other than "is any learning biologically neutral?" What we need to evaluate is whether the learning which occurs in the artificial environment is unbiased. As we saw above, Skinner set out to create an environment which neutralized species-specific contributions to learning. Our question now, in short, is did he succeed? Is the box biologically neutral?

Is the Skinner Box Biologically Neutral?

This is a question which has only begun to emerge in the last ten years. Despite intimations that the answer to the question should have been available in the literature, it took a particularly dramatic phenomenon to bring the question into focus. The phenomenon has come to be known as *autoshaping* (Brown & Jenkins, 1968). Autoshaping refers to a procedure with which the pigeon's key peck can be automatically shaped. A response key is periodically illuminated for a few seconds, and its illumination is followed by the delivery of food. After a number of such pairings of key light and food, the pigeon comes to peck the key, and continues pecking the key on trial after trial (automaintenance). This procedure seems little more than a convenient substitute for the standard procedure of shaping by successive approximation (Ferster & Skinner, 1957). All it is, after all, is an ordinary classical conditioning procedure; key light (CS) is paired with food (US), and elicits pecking (CR). However, a little reflection will reveal the significance of the fact the key pecks can be classically conditioned for much of what has been discussed above. First of all, the responses which result from classical conditioning procedures are not unbiased; they bear a direct relation to the US. This is true in the case of salivation in dogs, and it is true in the case of key pecking in pigeons. Jenkins and Moore (1973) have shown that when the US is food, pigeons make feeding pecks at the key, and when the US is water, pigeons make drinking pecks at the key (see Hearst & Jenkins, 1974; Schwartz & Gamzu, 1977, for reviews). We argued above that, in order for the set of definitions which guides the analysis of behavior to be nontautological, the members of the class of operants must be interchangeable with each other, i.e., they must bear no intrinsic relation to the reinforcer. But if key pecks are classically conditioned CRs, they do bear an intrinsic relation to the reinforcer.

It might be argued that even though the first key pecks that occur are the result of classical conditioning, the pecks are followed closely in time by food, and it is this adventitious, or superstitious relation between pecks and their consequences which maintains responding (Skinner, 1948b). If this were true, the problems posed for the analysis of behavior by autoshaping would be minimal. But it is not. In what is perhaps the most dramatic experiment on autoshaping which has been conducted, Williams and Williams (1969) arranged contingencies so that if the pigeon did not peck the lit key during a trial, food was delivered; if the pigeon did peck the key, food was omitted. This procedure insured that key pecks could never be followed by food. Key pecks, if under operant control, would certainly be eliminated by this omission procedure. On the other hand, if key pecks were under control of the classical conditioning, CS–US relation, they would continue to occur, as Sheffield (1965) has shown with conditioned salivation in dogs in an identical procedure. What Williams and Williams found, and what has been replicated many times since, (see

Schwartz & Gamzu, 1977) is that key pecking persisted despite the negative consequences for many, many sessions. Indeed, the experimenters stopped the experiment before the pigeons stopped pecking the key. They did not peck on every trial, but they did peck on 50–90% of the trials, thereby significantly decreasing the number of food deliveries they received. The message is clear; pigeons cannot withold key pecks in order to procure food. The findings of Williams and Williams generated many more experiments, nearly all of which pointed to the seemingly inevitable conclusion that the key peck is sensitive to and controlled by classical conditioning operations. Not only does key pecking bear a special relation to food reinforcement, but it does not appear to be under voluntary control, at least not all the time. The defining characteristic of operants is that they are sensitive to and controlled by their consequences. The omission phenomenon shows that key pecking may not belong to the class of operants. More recent research suggests that the same conclusions may be drawn about lever pressing in rats (Peterson, Ackil, Frommer, & Hearst, 1972; Stiers & Silberberg, 1974). Yet key pecking in pigeons and lever pressing in rats have been the two operants whose investigation has led to most of what we take to be general principles of operant conditioning.

And there is more. Bolles (1970) has argued, with impressive evidence, that the single most important variable in the study of avoidance learning is the required operant. If the operant bears a relation to the organism's defensive behaviors in nature, it will be learned rapidly; if not, it will be learned slowly, or perhaps not learned at all. Thus, for example, though pigeons can readily learn to hop on a treadle, or flap their wings, or raise their heads, or fly to avoid electric shock, they learn to peck a key to avoid shock only after hours of painstaking training (Hineline & Rachlin, 1969). Without this training they do not seem to learn at all (e.g., Schwartz, 1973). There is even evidence that pigeons that have been trained to peck a key for food, when shifted to an escape and avoidance procedure, will stop pecking the key even though they experience many instances of successful escape and avoidance of shock as a consequence of key pecks (Schwartz & Coulter, 1973). The same sorts of effect, as discussed by Bolles, are observed with rats.

And there is still more. Not only is there a special relation between operant and reinforcer, but there also seems to be a special relation between discriminative stimulus and reinforcer. The belongingness which characterizes taste-aversion learning in rats also characterizes key pecking for food in pigeons. It has been shown that pigeons are predisposed to associate visual stimuli with food and auditory stimuli with shock, even when the situation is arranged to promote the opposite associations (Foree & LoLordo, 1973, 1975; LoLordo, 1971; LoLordo, McMillan, & Riley, 1974; Schwartz, 1976).

All this evidence makes it abundantly clear that the standard methods of operant-conditioning research do not succeed in neutralizing the biological predispositions of the organisms under investigation; in short, the box is not biologically neutral. This fact, coupled with the possibility that learning in the natural environment is often not biologically neutral, has led some investigators to doubt that the quest for general laws of the control of behavior is a sensible one (Rozin & Kalat, 1971; Seligman, 1970; Seligman & Hager, 1972; Shettleworth, 1972). The alternative, of uncovering the "adaptive specializations is learning" (Rozin & Kalat, 1971) which characterize particular species, is likely to provide a more accurate picture of the control of behavior under naturalistic conditions. At the same time, however, it is likely to undermine the justification for extrapolation of principles of behavior developed in the study of pigeons' key pecking or rats' lever pressing to human behavior.

Is it necessary to come to such extreme conclusions about the generality of what goes on in the operant-conditioning chamber on the basis of the evidence sketched above? Is it not possible that even though the box permits the intrusion of species-specific predispositions, these predispositions have only a minor influence on the nature of the functional relations revealed in operant-conditioning research? The answer to this question seems to be yes. Species-specific predispositions seem to influence the functional relations one observes only some of the time. Maintenance of responding by most schedules of reinforcement seems unaffected by whether the recorded operant is specialized. But there are exceptions (the differential reinforcement of low rate [DRL] schedule; Hemmes, 1970; Schwartz & Williams, 1971). Many of the phenomena observed in discrimination-learning research seem uninfluenced by species-specific predispositions. But again there are exceptions (the phenomenon of behavioral contrast; see Schwartz & Gamzu, 1977 for a review). Thus, it seems that only a detailed understanding of the biological and environmental contributions to the control of any operant will enable one to determine which functional relations are general and which depend on the nature of the stimulus-operant-reinforcer relation.

To summarize this section, it is clear that many of the experimental situations we have studied have the potential to allow intrusions of species-specific behavior patterns. The central problem lies in understanding just which features of phenomena are attributable to general principles, and which are attributable to situation or species-specific ones. At this time, it seems virtually impossible to solve this problem, or, more generally, to make *a priori* determinations of which situations will generate which species-specific behaviors. We are forced either to make educated guesses or to await the discovery of phenomena which do not fit our theories, and which demand an assessment of potential biological influences.

Implications of Specialized Learning for Extensions of Operant Conditioning Principles to Human Affairs

The point of developing operant-conditioning methods was to prevent the occurrence of species-specific behaviors, not to deny either their existence or their importance. Skinner himself has stated quite clearly any number of times (e.g., 1966) that phylogenetic determinants of behavior are both real and significant. It is just that he and others were interested in a different class of determinants of behavior. The important point is that the method was so successful that it has taken some forty years for investigators to realize that the box does not prevent the intrusion of species-specific predispositions. In a similar way, students of social exchange, or practitioners of behavioral technology, have created experimental and therapeutic situations which are especially amenable to analysis in terms of operant-conditioning principles. In the past, one could study social interaction under artifical conditions secure in the belief that since the laboratory principles on which the analysis was based were general, the same principles applied to human behavior would be general as well. The upshot of recent developments in the animal laboratory is that this confidence in generality is unwarranted. Consider just one thorny problem in the operant analysis of human behavior: the problem of identifying reinforcers. It is clear that, since people are rarely food-and-water deprived, the reinforcers for their behaviors will be different from the ones typically employed in animal research. This granted, how do we find out what the reinforcers of human behavior are? The answer to this question, in both animal and human research, has been that if a stimulus increases the frequency of the behavior which precedes it, it is, by definition, a reinforcer. This is the tautology which Meehl (1950) tried to conquer with the principle of transsituationality. But there is now good reason to believe that reinforcers are not uniformly transsituational; that the particular relation between operant and reinforcer in any experiment has a major influence on the functions one obtains. If this is true in the animal laboratory, what confidence can one have that it is not true in the human laboratory? What is the evidence that social exchange research yields general principles?

The student of social exchange theory may read these arguments with a certain bemused interest and patience, wondering all the while how any of it makes a difference. Social exchange theory is, after all, a going concern; though its initial development depended upon what was going on in the pigeon laboratory, it now has its own data base, its own set of definitions, and its own general principles. If it turns out that what has been happening in the animal laboratory all these years is not what it first appeared to be, what difference does that make in the analysis of human social interaction?

This is a reasonable and difficult question. It seems clear that, as Skinner (1966) says, "What an organism does is a fact about that organism" (p. 1211). Thus, the findings of social exchange researchers need not be influenced by the developing revolution in our understanding of what goes on in the Skinner box. The problems posed for social exchange theory (or any theory based upon the data from the conditioning laboratory) are far more subtle. They have to do with what we as investigators take to be facts, and with how our methods influence—even determine—the kinds of facts we obtain. The methods of operant conditioning *create* phenomena. If the phenomena created are reflections of what goes on outside the laboratory, there is no problem. However, if what gets created in the laboratory is not a reflection of behavior control in the natural environment, then our methods may be providing us with a seriously distorted set of principles. This was the Brelands' argument. Their concern was not with the validity of operant conditioning principles *per se,* but with the validity of any principles derived from a method which systematically prevented the occurrence of powerful and important species-specific behaviors. The point was not that the law of effect did not work, but that it did not *always* work. And a method which failed to detect the boundaries of applicability of its general principles might lead to serious misrepresentations of those principles.

In the domain of human behavior, the risk involved in ignoring species-specific predispositions seems minor. It is clear that human behavior is much less dependent on these predispositions than is the behavior of pigeons and rats. However, operant-conditioning methods systematically exclude from consideration variables in addition to the species' biological predispositions. And some of these variables may play a significant—even a determining—role in much human behavior. If so, then the human "operant-conditioning chamber" (i.e., research done within the operant-theoretical framework) may be producing distortion which is just as profound as the distortion created in the pigeon chamber.

To make the discussion less hypothetical, let us consider what I take to be a concrete instance of distortion of our understanding of human behavior which results from an operant analysis, strictly applied. Let us return for a moment to the definition of the operant developed by Skinner. Skinner defined the operant with an eye toward functional utility. He saw the difficulty in attempting to identify behavioral units independent of environmental context, and he therefore emphasized the functional relations between behavior and environment (Skinner, 1935). An operant was defined on the basis of those properties on which reinforcement was dependent. Such a functional definition was successful if "the entity which it described gave smooth curves for the dynamic laws of the reflex" (Skinner, 1938, p. 37).

As we have seen above, this definition creates an interdependence between operant and reinforcer. As a result, it is necessary, in order for the functional relations one finds to have any generality, that an operant, as defined by Skinner, be a good operant (i.e., yield smooth curves) in combination with any known reinforcer. This is what makes the operant an unbiased behavioral unit. What this definitional problem implies is that the reinforcer must always be *extrinsic* to the operant. It simply makes no sense within the framework to claim that some behaviors are self-reinforcing. Behaviors are defined as discrete units *in terms of* their consequences; they cannot *be* their consequences. Now, as we know, many operants have been defined in this way and studied, and yielded smooth curves. One can observe the creation of an operant as a new behavioral unit as it develops. An organism enters the experimental situation with a certain genetic and experimental character. Preorganized units of behavior already exist. The arbitrary designation of an operant (e.g., lever press) cuts across preestablished behavioral units and creates a new one. Early in training, the operant is extremely variable in topography. It seems apparent that many occurrences are accidental consequences of the active organism's moving in tune to its own drummer. Gradually, as the law of effect exerts its influence, the variability decreases, an efficient topography develops, experimental control is established, and, with it, a new unit of behavior. It seems reasonable that this process of creating new units of behavior, defined in terms of their consequences, mirrors the organization of much of human behavior. Many human acts are arbitrary, and often they are organized and defined precisely in terms of their consequences. The reinforcing agents of a culture may in this way have a determining influence on the organization of human behavior. Thus, assembly-line workers will develop highly stereotyped and efficient behavioral units, secretaries will develop typing behavior and type without really reading the material they are typing, athletes will develop smooth and efficient motor patterns, students will learn the most effective strategies of study in preparing for examinations, and so on. There is no question that one *can* establish efficient and stereotyped behavioral units by improving extrinsic contingencies of reinforcement on behavior. There also seems to be little doubt that our culture operates in precisely this way. Most human activity is reinforced by stimuli which bear no intrinsic relation to the activity itself.

The question we must address is: Does the fact that behavior *can* be controlled by extrinsic consequences imply that in the ordinary course of events it always *is* controlled by extrinsic consequences? There is growing evidence that the answer to this question is no. There seem to be many human behaviors which are "intrinsically motivated" (Deci, 1975). For these behaviors, it is the mere occurrence or execution of the activity which sustains it; extrinsic consequences seem to play no role. Now one could simply acknowledge the existence of intrinsic motivation, as Skinner acknowledges the existence of species-specific behavioral predispositions, and one could admit that such intrinsically motivated behaviors are outside the domain of operant analysis, and then one could continue to pursue the operant analysis of those behaviors which are controlled by extrinsic consequences. Such a strategy would mirror the strategy employed in the animal laboratory. The trouble is that this strategy will not work. There are now impressive indications that when behavior which seems to be intrinsically motivated is paid off with extrinsic reinforcement, the extrinsic-reinforcement contingencies gain control of the behavior, and undermine, or compete with, the intrinsic source of control. This is the focus of much research currently being done on the "overjustification effect" (Deci, 1975; Kruglanski, 1975, Lepper & Greene, 1978). Colloquially, it seems that extrinsic reinforcements turn play into work. And they do so effectively. What this means is that, if one imposes an operant analysis of human behavior—if one brings behavior into the laboratory, and manipulates it with extrinsic-reinforcement contingencies—the analysis will be self-fulfilling. The very methods one uses will determine the effects one obtains. If one views human behavior as controlled by extrinsic consequences, and attempts to validate that view by imposing such consequences on particular bits of behavior, the behavior will be controlled by those consequences, and one's view will be confirmed. And the possibility that the very same behavior when it occurs in the natural environment is self-sustaining will go undetected. Furthermore, as operant-conditioning principles come to have greater and greater influence in applied settings, especially in education, and extrinsic contingencies gain control of more and more behavior, the "fact" that some behavior is intrinsically motivated may cease to be a fact. Token reinforcement in education may well control classroom behavior. In the process, intrinsic motivation to learn may disappear. An effective technology of employee management may keep people working at their jobs. In the process, enjoyment of work may disappear. The facts that (1) extrinsic rewards can gain control over intrinsically motivated behavior, and (2) the theoretical system which underlies operant-conditioning research excludes the study of intrinsically motivated behavior, taken together, suggest that the continued development of the operant analysis of human behavior may transform a valid but limited principle (that behavior *can* be controlled by extrinsic consequences) into a universal truth (that behavior *is* controlled by extrinsic consequences). The question we face is whether this operant view of the relation between behavior and consequence is one which we want to dominate our orientation to research, and ultimately, our culture (see Schwartz, Schuldenfrei, & Lacey, 1978).

This is certainly not inevitable, though it may seem so. At one time in history, the very notion of pleasure was bound up with the activities which produced it. Aristotle, in *Nichomachean Ethics*, argued that pleasure was not a process but an activity, and that every activity had its own proper pleasure. The idea that pleasure exists somehow apart from the acts which produce it is a modern one, arising from Utilitarianism. As time passes, and ideas change, the Aristotelian view may reappear. The dependence of any experimental inquiry upon the methods of operant conditioning seems to imply that the distinction between an act and the pleasure it produces is inevitable. If there is reason to doubt the inevitability and desirability of this state of affairs, there is reason to be concerned about the limitations on the nature of our understanding of behavior which are imposed by operant methods. This, it seems to me, is the most serious problem facing social exchange theory after a generation of interesting and productive research.

SUMMARY

In this paper, I have attempted to convey a feeling for the significant new directions in which the study of animal learning is moving, and to indicate the relevance of these new developments to the application of operant-conditioning principles to human behavior. The major points of the paper are these:

1. The theoretical framework on which the study of operant behavior rests is tautological.

2. What transforms the theory from a set of definitions into a set of testable hypotheses is the transsituationality, or generality, of empirical results.

3. The way to maximize generality is to arrange experimental situations so that their basic elements (stimuli, operants, reinforcers) are not intrinsically related.

4. This was the goal of Skinner's methods. The methods entailed the assumptions that (a) general principles of behavior exist; (b) species-specific determinants of behavior also exist; (c) these latter determinants can be neutralized by studying organisms in artificial environments, with the result that (d) the principles one obtains will be both transspecific and transsituational.

5. Recent research on instinctive drift and taste-aversion learning which provides clear evidence for specialized, species-specific learning abilities have raised serious questions about whether there are general principles of behavior control.

6. Recent research on autoshaping and related phenomena have suggested that even if general laws do exist, the operant-conditioning chamber may not be the appropriate context for discovering them.

7. The limits to generality of conditioning principles suggested by recent animal research raises doubts about the generality of principles obtained through application of operant methods to human behavior.

8. Although operant-conditioning studies with humans show that behavior *can* be controlled by reinforcement, they do not show that behavior ordinarily *is* controlled by reinforcement.

9. The significance of this distinction is highlighted by research on the overjustification effect, which shows that the imposition of extrinsic operant-reinforcement contingencies undermines the control of behavior by consequences intrinsic to the behavior. This research carries the implications that (a) operant analysis of human behavior in the laboratory may provide a systematic distortion of the control of behavior in the natural environment, and (b) the principles of operant analysis may be self-fulfilling.

The upshot of these arguments is that the theoretical foundation for the laboratory study of the control of behavior by operant contingencies of reinforcement may function not so much to mirror fundamental principles as to create them in its own image. When these studies are extended to the technology of behavior modification, they may function not to reveal a culture organized around operant principles, but to create one.

Exchange Theory
The Transient and the Enduring

KENNETH J. GERGEN

INTRODUCTION

Even the most casual observation of human interaction enables one to discern patterns of sequential activity. We observe X approach Y and call out in a friendly manner; Y thereupon smiles and inquires into X's health; X responds with a report on his physical well-being and inquires into Y's recent skiing experiences, and so on. One may also observe a certain degree of regularity or repetition in these patterns. We may be struck by the frequency with which a warm greeting on X's part precedes a friendly response on the part of Y, and that the same pattern can be located throughout society. It is, of course, just such sequential patterns that furnish the social theorist with the observation base undergirding his or her theoretical superstructure. Indeed the positivist–empiricist framework currently dominating the social sciences demands that one's theory furnish an accurate map of the regularities residing within the social sphere.

For the most part, theorists sharing the social exchange orientation have labored toward these traditional ends. Homans's (1974) formulation is said to be constituted by fundamental laws which rest on an extensive body of conditioning research. And, as Homans comments, empirical support for such propositions may be revealed in "continuous direct observation" (p. 7). In their initial exchange formulation, Thibaut and Kelley (1959) evidence a similar orientation. For example,

KENNETH J. GERGEN • Department of Psychology, Swarthmore College, Swarthmore, Pennsylvania 19081.
Preparation of the present manuscript was facilitated by a grant from the National Science Foundation (7809393). Portions of this chapter represent a revised treatment of an earlier paper (Gergen, 1977).

the function of the *comparison level*, like almost all aspects of the initial formulation, is said to be open to empirical test. One may essentially refer to ongoing patterns of action in determining the viability of the concept. In a similar manner, the equity model as summarized by Walster, Walster, and Berscheid (1978), indebtedness theory (cf. Greenberg, this volume), resource theory (cf. Foa & Foa, this volume), reciprocity theory (Gouldner, 1960), and other variations or elaborations on the exchange perspective employ observations, both rigorous and informal, to demonstrate the accuracy of the theoretical map in plotting the regularities in human interaction.

Yet, in part because of their commitment to a system of understanding that defines knowledge in terms of regularities, and in part because of the difficulties involved in identifying repetitive sequence, theorists share with others laboring in the positivist–empiricist vineyard an obtuse resistance to the fact that almost all regularities of interest are fundamentally ephemeral (Gergen, 1973). Clearly, whether X's warm greeting elicits a friendly response in Y is a matter of social history. Should a response be made at all, the range of actions in which Y may engage in response to X's greeting approaches infinity. Whether Y engages in a friendly interchange is primarily a function of the peculiar confluence of factors relevant to this particular relationship within the culture at a particular period.

To illustrate, let us consider Foa's (1971) classification of exchange patterns in society. Foa argues that there are essentially six types of resources exchanged by people in society, and that these six resource types may be arrayed in circular form about two orthogonal coordinates. Exchanges within society are said primarily to take place within a resource class or between commodities within the resource class and those adjoining it on either side (cf. Foa & Foa, this volume). Love is said to be one of the major resources, and it is most likely to be exchanged with love, or with status or services (the two adjacent resource types). By the same token, love will not be exchanged with money (its opposite on its coordinate), nor is it likely that love will be exchanged for goods or information—the two resource types most closely associated with money. Most of the Foas' data support these speculations—at least within currently selected samples. Yet, one can point to many exceptions to the theory, both in contemporary life and in earlier times. It was a major practice among Greek citizens, for example, to provide their romantic partners (the heterae) with money and goods in return for their favors. A similar relationship existed between the monied classes in Japan and their geisha. Likewise, for early Puritan society it would be difficult to generate evidence of common exchange between love and status, an exchange link favored by the present theory. In short, the exchange patterns upon which the contemporary formulation is based may be considered historically, culturally, and situationally specific. In like manner, whether one repeats an action for which he or she has been rewarded is also historically situated. One need not do so (unless the concept of reward or reinforcement is entirely circular), and there would appear to be numerous occasions in which people do not. Similarly, one may choose to respond in virtually any manner to an inequitable outcome, or to indebtedness. In no case do the patterns, norms, or endpoints of exchange seem genetically programmed.

To the extent that theories of social exchange are dependent on observed regularities within the culture, they are essentially documenting social history (Gergen, 1973). They primarily reflect the recurring patterns favored by the peculiar interplay of contemporary circumstance. Are contemporary exchange formulations thus delimited? Let us consider a second line of argument before attempting an answer.

Enlightenment Effects: Exchange Theory as Prescription

It would appear that social theories, once propounded, may become full participants in the confluence of contemporary events that support or fail to support various patterns of conduct. Once enlightened by theory, once acquainted with its predictions, one may chose to act in some other way than that dictated by the theory. Unlike the natural sciences, the communication of theory to persons furnishing the evidential grounds for the theory may alter their behavior so as to invalidate the initial premises. This is so in part because theories often contain strong value loadings; they carry implicit notions of "the good," and thus champion certain forms of activity while derogating others (cf. Gouldner, 1970). Because predictive theory grants the power of manipulation or exploitation to those who understand it and have means of implementation, these value implications take on special significance. In addition, the broad cultural commitment to "freedom" may negatively dispose people to theoretic encapsulation regardless of others' manipulative capacities. As research on psychological reactance suggests (Brehm, 1966; Wicklund, 1974), people may often strive to avoid the implications of a theory that reveals their behavior to be constrained. In all these regards theories may be influential in modifying human activity in such a way as to destroy the evidential grounds on which they are based.

It can be argued that the values implicit in exchange theory are minimal. What moral or ideological investments are discernible in such classic statements as "the more valuable to a man a unit of the activity another gives him, the more often he will emit activity rewarded by the activity of the other" (Homans, 1961, p. 56)? What groups are favored or denigrated by Thibaut and Kelley's (1959) statement "For a dyadic relationship to be viable it must provide rewards and/or economies in costs which compare favorably with those in other competing relationships or activities available to individual" (p. 49)? In spite of the dispassionate character of such formulations, it would appear that beneath the antiseptic patina lie a host of ideological or ethical implications. First there is the mechanistic form of such theorizing, one that treats the human as a passive automaton who merely responds to the reward/cost contingencies offered by the environment. Many find such views to be dehumanizing, robbing the individual of his or her capacities for responsible choice (cf. Harré & Secord, 1973). Further, the emphasis on the single individual's desire for maximal self-gain is viewed by many as socially alienating—setting people selfishly against each other—and thus militating against attempts to establish a cooperative society (cf. Sampson, 1978). The economic metaphor is also a source of displeasure to many. This marketplace mentality, it is said, encourages people to view each other as mere commodities to be bought and sold. As Plon (1976) has argued, the exchange orientation also ignores the fundamental conflicts between economic classes, and the inequitable distribution of power and reward in society. In ignoring such matters the theory lends tacit support to the status quo. Many would disagree with various of these charges (cf. Deutsch, 1974). However, such disagreement does not detract from the significance of the critiques: to the extent that people find the theory to be ideologically or ethically partial, it is effectively so.

There are other reasons people might wish to avoid behaving as exchange theory might predict. Frequently, the theory informs one that if he or she does X, there is a strong likelihood of obtaining Y from another person. If an employer wishes to increase worker productivity, for example, he or she may do so by increasing the workers' feelings of obligation. In this way, the theory sets the stage for interpersonal manipulation and exploitation. On a more general level, the theory informs us that others are bent on maximizing their profit in their relations with us. It argues that others will sacrifice as little as possible for us while attempting to gain maximally for themselves. Although such assumptions need not connote a war of all against all (Gergen, Barton, & Gergen, 1974), to the extent that they do, we may either gird ourselves for battle (thereby validating the theory solely because of its existence), or attempt to alter the human condition so that the assumptions are no longer accurate.

As a general surmise, it may be argued that the more closely tied to a given empirical operation, the more vulnerable the formulation to enlightenment effects. Many exchange-theory assumptions are sufficiently abstract that precise identification of exemplars is often very difficult. For example, one can not be sure what constitutes "exploitation," nor how to combat it in any given situation. The concept of exploitation is highly abstract, and thus difficult to illustrate with assuredness in any given circumstance. For the less abstract propositions, both the desirable and the undesirable features of social life become more manifest. For instance, numerous studies demonstrate the power of social approval in shaping behavior (cf. Crowne & Marlowe, 1964). Social approval (in terms of liking, love, respect, etc.) may be viewed as a major commodity exchanged between people (cf. Foa, 1971). However, once the power of approval becomes common knowledge, the stage is set for social change. In the same way that advertisers utilize their knowledge of social reinforcers to manipulate purchasing behavior, people may begin to utilize social approval (often simulated) to achieve their ends with others. Dale Carnegie's classic *How to Win Friends and Influence People*, among others, specifically recommends such tactics. And, in the same way one insulates oneself against being manipulated by the advertising gimmicks of the mass media, one may also harden him or herself to the effects of others' regard. Senior members in status hierarchies already appear sensitized to the use of positive regard by their subordinates (cf. Blau, 1964; Jones, Gergen & Davis, 1962; Schopler 1965). It is also interesting to note an increasing distrust of expressions of warmth (e.g., hugging, kissing, verbal praise) among those working in encounter or sensitivity groups; what was once viewed as a primary liberating force is now frequently seen as crass and cloying manipulation (Back, 1973). With the specification of the exchange properties, patterns of behavior are not likely to remain stable. There is good reason to conclude, then, that with respect to its dependence on empirical observation, the exchange formulation is essentially rooted to historical circumstance.

LEVEL OF ABSTRACTION AND THE INCORPORATION OF CHANGE

The thrust of the present arguments can be blunted in one important way. The more abstract one's theoretical terms, the more diverse facts one can incorporate, both across time and circumstance.

At the most abstract level, a theory which stated simply that "events follow events," could not be invalidated—regardless of epoch or culture. Less abstract theories, those which are tied more closely to specific observables (e.g., "poor communication links between parents and offspring precipitate the high rate of drug use") may be outdated within a brief period of time. Many of the exchange suppositions are of the more abstract variety. To say that people will behave in such a way as to achieve maximum rewards at minimum cost indeed has the ring of universal truth about it. Utilizing this assumption, it is possible to incorporate virtually all contemporary behavior, as well as those actions specifically attempting to destroy the validity of the general assumption. All the exchange theorist need do is to note that the character of rewards and costs has changed in the latter case. The existence of the theory may have changed people's ideas about what is valuable or desirable—but it does not change the seeming fact that people are bent on achieving what to them is valuable or desirable.

Yet, within the positivist–empiricist tradition, this appeal to high-order abstraction is highly unsatisfactory. One of the major criticisms of the seminal formulations of social exchange is that they contain few particulars; the formulations themselves contain few predictions, and thus remain virtually untestable. As Davis (1962) has said of Homans's theory, "There are a large number of general statements about relationships, but few or no propositions about specific variables for which the propositions are true. In neither case can one make predictions about empirical events from the theory alone" (p. 458). In effect, the exchange-theory assumptions are without consequence until they are tied to specific, concrete variables. The statement that persons seek maximal reward at minimal cost gains impetus only when one is able to specify what is both profitable and costly. It is at this latter level, of course, that the earlier arguments are most congent. As soon as the theory is tied to observables, and one begins to speak of the rewarding effects of a pleasant smile, a pat on the back, or a dollar bill, both enlightenment effects and shifts in historical circumstance become functional.

These various arguments leave us with a peculiar irony; highly abstract theories may be true for all time, but fail to predict any particular time. Postulates may encompass all periods and cultures, but their validity may only be assessed retrospectively.

Wedded to the difficulty of proving or disproving abstract theory is that of accumulating knowledge. The traditional positivist view of scientific theory holds that one derives hypotheses from the general theory, tests these hypotheses against unbiased observation, and either confirms, rejects, or revises the initial theory accordingly. It is on the basis of this process that we speak of accumulating knowledge. We believe that through continuous tests and revisions our theoretic knowledge becomes an increasingly better approximation of reality.

This view is seriously challenged by the arguments for historical perishability. Given changing patterns of social behavior, a specific derivation may be confirmed in one era, and rejected in another. An employer who increases his or her subordinates' pay may increase their morale at one period and decrease it by the same action in another; we may feel uncomfortable when we derive higher payoff than others for the same effort at one period, and exalt in the same outcome at another. Because confirmations and disconfirmations may vary with historical period, data can scarcely be used to increase or decrease one's confidence in the basic theory, nor to revise it in any essential way. Abstract theories thus do not enable one to accumulate knowledge in the traditional sense. Support can be generated for virtually any coherent theory of human behavior—at some time or place. Disconfirmations may be obtained as well. In any case we do not progress toward an inevitable state of improved knowledge.

This general line of argument has met with resistance. It has been argued (cf. Maris, 1976, Schlenker, 1974) that the changing character of confirmation poses no special problems for the theory builder. In fact, disconfirmation over time can occasion the further differentiation or elaboration of the theory. If increased pay produces increased productivity and morale in one period, and a decrease in morale at another, it simply suggests to the theorist that an additional parameter must be added to the theory. In this case, for example, the initial proposition might be differentiated further by saying that the positive relationship between monetary reward and morale is moderated by the recipients' perception of the donor. Under conditions in which the donor is valued positively, enhanced reward causes an increase in morale; when sentiments toward the donor are negative, the reverse will hold true.

Unfortunately, this refutation is misleadingly optimistic. If a given pattern of social behavior disappears from view, or its reversal begins to emerge in a culture, the question of identifying the significant moderator is virtually insoluble. Historical change presents us with infinite confounds; the events preceding sequence x and its reversal, not x, differ in so many ways (not the least of which may be that sequence x precedes not x), that the key parameter or the critical moderator is almost wholly obscured. Gillig and Greenwald (1974) have noted, for example, that between 1939 and 1958 some ten experiments yielded support for the general proposition that people learn more easily and forget less rapidly material that agrees with their values than that which is contravaluent. Yet, after 1963 almost all research on this topic failed to yield support for the proposition. At least five experiments were unable to achieve the earlier results. O'Leary (1972) has also been unable to replicate the famous "Hawthorne effect." Why are such phenomena discontinuous? Numerous coherent explanations can be generated. Yet, because of the countless differences between the present social context and that of earlier years, such explanations must remain merely conjectural.

A second difficulty with the argument for historical elaboration of theory revolves around the traditional criterion of truth value. If one's theory fails to predict, or the data are opposite from that predicted, the theory can either be scrapped or altered so as to accommodate the observations. Although there are no satisfactory procedures for determining whether to abandon or alter, special perils attend the consistent use of the latter alternative. To the extent that disconfirmations are consistently followed by modifications of the theory, the theory is untestable. If one accepts all confirmations of a proposition as support, and employs qualifications with each disconfirmation, then disconfirmation of the theory is impossible.

THEORETICAL UTILITY AND THE EXCHANGE ORIENTATION

Thus far, it has been argued that exchange theory contains ingredients—including value biases and behavioral directives—that are inimical to its longevity. Further, whenever the theory is linked to observables, its predictive capacity is severely threatened. Empirical research within the orientation, as in the case of other abstract theories of social behavior, does not lend itself to the task of accumulating knowledge. If theories of social behavior are of limited predictive value and cannot be "perfected" through the accumulation of further fact, should scientists give up their attempts to construct and verify such theories? Perhaps their efforts would be better devoted to building actuarial models for predicting world events of significance (e.g., crime, violence, charity support). Both the parameters of such models as well as their values could be altered over time as social monitoring revealed systemic changes. Although theoretically uncommitted actuarial models may have great social utility, the present arguments are in no way intended as a denigration of general theory in the social sciences. Neither "truth value" nor predictive utility need serve as the most significant crucibles for general theory. Theory should continue to play a vital role in the social sciences. Six fundamental functions may be described, and the exchange orientation may be viewed in relation to each.

The Explanatory Function

Initially it is commonly assumed that the major function of theory is *to explain*, or, as Toulmin (1961) has put it, "To make Nature intelligible." Two forms of explanation may be commonly distinguished: *descriptive* and *interpretive*. The former provides a systematic account of *what leads to what* in social life. It specifies the functional relationships between antecedents and consequences. A descriptive explanation of aggression would provide an elaborate account of the necessary and sufficient conditions for engendering or curtailing aggressive behavior; if prosocial behavior were understood in the descriptive sense, we would have at our disposal a list of all factors operating independently and interactively to enhance or reduce altruism. In pure form we seldom encounter descriptive explanations in social psychology. They are more frequent in applied settings or in the Skinnerian tradition. In educational settings, for example, investigators might wish to identify student characteristics predicting academic success or failure; in large-scale organizations, various measures might be used to develop a model predicting job performance; on the national level, administrators might wish to identify areas in which racial violence will erupt, and so on. For the Skinnerian, the specification of the necessary and sufficient conditions under which varying behaviors will occur furnishes the ultimate explanation of the behavior.

For most people, however, descriptive explanation of social action is not wholly satisfying. We not only wish to know about what leads to what, but *why* the patterns of events exist as they do. It is insufficient to be told that the mere presence of weapons in a given setting is sufficient to increase aggression. We wish to know why this should be so, and move on to form interpretations of the effects of past conditioning, the salience of cues associated with aggression, the arousal value of aggressive stimuli, and so on. Similarly, we form interpretations of why certain factors seem to influence prosocial behavior, and if we were in educational or business administration, we might wish to develop explanations as to why the successful predictors in our models proved effective.

Where prediction is critical, descriptive and interpretative explanations may play entirely different roles. If one is interested in predicting suicide rates, violent crime, charity giving, or participation in activistic movements, for example, reliance will inevitably be placed on current interpretations of social life (including those of interpretive social theory) as an aid in searching for and identifying the significant predictors. Clearly, one cannot begin the task of prediction by considering everything. Once the factors are identified empirically, descriptive explanation provides a mapping of these predictors, and can be of immediate and widespread usage. The descriptive explanation in no sense validates the interpretive explanation, although the latter may cause the investigator to sharpen his or her predictors over time, or to explore more deeply the conditions under which the predictors remain useful. At the same time, descriptive explanation is highly subject to the vicissitudes of history. The factors associated with suicide, crime, charity giving, and so on, undoubtedly change over the course of time, and if descriptive explanation is to be useful, its validity must be constantly checked against reality. Interpretive explanation, on the other hand, will always elude the attempt at empirical validation (Gergen, 1978). Any reasonable interpretation can be demonstrated empirically, and no set of empirical findings is without multiple explanations.

In present terms, exchange theory possesses both interpretive and descriptive components. The greatest emphasis by far, however, is on interpretation. Although Homans's brand of exchange theory owes much to the Skinnerian tradition, its major attempt is to explain why social life proceeds as it does. In its explanation of the self-serving character of motivation, the learning of payoff values, the need to equate rewards and costs, and so on, the theory makes intelligible a broad array of social activities. It gives us a sense of understanding, and thereby generates intellectual satisfaction and stimulation. In its interpretive capacity, it would be difficult to argue that exchange theory is necessarily superior to its competitors. Freudian theory, cognitive theory, role theory, and so on, all provide reasonably satis-fying explanations of many types of social activities. They all proceed with sufficient logic and clarity of exposition that they enable us to comprehend, and they are all relevant to an extremely broad array of events. As we shall see, however, the issue of theoretic superiority may be less important than the fact that the theory exists as a viable competitor at all. Its presence as a catalytic and compelling alternative may in itself be sufficient.

The Sensitizing Function

Both in their descriptive and interpretive roles, theories of social behavior can play an immensely valuable role as sensitizing devices. From moment to moment we face continuous demands for action, whether in the intense interpersonal encounter, or in the halls of government. Seldom, however, can we rely on social theory for making precise predictions about the consequences of a given action. Because of cross-time alteration in social pattern and the unique configuration of each new experience, previous descriptive accounts may no longer be predictive; previous explanations may no longer be relevant. However, both description and explanation can direct our attention to factors or processes of potential importance.

Is exchange theory superior to its competitors in its sensitizing function? This question is largely inappropriate, as competing theoretical accounts typically guide one's attentions in differing directions. Both the domain of relevant antecedents for any given range of phenomena, and the range of phenomena one hopes to understand, may vary widely. Theories may thus be compared more usefully with respect to the kinds of factors, processes, or phenomena to which they sensitize one than in their overall degree of sensitization. In this respect, the exchange orientation has much to commend it.

At the outset, the orientation suggests that, in understanding any given action or pattern of behavior, one shall search for the manner in which the contemporary context furnishes rewards for such activity. Rather than focusing on the early history of the individual, the "formative period," or on the vicissitudes of psychological dynamics, one's attentions are directed to the contemporary payoffs furnished by other people. The father who finds his adolescent son continuously disobeying his wishes might, from the exchange standpoint, inquire into the payoffs he can and does provide for his son, as well as those provided for his son by others. Exchange theory may suggest that he search for ways of increasing the profitability of his son's behaving in the more acceptable ways, or reducing the profit to be gained by catering to a peer group that favors disobedience. For the individual desiring advancement in an organization, exchange theory would suggest that thorough consideration be given to the ways in which his or her behavior is profitable or costly to superiors in the organization. This would entail not only an analysis of the range of professional and personal needs of those in power, but of his or her own ability and motivation to fulfill these needs. In both instances, the interpretive component of exchange theory may be highly useful. On the more descriptive level, a plant owner who wishes to reward those in one section of the plant for their exceptional work might pause in light of the exchange predictions concerning distributive justice. If all workers in other sections do not agree that the rewarded group is superior to them, the theory would suggest that considerable antagonism would develop in the nonrewarded group. Such a prediction cannot be made with confidence; rather, the theory serves as a sensitizer to what may happen in this case.

The sensitization function played by the exchange orientation is hardly exhausted in its focus on the payoffs in ongoing relations. In the Kelley & Thibaut (1978) formulation great stress is placed on patterns of *interdependency*. Rather than viewing each action as a function of particular payoffs, the emphasis is placed on patterns of interdependent payoff. From this vantage point, the unit of interest is no longer the single individual, but the dyad or the group which collectively sustains various patterns of behavior. Responsibility for any individual's behavior is thus shifted from the single individual to the group or groups in which membership is held. The exchange metaphor has also been useful in generating sensitization to various normative agreements concerning appropriate or desirable exchanges within a culture. Concepts such as the reciprocity norm, equity, and equality all become means of sensitizing one to common forms of exchange.

This is not to say that, as a sensitizing device, exchange theory is wholly free from ambiguity. One of the major problems in using the theory as a conceptual lever is the difficulty of assessing total rewards and costs in any situation. First, there is the problem of reducing all outcomes to a common standard. In economic theory all outcomes may be converted to monetary value, and the task is relatively simple. One may ask how much monetary value each of a given set of alternatives might have. However, exchange theory furnishes no such common standard, and it is thus very difficult to define the basis on which a person would select, for example, an embrace, as opposed to a piece of advice, praise, or money. Second, there is the problem of determining what is rewarding or costly to the individual in any given situation. Any given outcome may have multiple rewards and costs attached, each of which may advance or recede in cognizance (both for researcher and actor alike) over time. It would appear that one might even choose to carry out an action when the precise gains or losses in doing so had ceased to be apparent. Attendance at most social gatherings, for example, is an action the anticipated rewards and costs of which are often fraught with just such ambiguity. One attends, but really is not sure *why* he or she is doing so. Finally, it is difficult to understand how one integrates into a single solution the multiple payoffs derived from any single source. There is little reason to suspect that one typically adds and subtracts rewards and costs in simple fashion. The previously mentioned problem of the lack of common standard alone suggests that such simple processing is doubtful. Rather, individual action seems marked by vacillation, conflict, and rationalization (Gergen, 1969). Thus, although the exchange orientation has much to offer as a sensitizing device, it must be viewed as one of a range of necessary and valuable competitors.

The Organization of Experience

In one's initial attempts to understand a phenomenon, one is often faced with a tangled and fragmentary array of mixed impressions. Classic scientific procedures entail, as an initial step, a classification or sorting of such phenomena. By sorting the confusing array into discriminately different categories, one positions oneself for analytic inquiry; one may begin to ask questions about sequence and function. Exchange theory offers a highly useful vehicle for converting "noise" to "information," flux to order, or confusion to comprehension. The Kelley & Thibaut (1978) exchange matrix, the Foas' analysis of the structure of exchange patterns (this volume), Blau's (1964) analysis of the forms of reward and cost, are all exemplary in this respect. Such theoretical lenses are potent in their capacity to transform the seemingly haphazard character of social life into an ordered array.

The critic may argue that, in its highly abstract mold, the exchange orientation goes no further than specifying that various behaviors do have payoff values; little elaboration is undertaken of the specific payoff values attached to various types of behaviors. The theoretical lens provides order, but does not inform us as to what aspects of the order are critical. However, in light of our earlier arguments concerning historical perishability, this shortcoming may, in fact, be one of the chief advantages of the perspective. First, it should be noted that any attempt to specify the payoff values for various behaviors is likely to be of short-term utility. The evolution of styles, social understanding, technology, and so on are consistently altering the payoff value of various activities for various people. Unlike the physical sciences, the social sciences cannot furnish a historically enduring inventory of basic behavior units, nor can they specify what value various behaviors may have for people over time. Both behavior patterns and their value are in a constant state of change.

However, because of its highly abstract composition, exchange theory can accommodate the multiple and shifting array of human activity as it unfolds over time. Its terms are sufficiently flexible that, with a modicum of exertion, one can discern their application in almost any encounter. One may locate the reward and cost aspects of virtually any action, potential exchanges of reward and cost among actors, and the development and termination of normative agreements regarding proper exchange. Because of the abstract character of its terms, the theory may be uniquely qualified as a unifying force within contemporary social psychology.

In contrast, the major share of the research in the field is based on far more delimited models, and such research leads typically toward increased circumscription and delimited application. To illustrate, we may consider the twenty-year debate over the proper interpretation of role-playing effects in attitude-change research. Early research by Janis and King (1954) indicated that the active espousal of a position had a greater impact on attitudes than passive exposure to the same arguments. In presenting the arguments, the individual appears to convince himself of their validity. To explain this phenomenon, Hovland, Janis, & Kelly (1953) argued that, in readying oneself for the presentation, one scans his or her memory for facts or arguments that will lend support to what he or she is about to say. This *biased scanning* increases the salience of supporting arguments, and thus makes the position seem more tenable. Dissonance theorists, however, were not content with such an explanatory model, and reinterpreted the early findings (cf. Brehm, 1960). They argued that, when the individual confronts his or her overt arguments for x and subject belief of *not* x, cognitive dissonance is generated. Since the overt actions cannot be denied easily, dissonance reduction favors a modification of cognition in the direction of an increased commitment to this position. Later, Bem (1972) refuted this explanation, and argued that role-playing effects are not generally the result of dissonance reduction, but of self-observation. Using an alternative model, Bem argued that the individual may not be quite sure of his or her beliefs, and as a result of observing oneself maintain a position, one learns what it is that he or she must have believed.

The result of these competing explanations has been a plethora of critical experiments, critiques and countercritiques (cf. Brehm, 1965; Collins, 1969; Elms & Janis, 1965; Janis & Gilmore, 1965). Researchers within each orientation attempted vainly to demonstrate the truth of their position and the fallacious claims of their competitors. As we might expect from the present standpoint, resolution of the dilemma never occurred. From the exchange viewpoint, there is little to be gained from such dispute. Rather, the exchange theorist might ask about the range of potential payoffs operating in the role-playing situation to induce change. A partial answer might include the possibility of biased scanning (so as not to be found wanting if questioned about the position), dissonance reduction (as reducing dissonance clearly has payoff value to many people), as well as self-observation (as many people are rewarded for having an acceptable self-assessment). And, too, from the exchange viewpoint, there may be further payoffs to consider as well. For example, the individual may also gain in fantasizing about the social approval to be achieved by doing a good job or presenting a position (thereby producing a positive association to the position). Or, in presenting the arguments, one may gain feelings of self-confidence or enhanced perception of competence, again embedding the position in an aura of positive sentiment. From the exchange position, all such explanations may be relevant, as payoff processes underlying any behavior may be multiple. Further, the weight attached to each of these processes may vary within the same individual during the course of an experiment; the weights may vary from one person to another within the culture; and they may vary in their cultural distribution across time. The miniature models need not be viewed as mutually exclusive, from the exchange standpoint, but as each capturing a potential aspect of the total payoff matrix. The attempt to perform a critical experiment is largely wasted effort.

The Integration Function

Stephen Toulmin (1961) has remarked that within the sciences the "greatest fame is reserved for those who conceive new frameworks of fundamental ideas, and so integrate apparently disconnected branches of science" (p. 109). In part, such integration may be honored for its intellectual stimulation; the theorist unites previously disparate entities or frameworks, and in doing so challenges the imagination, and creates new puzzles to be solved. However, the theoretical integration of previously disconnected entities (and here we should not limit ourselves to "apparently disconnected branches of science") has additional advantages of considerable importance. We have already spoken of the sensitization function of theory. When two or more disconnected entities can be integrated within the same framework, or two or more branches of science become articulated through general integrative theory, the result may often be an enormous increase in sensitization. (We shall illustrate this point shortly in the case of exchange theory.) And, too, integrative theory often acts as a catalyst for the dissemination and adaptation of new research techniques. A theory that can span both micro and macro social processes, for instance, suggests to those in the former area that the methods in the latter may be relevant to exploring problems in which they are interested, and vice versa. Thus, experimentalists may begin to consider the potential of surveys or field observation for their own work, or may develop experimental survey methods or experimentation in field settings. Integrative theory thus opens the door to new theoretical and methodological insights.

With respect to integration, exchange theory must be ranked as one of the most significant social theories of the era. Freudian theory, Parsons's theory of action, and general systems theory are perhaps the only existing competitors in this respect. Exchange theory has been employed as a means of understanding various problems in almost all branches of the social sciences. The social exchange framework has been used to understand personality functioning, small-group inter- action, leadership, organizational behavior, social customs across cul- tures, social institutions in Western society, the development of legal codes, political behavior, and international relations, to name but a few. With each application, the potential of those in other disciplines is enhanced. For the investigator of personality function, for example, an exchange model of leadership may provoke consideration of the function of dominance in influencing personal dispositions; an ex- change model of political behavior may challenge the same investigator to consider the function of personal dispositions in the political spectrum; application in the cross-cultural area may suggest that the same investigator's work should be expanded to include the cultural context. The investigator of small groups could be moved by research into exchange processes governing legal behavior to consider new distinctions or processes influencing norm governance in the small group, or motivated by research on exchange between nations to think about the relations between small groups or cliques within a group in a similar manner. In each case, the integration may sensitize the investigator to new possibilities, both empirical and theoretical. Be- cause of the abstract character of the exchange orientation, it has lent itself to wide-ranging application in the social sciences, and as a result has been a powerful force for integration within the sciences.

The Generative Function

As Donald Campbell (1975) has argued, scientific theories are largely based upon commonly shared assumptions about the nature of reality. No less in the social sciences, most social theories rest upon widely shared notions about the composition of social life. In many cases, the scientific theory may be viewed as little more than a formalized rendering of popular beliefs within the culture. In opting for such "syntheses of common sense," the theorist is not necessarily acting dysfunctionally. A social theory that violates too many of the common sense assumptions of the culture is not likely to gain accept- ability, regardless of the empirical support generated by the scientist. As Kuhn (1962) and Feyerabend (1975) have pointed out, the accepta- bility of a theory may not be so much dependent on its empirical support as it is on its relationship to the popular intellectual supposi- tions of the day.

At the same time, a number of perils attend a commitment to any particular theory of social behavior. First, as we have seen, patterns of social behavior in a society are constantly emerging; in contrast, theory tends to remain stagnant. In the social sciences, theories are seldom altered as a function of disconfirming observations, and in their very statement (e.g., *X* is a function of *Y*) they suggest a transhistorical validity that is misleading. In addition, all theories represent artificial constructions of reality. As such, any given theory dismisses much that could be relevant to making any given decision, and renders one insensitive to entire domains of potentially significant experience. Although any given theory may sensitize us to certain factors, it simultaneously desensitizes us or directs our attention away from a host of potential competitors. Finally, since theories are formed essentially of abstract concepts, they miss what may be very important differences among entities within any class. A theory of American culture misses important differences among individual geographic locations; a theory of West Coast culture misses significant differences between urban and rural populations; a theory of urban populations misses differences between racial groups; a theory of urban black culture misses important occupational and sex differences; and so on. All abstract classes stop short of the individual.

Given these various shortcomings, commitment to any given theory within the social sciences is perilous. A premium is to be placed on developing theories whose major intent is to unsettle common ways of viewing reality and the theoretical superstructures resting on such common assumptions. Theories that combat common understanding may generate intellectual stimulation, open the individual to new realms of observations, enhance the range of one's sensitivities, and allow one a more differentiated understanding of social action. In effect, theories may play a *generative function* (Gergen, 1978), formulating new alternatives for social action.

In terms of the generative function, exchange theory possesses both advantages and shortcomings. In its placement of hedonistic motivation at the center of human activity, the theory is essentially cemented to common understanding within the culture. The theory is appealing to many people precisely because it does seem "so sensible," and this sensibility essentially reflects its congruence with common views of human action. At the same time, when this essential hedonistic assumption is elaborated in full measure, intellectually radicalized, the theory begins to have profound generative effects. One of the most potent examples has been furnished by Skinner (1971) in his exegesis on freedom and dignity. By extending the behaviorist treatment (a form of "externalized hedonism") to its logical conclusions, one must begin to question the social utility of these culturally honored ideals.

One begins to see possible shortcomings as well as alternatives, and in this manner the theory becomes generative. Similar though less pronounced effects have occurred in domains where romantic or idealized views of human motivation prevail. In romantic relations, for example, participants may be highly unsettled when pressed into identifying their own needs, the payoff value of their partner's behavior, and the character of the exchange in which they are engaged. Similarly, scientists have often reacted defensively when the exchange analysis is focused on various forms of prosocial behavior, such as charity or helping in emergencies (cf. Berkowitz, 1972). The exchange formulation would undoubtedly produce similar reactions when applied to religious behavior, martyrdom, and mother–child relations. Where the application of the analysis most irritates, the theory may prove most generative in its effects.

The Value-Sustaining Function

Attention was directed earlier to the prescriptive implications of the exchange formulation. In spite of the attempt by seminal thinkers in this domain to develop wholly descriptive formulations, we saw that the fundamentals of the theory carried with them "ought" implications. Such implications are hardly exclusive to exchange theory, as, indeed, all theories of human affairs are intrinsically value-laden (cf. Gouldner, 1970; Sampson, 1978). Exchange theorists need not be defensive concerning the prescriptive aspect of the formulation *per se*, for in the manner in which it directs attention, in the blindnesses which it creates, and in the terms selected for representation, exchange theory is similar to all theoretical formulations. Rather than viewing the prescriptive penumbra of descriptive theory as a potential threat to scientific purity, it may be argued that one of the chief functions of theory is that of molding social patterns in valued directions. As we have seen, general theories are minimally useful as predictive devices, and not fundamentally open to validation or falsification. With the stress on objectivity thus removed, one must ask what form of subjectivity is favored by a given theory. Theories may thus be judged "good" or "evil" depending on the form of the good which they happen to sustain.

In this light, one must take seriously the above criticisms voiced by those who find the exchange orientation to favor an inhumane social attitude. As we saw, from certain standpoints the theory appears to invite a calculated appraisal of the costs and benefits to be obtained from others, and thus alienates people from each other. To the extent that one is opposed to inhumane attitudes, calculated appraisals, and social alienation, the theory may be legitimately suspect. But are these criticisms well taken? If the full implication of the theory is considered, one may indeed conclude that, at base, the exchange orientation raises one's conscience concerning the interdependency of all people. Much of the bargaining literature, for example, has been explicitly concerned with the problem of social exploitation, and with some explicitness has championed the cause of cooperation among people (cf. Deutsch, 1975). Hardin's (1968) trenchant essay on the "tragedy of the commons" makes use of the exchange metaphor, and employs its logic to argue for a "fundamental extension of morality." As he and others have argued, self-interest is best served by an interest in the collectivity. In effect, only at the most superficial level does exchange theory favor social alienation. When deeply considered, one may begin to sense the necessity for a community of all.

Conclusion

This paper has attempted to deal with the place of social theory under conditions of steadily emerging configurations of social behavior. We have singled out exchange theory as a critical case, and have asked whether the validity of the theory can be maintained across changing time and circumstance. Could we hope to accumulate further knowledge that would allow us steadily to improve the validity of the theory? Our discussion revealed that, to the extent the theory makes specific predictions, its longevity cannot be assured. In addition, there is little to be gained in the attempt to sharpen its predictive capabilities through widespread empirical endeavors. The same may be said as well for other general theories of social conduct. However, we also argued that the criterion of predictive validity is only one, and perhaps the poorest, criterion on which to judge a theory of social behavior. Six functions of social theory were then outlined. First, theories are of inestimable value in making reality intelligible and in providing one with interpretations of why events fit together as they do. Second, theories can also be extremely useful as sensitizers to events that may occur under varying circumstances. Further, theories may organize experience, thus converting the flux of passing events to meaningful analytic units, and they may integrate such analyses as they emerge in seemingly disparate domains. Fifth, theory may serve a generative function, throwing into question prevailing assumptions within the culture, and elucidating significant alternatives. Finally, theories may legitimately be employed to sustain value commitments within society.

Viewing exchange theory in these terms, the orientation may be viewed as transhistorically viable. In its highly abstract level of formulation, it provides an intelligibility that can cut across historical circumstance. In contrast to the small models dominating the field over the past two decades, exchange theory can account for almost all social phenomena. The theory also serves well in its role as organizer of experience and social sensitizer; it is especially useful in pointing up relationships among highly diverse phenomena. When its implications are extended, the exchange formulation may have significant generative effects. And, when properly elaborated, the formulation may serve humane ends. These functions may continue to be served even after today's patterns of relationship become the future's caricature.

References

ABRAHAMSSON, B. Homans on exchange: Hedonism revived. *American Journal of Sociology*, 1970, *76*, 273–285.

ADAMS, J. S. Toward an understanding of inequity. *Journal of Abnormal and Social Psychology*, 1963, *67*, 422–436.

ADAMS, J. S. Inequity in social exchange. In L. Berkowitz (Ed.), *Advances in experimental social psychology* (Vol. 2). New York: Academic, 1965.

ADAMS, J. S., & FREEDMAN, S. Equity theory revisited: Comments and annotated bibliography. In L. Berkowitz & E. Walster (Eds.), *Advances in experimental social psychology* (Vol. 9). New York: Academic, 1976.

ADAMS, J. S., & JACOBSEN, P. R. Effects of wage inequities on work quality. *Journal of Abnormal and Social Psychology*, 1964, *69*, 19–25.

ADAMS, J. S., & ROSENBAUM, W. E. The relationship of worker productivity to cognitive dissonance about wage inequity. *Journal of Applied Psychology*, 1962, *46*, 161–164.

ALLEN, F. L. The big change in suburbia. *Harper's Magazine*, June/July, 1954.

ALLEN, V. L. Situational factors in conformity. In L. Berkowitz (Ed.), *Advances in experimental social psychology*. (Vol. 2). New York: Academic, 1965.

ALLPORT, F. H. *Social psychology*. Boston: Houghton Mifflin, 1924.

ALLPORT, G. W. *Pattern and growth in personality*. New York: Holt, Rinehart & Winston, 1961.

ALVAREZ, R. Informal reactions to deviance in simulated work organizations: A laboratory experiment. *American Sociological Review*, 1968, *33*, 895–912.

ALVES, W. M., & ROSSIE, P. H. Who should get what? Fairness judgments of the distribution of earnings. *American Journal of Sociology*, 1978, *84*, 541–564.

ANDERSON, L. R., & FIEDLER, F. E. The effect of participatory and supervisory leadership on group creativity. *Journal of Applied Psychology*, 1964, *48*, 227–236.

ANDERSON, N. H. Cognitive algebra: Integration theory applied to social attribution. In L. Berkowitz (Ed.), *Advances in experimental social psychology* (Vol. 7). New York: Academic, 1974.

ARISTOTLE. *Nicomachean ethics* (M. Ostwald, trans.). New York: Bobbs-Merrill, 1962.

ARONSON, E. Some antecedents of interpersonal attraction. In W. J. Arnold & D. Levine (Eds.), *Nebraska Symposium on Motivation*. Lincoln: University of Nebraska Press, 1969.

ATKINSON, J. W. *An introduction to motivation*. Princeton: Van Nostrand, 1964.

BACK, K. W. *Beyond words*. Baltimore: Penguin, 1973.

BALES, R. F. *Interaction process analysis*. Cambridge, Mass.: Addison-Wesley, 1950.

BALES, R. F., & SLATER, P. E. Role differentiation in small decision-making groups. In T. Parsons & R. F. Bales (Eds.), *Family, socialization and interaction process*. New York: Free Press, 1955.

BARBER, B., & LOBEL, L. S. Fashion in women's clothes and the American social system. *Social Forces*, 1952, *31*, 124–131.

BARNARD, C. I. *The functions of the executive.* Cambridge: Harvard University Press, 1938.

BARON, R. S. Anonymity, de-individuation, and aggression. Unpublished doctoral dissertation, University of Minnesota, 1970.

BAR-TAL, D., & GREENBERG, M. S. Effect of passage of time on reactions to help and harm. *Psychological Reports*, 1974, *34*, 617–618.

BAUER, R. A. The obstinate audience: The influence process from the point of view of social communication. *American Psychologist*, 1964, *19*, 319–328.

BAVELAS, A., HASTORF, A. H., GROSS, A. E., & KITE, W. R. Experiments on the alteration of group structure. *Journal of Experimental Social Psychology*, 1965, *1*, 55–70.

BEADLE, M. The game of the name. *New York Times Magazine*, October 21, 1973, pp. 38, 132.

BECKER, H. P. *Man in reciprocity.* New York: Praeger, 1956.

BEFU, H. Gift giving and social reciprocity in Japan, an exploratory statement. *France/ Asie*, 1966, *188*, 161–177.

BEFU, H. *Japan, an anthropological introduction.* San Francisco: Chandler, 1971.

BEM, D. J. Self perception theory. In L. Berkowitz (Ed.), *Advances in experimental social psychology.* New York: Academic, 1972.

BEM, S. L. Sex role adaptability: One consequence of psychological androgyny. *Journal of Personality and Social Psychology*, 1975, *31*, 634–643.

BENEDICT, R. *The chrysanthemum and the sword.* Cleveland & New York: World, 1967. (Originally published 1946).

BENNETT, J. W.The significance of the concept of adaptation for contemporary sociocultural anthropology. *Proceedings of VIIIth Congress of Anthropological and Ethnological Sciences*, 1970, *3*, 238–241.

BENSON, J. K. The interorganizational network as a political economy. *Administrative Science Quarterly*, 1975, *20*, 229–249.

BERGER, J., ZELDITCH, M., ANDERSON, B., & COHEN, B. P. Structural aspects of distributive justice: A status value formulation. In J. Berger, M. Zelditch, & B. Anderson (Eds.), *Sociological theories in progress* (Vol. 2). Boston: Houghton, Mifflin, 1972.

BERKOWITZ, L. Social norms, feelings and other factors affecting helping and altruism. In Berkowitz L. (Ed.), *Advances in experimental social psychology* (Vol. 6). New York: Academic, 1972.

BERKOWITZ, L., & FRIEDMAN, P. Some social class differences in helping behavior. *Journal of Personality and Social Psychology*, 1967, *5*, 217–225.

BERKOWITZ, L., & WALKER, N. Laws and moral judgments. *Sociometry*, 1967, *30*, 410–422.

BERKOWITZ, L., & WALSTER, E. (Eds.), *Advances in experimental social psychology* (Vol. 9). New York: Academic, 1976.

BERLYNE, D. E. *Conflict, arousal and curiosity.* New York: McGraw-Hill, 1960.

BERSCHEID, E., & WALSTER, E. H. *Interpersonal attraction* (2nd ed.). Reading, Mass.: Addison-Wesley, 1978.

BERTALANFFY, L. VON. *General system theory.* New York: Braziller, 1968.

BERTALANFFY, L. VON. *Perspectives on general system theory.* New York: Braziller, 1975.

BLAU, P. M. *Exchange and power in social life.* New York: Wiley, 1964.

BLAU, P. M. Comment. In R. Borger & F. Cioffi (Eds.), *The behavioral sciences.* Cambridge: Cambridge University Press, 1970.

BOFFEY, P. M. Energy research: A harsh critique says federal effort may backfire. *Science*, 1975, *190*, 535–537.

BOLITHO, W. *Twelve against the gods.* New York: Readers Club, 1941. (Originally published 1929.)

BOLLES, R. C. Species-specific defense reactions and avoidance learning. *Psychological Review*, 1970, *77*, 32–48.

BOULDING, K. E. An economist's view of Homans' *Social behavior: Its elementary forms. American Journal of Sociology*, 1962, *67*, 458–461. (a)

BOULDING, K. E. The relations of economic, political and social systems. *Social and Economic Studies*, 1962, *11*, *4*, 351–362. (b)

BOULDING, K. E. *The economy of love and fear.* Belmont, Calif.: Wadsworth, 1973.

BRANDT, J. M., & FROMKIN, H. L. A survey of unique attitudes among college students: A state of pluralistic ignorance. Unpublished manuscript, Purdue University, 1975.

BREER, P. E., & LOCKE, E. A. *Task experience as a source of attitudes.* Homewood, Ill.: Dorsey Press, 1965.

BREHM, J. W. A dissonance analysis of attitude-discrepant behavior. In M. J. Rosenberg, C. I. Hovland, W. J. McGuire, R. P. Abelson, and J. W. Brehm (Eds.), *Attitude organization and change.* New Haven: Yale University Press, 1960.

BREHM, J. W. Comment on counter-norm attitudes induced by consonant versus disconsonant conditions of role-playing. *Journal of Experimental Research in Personality*, 1965, *1*, 61–64.

BREHM, J. W. *A theory of psychological reactance.* New York: Academic, 1966.

BREHM, J. W., & COLE, A. H. Effect of a favor which reduces freedom. *Journal of Personality and Social Psychology*, 1966, *3*, 420–426.

BRELAND, K., & BRELAND, M. The misbehavior or organisms. *American Psychologist*, 1961, *16*, 681–684.

BRICKMAN, P. *Effects of outcome distribution and mode of comparison on two kinds of satisfaction.* Unpublished manuscript, Northwestern University, 1972.

BRICKMAN, P. *Varieties of equality.* Unpublished manuscript, Northwestern University, 1973.

BRICKMAN, P., & CAMPBELL, D. T. Hedonic relativism and planning the good society. In M. H. Appley (Ed.), *Adaptation-level theory: A symposium.* New York: Academic, 1971.

BROCK, T. C. Implications of commodity theory for value change. In A. G. Greenwald, T. C. Brock, and T. M. Ostrom (Eds.), *Psychological foundations of attitudes.* New York: Academic, 1968.

BROCK, T. C., EDELMAN, S. K., EDWARDS, D. C., & SCHUCK, J. R. Seven studies of performance expectancy as a determinant of actual performance. *Journal of Experimental Social Psychology*, 1965, *1*, 295–310.

BROWN, J. F. *Psychology and the social order.* New York: McGraw-Hill, 1936.

BROWN, P. L., & JENKINS, H. M. Auto-shaping of the pigeon's key peck. *Journal of the Experimental Analysis of Behavior*, 1968, *11*, 1–8.

BROWN, R., & FORD, M. Address in American English. *Journal of Abnormal and Social Psychology*, 1961, *72*, 375–385.

BUCHLER, I. R., and NUTINI, H. G. Introduction. In I. R. Buchler & H. G. Nutini (Eds.), *Games theory in the behavioral sciences.* Pittsburgh: University of Pittsburgh Press, 1969.

BUCKLEY, W. *Sociology and modern systems theory.* Englewood Cliffs, N. J.: Prentice-Hall, 1967.

BUCKLEY, W. (Ed.). *Modern systems research for the behavioral scientist.* Chicago: Aldine, 1968.

BUGENTAL, J. G., & ZELEN, S. L. Investigations into the "self concept": I: The W–A–Y technique. *Journal of Personality*, 1949–1950, *18*, 483–498.

BURKE, P. J. Authority relations and descriptive behavior in small discussion groups. *Sociometry*, 1966, *29*, 237–250.

BYRNE, D. *The attraction paradigm.* New York: Academic, 1971.

CALHOUN, J. B. Population density and social pathology. *Scientific American,* 1962, *206,* 139–146.

CAMPBELL, D. T. Qualitative knowing in action research. *The Journal of Social Issues,* 1975.

CAMUS, A. *The rebel.* New York: Vintage, 1956.

CANCIAN, F. *Economics and prestige in a Maya community: The religious cargo system in Zinacantan.* Stanford: Stanford University Press, 1965.

CANNAVALE, F. J., SCARR, H. A., & PEPITONE, A. Deindividuation in the small group: Further evidence. *Journal of Personality and Social Psychology,* 1970, *16,* 144–147.

CARPENTER, C. R. Societies of monkeys and apes. In C. H. Southwick (Ed.), *Primate social behavior.* Princeton: Van Nostrand, 1963.

CARSON, R. C. *Interaction concepts of personality,* Chicago: Aldine, 1969.

CASTRO, M. A. C. Reactions to receiving aid as a function of cost to donor and opportunity to aid. *Journal of Applied Social Psychology,* 1974, *4,* 194–209.

CHADWICK-JONES, J. K. *Social exchange theory: Its structure and influence in social psychology.* New York: Academic, 1976.

CHOMSKY, N. Review of B. F. Skinner's *Verbal behavior. Language,* 1959, *35,* 26–58.

CHRISTIE, R., & GEIS, F. L. *Studies in Machiavellianism.* New York: Academic, 1970.

CLARK, P. B., & WILSON, J. O. Incentive Systems: A theory of organizations. *Administrative Science Quarterly,* 1961, *6,* 129–166.

COLEMAN, J. S. Collective decisions. *Sociological Inquiry,* 1964, *34,* 166–181. (a)

COLEMAN, J. S. *Introduction to mathematical sociology.* New York: Free Press, 1964. (b)

COLEMAN, J. S. Foundations for a theory of collective decisions. *American Journal of Sociology,* 1966, *71,* 615–627.

COLEMAN, J. S. *The mathematics of collective action.* Chicago: Aldine, 1973.

COLLINS, B. E. The effects of monetary inducements on the amount of attitude change produced by forced compliance. In A. C. Elms (Ed.), *Role playing, reward and attitude change.* New York: Van Nostrand, 1969.

CROWNE, D. P., & MARLOWE, D. *The approval motive: Studies in evaluative dependence.* New York: Wiley, 1964.

CURRY, R. L., & WADE, L. L. *A theory of political exchange: Economic reasoning in political analysis.* Englewood Cliffs, N.J.: Prentice-Hall, 1968.

CYERT, R. M., & MARCH, J. G. *A behavioral theory of the firm.* Englewood Cliffs, N. J.: Prentice-Hall, 1963.

DANIELS, A. H. Fashion merchandising. *Harvard Business Review,* 1951, *29,* 51–60.

DANSEREAU, F., JR., GRAEN, G., & HAGA, W. S.A vertical dyad linkage approach to leadership within formal organizations: A longitudinal investigation of role making. *Organizational Behavior and Human Performance,* 1975, *13,* 46–78.

DAVIS, J. A. A sociologist's view of Humans' *Social behavior: Its elementary forms. American Journal of Sociology,* 1962, *67,* 454–458.

DECI, E. *Intrinsic motivation.* New York: Plenum, 1975.

DEUTSCH, M. Homans in the Skinner box. *Sociological Inquiry,* 1964, *34,* 156–165.

DEUTSCH, M. Critique: On cursing the darkness versus lighting a candle. In L. Strickland, F. Aboud, & K. Gergen (Eds.), *Social psychology in transition.* New York: Plenum, 1974, pp. 95–102.

DEUTSCH, M. Equity, equality, and need: What determines which value will be used as the basis for distributive justice? *Journal of Social Issues,* 1975, *31,* 137–149.

DEUTSCH, M., & KRAUSS, R. M. *Theories in social psychology.* New York: Basic, 1965.

DIPBOYE, R. L., & FROMKIN, H. L. *The dating game: The effects of interpersonal undistinc-*

tiveness on the avoidance of conformity as a self presentation tactic. Paper presented at Midwestern Psychological Association Convention, Cleveland, Ohio, May 1972.

Donnenwerth, G. V., & Foa, U. G. Effect of resource class on retaliation to injustice in interpersonal exchange. *Journal of Personality and Social Psychology,* 1974, *29,* 785–793. (Also summarized in Foa & Foa, 1974, pp. 187–190.)

Dore, R. P. *City life in Japan.* Berkeley & Los Angeles: University of California Press, 1959.

Douvan, E. Interpersonal relationships—some questions and observations. In G. Levinger & H. L. Raush (Eds.), *Close relationships: Perspectives on the meaning of intimacy.* Amherst: University of Massachusetts Press, 1977.

Duval, S. *Conformity on a visual task as a function of personal novelty on attitudinal dimensions and being reminded of the object status of self.* Unpublished doctoral dissertation, University of Texas, 1972.

Duval, S., & Wicklund, R. A. *A theory of objective self awareness.* New York: Academic, 1972.

Easton, D. *A system analysis of political life.* New York: Wiley, 1965.

Ekeh, P. P. *Social exchange theory: The two traditions.* Cambridge: Harvard University Press, 1974.

Elms, A. C., & Janis, I. L. Counter-norm attitudes induced by constant versus dissonant conditions of role-playing. *Journal of Experimental Research in Personality,* 1965, *1,* 50–60.

Emerson, R. Power dependence relations. *American Sociological Review,* 1962, *27,* 31–40.

Emerson, R. M. Operant psychology and exchange theory. In R. L. Burgess & D. Bushell (Eds.), *Behavioral sociology. The experimental analysis of social process.* New York: Columbia University Press, 1970.

Emerson, R. M. Exchange theory, Part I: A psychological basis for social exchange. In J. Berger, M. Zelditch, Jr., & B. Anderson (Eds.), *Sociological theories in progress* (Vol. 2). Boston: Houghton, Mifflin, 1972. (a)

Emerson, R. M. Exchange theory, Part II: Exchange relations and networks. In J. Berger, M. Zelditch, Jr., & B. Anderson (Eds.), *Sociological theories in progress* (Vol. 2). Boston: Houghton, Mifflin, 1972. (b)

Emerson, R. M. Social exchange theory. In A. Inkeles, J. Coleman, & N. Smelser (Eds.), *Annual review of sociology* (Vol. 2). Palo Alto: Annual Reviews Inc., 1976.

Emery, F. E., & Trist, E. L. The causal texture of organizational environments. *Human Relations,* 1965, *18,* 21–32.

Erskine, H., & Siegel, R. L. Civil liberties and the American public. *Journal of Social Issues,* 1975, *31,* 13–29.

Evans, W. M. The organization-set: Toward a theory of interorganizational relations. In J. D. Thompson (Ed.), *Approaches to organizational design.* Pittsburgh: University of Pittsburgh Press, 1966.

Evans, M. G. The effects of supervisory behavior on the path–goal relationship. *Organizational Behavior and Human Performance,* 1970, *5,* 277–298.

Farb, P. *Man's rise to civilization as shown by the Indians of North America from primeval times to the coming of the industrial state.* New York: Dutton, 1968.

Ferster, C. B., & Skinner, B. F. *Schedules of reinforcement.* New York: Appleton-Century-Crofts, 1957.

Festinger, L. *A theory of cognitive dissonance.* Evanston, Ill: Row Peterson, 1957.

Festinger, L., Pepitone, A., & Newcomb, T. Some consequences of deindividuation in a group. *Journal of Abnormal and Social Psychology,* 1952, *47,* 382–389.

Feyerabend, P. K. Explanation, reduction and empiricism. In H. Feigl & G. Maxwell

(Eds.), *Minnesota studies in the philosophy of science*. Minneapolis: University of Minnesota Press, 1962.

FEYERABEND, P. *Against method*. London: Verso, 1975.

FIEDLER, F. E. The contingency model: A theory of leadership effectiveness. In H. Proshansky & B. Seidenberg (Eds.), *Basic studies in social psychology*. New York: Holt, Rinehart & Winston, 1965.

FIEDLER, F. E. *A theory of leadership effectiveness*. New York: McGraw-Hill, 1967.

FIEDLER, F. E. The contingency model—New directions for leadership utilization. *Journal of Contemporary Business*, 1974, *3*, 65–79.

FINKIN, M. W. A judge in one's own case? *Academe*, 1975, *9*, 8.

FISHMAN, J. A. *Language and nationalism: Two integrative essays*. Rowley, Mass.: Newburg House, 1972.

FLEISHMAN, E. A., HARRIS, E. F., & BURTT, H. E. *Leadership and supervision in industry*. Columbus: Bureau of Educational Research, Ohio State University, 1955.

FOA, U. G. Interpersonal and economic resources. *Science*, 1971, *171*, 345–351.

FOA, U. G., & FOA, E. B. *Societal structures of the mind*. Springfield, Ill: Thomas, 1974.

FOREE, D., & LoLORDO, V. M. Attention in the pigeon: The differential effects of food getting vs. shock avoidance procedures. *Journal of Comparative and Physiological Psychology*, 1973, *85*, 551–558.

FOX, R. C., & SWAZEY, J. P. *The courage to fail: A social view of organ transplants and dialysis*. Chicago: University of Chicago Press, 1974.

FRIEDLAND, N., THIBAUT, J., & WALKER, L. Some determinants of the violation of rules. *Journal of Applied Social Psychology*, 1973, *3*, 103–118.

FRIEZE, I. H., & WEINER, B. Cue utilization and attributional judgments for success and failure. *Journal of Personality*, 1971, *39*, 591–606.

FROMKIN, H. L. *Affective and valuational consequences of self-perceived uniqueness deprivation*. Unpublished doctoral dissertation, Ohio State University, 1968.

FROMKIN, H. L. The effects of experimentally aroused feelings of undistinctiveness upon valuation of scarce and novel experiences. *Journal of Personality and Social Psychology*, 1970, *16*, 521–529.

FROMKIN, H. L. *A social psychological analysis of diffusion and adoption of new products from a uniqueness motivation perspective*. Paper presented at the Association for Consumer Research, University of Maryland, College Park, September 1971.

FROMKIN, H. L. Feelings of interpersonal undistinctiveness: An unpleasant affective state. *Journal of Experimental Research in Personality*, 1972, *6*, 178–185. (a)

FROMKIN, H. L. *The "irrationality" of "economic man": A psychological view of scarcity*. Paper presented in symposium at the 80th Annual Convention of the American Psychological Association, Honolulu, September 1972. (b)

FROMKIN, H. L. *The psychology of uniqueness: Avoidance of similarity and seeking of differentness*. Paper No. 438, Institute for Research in the Behavioral, Economic, and Management Sciences, Lafayette, Ind.: Purdue University, 1973.

FROMKIN, H. L., & BROCK, T. C. A commodity theory analysis of persuasion. *Representative Research in Social Psychology*, 1971, *2*, 47–57.

FROMKIN, H. L., & BROCK, T. C. Erotic materials: A commodity theory analysis of availability and desirability. *Journal of Applied Social Psychology*, 1973, *3*, 219–231.

FROMKIN, H. L., & DEMMING, B. *A survey of retrospective reports of feelings of uniqueness*. Unpublished manuscript, Ohio State University, 1967.

FROMKIN, H. L., OLSON, J. C., DIPBOYE, R. L., & BARNABY, D. *A commodity theory analysis of consumer preferences for scarce products*. Paper presented at the American Psychological Association Convention, Washington, D.C., September 1971.

FROMKIN, H. L., BRANDT, J., DIPBOYE, R. L., & PYLE, M. *Number of similar strangers and feelings of undistinctiveness as boundary conditions for the similarity attraction relationship: A bridge between "different sandboxes."* Paper No. 478, Institute for Research in the Behavioral, Economic and Management Sciences, Lafayette, Ind.: Purdue University, 1974.

GANS, H. J. *The Levittowners: Ways of life and politics in a new suburban community.* New York: Vintage, 1967.

GARCIA, J., & KOELLING, R. Relation of cue to consequence in avoidance learning. *Psychonomic Science,* 1966, *4,* 123–124.

GARRETT, J., & LIBBY, W. L., JR. Role of intentionality in mediating responses to inequity in the dyad. *Journal of Personality and Social Psychology,* 1973, *28,* 21–27.

GEORGIOU, P. The goal paradigm and notes towards a counter paradigm. *Administrative Science Quarterly,* 1973, *18,* 291–310.

GEORGOPOULOS, B. S., MAHONEY, G. M., & JONES, N. W., JR. A path–goal approach to productivity. *Journal of Applied Psychology,* 1957, *41,* 345–353.

GERARD, H. B. The anchorage of opinions in face-to-face groups. *Human Relations,* 1954, *7,* 313–325.

GERGEN, K. J. *The Psychology of Behavior Exchange.* Reading, Mass.: Addison-Wesley, 1969.

GERGEN, K. J. Social psychology as history. *Journal of Personality and Social Psychology,* 1973, *26,* 309–320.

GERGEN, K. J. *Experimentation in social psychology: A reappraisal.* Unpublished manuscript, 1975.

GERGEN, K. J. Social exchange theory in a world of transient fact. In E. Hamblin & J. Kunkel (Eds,) , *Behavioral theory in sociology.* New Brunswick, N.J.: Transaction, 1977.

GERGEN, K. J. Toward generative theory. *Journal of Personality and Social Psychology,* 1978, *36,* 1344–1360.

GERGEN, K. J. The emerging crisis in life-span developmental theory. In P. Baltes & O. Brim (Eds.), *Life-span development and behavior* (Vol. 12). New York: Academic, in press.

GERGEN, K. J., & GERGEN, M. M. International assistance from a psychological perspective. In *1971 Yearbook of World Affairs* (Vol. 25). London: Institute of World Affairs, 1971.

GERGEN, K. J., BARTON, W., & GERGEN, M. M. Exchange and strategy in social life. In K. J. Gergen (Ed.), *Social psychology, explorations in understanding.* Del Mar, Calif.: CRM Books, 1974.

GERGEN, K. J., MORSE, S. J., & BODE, K. A. Overpaid or overworked? Cognitive and behavioral reactions to inequitable rewards. *Journal of Applied Social Psychology,* 1974, *4,* 259–274.

GERGEN, K. J., ELLSWORTH, P., MASLACH, C., & SEIPEL, M. Obligation, donor resources and reactions to aid in three cultures. *Journal of Personality and Social Psychology,* 1975, *31,* 395–400.

GERGEN, K. J., MORSE, S. J., & GERGEN, M. M. Behavior exchange in cross-cultural perspective. In H. Triandis (Ed.), *Handbook of cross-cultural psychology.* New York: Allyn & Bacon, 1979.

GILLIG, P. M., & GREENWALD, A. G. Is it time to lay the sleeper effect to rest? *Journal of Personality and Social Psychology,* 1974, *29,* 132–139.

GOLDBERG, G. G. *Effects of consistent and inconsistent expectancy scores on reactions to disconfirmation.* Unpublished master's thesis, Northwestern University, 1973.

GOLDIN, J., LEVINGER, G., & HUESMANN, L. R. *Progress in a romantic relationship: A computer simulation.* Unpublished paper, University of Massachusetts, Amherst, 1975.

GOODMAN, P. S., & FRIEDMAN, A. An examination of Adams' theory of inequity. *Administrative Science Quarterly,* 1971, *16,* 271–288.

GORANSON, R. E., & BERKOWITZ, L. Reciprocity and responsibility reactions to prior help. *Journal of Personality and Social Psychology,* 1966, *3,* 227–232.

GORDON, L. V., MEDLAND, F. F. The cross-group stability of peer ratings of leadership potential. *Personnel Psychology,* 1965, *18,* 173–177.

GOTTMAN, J. L., NOTARIUS, C., MARKMAN, H., BANK, S., YOPPI, B., & RUBIN, M. E. Behavior exchange theory and marital decision making. *Journal of Personality and Social Psychology,* 1976, *34,* 14–23.

GOULDNER, A. W. The norm of reciprocity: A preliminary statement. *American Sociological Review,* 1960, *25,* 161–178.

GOULDNER, A. W. *The coming crisis of Western sociology.* New York: Basic, 1970.

GOULDNER, A. W. The importance of something for nothing. In A. W. Gouldner, *For sociology.* London: Allen Lane, 1973.

GRABURN, N. H. H. *Taqagmiut Eskimo kinship terminology.* Ottawa: Northern Coordination and Research Center, Department of Northern Affairs and Natural Resources (NCRC–64–1), 1964.

GRABURN, N. H. H. Eskimo law in light of self and group interest. *Law and Society Review,* 1969, *4,* 45–60. (a)

GRABURN, N. H. H. Eskimos without igloos. *Social and economic development in Sugluk.* Boston: Little, Brown, 1969. (b)

GRABURN, N. H. H. Traditional economic institutions and the acculturation of Canadian Eskimo. In G. Dalton (Ed.), *Studies in economic anthropology.* Washington, D. C.. American Anthropological Association, 1971.

GRAEN, G. Role-making processes within complex organizations. In M. D. Dunnette (Ed.), *Handbook of industrial and organizational psychology.* Chicago: Rand-McNally, 1975.

GRAY, D. Some comments concerning Maris on "logical adequacy." *American Sociological Review,* 1971, *36,* 706–709.

GREENBERG, D. S. Peer review under fire. *Science Digest,* 1975, *78,* 77–78.

GREENBERG, J., & LEVENTHAL, G. S. Equity and the use of overreward to motivate performance. *Journal of Personality and Social Psychology,* 1976, *34,* 179–190.

GREENBERG, M. S. A preliminary statement on a theory of indebtedness. In M. S. Greenberg (Chair), *Justice in social exchange.* Symposium presented at the meeting of the Western Psychological Association, San Diego, March 1968.

GREENBERG, M. S., & BAR-TAL, D. Indebtedness as a motive for the acquisition of "helpful" information. *Representative Research in Social Psychology,* 1976, *7,* 19–27.

GREENBERG, M. S., & FRISCH, D. M. Effect of intentionality on willingness to reciprocate a favor. *Journal of Experimental Social Psychology,* 1972, *8,* 99–111.

GREENBERG, M. S., & SAXE, L. Importance of locus of help initiation and type of outcome as determinants of reactions to another's help attempt. *Social Behavior and Personality,* 1975, *3,* 101–110.

GREENBERG, M. S., & SHAPIRO, S. P. Indebtedness: An adverse aspect of asking for and receiving help. *Sociometry,* 1971, *34,* 290–301.

GREENBERG, M. S., BLOCK, M. W., & SILVERMAN, M. A. Determinants of helping behavior: Person's rewards versus other's costs. *Journal of Personality,* 1971, *39,* 79–93.

GREENBERG, M. S., MOWREY, J., STEINBERG, R., & BAR-TAL, D. *The perception of indebtedness.* Unpublished manuscript, University of Pittsburgh, 1974.

GREENE, C. N. The reciprocal nature of influence between leader and subordinate. *Journal of Applied Psychology*, 1975, *60*, 187–193.

GREENGLASS, E. R. Effects of prior help and hindrance on willingness to help another: Reciprocity or social responsibility, *Journal of Personality and Social Psychology*, 1969, *11*, 224–231.

GREENWALD, A. G. *Consequences of prejudice against the null hypothesis.* Unpublished manuscript, Ohio State University, 1973.

GROSS, A. E., & LATANÉ, J. Receiving help, reciprocation, and interpersonal attraction. *Journal of Applied Social Psychology*, 1974, *4*, 210–223.

GROSS, A. E., & SOMERSAN, S. *Helper effort as an inhibitor of helpseeking.* Paper presented at the meeting of the Psychonomic Society Boston, November 1974.

GUSTAFSON, T. The controversy over peer review. *Science*, 1975, *190*, 1060–1066.

HAMBLIN, R. L., & CROSBIE, P. V. Anomie and deviance. In R. L. Hamblin & J. H. Kunkel (Eds.), *Behavioral theory in sociology.* New Brunswick, N. J.: Transaction Books, 1977.

HAMBLIN, R. L., & KUNKEL, J., (Eds.). *Behavioral theory in sociology.* New Brunswick, N. J.: Transaction Books, 1977.

HAMMER, T. H., & DACHLER, H. P. A test of some assumptions underlying the path goal model of supervision: Some suggested conceptual modifications. *Organizational Behavior and Human Performance*, 1975, *14*, 60–75.

HAMNER, W. C. Reinforcement theory and contingency management in organizational settings. In H. Tosi & W. C. Hamner (Eds.), *Organizational behavior and management.* Chicago: St. Clair Press, 1974.

HARDIN, G. The tragedy of the commons. *Science*, 1968, *162*, 1243–1248.

HARLOW, H. F., & SUOMI, S. J. Nature of love—simplified. *American Psychologist*, 1970, *25*, 161–168.

HARRÉ, R., & SECORD, P. *The explanation of social behavior.* Totowa, N. J.: Rowman & Littlefield, 1973.

HARRIS, R. J. Handling negative inputs: On the plausible equity formulae. *Journal of Experimental Social Psychology*, 1976, *12*, 194–209.

HARSANYI, J. C. A bargaining model for social status in informal groups and formal organizations. *Behavioral Science*, 1966, *11*, 357–369.

HEARST, E., & JENKINS, H. M. *Sign tracking: The stimulus-reinforcer relation and directed action.* Austin, Texas: Psychonomic Society, 1974.

HEATH, A. *Rational choice and social exchange: A critique of exchange theory.* Cambridge: Cambridge University Press, 1976.

HEIDER, F. *The psychology of interpersonal relations.* New York: Wiley, 1958.

HELSON, H. *Adaptation-level theory.* New York: Harper, 1964.

HEMMES, N. *DRL efficiency depends upon the operant.* Paper presented at the Psychonomic Society, San Antonio, Texas, 1970.

HEMPHILL, J. K. Why people attempt to lead. In L. Petrullo & B. M. Bass (Eds.), *Leadership and interpersonal behavior.* New York: Holt, 1961.

HENRY, J. "The economics of Pilaga food distribution," *American Anthropologist, 53*, 1951, 187–219.

HICKSON, D. J., HININGS, C. R., LEE, C. A., SCHENCK, R. E., & PENNINGS, J. M. A strategic contingencies theory of intraorganizational power. *Administrative Science Quarterly*, 1971, *16*, 216–229.

HINELINE, P. N., & RACHLIN, H. Escape and avoidance of shock by pigeons pecking a key. *Journal of the Experimental Analysis of Behavior*, 1969, *12*, 533–538.

HINNINGS, C. R., HICKSON, D. J., PENNINGS, J. N., & SCHNECK, R. E. Structural conditions of intraorganizational power. *Administrative Science Quarterly,* 1974, *19,* 22–44.

HINTON, B. L., & BARROW, J. C. The superior's reinforcing behavior as a function of reinforcements received. *Organizational Behavior and Human Performance,* 1975, *14,* 123–143.

HOBBES, T. *Leviathan.* (M. Oakeshott, Ed.). Oxford: Blackwell, 1960. (Originally published 1651.)

HOFFMAN, L. R. Group problem solving. In L. Berkowitz (Ed.), *Advances in experimental social psychology* (Vol. 2). New York: Academic, 1965.

HOGBIN, H. I. Polynesian ceremonial gift exchange. In A. Howard (Ed.), *Polynesia: Readings on a culture area.* San Francisco: Chandler, 1971.

HOLLANDER, E. P. Conformity, status, and idiosyncrasy credit. *Psychological Review,* 1958, *65,* 117–127.

HOLLANDER, E. P. Competence and conformity in the acceptance of influence. *Journal of Abnormal and Social Psychology,* 1960, *61,* 361–365.

HOLLANDER, E. P. Emergent leadership and social influence. In L. Petrullo & B. M. Bass (Eds.), *Leadership and interpersonal Behavior.* New York: Holt, Rinehart & Winston, 1961. (a)

HOLLANDER, E. P. Some effects of perceived status on responses to innovative behavior. *Journal of Abnormal and Social Psychology,* 1961, *63,* 247–250. (b)

HOLLANDER, E. P. *Leaders, groups, and influence.* New York: Oxford University Press, 1964.

HOLLANDER, E. P. Processes of leadership emergence. *Journal of Contemporary Business,* 1974, *3,* 19–33.

HOLLANDER, E. P. Independence, conformity and civil liberties: Some implications from social psychological research. *Journal of Social Issues,* 1975, *31,* 55–67.

HOLLANDER, E. P. *Leadership dynamics: A practical guide to effective relationships.* New York: Free Press, 1978.

HOLLANDER, E. P., & JULIAN, J. W. Contemporary trends in the analysis of leadership processes. *Psychological Bulletin,* 1969, *71,* 387–397.

HOLLANDER, E. P., & JULIAN, J. W. Studies in leader legitimacy, influence, and innovation. In L. Berkowitz (Ed.), *Advances in experimental social psychology* (Vol. 5). New York: Academic, 1970.

HOLLANDER, E. P. & JULIAN, J. W. A further look at leader legitimacy, influence, and innovation. In L. Berkowitz (Ed.), *Group Processes.* New York: Academic, 1978.

HOLLANDER, E. P., & MARCIA, J. E. Parental determinants of peer-orientation and self-orientation among preadolescents. *Developmental Psychology,* 1970, *2,* 292–302.

HOLLANDER, E. P., & WILLIS, R. H. Conformity, independence and anticonformity as determiners of perceived influence and attraction. In E. P. Hollander, *Leaders, groups, and influence.* New York: Oxford University Press, 1964.

HOLLANDER, E. P., & WILLIS, R. H. Some current issues in the psychology of conformity and nonconformity. *Psychological Bulletin,* 1967, *68,* 62–76.

HOLLANDER, E. P., FALLON, B. J., & EDWARDS, M. T. Some aspects of influence and acceptability for appointed and elected group leaders. *Journal of Psychology,* 1977, *95,* 289–296.

HOLLNSTEINER, M. R. Reciprocity in the lowland Philippines. In D. L. Lynch (Ed.), *Four readings on Philippine values.* Quezon City, Philippines: Ateneo de Manila University Press, 1964.

HOMAN, P. T., HART, A. G., & SAMETZ, A. W. *The economic order.* New York: Harcourt, Brace, 1958.

HOMANS, G. C. Social behavior as exchange. *American Journal of Sociology,* 1958, *63,* 597–606.

HOMANS, G. C. *Social behavior: Its elementary forms.* New York: Harcourt, Brace, & World, 1961.

HOMANS, G. C. Commentary. *Sociological Inquiry,* 1964, *34,* 221–231.

HOMANS, G. C. *The nature of social science.* New York: Harcourt, Brace, & World, 1967.

HOMANS, G. C. The relevance of psychology to the explanation of social phenomena. In R. Borger & F. Cioffi (Eds.), *The behavioral sciences.* Cambridge: Cambridge University Press, 1970.

HOMANS, G. C. Commentary. In H. Turk & R. L. Simpson (Eds.), *Institutions and social change: The sociologies of Talcott Parsons and George C. Homans.* Indianapolis: Bobbs-Merrill, 1971.

HOMANS, G. C. *Social behavior: Its elementary forms* (Rev. ed.). New York: Harcourt Brace Jovanovich, 1974.

HOMANS, G. C. Commentary. In L. Berkowitz & E. Walster (Eds.), *Advances in experimental social psychology* (Vol. 9). New York: Academic, 1976.

HOMANS, G. C., & SCHNEIDER, D. M. *Marriage, authority and final causes: A study of unilateral cross-cousin marriage.* Glencoe, Free Press, 1955.

HOUSE, R. J. A path–goal theory of leader effectiveness. *Administrative Science Quarterly,* 1971, *16,* 321–338.

HOUSE, R. J., & DESSLER, G. The path–goal theory of leadership: Some *post hoc* and a priori tests. In J. G. Hunt, & L. L. Larson (Eds.), *Contingency approaches to leadership.* Carbondale: Southern Illinois University Press, 1974.

HOVLAND, C. I., JANIS, I. L., & KELLEY, H. H. *Communication and persuasion.* New Haven: Yale University Press, 1953.

HOWARD, J. W., & DAWES, R. M. Linear prediction and marital happiness. *Personality and Social Psychology Bulletin,* 1976, *2,* 478–480.

HUESMANN, L. R., & LEVINGER, G. Incremental exchange theory: A formal model for progression in dyadic interaction. In L. Berkowitz & E. Walster (Eds.), *Advances in experimental social psychology* (Vol. 9). New York: Academic, 1976.

HUESMANN, L. R., LONG, P. E., & LEVINGER, G. *RELATE: A computer program for simulating dyadic interaction.* Technical Report, University of Illinois, Chicago Circle, 1975.

HUSTON, T. L. (Ed.). *Foundations of interpersonal attraction.* New York: Academic, 1974. (a)

HUSTON, T. L. A perspective on interpersonal attraction. In T. L. Huston (Ed.), *Foundations of interpersonal attraction.* New York: Academic, 1974. (b)

IHINGER, M. The referee role and norms of equity: A contribution toward a theory of sibling conflict. *Journal of Marriage and the Family,* 1975, *37,* 515–524.

ILCHMAN, W. F., & UPHOFF, N. T. *The political economy of change.* Berkeley: University of California Press, 1969.

JABLONSKY, S. F., & DEVRIES, D. L. Operant conditioning principles extrapolated to the theory of management. *Organizational Behavior and Human Performance,* 1972, *7,* 340–358.

JACOBS, D. Dependency and vulnerability: An exchange approach to the control of organizations. *Administrative Science Quarterly,* 1974, *19,* 45–59.

JACOBS, T. O. *Leadership and exchange in formal organizations,* Alexandria, Va.: Human Resources Research Organization, 1971.

JAMES, W. *Principles of Psychology* (Vol. 1). New York: Holt, 1890.

JANIS, I. L., & GILMORE, J. B. The influence of incentive conditions on the success of role-playing in modifying attitudes. *Journal of Personality and Social Psychology,* 1965, *1,* 17–27.

JANIS, I. L., & KING, B. T. The influence of role-playing on opinion change. *Journal of Abnormal and Social Psychology,* 1954, *49,* 211–218.

JENKINS, H., & MOORE, B. R. The form of the auto-shaped response with food or water reinforcers. *Journal of the Experimental Analysis of Behavior*, 1973, *20*, 163–181.

JOHNSGARD, P. A. *Animal behavior*. Dubuque, Iowa: Brown, 1967.

JOHNSON, C. D., GORMLY, J., & GORMLY, A. Disagreements and self esteem: Support for the competence-reinforcement model of attraction. *Journal of Research in Personality*, 1973, *7*, 165–172.

JONES, B. D., & KAUFMAN, C. The distribution of urban public services: A preliminary model. *Administration and Society*, 1974, *6*, 337–360.

JONES, E. E. *Ingratiation: A social psychological analysis*. New York: Appleton-Century-Crofts, 1964.

JONES, E. E. Conformity as a tactic of ingratiation. *Science*, 1965, *149*, 144–150.

JONES, E. E., & DAVIS, K. E. From acts to dispositions. In L. Berkowitz (Ed.), *Advances in experimental social psychology* (Vol. 2). New York: Academic, 1965.

JONES, E. E., & GERARD, H. B. *Foundations of social psychology*. New York: Wiley, 1967.

JONES, E. E., GERGEN, K. J., & DAVIS, K. E. Some determinants of reactions to being approved or disapproved as a person. *Psychological Monographs*, 1962, *76*, No. 2, Whole No. *521*.

JULIAN, J. W., HOLLANDER, E. P., & REGULA, C. R. Endorsement of the group spokesman as a function of his source of authority, competence, and success. *Journal of Personality and Social Psychology*, 1969, *11*, 42–49.

KAHN, A. Reactions to generosity or stinginess from an intelligent or stupid work partner: A test of equity theory in a direct exchange relationship. *Journal of Personality and Social Psychology*, 1972, *21*, 116–123.

KAHN, A., & TICE, T. E. Returning a favor and retaliating harm: The effects of stated intentions and actual behavior. *Journal of Experimental Social Psychology*, 1973, *9*, 43–56.

KALAT, J. W., & ROZIN, P. "Salience": A factor which can override temporal contiguity in taste-aversion learning. *Journal of Comparative and Physiological Psychology*, 1970, *71*, 192–197.

KARPEL, M. Individuation: From fusion to dialogue. *Family Process*, 1976.

KATZ, D. The functional approach to the study of attitudes. *Public Opinion Quarterly*, 1960, *24*, 163–204.

KATZ, D., & KAHN, R. L. *The social psychology of organizations*. New York: Wiley, 1966.

KATZ, D., & STOTLAND, E. A preliminary statement to a theory of attitude structure and change. In S. Koch (Ed.), *Psychology: A study of a science* (Vol. 3). New York: McGraw-Hill, 1959.

KATZ, E., & LAZARSFELD, P. F. *Personal Influence*. Glencoe, Ill.: Free Press, 1955.

KAUFMANN, H. Legality and harmfulness of a bystander's failure to intervene as determinants of moral judgment. In J. Macaulay & L. Berkowitz (Eds.), *Altruism and helping behavior*. New York: Academic, 1970.

KAUT, C. *Utang na loob*, a system of contractual obligation among Tagalogs. *Southwestern Journal of Anthropology*, 1961, *17*, 256–272.

KELLEY, H. H. Attribution theory in social psychology. In D. Levine (Ed.), *Nebraska symposium on motivation* (Vol. 15). Lincoln: University of Nebraska Press, 1967.

KELLEY, H. H. *Attribution in social interaction*. Morristown, N. J.: General Learning Press, 1971.

KELLEY, H. H., & THIBAUT, J. W. *Interpersonal relations: A theory of interdependence*. New York: Wiley, 1978.

KENISTON, K. Dissenting youth and the new society. In A. Kaplan (Ed.), *Individuality and the new society*. Seattle: University of Washington Press, 1970.

KERCKHOFF, A. C. The social context of interpersonal attraction. In T. L. Huston (Ed.), *Foundations of interpersonal attraction.* New York: Academic, 1974.

KLAPP, O. E. *Collective search for identity.* New York: Holt, Rinehart & Winston, 1969.

KOLENDA, P. M. Toward a model of the Hindu Jajmani system. *Human Organization,* 1963, *22,* 11–31.

KOMORITA, S. S., & CHERTKOFF, J. M. A bargaining theory of coalition formation. *Psychological Review,* 1973, *80,* 149–162.

KRECH, D., KRUTCHFIELD, R. S., & BALLACHEY, E. L. *Individual in society.* New York: McGraw-Hill, 1962.

KRISTOL, I. What's bugging the students. In Editors of the *Atlantic Monthly* (Eds.), *The troubled campus.* Boston: Little, Brown, 1966.

KRUGLANSKI, A. W. The endogenous–exogenous partition in attribution theory. *Psychological Review,* 1975, *82,* 387–406.

KUHN, T. S. *The structure of scientific revolutions.* Chicago: University of Chicago Press, 1962.

LASZLO, E. (Ed.). *The relevance of general systems theory.* New York: Braziller, 1972.

LATANÉ, B., & DARLEY, J. M. Bystander "apathy." *American Scientist,* 1969, *57,* 244–268.

LATANÉ, J. *Some determinants of favor acceptance.* Paper presented at the meeting of the Eastern Psychological Association, Washington, D. C., May 1973.

LAWLER, E. E. *Pay and organizational effectiveness: A psychological view.* New York: McGraw-Hill, 1971.

LAWRENCE, P. R., & LORSCH, J. W. *Organization and environment.* Homewood, Ill.: Irwin, 1969.

LEACH, E. R. The structural implications of matrilateral cross-cousin marriage, *Journal of the Royal Anthropological Institute,* 1951, *81,* 24–53.

LEARY, T. *Interpersonal diagnosis of personality.* New York: Ronald, 1957.

LEBRA, T. S. Reciprocity and the asymmetric principle, an analytical reappraisal of the concept of "On." *Psychologia,* 1969, *12,* 129–138.

LEBRA, T. S. Compensative justice and moral investment among Japanese, Chinese and Koreans. *The Journal of Nervous and Mental Disorders,* 1973, *157,* 278–291.

LEMAINE, G. Social differentiation and social originality. *European Journal of Social Psychology,* 1974, *4,* 17–52.

LEMERT, E. M. *Human deviance, social problems, and social control* (2nd ed.). Englewood Cliffs, N. J.: Prentice-Hall, 1972.

LEMPERT, R. Norm-making in social exchange: A contract law model. *Law and Society Review,* 1972, *6,* 1–32.

LEPPER, M. R., & GREENE, D. (Eds.). *The hidden costs of reward.* Hillsdale, N. J.: Erlbaum, 1978.

LERNER, M. J. Observer's evaluation of a victim: Justice, guilt, and veridical perception. *Journal of Personality and Social Psychology,* 1971, *20,* 127–135.

LERNER, M. J. The justice motive: "Equity" and "parity" among children. *Journal of Personality and Social Psychology,* 1974, *29,* 539–550. (a)

LERNER, M. J. Social psychology of justice and interpersonal attraction. In T. L. Huston (Ed.), *Foundations of interpersonal attraction.* New York: Academic, 1974. (b)

LERNER, M. J., & LICHTMAN, R. R. Effects of perceived norms on attitudes and altruistic behavior toward a dependent other. *Journal of Personality and Social Psychology,* 1968, *9,* 226–232.

LEVENTHAL, G. S. The distribution of rewards and resources in groups and organizations. In L. Berkowitz & E. Walster (Eds.), *Advances in experimental social psychology.* (Vol. 9). New York: Academic, 1976. (a)

LEVENTHAL, G. S. Fairness in social relationships. In J. W. Thibaut, J. T. Spence, & R. C.

Carson (Eds.), *Contemporary topics in social psychology*. Morristown, N. J.: General Learning Press, 1976. (b)

LEVENTHAL, G. S., & WHITESIDE, H. D. Equity and the use of reward to elicit high performance. *Journal of Personality and Social Psychology*, 1973, *25*, 75–83.

LEVENTHAL, G. S., ALLEN, J., & KEMELGOR, B. Reducing inequity by reallocating rewards. *Psychonomic Science*, 1969, *14*, 295–296.

LEVENTHAL, G. W., WEISS, T., & LONG, G. Equity, reciprocity, and reallocating the rewards in the dyad. *Journal of Personality and Social Psychology*, 1969, *13*, 300–305.

LEVENTHAL, G. S., MICHAELS, J. W., & SANFORD, C. Inequity and interpersonal conflict: Reward allocation and secrecy about rewards as methods of preventing conflict. *Journal of Personality and Social Psychology*, 1972, *23*, 88–102.

LEVINE, S., & WHITE, P. E. Exchange as a conceptual framework for the study of interorganizational relationships. *Administrative Science Quarterly*, 1960–1961, *5*, 583–601.

LEVINGER, G. A three-level approach to attraction: Toward an understanding of pair relatedness. In T. L. Huston (Ed.), *Foundations of interpersonal attraction*. New York: Academic, 1974.

LEVINGER, G. A social psychological perspective on marital dissolution. *Journal of Social Issues*, 1976, *32*, (1), 21–47.

LEVINGER, G., & SNOEK, J. D. *Attraction in relationship: A new look at interpersonal attraction*. Morristown, N. J.: General Learning Press, 1972.

LÉVI-STRAUSS, C. *The elementary structures of kinship*. Boston: Beacon, 1949. (Republished, 2nd ed., 1969).

LÉVI-STRAUSS, C. *Les structures élémentaires de la parenté*. Paris: Presses Universitaires de France, 1949.

LÉVI-STRAUSS, C. Social structure, In A. L. Kroeber (Ed.), *Anthropology Today*. Chicago: University of Chicago Press, 1953.

LINTON, R. *The cultural background of personality*. New York: Appleton-Century-Crofts. 1945.

LIPSET, S. M., TROW, M. A., & COLEMAN, J. S. *Union democracy and secondary organization*. In W. Petersen (Ed.), *American social patterns*. Garden City, N. Y.: Doubleday, 1956.

LIPSHITZ, R., & FROMKIN, H. L. A construct validity method for scale development. *Journal of Applied Psychology*, 1976.

LISKA, A. E. Uses and mis-uses of tautologies in social psychology. *Sociometry*, 1969, *32*, 444–457.

LoLORDO, V. M. Facilitation of food reinforced responding by a signal for free food. *Journal of the Experimental Analysis of Behavior*, 1971, *15*, 49–55.

LoLORDO, V. M., McMILLAN, J. C., & RILEY, A. L.The effects upon food reinforced pecking and treadle-pressing of auditory and visual signals for response independent food. *Learning and Motivation*, 1974, *5*, 24–41.

LONGABAUGH, R. A. A category system for coding interpersonal behavior as social exchange. *Sociometry*, 1963, *26*, 319–344.

LORENZ, K. *Evolution and the modification of behavior*. Chicago: University of Chicago Press, 1965.

LOURENCO, S. V., & GLIDEWELL, S. C. A dialectical analysis of organizational conflict. *Administrative Science Quarterly*, 1975, *20*, 489–508.

LUTHANS, F., & KREITNER, R. *Organizational behavior modification*. Glenview, Ill.: Scott, Foresman, 1975.

MACAULAY, S. Non-contractual relations in business: A preliminary study. *American Sociological Review*, 1963, *28*, 55–69.

MALINOWSKI, B. *Argonauts of the western Pacific.* New York: Dutton, 1922.

MALINOWSKI, B. *Crime and custom in savage society.* London: Kegan Paul, 1926.

MANIS, M. Social psychology and history: A symposium. *Personality and Social Psychology Bulletin,* 1976, *2*, 371–372.

MANN, R. D. A review of the relationships between personality and performance in small groups. *Psychological Bulletin,* 1959, *56*, 241–270.

MARCH, J. G., & SIMON, H. A. *Organizations.* New York: Wiley, 1958.

MARIS, R. The logical adequacy of Homans's social theory. *American Sociological Review,* 1970, *35*, 1069–1081.

MAUSS, M. Essai sur le don, forme et raison de l'échange dans les sociétés archaïques. *Année Sociologique,* n. s., 1925, *1*, 30–186.

MAUSS, M. *The Gift.* Glencoe, Ill.: Free Press, 1954. (Republished, New York: Norton, 1967.) Translation of Mauss (1925) by I. Cunnison.

McCALL, D. B. Profit: Spur for solving social ills. *Harvard Business Review,* 1973, May–June, *46–48, 50, 52, 54,* 180–181.

McCLELLAND, D. C. Toward a theory of motive acquisition. *American Psychologist,* 1965, *20,* 321–333.

McCLELLAND, D. C., & WINTER, D. G. *Motivating economic achievement.* New York: Free Press, 1969.

McKENZIE, R. B., & TULLOCK, G. *The new world of economics.* Homewood, Ill.: Irwin, 1975.

MEEHL, P. E. On the circularity of the law of effect. *Psychological Bulletin,* 1950, *47,* 52–75.

METCALFE, J. L. Systems models, economic models and the causal texture of organizational environments: An approach to macro-organization theory. *Human Relations,* 1974, *27,* 639–663.

MEZZROW, M., & WOLFE, B. *Really the blues.* New York: Doubleday, 1972.

MILGRAM, S., & TOCH, H. Collective behavior: Crowds and social movements. In G. Lindzey & E. Aronson (Eds.), *The handbook of social psychology* (2nd ed., Vol. IV). Reading, Mass.: Addison-Wesley, 1969.

MINDLIN, S. E., & ALDRICH, H. Interorganizational dependence: A review of the concept and a reexamination of findings of Aston group. *Administrative Science Quarterly,* 1975, *20,* 382–392.

MINER, J. B. Management appraisal: A review of procedures and practices. In H. L. Tosi, R. J. House, & M. D. Dunnette (Eds.), *Managerial motivation and compensation.* East Lansing: Michigan State University Business Studies, 1972.

MORRIS, S. C. III, & ROSEN, S. Effects of felt adequacy and opportunity to reciprocate on help seeking. *Journal of Experimental Social Psychology,* 1973, *9,* 265–276.

Ms. Magazine, 1973, *11,* 97–100.

MUIR, D. E., & WEINSTEIN, E. A. The social debt: An investigation of lower-class and middle-class norms of social obligation. *American Sociological Review,* 1962, *27,* 532–539.

MULKAY, M. J. *Functionalism, exchange and theoretical strategy.* New York: Schocken, 1971.

MURSTEIN, B. I. (Ed.), *Theories of attraction and love.* New York: Springer, 1971.

MURSTEIN, B. I. *Who will marry whom? Theories and research in marital choice.* New York: Springer, 1976.

NEMETH, C. Effects of free versus constrained behavior on attraction between people. *Journal of Personality and Social Psychology,* 1970, *15,* 302–311.

NIMMER, R. T. The system impact of criminal justice reforms. In J. L. Tapp & F. J. Levine (Eds.), *Law, justice, and the individual in society.* New York: Holt, Rinehart & Winston, 1977.

NORD, W. R. Beyond the teaching machine: The neglected area of operant conditioning in the theory and practice of management. *Organizational Behavior and Human Performance*, 1969, 4, 375–401. (a)

NORD, W. R. Social exchange theory: An integrative approach to social conformity. *Psychological Bulletin*, 1969, 71, 174–208. (b)

O'LEARY, V. E. The Hawthorne effect in reverse: Trainee orientation for the hard-core unemployed woman. *Journal of Applied Psychology*, 1972, 56, 491–494.

ORGAN, D. W. Social exchange and psychological reactance in a simulated superior–subordinate relationship. *Organizational Behavior and Human Performance*, 1974, 12, 132–142.

PARSONS, T. *The social system*. Glencoe, Ill.: Free Press, 1951.

PARSONS, T. Family structure and the socialization of the child. In T. Parsons & R. F. Bales (Eds.), *Family, socialization and interaction process*. Glencoe, Ill.: Free Press, 1955.

PARSONS, T., SHILS, E. A., & OLDS, J. Values, motives, and systems of action. In T. Parsons & E. A. Shils (Eds.), *Toward a general theory of action*. New York: Harper & Row, 1951.

PATCHEN, M. *The choice of wage comparisons*. Englewood Cliffs, N. J.: Prentice-Hall, 1961.

PEPINSKY, P. N., HEMPHILL, J. K., & SHEVITZ, R. N. Attempts to lead, group productivity, and morale under conditions of acceptance and rejection. *Journal of Abnormal and Social Psychology*, 1958, 57, 47–54.

PETERSON, G. C., ACKIL, J. E., FROMMER, G. P., & HEARST, E. S. Conditioned approach and contact behavior toward signals for food or brain stimulation reinforcement. *Science*, 1972, 177, 1009–1011.

PFEFFER, J. Size, composition, and function of hospital boards of directors: A study of organization–environment linkage. *Administrative Science Quarterly*, 1973, 18, 349–364.

PFEFFER, J., & SALANCIK, G. R. Organizational decision making as a political process: The case of a university budget. *Administrative Science Quarterly*, 1974, 19, 135–151.

PITTS, J. R. The hippies as contra meritocracy. *Dissent*, 1969, 16, 326–337.

PLON, M. *La théorie des jeux: Une politique imaginaire*. Paris: F. Maspero, 1976.

PONDY, L. R. Toward a theory of internal resource-allocation. In M. N. Zald (Ed.), *Power in organizations*. Nashville: Vanderbilt University Press, 1970.

PORTER, L. W., & LAWLER, E. E. *Managerial attitudes and performance*. Homewood, Ill.: Irwin-Dorsey, 1968.

PRICE, R. On Maris and the logic of time. *American Sociological Review*, 1971, 36, 711–713.

PRITCHARD, R. D. Equity theory: A review and critique. *Organizational Behavior and Human Performance*, 1969, 4, 176–211.

PRUITT, D. G. Reciprocity and credit building in a laboratory dyad. *Journal of Personality and Social Psychology*, 1968, 8, 143–147.

PRUITT, D. G. Indirect communication and the search for agreement in negotiation. *Journal of Applied Social Psychology*, 1971, 1, 205–239.

PRUITT, D. G. Methods for resolving differences of interest: A theoretical analysis. *Journal of Social Issues*, 1972, 28, 133–154.

PRYOR, F. L. *The origins of the economy: A comparative study of distribution in primitive and peasant economies*. New York: Academic, 1978.

RAPOPORT, A., & CHAMMAH, A. M. *Prisoner's dilemma*. Ann Arbor: University of Michigan Press, 1965.

RAUSCH, H. L., BARRY, W. A., HERTEL, R. K., & SWAIN, M. *Communication, conflict, and marriage*. San Francisco: Jossey-Bass, 1974.

RAWLS, J. *A theory of justice*. Cambridge: Harvard University Press, 1971.

READ, P. B. Source of authority and legitimation of leadership in small groups. *Sociometry,* 1974, *37,* 189–204.

REGAN, D. T. Effects of a favor and liking on compliance. *Journal of Experimental Social Psychology,* 1971, *7,* 627–639.

REGULA, R. C., & JULIAN, J. W. The impact of quality and frequency of task contributions on perceived ability. *Journal of Social Psychology,* 1973, *89,* 115–122.

REICH, C. *The greening of America.* New York: Randon House, 1970.

REIS, H. T., & GRUZEN, J. *On mediating equity, equality and self-interest: The role of self-presentation in social exchange.* Unpublished manuscript, University of Rochester, 1975.

REVUSKY, S. H., & GARCIA, J. Learned associations over long delays. In G. H. Bower & J. T. Spence (Eds.), *The Psychology of learning and motivation* (Vol. IV). New York: Academic, 1970.

ROBOLOS, Z. M. Promissory and debt aspects of the folk ritual in Misamis Oriental. *Philippine Sociological Review,* 1964, *12,* 95–101.

ROMER, D., BONTEMPS, M., FLYNN, M., MCGUIRE, T., & GRUDER, C. L. The effects of status similarity and expectation of reciprocation upon altruistic behavior. *Personality and Social Psychology Bulletin,* 1977, *3,* 103–106.

ROSMAN, A., & RUBEL, P. G. *Feasting with mine enemy, rank and exchange among Northwest Coast societies.* New York: Columbia University Press, 1972. (a)

ROSMAN, A., & RUBEL, P. G. The potlatch, a structural analysis. *American Anthropologist,* 1972, *74,* 658–671. (b)

ROSNOW, R. L. The prophetic vision of Giambattista Vico: Implications for the state of social psychological theory. *Journal of Personality and Social Psychology,* 1978, *36,* 1322–1331.

ROSSI, A. S. *Discussion of "Perspectives on close relationships."* Presented at Symposium on Close Relationships, Amherst, Mass., 1974.

ROZIN, P. The evolution of intelligence and access to the cognitive unconscious. In. E. Stellar & J. M. Sprague (Eds.), *Progress in psychobiology and physiological psychology.* New York: Academic, 1976.

ROZIN, P. & KALAT, J. W. Specific hungers and poison avoidance as adaptive specializations of learning. *Psychological Review,* 1971, *78,* 459–486.

RUBEL, P. G., & ROSMAN, A. Potlatch and sagali, the structure of exchange in Haida and Trobriand societies. *New York Academy of Sciences, Transactions,* (Ser. II.), 1970, *32,* 732–742.

RUBEL, P. G., & ROSMAN, A. Potlatch and hakari, an analysis of Maori society in terms of the potlatch model. *Man,* 1971, *6,* 660–673.

RUBIN, Z. *Liking and loving: An invitation to social psychology.* New York: Holt, Rinehart, & Winston, 1973.

RUBIN, Z. *Becoming intimate.* Unpublished chapter. Harvard University, 1974.

RUDRASWAMY, V. An investigation of the relationship between perceptions of status and leadership attempts. *Journal of the Indian Academy of Applied Psychology,* 1964, *1,* 12–19.

SAHLINS, M. *Stone age economics.* Chicago: Aldine, 1972.

SALANCIK, G. R., & PFEFFER, J. The bases and use of power in organizational decision making: The case of a university. *Administrative Science Quarterly,* 1974, *19,* 453–473.

SAMPSON, E. E. Status congruence and cognitive consistency. *Sociometry,* 1963, *26,* 146–162.

SAMPSON, E. E. Studies of status congruence. In L. Berkowitz (Ed.), *Advances in experimental social psychology* (Vol. 4). New York: Academic, 1969.

SAMPSON, E. E. Psychology and the American ideal. *Journal of Personality and Social Psychology,* 1977, *35,* 767–782.

SAMUEL, W. In further support of the Adams ratio: A reply to Dr. G. William Walster. *Personality and Social Psychology Bulletin,* 1976, *2,* 45–46. (a)

SAMUEL, W. Suggested amendments to "new directions in equity research." *Personality and Social Psychology Bulletin,* 1976, *2,* 36–39. (b)

SANFORD, F. H. *Authoritarianism and leadership.* Philadelphia: Institute for Research in Human Relations, 1950.

SARBIN, T. R., & ALLEN, V. L. Role theory. In G. Lindzey & E. Aronson (Eds.), *Handbook of social psychology* (2nd ed., Vol. I). Reading, Mass.: Addison-Wesley, 1968.

SARNOFF, I. Psychoanalytic theory and social attitudes. *Public Opinion Quarterly,* 1960, *24,* 251–279.

SCHACHTER, S. The interaction of cognitive and physiological determinants of emotional state. In L. Berkowitz (Ed.), *Advances in experimental social psychology* (Vol. I). New York: Academic, 1964.

SCHEIN, E. H. Organizational socialization and the profession of management. *Industrial Management Review,* 1968, *9,* 1–6.

SCHLENKER, B. R. Social psychology and science. *Journal of Personality and Social Psychology,* 1974, *29,* 1–15.

SCHMITT, D. R., & MARWELL, G. Cooperation and the human group. In R. Hamblin & J. Kunkel (Eds.), *Behavioral theory in sociology.* New Brunswick, N. J.: Transaction Books, 1977.

SCHNEIDER, H. *Economic man: The anthropology of economics.* New York: Free Press, 1974.

SCHNEIER, C. E. Behavior modification in management: A review and critique. *Academy of Management Journal,* 1974, *17,* 528–548.

SCHOPLER, J. Social power. In L. Berkowitz (Ed.), *Advances in experimental social psychology.* (Vol. 2). New York: Academic, 1965.

SCHOPLER, J. An attribution analysis of some determinants of reciprocating a benefit. In J. Macaulay & L. Berkowitz (Eds.), *Altruism and helping behavior.* New York: Academic, 1970.

SCHOPLER, J., & THOMPSON, V. D. Role of attribution processes in mediating amount of reciprocity for a favor. *Journal of Personality and Social Psychology,* 1968, *10,* 243–250.

SCHWARTZ, B. Maintenance of key pecking by a food avoidance but not a shock avoidance contingency. *Animal Learning and Behavior,* 1973, *1,* 164–166.

SCHWARTZ, B. On going back to nature: A review of Seligman and Hager's *Biological boundaries of learning. Journal of the Experimental Analysis of Behavior,* 1974, *21,* 183–198.

SCHWARTZ, B. Positive and negative conditioned suppression in the pigeon: Effects of the locus and modality of the CS. *Learning and Motivation,* 1976, *7,* 86–100.

SCHWARTZ, B., & COULTER, G. A failure to transfer control of key pecking from food reinforcement to escape from and avoidance of shock. *Bulletin of the Psychonomic Society,* 1973, *1,* 307–309.

SCHWARTZ, B., & GAMZU, E. Pavlovian control of operant behavior: An analysis of autoshaping and its implications for operant conditioning. In W. K. Honig & F. R. Staddon (Eds.), *Handbook of operant behavior.* Englewood Cliffs, N. J.: Prentice-Hall, 1977.

SCHWARTZ, B., & WILLIAMS, D. R. Discrete-trials spaced responding in the pigeon: the dependence of efficient performance on the availability of a stimulus for collateral pecking. *Journal of the Experimental Analysis of Behavior,* 1971, *16,* 155–160.

SCHWARTZ, B., SCHULDENFREI, R., & LACEY, H. Operant psychology as factory psychology. *Behaviorism,* 1978, *6,* 239–254.

SCHWARTZ, S. H. Awareness of consequences and the influence of moral norms on interpersonal behavior. *Sociometry*, 1968, *31*, 355–369. (a)

SCHWARTZ, S. H. Words, deeds, and the perception of consequences and responsibility in action situations. *Journal of Personality and Social Psychology*, 1968, *10*, 232–242. (b)

SCHWIMMER, E. G. *Exchange in the social structure of the Orokaiva.* Unpublished doctoral dissertation, University of British Columbia, 1970.

SCHWIMMER, E. G. *Exchange in the social structure of the Orokaiva: Traditional and emergent ideologies in the northern district of Papua.* New York: St. Martin's Press, 1974.

Science. Nuclear foes fault *Scientific American's* editorial judgment in publishing a recent article by Nobel laureate Hans Bethe, 1976, *191*, 1248–1249.

SEARS, D. O. Political behavior. In G. Lindzey & E. Aronson (Eds.), *The handbook of social psychology* (2nd ed., Vol. 5). Reading, Mass.: Addison-Wesley, 1969.

SECORD, P. F., & BACKMAN, C. W. *Social psychology.* New York: McGraw-Hill, 1964.

SELBY, H. A. Continuities and prospects in anthropological studies. In A. Fischer (Ed.), *Current directions in anthropology.* (American Anthropological Association Bulletin, Vol. 3, No. 3, part 2.) Washington, D. C.: American Anthropological Association, 1970.

SELIGMAN, M. E. P. On the generality of laws of learning. *Psychological Review,* 1970, *77*, 406–418.

SELIGMAN, M. E. P., & HAGER, J. L. (Eds.), *Biological boundaries of learning.* New York: Appleton-Century-Crofts, 1972.

SELZNICK, P. *Leadership in Administration.* Evanston, Ill.: Row, Peterson, 1957.

SHAW, M. E., & COSTANZO, P. R. *Theories of social psychology.* New York: McGraw-Hill, 1970.

SHEFFIELD, F. K. Relation between classical conditioning and instrumental learning. In W. F. Prokasy (Ed.), *Classical conditioning.* New York: Appleton-Century-Crofts, 1965.

SHETTLEWORTH, S. Constraints on learning. In D. S. Lehrman, R. A. Hinde, and E. Shaw (Eds) , *Advances in the study of behavior* (Vol. 4). New York: Academic, 1972.

SIMMEL, G. *The web of group affiliations.* (R. Bendix, Trans.). Glencoe, Ill.: Free Press, 1955.

SIMMEL, G. Fashion. *American Journal of Sociology,* 1956, *62*, 541–548.

SIMON, H. A. *Administrative Behavior* (2nd ed.). New York: Macmillan, 1957.

SIMPSON, R. L. *Theories of social exchange.* Morristown, N. J.: General Learning Press, 1972.

SINGER, J. E., BRUSH, C. A., & LUBLIN, S. C. Some aspects of deindividuation: Identification and conformity. *Journal of Experimental Social Psychology,* 1965, *1*, 356–378.

SKINNER, B. F. The generic nature of the concepts of stimulus and response. *Journal of General Psychology,* 1935, *12*, 40–65.

SKINNER, B. F. *The behavior or organisms.* New York: Appleton-Century-Crofts, 1938.

SKINNER, B. F. *Walden two.* New York: Macmillan, 1948. (a)

SKINNER, B. F. "Superstition" in the pigeon. *Journal of Experimental Psychology,* 1948, *38*, 168–172. (b)

SKINNER, B. F. *Science and human behavior.* New York: Free Press, 1953.

SKINNER, B. F. *Verbal behavior.* New York: Appleton-Century-Crofts, 1957.

SKINNER, B. F. The phylogeny and ontogeny of behavior. *Science,* 1966, *153*, 1205–1213.

SKINNER, B. F. *The technology of teaching.* New York: Appleton-Century-Crofts, 1968.

SKINNER, B. F. *Contingencies of reinforcement: A theoretical analysis.* New York: Appleton-Century-Crofts, 1969.

SKINNER, B. F. *Beyond freedom and dignity.* New York: Knopf, 1971.

SMITH, A. *The theory of moral sentiments.* London: George Bell & Sons, 1892.

SMITH, M., BRUNER, J., & WHITE, R. *Opinions and personality.* New York: Wiley, 1956.

SMITH, M. B. Perspectives on selfhood. *American Psychologist,* 1978, *33,* 1053–1963.

SORRENTINO, R. M., & BOUTILLIER, R. G. The effect of quantity and quality of verbal interaction on ratings of leadership ability. *Journal of Experimental Social Psychology,* 1975, *11,* 403–411.

STAATS, A. W. *Social behaviorism.* Homewood, Ill.: Dorsey, 1975.

STAPLETON, R. E., NACCI, P., & TEDESCHI, J. T. Interpersonal attraction and the reciprocation of benefits. *Journal of Personality and Social Psychology,* 1973, *28,* 199–205.

STAW, B. M., & SZWAJKOWSKI, E. The scarcity–munificence component of organizational environments and the commission of illegal acts. *Administrative Science Quarterly,* 1975, *20,* 345–354.

STEINER, I. D. Task-performing groups. In J. W. Thibaut, J. T. Spence, & R. C. Carson (Eds.), *Contemporary topics in social psychology.* Morristown, N. J.: General Learning Press, 1976.

STIERS, M., & SILBERBERG, A. Autoshaping and automaintenance of lever contact responses in rats. *Journal of the Experimental Analysis of Behavior,* 1974, *22,* 497–506.

STOGDILL, R. M. Personal factors associated with leadership. *Journal of Psychology,* 1948, *25,* 35–71.

STONE, C. P. Appearance and the self. In A. M. Rose (Ed.), *Human behavior and social processes.* Boston: Houghton, Mifflin, 1962.

STRAUSS, A. L. *Mirrors and masks: The search for identity.* Glencoe, Ill.: Free Press, 1959.

SZYBILLO, G. J. *The effects of price and scarcity on the valuation of fashions by fashion opinion leaders and nonopinion leaders.* Unpublished doctoral dissertation, Purdue University, 1973.

TANNEBAUM, A. S. Unions. In J. G. March (Ed.) , *Handbook of organizations.* Chicago: Rand McNally, 1965, pp. 710–763.

TANNEBAUM, A. S. *Control in organizations.* New York: McGraw-Hill, 1968.

TEICHMAN, M., & FOA, U. G. Effect of resources similarity on satisfaction with exchange. *Social Behavior and Personality,* 1975, *3,* 213–224. Also summarized in Foa and Foa, 1974, pp. 204–209.

TERREBERRY, S. The evolution of organizational environments. *Administrative Science Quarterly,* 1968, *12,* 590–613.

TESSER, A., GATEWOOD, R., & DRIVER, M. Some determinants of gratitude. *Journal of Personality and Social Psychology,* 1968, *9,* 233–236.

THIBAUT, J. W., & FAUCHEUX, C. The development of contractual norms in a bargaining situation under two types of stress. *Journal of Experimental Social Psychology,* 1965, *1,* 89–102.

THIBAUT, J. W., & KELLEY, H. H. *The social psychology of groups.* New York: Wiley, 1959.

THIBAUT, J., & GRUDER, C. L. Formation of contractual agreements between parties of unequal power. *Journal of Personality and Social Psychology,* 1969, *11,* 59–65.

THIBAUT, J., FRIEDLAND, N., & WALKER, L. Compliance with rules: Some social determinants. *Journal of Personality and Social Psychology,* 1974, *30,* 792–801.

THIBAUT, J., WALKER, L., LATOUR, S., & HOULDEN, P. Procedural justice as fairness. *Stanford Law Review,* 1974, *26,* 1271–1289.

THOMPSON, J. D. *Organizations in action.* New York: McGraw-Hill, 1967.

TORNOW, W. W. The development and application of an input–output moderator test on the perception and reduction of inequity. *Organizational Behavior and Human Performance,* 1971, *6,* 614–638.

TOULMIN, S. *Foresight and understandings: An inquiry into the aims of science.* London: Hutchinson, 1961.

TRIANDIS, H. C. Some universals of social behavior. *Personality and Social Pscyhology Bulletin,* 1978, *4,* 1–16.

TURNER, S. The logical adequacy of "the logical adequacy of Homans' social theory." *American Sociological Review,* 1971, *36,* 709–711.

VEBLEN, T. *The theory of the leisure class.* New York: Random House, 1931.

VROOM, V. H. *Work and motivation.* New York: Wiley, 1964.

VROOM, V. H. Industrial social psychology. In G. Lindzey & E. Aronson (Eds.), *The handbook of social psychology* (2nd ed., Vol. 5). Reading, Mass.: Addison-Wesley, 1969.

VROOM, V. H., & YETTON, P. H. *Leadership and decision-making.* Pittsburgh: University of Pittsburgh Press, 1973.

WAHRMAN, R., & PUGH, M. D. Competence and conformity: Another look at Hollander's study. *Sociometry,* 1972, *35,* 376–386.

WAHRMAN, R., & PUGH, M. D. Sex, nonconformity and influence. *Sociometry,* 1974, *37,* 137–147.

WALDMAN, S. R. Exchange theory and political analysis. *Sociological Inquiry,* 1970, *42,* 101–128.

WALKER, L., LaTOUR, S., LIND, E. A., & THIBAUT, J. Reactions of participants and observers to modes of adjudication. *Journal of Applied Social Psychology,* 1974, *4,* 295–310.

WALSTER, E. BERSCHEID, E., & WALSTER, G. W. New directions in equity research. *Journal of Personality and Social Psychology,* 1973, *25,* 151–176.

WALSTER, E., PILIAVIN, J., & WALSTER, G. W. The hard-to-get woman. *Psychology Today,* 1973, *7,* 80–83.

WALSTER, E., WALSTER, G. W., PILIAVIN, J., & SCHMIDT, L. "Playing hard to get": Understanding an elusive phenomenon. *Journal of Personality and Social Psychology,* 1973, *26,* 113–121.

WALSTER, E., WALSTER, G. W., & BERSCHEID, E. *Equity: Theory and research.* Boston: Allyn & Bacon, 1978.

WALSTER, G. W. Reply to Dr. William Samuel: Suggested amendments to new directions in equity research. *Personality and Social Psychology Bulletin,* 1976, *2,* 40–44.

WATSON, R. L., JR. Investigation into deindividuation using a cross-cultural survey technique. *Journal of Personality and Social Psychology,* 1973, *25,* 342–345.

WEICK, K. E. The concept of equity in the perception of pay. *Administrative Science Quarterly,* 1966, *11,* 414–439.

WEICK, K. E. Middle range theories of social systems. *Behavioral Science,* 1974, *19,* 357–367.

WEIR, H. B. *Deprivation of the need for uniqueness and some variables moderating its effects.* Unpublished doctoral dissertation, University of Georgia, 1971.

WHITE, P. E. Intra- and interorganizational studies: Do they require separate conceptualizations. *Administration & Society,* 1974, *6,* 107–152. (a)

WHITE, P. E. Resources as determinants of organizational behavior. *Administrative Science Quarterly,* 1974, *19,* 366–379. (b)

WHITLEY, B. E., JR. A role theory model of trait evaluation. Unpublished master's thesis, University of Pittsburgh, 1979. (a)

WHITLEY, B. E., JR. Sex roles and psychotherapy: Where they stand now. *Psychological Bulletin,* 1979, *86,* 1309–1321. (b)

WHITTEN, N. E., JR., & WHITTEN, D. S. Social strategies and social relationships. In B. J. Siegel (Ed.), *Annual Review of Anthropology,* Palo Alto: Annual Reviews, 1972.

WHYTE, W. F. *Street corner society.* Chicago: University of Chicago Press, 1955.

WICKLUND, R. *Freedom and reactance.* Potomac, Md.: Erlebaum, 1974.

WIGGINS, J. A., DILL, F., & SCHWARTZ, R. D. On "status-liability." *Sociometry,* 1965, *28,* 197–209.

WILCOXIN, H. C., DRAGOIN, W., & KRAL, P. Illness-induced aversions in rats and quail: Relative salience of visual and gustatory cues. *Science,* 1971, *171,* 826–828.

WILKE, H., & LANZETTA, J. T. The obligation to help: The effects of amount of prior help on subsequent helping behavior. *Journal of Experimental Social Psychology,* 1970, *6,* 488–493.

WILLIAMS, D. R., & WILLIAMS, H. Automaintenance in the pigeon: Sustained pecking despite contingent non-reinforcement. *Journal of the Experimental Analysis of Behavior,* 1969, *12,* 511–520.

WILLIAMSON, O. E. *The economics of discretionary behavior: Managerial objectives in a theory of the firm.* New York: Prentice-Hall, 1964.

WILLIS, R. H. Two dimensions of conformity–nonconformity. *Sociometry,* 1963, *26,* 499–513.

WILLIS, R. H. Conformity, independence, and anticonformity. *Human Relations,* 1965, *18,* 373–388.

WILLIS, R. H., & HOLLANDER, E. P. An experimental study of three response modes in social influence situations. *Journal of Abnormal and Social Psychology,* 1964, *69,* 150–156. (a)

WILLIS, R. H., & HOLLANDER, E. P. Supplementary note: Modes of responding in social influence situations. *Journal of Abnormal and Social Pschology,* 1964, *69,* 157. (b)

WILLIS, R. H., & OLSON, J. E. Partner markets: Perfect competition under strict indivisibility. (Working Paper 314.) Pittsburgh: Graduate School of Business, University of Pittsburgh, 1978.

WINCH, R. F. *Mate-selection: A study of complementary needs.* New York: Harper, 1958.

YUCHTMAN, E. Reward distribution and work-role attractiveness in the Kibbutz— Reflections on equity theory. *American Sociological Review,* 1972, *37,* 581–595.

YUCHTMAN, E., & SEASHORE, S. E. A system resource approach to organizational effectiveness. *American Sociological Review,* 1967, *32,* 891–903.

ZALD, M. N. *Organizational change: The political economy of the Y.M.C.A.* University of Chicago Press, 1970. (a)

ZALD, M. N. Political economy: A framework for comparative analysis. In M. N. Zald (Ed.), *Power in organizations.* Nashville: Vanderbilt University Press, 1970. (b)

ZALEZNIK, A. Review of *The social psychology of organizations,* by Katz and Kahn. *Administrative Science Quarterly,* 1967, *11,* 682–691.

ZDEP, S. M., & OAKES, W. I. Reinforcement of leadership behavior in group discussion. *Journal of Experimental Social Psychology,* 1967, *3,* 310–320.

ZELLINGER, D., FROMKIN, H. L., SPELLER, D., & KOHN, C. A commodity theory analysis of the effects of age restrictions upon the desire to obtain pornographic materials. *Journal of Applied Psychology,* 1975.

ZELLMAN, G. L. Antidemocratic beliefs: A survey and some explanations. *Journal of Social Issues,* 1975, *31,* 31–53.

ZILLER, R. C. Individuation and socialization. *Human Relations,* 1964, *17,* 344–360.

ZILLER, R. C. Towards a theory of open and closed groups. *Psychological Bulletin,* 1965, *64,* 164–182.

ZIMBARDO, P. G. The human choice: Individuation, reason and order versus deindividuation, impulse and chaos. In W. J. Arnold and D. Levine (Eds.), *Nebraska Symposium on Motivation,* 1969 (Vol. 17). Lincoln: University of Nebraska Press, 1970.

Index

Adams, J. S., 4, 21–22, 28, 96–98
Altruism, 5, 217, 235
  and exchange theory, 89–90, 126
Applications, 95–99
  as descriptive theoretical extensions, 94, 95
Attraction, *See* Social attraction
Attribution theory, 7, 15, 99, 108, 144–145
Authority, 105, 114, 116, 134. *See also* Power; Influence
  legitimacy, 105, 109–110, 113, 133
  responsibility, 115

Berscheid, E., 4, 22, 28, 52, 96, 262
Blau, P. M., 1, 4, 14, 27, 57, 80, 107, 120, 129–130, 132, 136–138, 191–194, 212, 265, 273

Coercion. *See* Compliance; Influence; Power
Cognitive dissonance, 21, 274
Commitment, 115
Communication, 107–108, 110, 183
Comparison level, 176–177, 262
Comparison level for alternatives, 160–161
Compatibility, 100–101, 148–163. *See also* Complementarity
  components of, 149–154
  intrinsic, 148–149, 155, 157, 160–162
  overall, 149, 154–158
  relative, 154
Competition, 125, 152. *See also* Conflict; Cooperation
  perfect competition, classical model of, 148
Complementarity, 150–154, 158
  need–complementarity, 150, 153–154, 158

Complementarity (*cont.*)
  resource–complementarity, 153–154
  similarity and other patterns of, 150–154
Compliance. *See* Conformity
Conflict, 96, 131, 154. *See also* Competition; Cooperation
Conformity, 57–59, 61, 63, 68–69, 75, 107, 109–110, 113, 125. *See also* Influence
  compliance, 61
  deviance, 101, 112
  independence, 113
  nonconformity, 60, 106, 111–113
Cooperation, 128, 132–135. *See also* Competition
Courtship, 180. *See also* Social attraction

Decision making, 44, 114, 116, 136–137
Dependence. *See* Power
Deviance. *See* Conformity
Dissonance. *See* Cognitive dissonance
Distributive fairness, 2, 29–43. *See also* Procedural fairness
  concern about, 48–53
  contributions rule, 29–34
  equality rule, 30–32
  needs rule, 31–32
  other rules, 31–34
Distributive justice, 28–29, 136–137. *See also* Equity; Equity theory

Equity, 29, 103, 117–118, 137, 162. *See also* Distributive fairness; Distributive justice; Equity theory; Exchange
  hypothetical, 153
  procedural. *See* Procedural fairness
  ratio, definition of, 97
  role reversal test, 153

Equity theory, 28–29, 33–34, 52. *See also* Equity
Esteem. *See* Status
Exchange, 88, 100, 112, 115, 1?4, 141–188, 208–209. *See also* Gift exchange; Social exchange theory
  collectivistic, 120, 132–133, 138, 193
  dyadic, 141–188
  generalized, 135, 138, 188, 194, 217
  and grants, 126, 134–155
  incremental, 165–188
  indirect, 18–20, 24
  individualistic, 135–138, 193
  intergroup, 100
  interorganizational, 125–129
  intraorganizational, 133–136
  rate of, 97–100, 113, 162
  rules of, 202–203
  and univocal reciprocity, 134
Exchange theory. *See* Social exchange theory
Expectations, 107, 111, 114, 116, 137, 142–145, 172
  mathematical, 143
  normative (prescriptive), 143–144. *See also* Roles; Social norms
  predictive, 143–144

Festinger, L., 21, 74

Gift exchange, 23, 25, 190–202, 205, 208–210, 216–218, 227–229, 234–235
Gouldner, A. W., 1, 4–6, 15, 23, 195, 199–202, 262–263, 278

Heider, F., 5, 108
Homans, G. C., 1–2, 4, 14, 27–28, 33, 57–58, 107, 120, 132, 136–138, 174, 189–194, 199, 211–213, 239–240, 261, 264, 266

Idiosyncrasy credit. *See* Status
Incremental exchange theory, 165–188. *See also* RELATE model
  gradient effects, 176–177
  interaction, state of, 165
  involvement, level of, 165
  payoff matrix, 166–167
  transition matrix, 168
Indebtedness, 1
  assessment of magnitude, 11–21
  comparison with inequity, 21–23

Indebtedness (*cont.*)
  cultural variations, 23–25
  definition of, 3–4
  determinants of, 4–11
Inequity theory. *See* Equity theory
Influence, 103, 106–115. *See also* Power; Influence
  ingratiation, 52, 113
Instinctive drift, 246–248
Interpersonal attraction. *See* Social attraction

Jones, E. E., 7, 15, 52, 113, 175
Justice. *See* Distributive justice; Equity; Equity theory

Kelley, H. H., 1–2, 15, 27, 107–108, 120, 132, 151, 166, 168, 174–176, 189–190, 193–194, 261–264, 272–273

Leadership, 99–100, 103–118, 137
  appointed and elected, 111, 114–115
  approaches to, 103–110, 276
  effectiveness, 108, 111, 115–118
  and idiosyncrasy credit, 99–100, 105–106, 110–118
  and innovation, 106, 110–118
  leader attributes, 107, 116–117
Lévi-Strauss, C., 120, 135, 193, 198–199, 207–213, 217
Loners. *See* Markets, loners

Markets, 129, 132–134, 147–163
  loners, 101, 148, 159–163
  organizations as markets, 132–133
  partner markets, 147–163
Marriage, 207–210. *See also* Courtship; Social attraction
Mauss, M., 23, 198–199, 201–202, 207–210, 215–218, 224, 226, 229, 235
Measurement, 96–98, 170, 173
Methodology. *See* Measurement
Micro and macro levels, 100–101, 119–121, 127, 132, 135–138

Nonconformity. *See* Conformity
Norms. *See* Social norms

Obligations, 1, 10, 12–13, 143, 161, 200–202, 234
Operant conditioning, 137, 195–196, 239–260
  ethological approach, 245–246

Organizations, 98–100, 112, 120–140
    interaction with environment, 122,
        124–125, 129–131
    interorganizational exchange, 125–129
    intraorganizational exchange, 133–136

Partner markets. *See* Markets
Payoffs, 99–101, 187, 275
    matrix, 151, 166, 275
Power, 44, 118, 125, 128–130, 133, 137,
        175. *See also* Authority; Influence
    strategies, 128, 133
Preferences. *See also* Utility
    partner preferences, 147, 155, 158
    preference structure, 147–163
    task preference, 153
    SV-matchers, 147–163
    SV-strivers, 147–163
Prisoner's Dilemma, 134–169
Procedural fairness, 34–55, 112
    components of, 37–39
    concern about, 48–53
    rules of, 39–46
Prosocial behavior. *See* Altruism

Rationality, 126
Reciprocity, 14–20, 126, 135, 153,
        166–167, 182, 188, 194–195. *See also*
        Social norms, reciprocity
    anthropological approaches, 135,
        215–218
    attraction-mediated, 15, 153
    and kinship distance, 217–218,
        229–233
Reinforcement, 109–110, 242–245,
        250–255
    intrinsic vs. extrinsic, 256–258
RELATE model, 168–186. *See also*
        Incremental exchange theory
    first version (John & Susan), 170–178
    revised version (Keith & Terry),
        178–186
Relative deprivation, 176
Resource theory, 2, 77–94, 262–263
    applications, 94
    classes, 78–86
    recent developments, 90–91
Resources, 100, 106, 114–115, 121–130,
        145, 150, 155, 158. *See also* Resource
        theory; Rewards
    allocation, 107, 132–135
    discretionary, 134–136

Resources (*cont.*)
    flow, 119, 122, 125, 128, 131, 135–139
    resource-complementarity, 80,
        153–154
    resource–dependence model, 129
    resource–exchange (R–E) paradigm,
        100, 119–139
    resource position, 127
Rewards, 36–37, 50, 53, 58, 109, 118,
        122, 137–138, 144, 151, 155, 165,
        266. *See also* Reinforcement;
        Resources
    anticipatory, 155, 160
    attributional vs. direct, 176, 179
    behavioral vs. relational, 174
    gradients of, 176–177
    symbolic vs. concrete, 174
    universalistic vs. particularistic, 79–81
Risk. *See* Uncertainty, risks
Role-playing, 274
Roles, 9, 100, 109–112, 116–117, 141–163
    sex roles, 100, 141–163
Romantic attraction. *See* Social
        attraction; Courtship; RELATE model

Self-concept, 52, 64–67, 70–71, 74–75
Self-disclosure, 183
Self-perception, 59–63, 74, 274
Simulation, 161–162, 168–186
    computer. *See* RELATE model
    experimental, 161–162
Skinner, B. F., 239–246, 250–251,
        254–256, 259, 277
Skinner Box, 196, 250–255
Social approval, 58, 143–147, 174, 265
Social attraction, 100, 147–188. *See also*
        Courtship
    and similarity, 59–60, 150–154. *See*
        also Preferences, SV-matchers
    stability of, 100
Social exchange theory, 119–120, 162
    anthropological approach, 198–199
    calculation of rewards and costs, 190,
        272
    criticisms of, 75, 189–196, 261–268
    cultural frame of reference, 204–206,
        267
    definitions of, 189–190
    and economic theory, 100–101,
        120–121, 125, 128, 264
    and enlightenment effects, 196, 263

Social exchange theory (*cont.*)
  and game theory, 120
  and indirect exchange, 126
  level of abstraction and incorporation
    of change, 265–268
  logical structure, of theoretical
    propositions, 191
  motivational approach, 47, 195,
    206–207, 210–213
  and reductionism, 191–192. *See also*
    Micro and macro levels
  strategies of social exchange, 81–82,
    203–205
  structural approach, 195, 206–210
  theoretical utility of, 98–99, 196,
    268–279
Social influence. *See* influence
Social norms, 72, 100, 112, 126
  reciprocity, 4, 195, 199–202, 213
  social responsibility, 195
Status, 1, 4, 33, 66, 103–104, 106, 109,
    112–113, 136, 226, 234–235. *See also*
    Leadership
  achieved, 106, 110, 142–144
  ascribed, 110, 142–145
  and idiosyncrasy credit, 99–100,
    105–106, 110–118
  incongruence, 33, 136
Supply and demand, 64–65, 100–101,
    118–121, 129, 134, 147, 159–162

Systems, 115, 128. *See also* Markets
  general systems theory, 98–99,
    123–124, 138
  open systems model, 119, 129
  system progress, 103, 113, 118
Task, 109–110, 143–158
  difficulty, 144
  performance, 110, 143–147
  preferences, 153
  specialization, 133, 145
Taste-aversion learning, 248–250
Thibaut, J. W. (or J.), 1–2, 27, 35, 46,
    107, 120, 132, 151, 166, 168,
    174–176, 189–190, 193–194, 261,
    264, 272–273
Trust, 117, 126, 152–153, 265

Uncertainty, 107, 116–117, 133, 154
  risks, 143, 146, 193
Uniqueness, 2, 57–75
  attributes, 63–64
  commodity theory, 64–66
  deindividuation, 73–75
Utility, 168, 173, 176, 193. *See also*
  Preferences; Value

Value, 130, 136. *See also* Utility

Walster, E., 4, 22, 28, 52, 69–70, 96, 262
Walster, G. W., 4, 22, 28, 52, 69–70, 96,
    262